Self-Cultivation (修身) in Early China

SUNY series in Chinese Philosophy and Culture

Roger T. Ames, editor

Self-Cultivation (修身) in Early China

PAUL FISCHER

SUNY PRESS

Cover art: Image courtesy the Metropolitan Museum of Art. *Light Snow on the Mountain Pass*. Unidentified artist. China, late Ming (1368–1644)–early Qing (1644–1911) dynasty. Bequest of John M. Crawford Jr., 1988. Accession Number: 1989.363.168

唐人楊昇畫關山蒲雪圖, 宋御府所藏.
康熙丙午得見於長安借綠堂, 因以重價購得.
此畫有所賞心, 永寶. 沚鑑題.

Tang artist Yang Sheng painted this *Light Snow at Mt. Guan*, which was in the collection of the Song Imperial court.

In the *bingwu* year (1666 CE) of the Kangxi emperor, I was able to view [this painting] at the Borrowed Green Studio in Chang'an, and then purchased it for a hefty price.

This painting has something that appeals to the heart, and I will treasure it forever. Inscribed by Zhijian [i.e., Feng Xianshi 馮仙湜; fl. mid-17th to 18th cent.] Translation by (and thanks to) Yunchiahn Sena.

Published by State University of New York Press, Albany

© 2022 State University of New York

All rights reserved

Printed in the United States of America

No part of this book may be used or reproduced in any manner whatsoever without written permission. No part of this book may be stored in a retrieval system or transmitted in any form or by any means including electronic, electrostatic, magnetic tape, mechanical, photocopying, recording, or otherwise without the prior permission in writing of the publisher.

For information, contact State University of New York Press, Albany, NY
www.sunypress.edu

Library of Congress Cataloging-in-Publication Data

Name: Fischer, Paul, author.
Title: Self-cultivation in early China / Paul Fischer.
Description: Albany : State University of New York Press, 2022. | Series: SUNY series in Chinese philosophy and culture | Includes bibliographical references and index.
Identifiers: LCCN 2021051929 (print) | LCCN 2021051930 (ebook) | ISBN 9781438488332 (hardcover : alk. paper) | ISBN 9781438488356 (ebook) | ISBN 9781438488349 (pbk. : alk paper)
Subjects: LCSH: Ethics—China. | Conduct of life.
Classification: LCC BJ117 .F57 2022 (print) | LCC BJ117 (ebook) | DDC 170.951—dc23/eng/20220120
LC record available at https://lccn.loc.gov/2021051929
LC ebook record available at https://lccn.loc.gov/2021051930

10 9 8 7 6 5 4 3 2 1

"If the mind does not have its Heavenly wanderings, then the six senses will be mutually confused." (心無天遊，則六鑿相攘。)

—Zhuangzi 莊子

"As truth is gathered, I rearrange . . . inside out, outside in: perpetual change."

—Jon Anderson

Contents

Acknowledgments ... ix

Book Title Translations ... xi

Introduction ... 1

Part I. Person (人)

Chapter 1 Body (體) ... 33

Chapter 2 Nature (性) ... 77

Chapter 3 Mind (心) ... 101

Part II. Environment (地)

Chapter 4 Virtuosity (德) ... 143

Chapter 5 Timeliness (時) ... 191

Part III. Objects (物)

Chapter 6 Learning (學) ... 213

Chapter 7 Music (樂) ... 235

Part IV. Cosmos (天)

Chapter 8	Fate (命)	247
Chapter 9	Destiny (天)	271
Chapter 10	Spiritousness (神)	283
Works Cited		321
Index		331

Acknowledgments

I would like to thank the many very nice people I met during my years studying in China: teachers, fellow students, office workers, librarians, bookstore workers, cafeteria workers, bus drivers, taxi drivers, neighbors, shop owners, restaurant workers, tea shop servers, bartenders, barbers, bicycle-fixers, everyone who sold things at Beijing's Panjiayuan 潘家园 market, all those who gave me directions when I was lost (this was in the early 2000s, before cellphones with GPS were common), and all those who just walked up to me and started a conversation; all of those interactions were overwhelmingly positive and left a lasting impression that is somehow related to the theme of this book. I would in particular like to thank my fellow sinologist Lin Zhipeng 林志鹏 for his many years of help and friendship. I would also like to thank the Visiting Scholars Program of the International Center for Studies of Chinese Civilization (ICSCC) at Fudan University (复旦大学中华文明国际研究中心访问学者计划). Zhang Ke 章可 and Qian Yu 钱宇 of the ICSCC were especially gracious and helpful in facilitating my visit and the attendant conference in the summer of 2015. Six years later (while also attending to my day job), I have finally finished what I began that summer in Shanghai. I further thank another fellow sinologist, He Jianjun 何建軍, for his encouragement and friendship. Thanks also to Jimi, Jimmy, David, Steve, and Trey, for their spiritousness. Last, according to custom, but not least, ldl.

Book Title Translations

Because many of the primary sources in this monograph do not have single, agreed-upon English translations for titles, I will transliterate them throughout. I translate them here for the interested reader. For example, in the text, I refer to the *Shujing*, not the *Documents Classic*. Also, in the list below, there is a space between the Chinese words in the title which correspond to the translation (e.g., *Shu* for *Documents* and *jing* for *Classic*, below, but *Shujing* in the text). In the text, most of these spaces are omitted to follow convention (which is rather arbitrary).

Classics

Chun qiu 春秋 (Annals [of the state of Lu]; literally "Spring [and] Autumn")
Li ji 禮記 (Protocol Record)
Shi jing 詩經 (Odes Classic)
Shu jing 書經 (Documents Classic)
Xiao jing 孝經 (Filiality Classic)
Yi jing 易經 (Changes Classic)
Zhou li 周禮 (Zhou Protocols)

Scholars

All eponymous Scholars' texts end with "zi." Thus, *Mengzi* 孟子 (Scholar Meng), *Xunzi* 荀子 (Scholar Xun), and so forth. These need not be translated below. Other such texts include:

Chu ci 楚辭 (Chu Elegies)
Guo yu 國語 (State Sayings)

Han shi wai zhuan 韓詩外傳 ([Mr.] Han's Commentarial Account of the Odes)
Heng xian 恆先 (Abiding Antecedent), excavated, now in Shanghai Museum
Kong zi jia yu 孔子家語 (Scholar Kong's School Sayings)
Liu de 六德 (Six Virtuosities), excavated from Guodian
Lü shi chun qiu 呂氏春秋 (Mr. Lü's Annals)
Lun yu 論語 (Selected Sayings, aka Analects)
Mu tian zi zhuan 穆天子傳 (Biography of Heavenly Scion Mu)
Shang jun shu 商君書 (Lord Shang's Writings)
Tai yi sheng shui 太一生水 (The Great One Creates Water), excavated from Guodian
Wu xing 五行 (Five Conducts), excavated from Guodian
Xin yu 新語 (New Sayings)
Xing zi ming chu 性自命出 ([Human] Nature Derives from [Heaven's] Mandate), excavated from Guodian
Yan zi chun qiu 晏子春秋 (Scholar Yan's Annals)
Yu cong 語叢 (Sayings Thicket), in four parts; excavated from Guodian
Zhong xin zhi dao 忠信之道 (The Way of Loyalty and Trust), excavated from Guodian
Zuo zhuan 左傳 ([Mr.] Zuo's Account [of the Annals Classic])

Introduction

"Those who wish to achieve great things in the world must first cultivate themselves in private."

—*Xinyu* ch. 6

夫建大功於天下者，必先修於閨門之內。《新語。慎微》

Aim, Scope, Method

The aim of this book is to introduce a general, interested audience to the practice of self-cultivation (修身) in early China. Self-cultivation is a broad term that denotes a multi-faceted pursuit of three distinct but related goals: individual health, social harmony, and environmental concord. (Each of these can be further analyzed into more precise concerns; for example, individual health can be divided into physical and mental health; social harmony, into political stability and ethical pluralism, and so on.) "Self-cultivation" may be readily understood in English, but it is nevertheless an enigmatic term; while it is a central and rather well-understood term in the intellectual history of China, if not all of East Asia, it has no specific cultural traction in the West. The closest example in the West may be the ancient Greek idea of *eudaimonia* (well-being), but this remains a relatively unknown term outside of Classics or early Philosophy specialties. Thus, a better point of comparison for the Westerner may be soteriology, the study of how to be "saved." This comparison founders on the fact that early China had no "heaven" and "hell" with the religious sense that they commonly hold today, nor was there the idea of an eternal soul which would go to one of these places after death. But the comparison works well teleologically because self-cultivation and soteriology both occupy similar central places in the intellectual histories of the East and West. Early China has had an extensive and lasting influence on Chinese culture that extends to the present day. Meanwhile, modern China once again has an extensive and still-growing influence on the rest of the world. For anyone who is curious about global approaches to the meaning of life, then, an inquiry into the early Chinese approaches of self-cultivation should be of interest.

My general argument is that early Chinese self-cultivation is analyzable into the ten constituent parts that make up the ten chapters of this book. All ten of these topics are important and well-known in Chinese history. Thus, the broader theme of self-cultivation and the subsequent ten subjects are presented in terms that would immediately be recognizable to a literate ancient Chinese person. Likewise, these ten topics may be subsumed under four broad categories that are also traditional categories in the Chinese context: the person (人), the environment in general (地), particular objects (物), and the larger context of the cosmos (天). Self-cultivation that focuses on the "person" includes the body, human nature, and the mind. The "environment" includes virtuosity and timeliness. (I classify virtuosity under "environment" because virtuosity is primarily a social concern, and therefore most relevant to the social environment.) "Objects" pertain to those useful to a relevant task, like books that are necessary for learning, and instruments that are needed for music. Finally, relations with the "cosmos" may be considered via fate, destiny, and spiritousness.

In the chapters that follow, there are many primary-source quotations because these quotes constitute the evidence for my claims. It is important, for several reasons, to include the original Chinese in a discussion of these topics, along with the translations, even though my audience will probably be primarily Western and English-speaking. The most important reason is that the state of the field of Western sinology is not yet to a point where we all, or even most of us, have agreed upon standardized translations, even for central concepts. The field is simply still too young. So it is very helpful for those who can read Chinese, and even for those who cannot but are reading other monographs on early China, to know how I am translating. It also encourages those who are interested to learn a few key words, just as one might learn a few important words of Greek or Sanskrit to help in understanding those cultures; for example, *logos* (logic; word) or *duhkha* (dissatisfaction; out of alignment). There is also a growing number of Western students learning Chinese at college, for whom the inclusion of the Chinese will be a boon. Finally, there are a great many Chinese students who know or are learning English, who may be interested in this analysis. There is, to my knowledge, no Chinese language equivalent of this monograph.

The temporal scope of this book is "early China," and focus here is on the 350-year period from roughly 500–150 BCE, though I have taken into account texts from about 1000 BCE down to 139 BCE.[1] The reason for this temporal scope is that the primary sources of this inquiry are the "Scholars' texts" (子書) and, to a lesser extent, the classics that more or less precede them. This focus is inescapable because, out of all early Chinese literature, Scholars' texts are the most concerned with self-cultivation, broadly construed; the classics, despite being older and more authoritative, are much less concerned with this topic. In the time period delineated here, there are five classics and about twenty-five received Scholars' texts. In addition, there are another dozen "fragmented" Scholars' texts and another two dozen excavated Scholars' texts relevant to this survey.[2] These texts are foundational to much of Chinese intellectual history and to cultural history across East Asia.

Many students in the West are puzzled about where these Scholars' texts fit into Western academia: are they philosophy or religion or something else? It is curious that in China they are considered philosophy but in America they (or, at least, some of them) are considered religion.[3] Although both "philosophy" and "religion" are notoriously difficult to define (though

---

1. Precise dating of the earliest parts of the Chinese classics is impossible, and even accurate dating for most Scholars' texts is a fraught enterprise. The "roughly 1000 BCE" comes from the assumption that at least parts of some of the classics date to around the time when the Zhou dynasty (1045–256 BCE) displaced the Shang dynasty (1570–1045 BCE), that is, around 1045 BCE. The "139 BCE" is the date of the *Huainanzi* 淮南子, which is the last Scholars' text to be included in this survey. Dating early Chinese texts is also complicated by the fact that the contents of some texts were not all written at the same time; that is, some parts of a given text might have been added later, while other parts may have been altered—minimally or substantially—by later editors.

2. Briefly, "Scholars' texts" are what we might call "philosophy" or "intellectual history," while the five "classics" are on a variety of topics: political history (*Shujing*), poetry (*Shijing*), divination (*Yijing*), protocol (*Liji*), and court records for the state of Lu (*Chunqiu*). For more information on the received classics and Scholars' texts, see Michael Loewe, ed., *Early Chinese Texts: A Bibliographical Guide* (Berkeley: The Society for the Study of Early China, 1993).

3. "Philosophy" in Western academia usually means "Western Philosophy." There are, however, a handful of Philosophy departments in America which include Chinese philosophy. I might note that the classics and Scholars' texts are also central to a kind of "Classics" department in China called *Guo xue* 國學 that has no equivalent in Western academia; it is sort of like "intellectual history" within Chinese history.

the foundational definition of "philosophy" as "love of wisdom" is both simple and beautiful), the answer to the question above is: it depends on how you define "philosophy" and "religion." If you think that a "religion" necessarily includes one or more deities that want worshipping, as distinct from ancestors that want venerating, then this monograph is philosophy.[4] Nevertheless, the teachings of scholars like Kongzi[5] are typically taught in Religion courses in America.[6] In any case, the question does not in any way intrude upon this study. Chinese Scholars' texts are relevant to both philosophy and religion, as well as to intellectual history and literature.[7]

My methodology in this book is decidedly less historical and more philosophical. By this I mean that I focus more on ideas than on names and dates or on the contextualization or evolution of ideological debates (as important as these are). Take the following quotation, for example: "Yao asked Shun saying: 'What should be served?' Shun answered: 'Serve Heaven.' [Yao] asked: 'What should be made use of?' [Shun] answered: 'Make use of Earth.' [Yao] asked: 'What should we be devoted to?' [Shun] answered: 'Be devoted to the people.'" (堯問於舜曰：「何事？」舜曰：「事天。」問：「何任？」曰：「任地。」問：「何務？」曰：「務人。」)[8] This exchange is relevant to the present study because it highlights three central constituents of the early Chinese worldview: Heaven, Earth, and humans. It also reveals

---

4. For the difference between "worshipping" and "venerating," look into any account of the "Rites controversy" in 16th–18th century China.

5. I use "Kongzi" instead of "Confucius" because it is important to contextualize him as one "scholar," i.e., "zi" (子) among many. In fact, one might transcribe the Chinese as "Kong Zi" rather than "Kongzi" to show that the last two letters are in fact an honorific, but convention, and a desire to not give the impression that "Zi" is a surname, conspire to put them together.

6. For an excellent book on Ruist (Confucian) "a-theistic" religiosity, see Roger Ames, *Confucian Role Ethics: A Vocabulary* (Honolulu: University of Hawaii Press, 2011).

7. And to political history as well; see Yuri Pines, *Envisioning Eternal Empire: Chinese Political Thought of the Warring States Era* (Honolulu: University of Hawaii Press, 2009).

8. *Shizi* 尸子 ch. 9 (仁意). All translations are mine, mainly for the purpose of consistency, and I am greatly indebted to many previous translators. Translators often must choose between word-for-word accuracy and overall elegance; in this book I aim for the former. Words in brackets are added for correct English grammar, added clarity, or to provide context. However, some translated words are not, strictly speaking, in the Chinese and I do not bracket them. One example of this is in "If-then" sentences, where the Chinese has an implied "If" and an articulated "then" (則). A second example is the subject of verbs, which in the Chinese might be articulated at the beginning of the passage and only implied thereafter.

three important actions within that worldview: serving, using, and devotion. If this were a different kind of book, the focus may well be on the figures of Yao and Shun, since Yao and Shun are the fourth and fifth of the semi-legendary, mytho-historical "Five Thearchs" (五帝) that were said to rule before the first Chinese dynasty. Yao and Shun are very important to the cultural history of China, but their names, putative dates, and historicity are not central to the concern of this monograph and therefore discussion of these kinds of figures is curtailed in the following pages.

A second issue in differentiating philosophical from historical monographs is that ideas (and texts) are situated in a particular historical context but have a tendency to evolve. Of particular concern for the present study is the degree to which we should consider these self-cultivation practices as situated in the centuries during which the primary texts were written, the degree to which they were re-imagined in later Chinese cultural history, and the degree to which they may be relevant to a modern, Western reader.[9] As a sinologist, the first context has priority for me, but as a teacher of undergraduates, the second and third contexts inevitably come into play. Because this topic is already quite broad, for reasons of space, I will not consider the second context at all, interesting as it certainly is. And because of my imagined audience (of undergraduates), the third context may impinge upon the first more than some of my colleagues may find comfortable, but I hope they will remember my goals here. However, this is not an "either-or" problem whereby we must choose between reading ancient texts *only* as they related to their original audiences or construing them *only* as they match modern concerns.

For example, a primary aspirational figure since the time of Kongzi is the *junzi* 君子, which I translate as "noble person." While "person" is indeed an accurate translation of "*zi* 子," which here does not mean "scholar" (as it does with "Kong-zi"), but rather is an extrapolation from "child" or "son,"[10] it has been argued that "noble man" is a more honest translation, given

---

9. As Stephen Angle says, "There is an inevitable tension between historical fidelity and philosophical construction. The former pushes us toward carefully qualified, highly context-sensitive interpretations; the latter, toward generalization, loose paraphrase, and critical emendation. No matter what our goals, anyone dealing with an intellectual tradition finds him or herself pulled back and forth between these poles." Stephen Angle, *Sagehood: The Contemporary Significance of Neo-Confucian Philosophy* (New York: Oxford University Press, 2009), 5.

10. "*Junzi*" prior to Kongzi literally referred to the "child" or "son" of "noble," that is, high-ranking, parentage. Kongzi famously reconfigured the term to refer to any person of moral worth, much as an English "gentleman" from a landed estate eventually evolved into any person with manners.

that premodern China was patriarchal, and the likelihood of the authors of these texts assuming that a woman could be a "noble person" is quite small. Nevertheless, I translate it as "noble person" not because there was a slim possibility that at least some of these authors were more egalitarian than their peers, but because these texts, to the degree that they are received as relevant to a modern audience, can still speak to us. This is particularly true of a topic as perennial as self-cultivation. I realize that a desire to be "relevant" can be problematic; but regardless of my audience, I am an academic first, and it is my goal always to be historically accurate first, and relevant to a modern audience in their own terms second. I will, however, be both historically accurate *and* relevant to a modern audience—as with the translation of "noble person"—whenever I can.

A third methodological decision was to emphasize certain concepts by capitalizing the first letter of those words, as I have done with "Heaven" and "Earth" above. Chinese has no upper or lower case, so these emphases are only for Western audiences unfamiliar with such concepts. I have tried to keep this to a minimum, with only Scholars' texts, Heaven, Earth, the Way, Yin-Yang, the One, and the Great One so designated. Three of these will be discussed shortly. Two other terms that are quite important, and that have been capitalized by other authors, but not by me, include "virtuosity" (德) and "goodness" (仁). While I find that emphasizing some words in this way has pedagogical value, it should be remembered that the Chinese authors themselves did not, because they could not. Nevertheless, the decision to capitalize some terms and not others remains a subjective one.

A fourth methodological decision was to rely mostly on primary sources and to scale back the use of secondary sources, particularly those not in English.[11] This was done partially to make the work more accessible to non-specialists and partially because returning to the original sources is a fitting place to start. After all, most of the primary sources have been translated into English, whereas almost none of the secondary scholarship in Chinese has. Moreover, I think that text criticism—that is, paying close attention to language—is an extremely important skill. For example, what exactly *did* the authors of the American constitution's "Bill of Rights" mean in the single sentence of the Second Amendment? Or what *should* be the takeaway from the first verse of the "gospel" of John: "In the beginning

---

11. In anticipation of a potential criticism of this book as not explicitly engaging with the literature of the field, I want to emphasize that my *primary* intended audience consists of American undergraduates who, if my decade of teaching is anything to go by, are decidedly *not* interested in scholarly debate (at least, not in a book-length monograph).

was the *Logos*, and the *Logos* was with the Deity, and the *Logos* was the Deity?"[12] For close readers, even prepositions (such as "with" in the quote above) matter. Text criticism, in its simplest form, asks us to carefully consider such questions. Secondary sources are certainly invaluable for giving us more perspectives on these issues, but it is always good to begin at the beginning, which, in this case, are the primary sources.

Finally, a fifth method is my use of the "principle of charity," which is relatively standard in academia, but not quite as widespread outside of it.[13] Using this principle means that when one encounters two claims that do not seem to fit together but presumably ought to, then we will try, within reason, to make it work. For example, "desire" is a tricky topic in many East Asian intellectual traditions, and "knowledge" is problematized in the *Laozi*, which says that sages "cause the people to be without [contrived] knowledge and without [contrived] desire" (使民無知無欲).[14] Note the bracketed words that I added. Without them, the sentence implies (or might be taken to imply) that all knowledge and all desire are bad, given the correct assumption that sages, as aspirational figures, only do good things. But that would imply that the knowledge gained from reading the *Laozi* itself was bad, and that the ordinary desires for food and sleep are bad. One could, at this point, simply throw the books away for being ridiculous, but the "principle of charity" asks us to continue reading and see if the author says other things that would lead us to think that there are implied modifiers, like the two I added. Reading this sentence in the context of the rest of the chapter, which is about the effects of conspicuous consumption on society, one will see that the bracketed additions are justified. Authors do not always say what they mean, but sometimes it is worthwhile to try, charitably, to make sense of their words.

The "principle of charity," however, can backfire in two ways. Whenever one describes a large and complex topic, someone will almost inevitably say that the description is "reductive." This can mean that either the analysis is over-simplified or one-sided. Regarding oversimplification, given that I am analyzing a broad and multivalent topic which spans several centuries with an abundance of relevant primary sources, a degree of simplification is unavoidable, but it is my hope that what follows is not an *over*-simplification.

---

12. The biblical "John" 1:1.
13. This issue is sometimes articulated as a "hermeneutics of charity" versus a "hermeneutics of suspicion." On the other hand, it is possible that one can be too charitable. To paraphrase Saul Lieberman: "Nonsense is nonsense, but the *history* of nonsense is scholarship."
14. *Laozi* 老子 ch. 3.

The issue of one-sidedness does not, I think, apply to the present study, given that I focus on a specific area of intellectual history, and not on early Chinese culture in general.

Reasons for Writing

The primary reason for writing this book is to convey the breadth and importance of self-cultivation in early China to those who are interested. But there are other reasons why one might come to be interested in this topic. One is that it can increase "global-mindedness," that is, the attitude that we are all, in some sense, "global citizens." As Donald Munro said, "I must admit that I hope that the reader may seriously entertain and consider some of the assumptions behind the Chinese view of man and society. I hope so because I expect this will make his own reflections on social problems more flexible and rational, because he understands that there are other ways of looking at things."[15] Although he was writing about "social problems" and I am not (or, not directly), the idea still stands. Learning about other paradigms—cosmic, psychological, religious, philosophical—is useful for critically thinking about one's own paradigms.

Critical thinking is especially important, and especially difficult, on texts in which people are emotionally invested. And while Western readers typically may not attach much emotion to texts with which they are unfamiliar (how could they?), Scholars' texts do carry significant weight in China. Quoting Laozi in China is not unlike quoting Plato, or even the Bible, in the West. We might define "critical thinking" as the ability to identify and question our own assumptions, with the goal of either substantiating or altering them. In cross-cultural exchanges, this has the effect of moving our thinking from a zero-sum, black and white, "which narrative is true and which is false?" approach, to one that is centered on a multivalent, "let's weigh the evidence" attitude that may well result in critical-minded ambivalence. This way of thinking allows for a deeper engagement with global-mindedness, resulting in a kind of multicultural individual. Global-mindedness and critical thinking, then, should not just be thought of as providing paradigm foils for one's own cultural assumptions, that is, for checking ethnocentrism: expanding one's conceptual and literary repertoire is a worthy end in itself.

---

15. Donald Munro, *The Concept of Man in Contemporary China* (Ann Arbor: The University of Michigan Press, 1977), ix.

Historical-mindedness is another valuable cognitive skill that is strengthened by reading books like this one. History is the backbone of global-mindedness and is the material upon which critical thinking acts. Reading history, however, returns us to the problem of historical context and modern applicability. As G.E.R. Lloyd warns, "forcing issues by raising questions that are foreign to the actors' own views and concerns" can be a problem in monographs like this one, especially when considering ancient ideas that touch upon (or seem to touch upon) issues of contemporary relevance.[16] This is an issue even for literature that belongs to one's own culture. Is reading Jane Austen, for example, an exercise in romantic escapism or contemporary commentary? Surely it can be both. Further afield in both space and time, is it fair to ask if early Chinese authors would concede that a woman can be considered a "noble person"? They probably never gave such a question any thought. Although I do think it can be a valid exercise to interrogate antique writings with modern and alien questions,[17] this problem is (hopefully) avoided here by considering self-cultivation in Chinese terms. So, while the problem of context remains a live one, and very much worth considering, reading history, especially of cultures not one's own, presents unique opportunities for cultivating historical-mindedness. A thousand years ago, Lü Zuqian (1137–1181) gave us some advice on how to read history:

> Generally speaking, when [people] look at history, [they simply] look at [times of] order and take them to be orderly, and look at [times of] disorder and take them to be disorderly: [that is, they] look at one thing and just stop inquiring at that one thing. How could [they thus] attain historical-mindedness? [You should imagine yourself] as if you personally were in the midst of the situation, and look at the benefits and dangers of the matter, and the fortunes and misfortunes of the time. [You] must close the book and think about them yourself, prompt yourself to go through these matters, and [think about] what would have been the appropriate way to deal with them. If [you] are historical-minded in this way, then [your] learning will advance,

---

16. G.E.R. Lloyd, *Demystifying Mentalities* (Cambridge: Cambridge University Press, 1990), 10.

17. To stay with the Jane Austen example for just a moment longer, although the term "female gaze" does not appear in any of her works, or in any of the works of her contemporaries, having been coined much later, it seems to me a fair and interesting question to ask whether or not her novels do in fact articulate a "female gaze."

and [your] knowledge will increase, and [you] will experience growth.

(大抵看史，見治則以為治，見亂則以為亂，見一事則止知一事。何取觀史？如身在其中，見事之利害，時之禍患。必掩卷自思。使我遇此等事，當作何處之。如此觀史，學問亦可以進，智識亦可以高，方為有益。)[18]

In the following chapters, if you "prompt yourself to go through these matters," you may find much that is commendable, and much that you agree with. This, on the surface anyway, should be odd. What common ground could there possibly be between twenty-first-century Westerners and some philosophical-minded authors living two and a half thousand years ago, on the other side of the world? They certainly lived very different lives, so doesn't some of their advice sound suspiciously modern? I think the answer must lie in the modifier "philosophical-minded." Some things about the human condition remain relatively constant. How to take care of yourself would certainly count as one of them.

Another question arises: if ancient advice on self-cultivation is largely a matter of what we might now consider "common sense," why bother to read it? The aforementioned global-mindedness and historical-mindedness are two reasons. Another is that people seem to like to feel part of a larger narrative, a longer tradition, so it seems intrinsically interesting that a modern reader can connect with a culture so long ago and so far away.[19] But

---

18. Lü Zuqian 呂祖謙, *Lü Donglai wenji* 呂東來文集 (台北: 臺灣商務, 1968), 19:431; cf. Burton Watson in *Sources of Chinese Tradition: From Earliest Times to 1600*, eds. Wm. Theodore de Bary and Irene Bloom (New York: Columbia University Press, 1999), 660. Note: *zhi* 抵 (clap) is a loan graph for *di* 抵 (many); hereafter I will denote this by an X = Y construction, thus: 抵 = 抵.

19. For those who may think that "a culture so long ago and so far away" may have too little in common with "us" (however one might define that pronoun), I agree with Edward Slingerland's view: "When it comes to the study of early China, we need to acknowledge that the early Chinese were fellow *Homo sapiens*, with bodies and minds very much like ours, moving through a physical/cultural world that, because of convergent cultural evolution, was broadly similar to ours. They developed distinctive cultural ideas and practices, but these cultural forms remained ultimately grounded in shared human cognitive structures and adaptive challenges." Edward Slingerland, *Mind and Body in Early China: Beyond Orientalism and the Myth of Holism* (New York: Oxford University Press, 2019), 9–10.

of course it is highly unlikely that you will consider everything you read in this book to be unsurprising or "common sense." If that were the case, then I would not have written it.

Disparity of Sources

There are dozens of early Chinese Scholars' texts, most of which have been categorized as belonging to different schools of thought.[20] As such, many of these authors are often characterized as being "in conversation" with each other across the decades and centuries of our chosen time period. One might object that in the following pages I do not deal adequately with the "conversational" aspect of these sources, and that I do not pay sufficient attention to the disparity of my sources, insofar as some came to be considered more important than others. But while it is certainly true that many of these texts were, in some sense and to some degree, in conversation with one another, the details of their temporal precedence, and therefore the direction of the conversation, is open to considerable debate, and is far beyond the scope of this work.[21] Also, these conversations are not really relevant to my argument. Here, I only want to outline what self-cultivation meant in early China, not what it meant to a particular author or in a particular text. Likewise, which schools of thought emphasized which aspects of that outline are not of concern to my project. The narrative that I weave in the following pages does not hew to any one text or tradition and therefore is not "faithful" to any one of them. But that does not mean that this narrative is thereby compromised or somehow inauthentic. It is a work of syncretism,

---

20. The phrase "schools of thought," when applied to pre-Qin texts, has in recent decades become an item of contention for some scholars. In my view, the acceptability of this phrase usually hinges on the rhetorical problem of how one defines "school." If you agree with, for example, Kenneth Brashier's claim that "A school implies an institutionalism that includes a number of scholars consciously identifying with a particular idea system," then the phrase is probably inappropriate. (Kenneth Brashier, *Ancestral Memory in Early China*, Cambridge: Harvard University Asia Center, 2011, p. 6.) On the other hand, if you can countenance a "school of thought" as an analytic tool for recognizing similarities among texts, then it may be a useful construct. For my extended argument, see Paul Fischer, "The Creation of Daoism," *Journal of Daoist Studies* 8 (2015): 1–23.

21. For my thoughts on how early Chinese texts circulated and were reproduced, see Paul Fischer, "Authentication Studies (辨偽學) Methodology and the Polymorphous Text Paradigm," *Early China* 32 (2008–2009): 1–43.

considering a body of work from an intellectual milieu that very much valued syncretism. The various authors that I cite may well have disagreed about how to, say, best administer a country, but the concepts they used and the cultural norms they took for granted were to a very large degree unanimously shared. That continuity is what I draw from.

Another potential objection to broad surveys like this one is that the author may have cherry-picked the evidence for their claims. In a work this broad, there is no hope for demonstrably countering such a contention. For a narrower claim, one might marshal all the evidence and counterevidence and then proceed accordingly. Here I will make claims and adduce evidence, but a single monograph cannot include all possible counterevidence that would enable readers to draw their own conclusions. I am attempting to create a unified theory of self-cultivation, but there is a crucial difference between a scientific theory and an arts theory. While both are explanatory ideas originating from human creativity, the material world of science cannot be contradictory, while the imaginative world(s) of the arts can be, and usually is. Therefore, no single theory of self-cultivation in early China will ever account for all of the discrepancies of opinion among the sources. For what it is worth, despite the caveat of the "argument from authority" fallacy whereby students should not blindly trust authority figures, I have sought to be objective.

A slightly different potential objection is that I give short shrift to the supernatural, which may lead to the impression that early China was uncommonly secular. I have two replies to this. First, the supernatural simply does not play a very large role in this particular field of inquiry (i.e., self-cultivation), during this particular period of time, among the authors of the Scholars' texts. It is true that in later times, alchemy, for example—both the interior and exterior kinds—will become an important part of self-cultivation for a certain segment of the population. But that is a much later development. Second, more broadly, early Chinese Scholars' texts are in fact astonishingly, though not completely, secular. Reading them in isolation may well give the mistaken impression that early Chinese society as a whole seldom dealt with the supernatural. Other works on early Chinese cultural history will balance any such impression.[22] But, despite my comparing self-cultivation with soteriology above, it is not my goal here to

---

22. One such work is Poo Mu-chou 蒲慕州, *In Search of Personal Welfare: A View of Ancient Chinese Religion* (Albany: State University of New York Press, 1998).

give a balanced view of the supernatural in early China. Ultimately, any historical survey like this one will be a simplification. Despite academia's justifiable penchant for problematizing things, simplification has its place too.

Technical Terms

The mental paradigms through which we apprehend the world often come into focus when we learn about other cultures. Discovering these new paradigms, considering them, and juxtaposing them with one's own cultural paradigms is often a gradual process. To get us started, it would be a good idea to discuss the general contours of the early Chinese worldview. In the West, and extending eastward across the Indian subcontinent, there is an implicit understanding that there are one or more heavens above, and one or more hells below, with earth situated in between. Powerful deities that want worshipping reside in heaven, malevolent entities to be feared are in hell, and immortal human souls either go up to the one or down to the other after death. Early China does not share this paradigm. Looking at the scholars' literature as a whole, there is a heaven, but no one lives there, there is no hell, and human souls are not eternal.[23] Nothing in early Chinese culture was thought to be eternal; rather, the principle of ceaseless change and transformation is an underlying assumption among the authors we consider. The souls of humans may persist for a time after death, and humans that were powerful in life sometimes continued to be powerful after death, for a time, typically a few decades (though a precise time frame is never given). Local nature spirits were also thought to be active, and spirits and ancestors were both sacrificed to, at least by the royal family and other powerful clan patriarchs. What regular people believed and practiced is nearly impossible to discern because they typically did not leave records of such

---

23. Some early authors claim that royal ancestors "live" in Heaven, possibly as stars in the night sky. See, for example, *Shijing* 詩經 #235 (文王), where the dead Zhou King Wen is described as being "in Heaven" (于天). But whatever this implies, it is not really comparable to an idyllic abode of happiness where the souls of all morally good people go to reside; cf. Arthur Waley, *The Book of Songs: The Ancient Chinese Classic of Poetry* (1937; edited with additional translations by Joseph Allen; New York: Grove Press, 1996), 227. For more on the connection between ancestors and stars, see David Pankenier, *Astrology and Cosmology in Early China: Conforming Earth to Heaven* (Cambridge: Cambridge University Press, 2013).

things. But if the corpus of Scholars' texts is in any way representative of regular people and their beliefs (a claim that I am not making), then spirits and ancestors played a vanishingly small role in their lives.

These differences are important to remember because people naturally assume that other cultures are in fact similar to their own. So I want to reiterate that the early Chinese paradigm is not at all like the Western paradigm.[24] The authors who wrote the Scholars' texts, with very few exceptions, were quite uninterested in propitiating spirits or ancestors. It seems such sacrifices were the business of a tiny elite and not particularly relevant to the good life of the people. But it is quite possible that the corpus of Scholars' texts is *not* representative of regular people. There does exist a small amount of counterevidence to the claims just made about heaven and hell. There were those who did think that at least some people went to a kind of heaven, that there was a kind of Hades-like afterworld where souls might meet, and that it was potentially efficacious to sacrifice to certain spirits when you got sick.[25] I do not at all wish to sweep this evidence under the rug, but neither do I want to give the impression that we can comfortably use our cultural paradigms (in particular, the creator-deity, immortal souls, and eternal heaven or hell paradigm) to apprehend those of early China, particularly within the pursuit of self-cultivation. The differences clearly outweigh the similarities. Though there is no quick route to assessing all such differences and similarities, it will be beneficial to set the stage with a discussion of three things: Heaven and Earth, and the Way.

HEAVEN AND EARTH (天地)

Heaven and Earth constitute an indissoluble cosmic dyad. They comprise the widest parameters of the cosmos; nothing exists outside of them. No deities precede them, command them, or match them in any sense. They are responsible for the existence of everything, including humans.[26]

---

24. The "not at all" is, given what I just said in note 19, a hyperbolic rhetorical flourish. And yet, even upon reflection, I wish to keep this sentence as is, but want to note here that it is a pedagogical (and literary) device.

25. For more on these issues see, for example, Lai Guolong, *Excavating the Afterlife: The Archaeology of Early Chinese Religion* (Seattle: University of Washington Press, 2015).

26. This paradigm is, like most ancient cosmologies, earth-centric, and is not commensurate with our modern paradigm, in which the earth is but a tiny speck in the vast, star-filled cosmos.

Heaven and Earth arose spontaneously from primordial formlessness. They are uncaused and, though early China has no explicit cosmic eschatology, they will presumably someday return to homogenous formlessness. In the meantime, we live betwixt them, our heads wandering through the former, our feet roaming across the latter. Their primary accomplishments are the creation of the seasons (and phenology in general), and the foundation of the agricultural cycle that is, in turn, the foundation of human civilization.

There is no single creation story in early China that compares with the "Genesis" account in the West. There are, however, many shorter, almost off-handed, observations by a number of different authors. One reads: "When Heaven and Earth first began, Heaven rarefied and thereby was completed, Earth solidified and thereby was formed. The harmony of Heaven and Earth's union is the great mainstay of [all] living things." (天地有始，天微以成，地塞以形。天地合和，生之大經也。)[27] Much more will be said about the principle of harmony and its influence upon human society later. For now, let us stay focused on our two subjects. "Heaven is said to be open, Earth is said to be tranquil, thus they do not intrude [upon one another]." (天曰虛，地曰靜，乃不伐。)[28] This speaks to the grounds of their harmony, but in a more active vein, "Heaven is where *qi*-substance(s) all issues forth; Earth is the inevitability of [natural] principle(s)." (天者氣之所總出也，地者理之必然也。)[29] More than a thousand years later, "*qi*-substance" and "principle" came to form the foundation of Neo-Confucianism, the mainstay of intellectual history not only in Song dynasty (960–1279) China, but across all of East Asia. *Qi*-substance is what we might call "matter," except it is conceived as much more fluid, self-moving, and multivalent than lumpish "matter." (In fact, *qi* can be conceived of as a "process" as much as being a "substance," so "*qi*-fluctuating-substance" or "*qi*-process-substance" would be more accurate, albeit less wieldy.) Everything is made of it, even Heaven and Earth. Principle refers to the natural inclinations of things, both living and nonliving. It is a general term for what things do spontaneously when left to their own devices. We will return to these concepts in chapter 1.

---

27. *Lüshi chunqiu* 呂氏春秋 ch. 13.1 (有始); cf. John Knoblock and Jeffrey Riegel, *The Annals of Lü Buwei* (Stanford: Stanford University Press, 2000), 278.

28. *Guanzi* 管子 ch. 36 (心術上); cf. W. Allyn Rickett, *Guanzi: Political, Economic, and Philosophical Essays from Early China* (Princeton: Princeton University Press, 1985, 1998), 2:72.

29. *Heguanzi* 鶡冠子 ch. 11 (泰錄); cf. Carine Defoort, *The Pheasant Cap Master: A Rhetorical Reading* (Albany: State University of New York Press, 1997), 93.

Heaven and Earth, then, are both self-created and creators of other things. They are also exemplars for humans: "Heaven prevails with correctness; Earth prevails with equanimity; humans prevail with calm tranquility." (天主正，地主平，人主安靜。)³⁰ Our calm tranquility should be patterned on the correctness and equanimity of Heaven and Earth. One aspect of Heaven's correctness is its impartiality. "Heaven covers [all] without partiality; Earth bears [all] without partiality, the sun and moon shine [on all] without partiality, the four seasons proceed without partiality. [They] proceed with their virtuosities and the myriad things obtain consequent maturation with them." (天無私覆也，地無私載也，日月無私燭也，四時無私行也。行其德而萬物得遂長焉。)³¹ "Virtuosity" refers to the function of inanimate objects, the functional ability of living things, and the ethical virtues of humans. It combines the skill of a "virtuoso," the various "virtues," and the charisma of skillful and virtuous people. Another good translation might be "power." It is a very useful and very important term that we will meet quite often in the following pages. We are specifically asked to imitate the impartiality of the cosmic dyad: "How can we be selfless? By imitating the main precepts of Heaven and Earth." (庸能己無己乎？效夫天地之紀。)³² Further: "Those who can give without taking are the companions of Heaven and Earth." (能予而無取者，天地之配也。)³³ Heaven is rarified, open, correct, and impartial; it extrudes *qi*-substance and covers us. Earth is solid, tranquil, equanimous, and impartial; it conveys the inevitability of natural principles and it supports us. They act together in harmony. So far, so good.

Since they are responsible for the existence of everything, including people, in a sense they are like cosmic "parents." But the metaphor of "parents" raises the dicey question of the degree to which they are like Western deities, specifically the degree to which they are anthropomorphic. There are two answers to this question. The first is that they *used* to be conceived as more anthropomorphic but became less so over time, even to the point of not at all. There is more evidence for the anthropomorphism of Heaven, in particular, in the early years of the Zhou dynasty (1045–256 BCE) than in its later years, many centuries later. The second answer is: it depends on who you ask. It is like someone asking if Westerners think that "Mother

---

30. *Guanzi* ch. 49 (內業); cf. Rickett, *Guanzi*, 2:43.
31. *Lüshi chunqiu* ch. 1.5 (去私); cf. Knoblock and Riegel, *Lü Buwei*, 73.
32. *Guanzi* ch. 38 (白心); cf. Rickett, *Guanzi*, 2:90.
33. *Guanzi* ch. 2 (形勢); cf. Rickett, *Guanzi*, 1:77.

Nature" is an anthropomorphic deity. It is a common phrase, and some people do think of nature as a "her" and, in fact, there are plenty of people who worship "her," but I think most would agree that most Westerners use "Mother Nature" metaphorically, not literally. The same can be said of Heaven.

Heaven is fundamentally only one half of the cosmic dyad of Heaven and Earth, but like the "master" of a house in a patriarchal society, it gets much more press than its partner. In earlier texts, like the classics, several anthropomorphic actions and emotions are ascribed to Heaven. The *Shujing* says: "When Heaven looks down upon the people below, it measures their propriety, and sends down years that are either long-lasting or not long-lasting. It is not that Heaven causes people to die prematurely, [but rather that] people cut short their own lives/destinies." (惟天監下民，典厥義，降年有永有不永。非天夭民，民中絕命。)[34] The *Shijing* says: "Heaven protects and settles you with great security, causing you to have ample richness. [It is] why [your] blessings will not be eliminated, causing you much increase, so that everything will be abundant." (天保定爾，亦孔之固，俾爾單厚。何福不除，俾爾多益，以莫不庶。)[35] The *Yijing* says: "The way of Heaven is to send down help but [still] shine brightly, the way of Earth is to lie low but [still] send [things; e.g., plants] up. The way of Heaven is to take from [those who are] excessive and give to [those who are] humble, the way of Earth is to change [those who are] excessive and flow towards [those who are] modest." (天道下濟而光明，地道卑而上行。天道虧盈而益謙，地道變盈而流謙。)[36] These three classics should suffice to show a degree of anthropomorphism in early accounts of Heaven. While it may be easy to take the verbs "look" and "send down" as metaphorical, it is somewhat harder (though not impossible) to do this with "protect," "settle," and the rest.

The evidence in the preceding paragraph seems to present a clear picture of an anthropomorphic, deity-like Heaven. Yet these self-same writings undermine this conception by equating, in a sense, above with below. For example, the *Shujing* also says: "Heaven's keen hearing and sight derive from our people's keen hearing and sight [toward good rulers]; Heaven's discern-

---

34. *Shujing* 書經 ch. 24 (高宗肜日); cf. James Legge, *The Shoo King*, 2nd ed. (1894; rpt. Hong Kong: Hong Kong University Press, 1960), 264.

35. *Shijing* #166 (天保); cf. Waley, *The Book of Songs*, 138.

36. *Yijing* 易經 #15 (謙), "Tuan" (彖) commentary; cf. Richard Lynn, *The Classic of Changes: A New Translation of the* I Ching *as Interpreted by Wang Bi* (New York: Columbia University Press, 1994), 229.

ment and fearsomeness derive from our people's discernment and severity [toward bad rulers]. There is a connection between above and below, so be respectful, those who possess the soil [i.e., rulers]." (天聰明自我民聰明，天明畏自我民明威。達于上下，敬哉有土。)[37] What does it mean that the one "derives from" the other? And what is the nature of the "connection" between above and below? Literal-minded scholars say that an anthropomorphic Heaven simply sees what we see, but metaphorical-minded scholars say that "Heaven" here is a metaphor for "the will of the people." I find the metaphorical reading more persuasive, and suspect that later authors, who over time anthropomorphized Heaven less and less, would have read it this way.

Xunzi, in particular, thought that "Heaven" was just another name for "nature." He wryly observed: "[One] performs the summer rain sacrifice and it rains, but why? [I] say: there is no reason why. It is the same as if [one] did not perform the summer rain sacrifice and it rains." (雩而雨，何也？曰：無何也，猶不雩而雨也。)[38] A famously wise counselor named Guan Zhong concurred: "Qi Duke Huan asked Guan Zhong: 'What should kings revere?' [Guan Zhong] replied: 'Revere Heaven.' Duke Huan raised his head and looked at heaven. Guan Zhong said: 'What I mean by "Heaven" is not the blue-sky heaven. Kings should take the people to be Heaven.'" (齊桓公問於管仲曰：「王者何貴？」曰：「貴天。」桓公仰而視天。管仲曰：「所謂天，非蒼莽之天也。王者以百姓為天。」)[39] Here, too, a metaphorical reading whereby "to be" means "to be the same as" and not "to stand in for" makes more sense, for if Xunzi believed in Heaven as some kind of "higher power" that is concerned with human affairs, then this passage would be insulting to it. This may be a decidedly counterintuitive metaphor in the West, but in the East it has a pedigree stretching back over two thousand years.

The benevolence of an ostensibly anthropomorphic Heaven sometimes appears to have been doubted, but closer inspection usually reveals that humans deserved whatever disaster, natural or otherwise, had been visited

---

37. *Shujing* ch. 4 (皋陶謨); cf. Legge, *Shoo King*, 74.

38. *Xunzi* 荀子 ch. 17 (天論); cf. Eric Hutton, *Xunzi: The Complete Text* (Princeton: Princeton University Press, 2014), 179.

39. *Hanshi waizhuan* 韓詩外傳 ch. 4.18; cf. James Hightower, *Han Shih Wai Chuan: Han Ying's Illustrations of the Didactic Application of the Classic of Songs* (Cambridge: Harvard University Press, 1952), 144.

upon them.⁴⁰ The *Shijing* notes, bitterly, "Great Heaven is not fair, to send down these plentiful troubles. Great Heaven is not kind, to send down these great injustices." (昊天不傭，降此鞠訩。昊天不惠，降此大戾。)⁴¹ But these "troubles" and "injustices" may be contextualized as the result of poor rulership. Heaven was thought to grant a "mandate" to benevolent rulers, which could be withdrawn, resulting in human conflict—the overthrow of the dynasty, say—or natural disaster. Heaven, it seems, "helps" those who throw the bums out (i.e., it serves as a powerful metaphor supporting people who overthrow incompetent rulers). Elsewhere, Heaven is depicted as caring, even while intolerant of poor rulership. "Heaven's love for the people is deep. How could it allow one person to wantonly reign over the people, in order to indulge his excesses, and abandon the natures of Heaven and Earth? It certainly would not!" (天之愛民甚矣。豈其使一人肆於民上，以從其淫，而棄天地之性？必不然矣！)⁴²

The ideals of impartiality and love may seem contradictory, but Mozi combines them by saying that Heaven loves humans impartially, that "the sun shines on the evil as well as the good."⁴³ Laozi, too, notes that "The Heavenly way has no favorites, [but] it abides with competent people." (天道無親，常與善人。)⁴⁴ "Competence" does not necessarily carry moral overtones—though it may not necessarily exclude them either—but the

---

40. Usually, but not always: for the problem of an ostensibly "good" Heaven "allowing" bad things to happen to ostensibly good people, see Franklin Perkins, *Heaven and Earth are Not Humane: The Problem of Evil in Classical Chinese Philosophy* (Bloomington: Indiana University Press, 2014).

41. *Shijing* #191 (節南山); cf. Waley, *Book of Songs*, 166. See also *Shijing* #257 (桑柔) for similar complaints.

42. *Zuozhuan* 左傳 (襄公 14); cf. Stephen Durrant, Wai-yee Li, David Schaberg, *Zuozhuan: Commentary on the "Spring and Autumn Annals"* (Seattle: University of Washington Press, 2016), 2:1025.

43. *Mozi* 墨子 ch. 4 (法儀): "Heaven certainly wants people to mutually love and benefit one another and does not want people to mutually hate and rob one another. How do we know Heaven wants . . . [this]? Because it equally loves them and equally benefits them. How do we know . . . [this]? Because it equally causes them to have things and equally causes them to have food." (天必欲人之相愛相利，而不欲人之相惡相賊也。奚以知 . . . ？以其兼而愛之，兼而利之也．奚以知 . . . ？以其兼而有之，兼而食之也。) cf. John Knoblock and Jeffrey Riegel, *Mozi: A Study and Translation of the Ethical and Political Writings* (Berkeley: University of California, Berkeley, 2013), 59. The "sun shines on the evil . . ." quote is a common paraphrase of the biblical "Matthew" 5.45.

44. *Laozi* ch. 79.

emphasis is certainly on going about one's business intelligently.⁴⁵ Heaven is most concerned with practical things, like sufficient food for the people, harmony among people, and sacrificial "meals" for itself (provided only by rulers, not us regular folk). It does not ask to be worshipped or praised or loved. But, as mentioned above, it can mete out punishment for wrongdoing, that is, for incompetence.

One way that Heaven can intervene in human affairs is by allowing the overthrow of a bad ruler. Another, more common method, is by showing what might be called "displeasure" by allowing, or possibly even causing, natural disasters. Mozi was less concerned with bad rulers than with a defiant populace. This is why he focuses on people who do not "conform" to Heaven's mandated ruler, often known as a "Heavenly scion" (天子) rather than a "king" (王). For Mozi, rebelling against the ruler (at least, when it was not warranted) was as bad as rebelling against Heaven. "These days, if Heaven's stormy winds and bitter rains arrive in profusion, this is Heaven's way of punishing the people for not upwardly conforming with Heaven." (今若天飄風苦雨，潦潦而至者，此天之所以罰百姓之不上同於天者也。)⁴⁶

Xunzi, as we have seen, and quite possibly in "conversation" with Mozi, disagreed, saying: "When stars fall or trees groan, the people of the state are all afraid, saying: what is this? [I] say: it is nothing! It is [only] the changes of Heaven and Earth, the developments of Yin and Yang, and rare occurrences among things. It is okay to wonder at them, but not to fear them." (星隊木鳴，國人皆恐。曰：是何也？曰：無何也！是天地之變，陰陽之化，物之罕至者也。怪之，可也；而畏之，非也。)⁴⁷ Yin and Yang are the passive and active modes of *qi*-substance.⁴⁸ Heaven, with its constantly moving sun, moon, and stars, was seen as the epitome of Yang, while Earth, which in stillness accepts the quickening elements of rain and lightning (before later "giving birth" to the plants growing out of it), was seen as the epitome of Yin. Both of these will be discussed further in chapter 1. Here, the disparity of opinion on the anthropomorphic workings of Heaven and Earth is clearly evident.

---

45. "Competence," which may also be translated as "excellence" or "skill," is remarkably like the "virtue" that is the core of Robert Pirsig's *Zen and the Art of Motorcycle Maintenance* (1974). For a discussion on the possible amorality of some early Chinese texts like the *Laozi*, see Hans-Georg Moeller, *The Moral Fool: A Case for Amorality* (New York: Columbia University Press, 2009).

46. *Mozi* ch. 11 (尚同上); cf. Knoblock and Riegel, *Mozi*, 116.

47. *Xunzi* ch. 17 (天論); cf. Hutton, *Xunzi*, 17.

48. For a book-length analysis of Yin and Yang, see Robin Wang, *Yinyang: The Way of Heaven and Earth in Chinese Thought and Culture* (New York: Cambridge University Press, 2012).

Scholars' texts, however, were usually less interested in Heaven's perceived anthropomorphism and more interested in its orderliness. Like a conductor before a whirling orchestra, sun, moon, stars, and seasons all move in remarkably dependable and systematic ways. Think how hard it would be to plant and harvest crops if the seasons arrived haphazardly. Thanks, Heaven. This orderliness was thought to provide a pedagogical model: "Accord with the way of Heaven, return to the principles of things: investigate, examine, and study them, and when you finish, then start again." (因天之道，反形之理：督參鞠之，終則有始。)[49] The role of Heaven, and of Heaven and Earth, as the cosmic paradigm within which all other dramas, human and otherwise, unfold, will be a mainstay of this survey.

The Way (道)

"The way of Heaven" is a common trope in early China. Some authors drop the "of Heaven" part and refer to "the way" by itself. At other times authors posit a Way that is separate from, and prior to, Heaven. This causes a problem, however, because now some authors appear to conflate the "way of Heaven" with the "Way" that precedes Heaven, while others will assume the "Way" is, in some sense, superior. It is impossible to always know for sure when an author is referring to the "way of Heaven" but has dropped the "of Heaven" part and only written "way," but usually this can be inferred from context. Therefore, I will use a convention available in English, but not Chinese, and refer to the Way that is superior to Heaven as the "Way," while all other ways will just be a particular "way."

The Chinese word "way" (道) has semantic parameters similar to those in English. It includes a literal "way" or road that one can walk upon, as well as an extrapolated "way" of doing something, like playing the piano or administering a state, just as one may say in English. There is also one's personal way of living life, as well as a way that might be thought proper to all humans (or at least all humans in a given community). There is also an addition to the two ways from the previous paragraph: the way of Heaven, and the (cosmic) Way.[50] Thus, we already have six different "ways" to consider.

---

49. *Hanfeizi* 韓非子 ch. 8 (揚權); cf. Burton Watson, *The Basic Writings of Han Fei Tzu* (New York: Columbia University Press, 1964), 36. Note: 有 = 又.

50. It should also be noted that Chinese lacks the definite article "the" and the indefinite article "a," so writing in English of "a way" or "the way" is matter of interpretation that necessarily affects translation.

For some, there is a Way that is in some sense above and beyond the cosmic Heaven-Earth dyad.[51] They say that this Way is non-material, while Heaven is made of *qi*-substance, and for them the relationship between the Way and Heaven is conceived as something like that between gravity and the physical universe. Would gravity exist without a physical universe? If gravity is conceived as some kind of "law of nature," then I suppose it could, insofar as the law would exist, even if there was nothing for it to act upon. In the same manner, the Way is said to exist of its own accord: it is "based in itself and rooted in itself, before there was Heaven and Earth, from antiquity it assuredly existed." (自本自根，未有天地，自古以固存。)[52] Even more, this Way is said to have created Heaven and Earth.[53]

One question that often arises is: if the Way (or the way of Heaven) is responsible for the creation of everything, then we might call it the way of nature; and since humans are part of nature, then isn't everything we do a part of it? That is, is it possible to depart from the Way? The short answer to both is: it depends on how you conceive "part of" and "depart from." I do not mean to split hairs here, but this is a common, and sometimes contentious, question, and it deserves some attention. It may be helpful to think of the gravity analogy here: nothing made of matter can ever escape the effects of gravity, so in that sense we are always "part of" gravity and we cannot "depart from" it. But we can work "against" gravity by, say, carefully engineering a plane and continuously powering it with fuel to sustain flight. Similarly, the Way is inescapable, and we are always "part of" it (although, as with gravity, this is not a very good way of describing our relation to it), but we *can* act against it. Another common analogy of the Way is as the current of a river in which we are all swimmers: we cannot get out of the river (in this metaphor), but we *can* swim against the flow. Therefore, despite the ontological claim that the Way is the ultimate source of all things and is "in" everything, that does not mean that all human actions are in accord with it, as humans possess the peculiar capacity to act contrary to it.

---

51. "Way" in Chinese is transliterated as "dao," and some readers may have heard of a school of thought, or perhaps a religion, called Daoism. This is the same Dao. "Dao-ism" is "the way of the Way." In general, a Daoist will think that the Way is in some sense "higher" than Heaven, while a Ruist (i.e., Confucian) would think the Way *is* the way of Heaven. This is a useful rule of thumb, but it is not always clear.

52. *Zhuangzi* 莊子 ch. 6 (大宗師); cf. Burton Watson, *The Complete Works of Zhuangzi* (New York: Columbia University Press, 1968; 2013), 45.

53. *Guanzi* ch. 39 (水地): "The Way created Heaven and Earth." (道生天地。) cf. Rickett, *Guanzi*, 2:116.

There are two wrinkles to this explanation, however, depending on how one feels about free will and ethics. "Free will" is not a concept found in early Chinese writings, though "will" (志) and "intention" (意) are, so looking at them with this in mind is an alien imposition on the texts.[54] Nevertheless, if you do believe in free will, then you will probably blame free will as the thing responsible for humans acting against the Way, usually, if not always, under the sway of excessive emotions. It is probably better, however, not to take the "free will" approach, for two reasons. One is that "free will" is simply not part of the early Chinese vocabulary. A second is that, while a belief in free will is still the cultural default in the West, a growing number of people do not hold it.[55] Without free will, one can still act against the Way; it is just that blame is vitiated. In this paradigm, "misdeeds" are construed as being caused more by genetic or environmental factors rather than by a pristine "self" that can "freely choose" among options without significant influence from either biology or circumstance. People who intentionally act against the Way by acting against social harmony are still punished, in this paradigm, but they are punished by authorized members of society who carry feelings of regret, not revenge; they are punished with compassion, not moral outrage.[56] This brings us to the second wrinkle.

While "virtuosity" plays a central role in early Chinese thought, its connection to ethical virtue in texts that particularly prize the cosmic Way is, arguably, more tenuous. Following up on this claim, however, would lead us too far astray.[57] In any case, as with free will, some people do not accept a universal code of ethics, only a number of local, culture-specific, socially-conditioned ethics. So, if there is no such thing as universal ethics, then how can one act against a normative Way? As with the example of dealing with rule-breakers in a community that does not subscribe to the idea of free will, acting contrary to the Way is a matter of competence, not morality.[58] Incompetence, and particularly social incompetence that leads to disharmony

---

54. Insofar as "free will" is related to agency and the individual, see Erica Brindley, *Individualism in Early China: Human Agency and the Self in Thought and Politics* (Honolulu: University of Hawaii Press, 2010).
55. See, for example, Sam Harris, *Free Will* (New York: Free Press, 2012).
56. For more on this, see *Laozi* chs. 27, 49, 62, and 79.
57. For one articulation of this argument, see Moeller, *The Moral Fool*.
58. One problem in discussing this matter is the broad semantic parameters of the words like "good" and "bad," which can refer to the advisability, legality, or morality of a particular action, though these are three very different things.

among people, is against the Way, which is a way of graceful harmony, both among humans and between humans and the natural environment.

To reiterate, there are many "ways": a literal path; a "way" of doing something, like a particular way of playing the piano; a personal "way" of life; a communal "way" of living harmoniously; a way of Heaven; and a Way that is prior to, and logically separate from, Heaven. Nothing more need be said of the first two as they are not particularly relevant to the topic of self-cultivation. A personal way may be broadly charted: "That which is not appropriate to me, even though beneficial to me, I will not do. That which is not my way, even though beneficial to me, I will not accept." (非吾當，雖利不行。非吾道，雖利不取。)[59] However, in early China, one's personal way will almost certainly be presented as aligned with a more expansive way, as indicated by the very next sentence: "The best is to follow Heaven; the next best is to follow humans." (上之隨天，其次隨人。) Almost certainly, but not *always* certainly: recall that Xunzi was known for conceiving "Heaven" simply as "nature." For him, humans ought to follow a human way: "The way [of former kings] is not the way of Heaven, nor the way of Earth, but is that which *people* take to be the way, which is the way that noble people have made." (道者，非天之道，非地之道，人之所以道也，君子之所道也。)[60] He is clear that, while there may be as many "ways" as there are humans, there is only one correct human way, which here he calls the way of noble people, but elsewhere he calls the way of sagely people: "The world does not have two [correct, human] ways; sagely people are not of two minds." (天下無二道，聖人無兩心。)[61] This correct human way, then, is a human construction. Xunzi continues: "The mind is the artisan and governor of the [human] way." (心也者，道之工宰也。)[62]

---

59. *Guanzi* ch. 38 (白心); cf. Rickett, *Guanzi*, 2:86.

60. *Xunzi* ch. 8 (儒效); cf. Hutton, *Xunzi*, 55. Italics in translations are always mine because there are no italics in ancient Chinese. The "way of former kings" is, for Xunzi, assumed to be good.

61. *Xunzi* ch. 21 (解蔽); cf. Hutton, *Xunzi*, 224. The Chinese word *xin* 心 is a more expansive word than the English word "mind," insofar as it refers to both the cognitive functions associated with the mind as well as the emotional functions associated with the "heart." Thus, some translators use "heart-mind," but I find this a little awkward (even if more accurate), and thus typically translate this word simply as "mind," though in the relatively few cases when the physical heart or the emotions are the primary referent, then I translate it as "heart." (For the physical heart and the emotional "heart," see, for example, the translations at chap. 1, n. 111 and chap. 2, n. 13, respectively).

62. *Xunzi* ch. 22 (正名); cf. Hutton, *Xunzi*, 241.

This explains Kongzi's famous saying: "It is people that can broaden the way; it is not the way that broadens people." (人能弘道，非道弘人。)[63] Just how to construct this way, in order to broaden people, was the central concern for both these authors. Both of them looked outward, to historical precedent, as well as inward, to what they saw as human nature.

Some people disagreed with Xunzi and had a somewhat less optimistic view of human potential, at least in the aggregate, which is to say, as a society. Zhuangzi was one of these people. He said: "What do [we] call the 'way'? There is the Heavenly way and the human way. Being uncontrived yet honorable is the Heavenly way. Being contrived and attached is the human way. The ruler [should represent] the Heavenly way; the minister [should represent] the human way. The Heavenly way and the human way are far apart from each other. This really should be investigated." (何謂道？有天道，有人道。無為而尊者，天道也；有為而累者，人道也。主者，天道也；臣者，人道也。天道之與人道也，相去遠矣。不可不察也。)[64] Whereas Xunzi promoted an aspirational "human way," Zhuangzi diagnosed it as too contrived and instead posited the "Heavenly way"—which may be understood both as a cosmic way as well as the various "ways" of our individual destinies—as his aspirational way.

Other authors wrote of a way that precisely corresponds to neither Xunzi's nor Zhuangzi's but seems to synthesize the two with a human way that is nevertheless derived from Heaven. "[One of the things] that Heaven mandates is called [human] nature. That which follows [human] nature is called the [human] way. That which cultivates the way is called teaching. The way should not for an instant be departed from; [that which] may be departed from is not the way." (天命之謂性。率性之謂道。脩道之謂教。道也者，不可須臾離也；可離非道也。)[65] So, depending on the author, some-

---

63. *Lunyu* 論語 15.29; cf. Edward Slingerland, *Confucius: Analects with Selections from Traditional Commentaries* (Indianapolis: Hackett, 2003), 185. "*Lunyu*" is the Chinese name for the *Analects*.

64. *Zhuangzi* ch. 11 (在宥); cf. Watson, *Zhuangzi*, 83.

65. *Liji* 禮記 ch. 31 (中庸); cf. James Legge, *Li Chi: Book of Rites* (1885; rpt. New York: University Books, 1967), 2:300. The last sentence, which is a normative claim, is sometimes mistaken for an ontological claim. It does not help that the *bu ke* 不可 and *ke* 可 translated here as "should not" and "may" can also be translated as "cannot" and "can," respectively. But the context makes clear that this human way is derivative both of Heaven and (human) nature, and that it can be "cultivated" by us via learning. Therefore the last sentence can only mean that we *should not* depart from this way, not that we *cannot* depart from it.

times the way humans should follow is seen as deriving from a Way that is prior to Heaven and Earth, sometimes as modeled (and, in a metaphorical sense, "given") to us by Heaven, sometimes as derived from Heaven via our human nature and "cultivated" by learning, and sometimes as quite separate from Heaven and Heaven's way. Despite this ambiguity, it is clear that the "way" humans ought to follow was an important concern in early China.

In the previous section we saw that Heaven was described both as impartial and as impartially loving humans. The cosmic Way is described as impartial too, and it was also said to be partial to competent people, even within the same text. Zhuangzi, at least, is clear: "From the point of view of the Way, things are neither precious nor worthless." (以道觀之，物無貴賤。)[66] If we allow ourselves to conflate the Way with the way of Heaven for a moment, then Laozi uses a more trenchant image to say the same thing: "Heaven and Earth are not [contrivedly] good, [because] they take the myriad things to be as straw dogs." (天地不仁，以萬物為芻狗。)[67] "Straw dogs" are ceremonial objects that were honored before a sacrificial ceremony but subsequently either burned during the ceremony or discarded after it. For Laozi, unlike Mozi above, Heaven does not love us. The point here, however, is its impartiality, yet later in the same text it says, as we saw above, "The Heavenly way has no favorites, [but] it abides with competent people."[68] How might our "principle of charity" make sense of this? How can something both have "no favorites" but still "abide with" a certain group of people? Resolving this is not as difficult as it may appear. The Way—or Heaven, or nature—is the way it is regardless of what humans think, but a certain group of people are better able to see this way, adapt to it, work with it, and consequently benefit from it. The Heavenly way does not favor them, per se, rather, they have done the work of making the most of what we might call, for lack of a better word, reality.

There are three final points I want to make about the Way: it can make you happy, it can help your virtuosity, and it can be important for self-cultivation. First, though following the Way does not guarantee happiness, and indeed the general attitude towards all emotions in texts that extol the Way is one of detachment (more on this in chapter 3), happiness is an explicit prospect. "Those in ancient times who attained the Way were

---

66. *Zhuangzi* ch. 17 (秋水); cf. Watson, *Zhuangzi*, 129.
67. *Laozi* ch. 5.
68. *Laozi* ch. 79, cited in note 44 above.

happy in dire straits and also happy in smooth sailing, for their happiness was not derived from the dire straits or the smooth sailing." (古之得道者，窮亦樂，通亦樂，所樂非窮通也。)⁶⁹ This kind of happiness is certainly closer to cheerful equanimity than giddy delight, but it is a distinct side effect of working with the Way nonetheless.

Mere emotional happiness pales in comparison to the power of virtuosity in the intellectual milieu of early China. The *Laozi*, which has an alternate title of *The Way and Virtuosity Classic* (道德經), says: "The expression of great virtuosity follows only the Way." (孔德之容，惟道是從。)⁷⁰ Another passage shows that virtuosity is second only to the Way itself. "The Way produces them; virtuosity nurtures them; things shape them; circumstances complete them." (道生之，德畜之，物形之，勢成之。)⁷¹ "Them" refers to the "myriad things"—that is, to everything—and virtuosity is key to their development. Virtuosity is a concept that started out in early China as the charismatic leadership qualities that some rulers possessed, or wanted to possess.⁷² But, as with the evolution of the idea of a "noble person," "virtuosity" also evolved and came to refer to the "defining qualities" of anything. Yet virtuosity is not a passive agent, as it also refers to the potential that *could* define a person or thing, given the right circumstances and the will to see a given course of action through. We will investigate virtuosity in chapter 4; in the meantime, the *Laozi* is no doubt employing a bit of hyperbole when it announces "[If you] emphasize the accumulation of virtuosity, then anything is possible." (重積德則無不克。)⁷³

The focus of the present book is self-cultivation, and in this endeavor too, the Way plays an integral role (at least for those who acknowledge it). As virtuosity is an inner potential to be realized, the Way is like an energizing order in the world that can be interiorized and used. "As a general rule, the Way has no [fixed] position, [but in] a competent mind it securely dwells. . . . Cultivate the mind, make tranquil the intentions, then the Way

---

69. *Zhuangzi* ch. 28 (讓王); cf. Watson, *Zhuangzi*, 248. Chapters 18 and 21 even describe "full happiness" (至樂).

70. *Laozi* ch. 21.

71. *Laozi* ch. 51.

72. For an analysis of the evolution of the idea of "virtuosity" throughout the roughly 800-year-long Zhou dynasty, see Constance Cook, *Ancestors, Kings, and the Dao* (Cambridge: Harvard University Asia Center, 2017).

73. *Laozi* ch. 59.

can be attained." (凡道無所,善心安愛. . . . 修心靜音,道乃可得。)[74] What, exactly, can the Way be used *for*? For an individual, use it to increase your virtuosity, fulfill your potential, be content with fate, realize your destiny. For a society, use it for justice and harmony.

Imaginativeness, Applicability, and Metaphor

Many cultures have authoritative texts in their traditions of intellectual history. Given their importance in their respective cultures, it is notable that many, if not most, of these texts were written in a less-than-straightforward style. Such a style, which we might call "poetic," allows greater interpretive freedom. This freedom means the texts can appeal to a wider audience, which may be one reason why such works became authoritative in the first place. Regardless of how they came to be viewed as authoritative, these works are more difficult to analyze precisely because they were written this way. Using the "principle of charity" therefore becomes inevitable with these books. Some early Chinese Scholars' texts are more poetic than others, but none of them clearly and unambiguously explain their philosophies in plain language: not for their own, contemporary audience, and certainly not for audiences in other cultures thousands of years later. There are, therefore, a few things to keep in mind when we read these texts today: imaginativeness, applicability, and metaphor.

A lot of important intellectual work goes on in the imagination. When we "talk to ourselves" in our minds, we imagine the words being spoken. When we "picture" how an event occurred in the past, we imagine it in our "mind's eye." And when we relate to an authoritative figure—cultural, philosophical, religious—we may imagine an encounter with them. The same is true with ideas: when you first saw the word "self-cultivation" on the cover of this book, it is quite likely that your imagination led to you guess at what the contents would be. The texts of early Chinese intellectual history, both the classics and the Scholars' texts, like Western works of philosophy and religion, might be called "imaginative" insofar as they are not straightforward history, even though they may relate much historical information. It is unfortunate that "imaginative" usually means "creative" but "imaginary" usually means "fictional," precisely because authors of poetic works create scenarios that may well *derive* from historical events, but that

---

74. *Guanzi* ch. 49 (內業); cf. Rickett, Guanzi, 2:41–42. Note: 愛 = 處 or 薆; 音 = 意.

are articulated in a way to make a certain point, rather than to simply and accurately recount something that happened.

Early Chinese Scholars' texts vary considerably, just as, say, early Christian or early Buddhist texts do. As "John" is more poetic than the other biblical biographies of Jesus, and literarily quite different from both the letters and apocalyptic writings of the New Testament, so the *Laozi* is more poetic than other contemporaneous writings, never mentioning a single person or place by name, while the *Zhuangzi* has lots of made-up people and places—truly imaginary—with other Scholars' texts utilizing other narrative devices to make their points. It is important to keep the imaginative aspects of culturally authoritative writings in mind in order to avoid the assumption, the "false dichotomy," that such narratives are either fact or fiction. Sometimes they are both, to widely varying degrees. Faith groups within cultures tend to regard the authoritative writings with which they are familiar as fact, and all others as fiction. In a globalizing world that values fairness and a degree of objectivity, this tendency is not tenable. Assessing the historicity of a given text is an interesting and important scholarly enterprise, but the present book will, by design, quote from a number of sources, and may not pause to consider the degree of imaginativeness, of "poetry," that characterizes each one. This survey is a survey of ideas, and sometimes these ideas are couched in poetic language.

Applicability is another complication for culturally authoritative texts. As with the "principle of charity" and imaginativeness, applicability addresses another kind of "either-or" judgment. That is: does the entire text "apply" to modern readers, or only parts of the text? When modern Buddhists learn that there are a lot more rules for female nuns than for male monks, should the extra rules still apply to modern Buddhists, or were those extra rules only a reflection of the patriarchal time in which they were written? Similarly, when Paul wrote that women should "learn in silence with full submission" and should not "teach or have authority over a man," was that injunction meant only for his immediate audience, or does it apply to modern readers too?[75] Similarly, Kongzi said "Only women and petty people are difficult to provide for: [if one becomes too] close to them, then they become overly friendly, and [if one becomes too] distant from them, then they are resentful." (唯女子與小人為難養也：近之則不孫，遠之則怨。)[76]

---

75. The biblical "1st Timothy" 2:11–12.

76. *Lunyu* 17.25; cf. Slingerland, *Analects*, 211. Some commentators claim that this does not "apply" to all women, but only household maids. There is no way to know for sure.

Egalitarian readers, therefore, often have "applicability" problems like these with ancient authoritative texts. Resolving such problems is up to the reader but being aware of the issue is important.

A third potential complication is the question of when a text is being literal and when it should be read as metaphorical. Authors typically do not mark this distinction and, since human language is so imbued with metaphor, they may not always know themselves when they are writing with metaphor.[77] Often, especially with "poetic" narrative, the judgment of literal versus metaphorical must lie with the reader. Currently (i.e., in 2021), American Christians seem about evenly divided on whether the seven-day creation story in "Genesis" indicates a literal seven days or whether a "day" is a metaphor for a different unit of time. As noted above, some early Chinese authors, like Xunzi, interpreted "Heaven" as a metaphor for "nature." The degree to which early Chinese Heaven should be thought of as anthropomorphic will always remain an open question, since anthropomorphic language can always be read as metaphorical. Metaphor can be beautiful and evocative; academic analyses of metaphor, while not noted for their beauty and evocativeness in doing so, may nevertheless help reveal both.

---

77. The classic work on this is by George Lakoff and Mark Johnson, *Metaphors We Live By* (Chicago: University of Chicago Press, 1980). For something specific to early China, see Edward Slingerland, "Metaphor and Meaning in Early China," *Dao: A Journal of Comparative Philosophy* 10.1 (2011): 1–30.

PART I
PERSON (人)

Chapter 1

Body (體)

"If an action tires your body but puts your mind at ease, do it."

—*Xunzi* ch. 2 "Self-cultivation"

身勞而心安,為之。《荀子·修身》

Introduction

Humans are but one of the myriad things created by Heaven and Earth. We are not more important to this cosmic dyad, insofar as we are not more "precious" or "beloved" to them, but we do have what seems to be a unique opportunity to consciously work in cooperation with them. Xunzi said: "Heaven has its seasons, Earth has its resources, humans have their orderliness, and these are said to be able to form a triad." (天有其時,地有其財,人有其治,夫是之謂能參。)[1] Human orderliness, however, is not a given; it is a matter of cultivation. So, while humans are not really privileged in the larger scheme of things, self-cultivation presents us with the possibility to order ourselves and thereby come to enjoy a special relationship with the cosmos. Precisely what humans need to do to "have their orderliness" is the purview of this book. The first thing to understand about this process is that effort is required. According to Xunzi:

---

1. *Xunzi* 荀子 ch. 17 (天論); cf. Eric Hutton, *Xunzi: The Complete Text* (Princeton: Princeton University Press, 2014), 176.

Concentration and habituation are the means by which we develop our nature. Focusing on one thing and not two is the means by which we complete our accumulated [efforts]. *Habituation* can change our intentions and being comfortable [with such changes] over a period of time can [actually] change our substance. *Focusing* on one thing and not two may result in a connection with spiritous percipience and the creation of a triad with Heaven and Earth.

(注錯習俗，所以化性也。并一而不二，所以成積也。習俗移志，安久移質。并一而不二，則通於神明，參於天地矣。)[2]

"Concentration" entails both initial attention (注) and subsequent action (措), while "habituation" includes practice (習) as well as eventual adaptation (俗). We will read more about the "substance" that may be changed later in this chapter, and more about human nature and the possibility of spiritous perceptivity in chapters 2 and 10. Here I first want to highlight the role of initial human effort. The four-part program of attention, action, practice, and adaptation is a good way to begin. This chapter deals with the body, and the immediate goals of bodily self-cultivation are health and beauty. We will first turn our attention to the makeup of the human body before considering how to act with it. Briefly, our bodies are an arrangement of *qi*-substance(s), which we should want to operate, or "flow," smoothly.

As noted in the introduction, some of the ideas articulated in early Chinese philosophy are incompatible with one another. This is certainly the case with cosmology, but this incompatibility is probably nowhere more pointed than in descriptions of the human person. Such discrepancies exist in other cultures as well, and I am often amazed that this continues to be the case today. English-speakers routinely use words like "spirit" and "soul" and often assume their audience knows what these terms refer to, but upon further discussion it almost always becomes quite clear that these terms, and others like them, are hopelessly opaque. In America, where seventy percent of the population self-identify as "Christian," appeal to their use in authoritative texts is of little use. Jesus and Paul, like their audiences, apparently had no clear, agreed-upon definitions of these terms.[3] The same

---

2. *Xunzi* ch. 8 (儒效); cf. Hutton, *Xunzi*, 65. Note: 錯 = 措.
3. See Dale Martin, *The Corinthian Body* (New Haven: Yale University Press, 1995). The same could be said of the early Greek philosophers.

is true of early Chinese authors. So, while I wish to argue for a coherent theory of the cosmos and a coherent theory of the body, the latter will have a particularly large amount of counterevidence. But just as this problem has not prevented Christians from having coherent paradigms and plans of action, so it shall not prevent us either. The theory I present below is not meant to obscure the diversity of opinion on the subject, but rather to present a point of view—retrospective and imposed, to be sure, but also broadly accurate—from which we may begin our inquiry.

In this chapter we will consider early Chinese cosmology and anthropology, with the goal of assessing the parameters and particulars of physical self-cultivation. Though "cosmology" is intuitively distinct from "astronomy," there is no corresponding word relating to the human person, as distinct from "physiology." I use the word "anthropology" for the philosophical study of the human (Gr: *anthropo*: human; *-logy*: discussion of), even though it is already employed to describe non-Western sociology. "Cosmology" includes "astronomy," but also imaginative realms like "heaven" and "hell." Likewise, "anthropology" here includes "physiology," but also imaginative entities like "spirit" and "soul." Anthropology is derivative of cosmology because humans are derived from the cosmos. Our goal here is to come to an understanding of the mechanics of cosmology, and then anthropology, before turning to how specific humans can make use of their materiality to improve themselves.

In this chapter I argue for the following cosmo-anthropological theory. The cosmos is made of matter, which is called *qi*-substance (氣). I use the term "*qi*-substance" rather than "matter" or "substance" because it better conveys the self-moving dynamism of the Chinese idea of *qi*, which, in its primordial state, flows like water and drifts like clouds.[4] This *qi*-substance has either always existed or it arose spontaneously. It has a creative aspect called "essence" (精).[5] It also has active and passive states, with Yin 陰 denoting the passive and Yang 陽 denoting the active. Yin and Yang are states of *qi*-substance just as your body has states of passivity (sleep) and activity (waking). They

---

4. Other translations for *qi* 氣 include vapor, ether, breath, and *pneuma*, but I find these a little too insubstantial for describing the full spectrum of matter, which, in humans, would run from breath, through saliva, blood, and muscles, to bones, each being more "rarified" or "solidified" than the other.

5. The translation of *jing* 精 as "essence" is meant to convey a sense of "important and creative—and ever-changing—*qi*-substance" and should *not* be conflated with any permanent, Aristotelian sense of "essence" whereby "the essence of each thing is what it is said to be intrinsically" (Aristotle, *Metaphysics* 1029b).

alternate with and complement each other. Active and passive *qi*-substance spontaneously separated into Heaven and Earth, and Heaven and Earth spontaneously gave birth to the "myriad things" (萬物), that is, everything. The early Chinese cosmos is a harmonious entity—indeed, a complementary pair—and therefore the Greek *kosmos* (cosmos), as opposed to *khaos* (chaos), is a felicitous term for the Heaven-Earth dyad. The particular thing among the myriad things that we will focus on here is the human animal.

Humans experience Yin and Yang states not only while asleep and awake, but also in death and life. A living human body is composed of *qi*-substance, with its own biological creative aspect, also called "essence" (think of the creative potency of sperm and eggs). The creative aspect of one's intellectual life is "spirit" (神). The creative aspect of one's bodily (and, to a lesser extent, emotional) life is further split into a Yin-Yang pair of souls: the passive *po*-soul (魄) and the active *hun*-soul (魂). All these elements reside in one's "form" (形), or "body" (身; also translated as "person" or "self"). When a person dies, the *qi*-substance of the body and its biological essence simply rots, while the *hun*- and *po*-souls persist for a few years or decades and then dissipate. The spirit may or may not persist for a time after death. In no case are these entities thought to be "eternal" in the sense that they will never die or fade away. Therefore, the goal of self-cultivation is not to be found in the afterlife, but rather in life. Life proceeds best when *qi*-substance "flows" in and through us as smoothly and harmoniously as possible. The semantic parameters of these technical terms—essence, spirit, and *hun*- and *po*-souls—will become clear below.

Because bodily self-cultivation involves the physical body (which is made of *qi*-substance, characterized by Yin-Yang states), and the body is situated, both conceptually and physically, within the cosmos as a whole (that is, Heaven and Earth), this chapter must begin at the beginning, with cosmology, though this initially may feel a long way off from our topic.

Cosmology (天地學)

Probably the most famous "In the beginning . . ." account in early China comes from Laozi. Chapter 1 states: "'Formlessness' is the name of the beginning of Heaven and Earth." (無,名天地之始。)[6] *Laozi* chapter 40 reaffirms this: "The world's myriad things are produced in forms; form is produced from

---

6. Interpretations of *Laozi* chapter 1 are notoriously contentious. My explanation for this reading is in Paul Fischer, *The Annotated Laozi, or Daodejing* (forthcoming).

formlessness." (天下萬物生於有，有生於無。)[7] This does not describe a miraculous "something-from-nothing" event, but rather a spontaneous emergence of cosmos from chaos. No time frame is articulated; indeed, because classical Chinese does not have tense, the process is probably going to be an ongoing one. Such an ongoing process is indicated by the title of a short, archaeologically recovered text called *Hengxian* (*Abiding Antecedent*), obtained by the Shanghai Museum in 1994. It opens with a more detailed creation account.

> Abiding antecedence is without form, [but has] potential and is tranquil and open.[8] This potential is great potential, this tranquility is greatly tranquil, and this openness is greatly open. [It is] self-fulfilling and not self-constraining. Space arises, and when there is space then there is *qi*-substance; when there is *qi*-substance then there are forms; when there are forms then there are beginnings; and when there are beginnings then there is progress. When there was not yet Heaven and Earth: there was not yet arising, moving, emerging, or producing; open, tranquil, actively unified, and seemingly silent. Dark, tranquil, homogeneous, and still without any brightness, still without any abundant production. *Qi*-substance here is self-producing; the abiding does not produce *qi*-substance. *Qi*-substance here is self-producing and self-arising.
>
> (恆先無有樸靜虛。樸大樸，靜大靜，虛大虛。自厭不自忍。域作，有域焉有氣，有氣焉有有，有有焉有始，有始焉有往者。未有天地：未有作行出生，虛靜為一若寂。夢夢靜同，而未有明，未有滋生。氣是自生，恆莫生氣。氣是自生自作。)[9]

---

7. The word "formlessness" (無) is sometimes translated as "emptiness" or "nonbeing," but "the beginning" is better understood as a chaotic, undifferentiated mass that was subsequently organized.

8. This "openness" (虛) is similar to "potential," with both words abstracted from concrete objects. The word translated here as "potential" is also "unhewn wood" (樸), while the word for "open" is from an "empty" (虛) vessel or "an abandoned area" (墟): both can be construed as receptive and awaiting development.

9. Ma Chengyuan 馬承源, ed., *Shanghai bowuguan cang zhanguo Chu zhushu* 上海博物館藏戰國楚竹書, vol. 3 (上海: 上海古籍出版社, 2003), 105–06. The orthography of this text is uncertain, particularly in what follows this passage, but the opening section, quoted here, is mostly well-established. The biggest potential difference is that "space" (域) could be a more mysterious "something" (或), as these terms are interchangeable in early texts.

"Abiding antecedence" is not a common phrase in early Chinese texts, but it must refer to a time frame, a situation, or a principle, rather than an entity, so it is not a crucial component in analyzing the actors involved in creation.[10] First there is "space" (or "something"), which precedes and contains Heaven and Earth, but it seems to be a generic term, and not a technical term elaborated on in the early texts.[11] It simply "arises," or "unfolds," uncaused, from itself. The verb that describes the appearance of *qi*-substance is even more anodyne: when there is space, there just "is" (有) *qi*-substance. No description could be less dramatic. The cosmic development continues in this vein, with a "when there was X, then there was Y" chain of appearances: *qi*-substance, forms, beginnings, and progress. How can there be "forms" before the "beginnings" of things? It may be best to think of "forms" as primitive building blocks, like chemical elements, that may be used for the "beginnings" of things that then progress to interact with each other. Then the narrative stops and starts over again with "When there was not yet Heaven and Earth. . . ." We know the narrative is starting over again, not only because some of the adjectives used to describe the initial state are repeated ("tranquil" and "open"), but because it specifically says that "there was not yet arising," whereas in the previous sentence, space had already arisen. The concluding section both expands the description of the primal state and reiterates the self-arising of *qi*-substance, lest anyone think that perhaps it had been caused by some outside force or entity.

The "forms" that proceed from *qi*-substance may well refer to the Yin and Yang aspects of *qi*-substance, even though the passage does not specify *two* forms. The clearest evidence for the relationship between *qi*-substance and Yin-Yang is relatively late, from the Han dynasty, in a dictionary entry for "Earth." It says: "Earth: When original *qi*-substance first separated, clear and light Yang became Heaven, while turbid and heavy Yin became Earth, which are those by which the myriad things were laid out and delineated." (地：元气初分，清輕陽為天，濁重陰為地，萬物所陳列也。)[12] The rather clear implication in this passage is that Yang and Yin are adjectives modifying "original *qi*-substance," rather than entities separate from *qi*-substance. I think this is an important distinction to make, because once some people learn that active Yang in some ways "corresponds" to maleness and passive

---

10. It is possible that "abiding antecedence" is an appellation of the Way.
11. However, *Laozi* ch. 25 also describes Heaven and Earth as within "space."
12. Xu Shen 許慎 (55–149?), *Shuowen jiezi* 說文解字, (台北: 天工書局, 1991), 682上.

Yin to femaleness, there sometimes is a mistaken tendency to think that male and female are essentially "composed" of different stuff. But this is not the case: all humans (indeed, all things) are composed of *qi*-substance, but the early Chinese thought that males were more active, or aggressive, while females were more passive, or calm. Furthermore, males and females were not thought to be either one hundred percent Yang or Yin, just predominantly one or the other, with the goal—at least for those interested in self-cultivation—being a balance of both. That males and females may be predisposed to have more Yang or Yin is a descriptive generalization, not a prescriptive ideal. Laozi indicates this when he says: "The myriad things carry Yin on their backs and embrace Yang in front and blend [these two aspects of] *qi*-substance in order to be harmonious." (萬物負陰而抱陽，沖氣以為和。)[13] This implies both an inclusive balance and one that is contingent on our actions.

This characterization of Yin and Yang as "aspects" of *qi*-substance is, I believe, the best way to construe the relationship between them. Another, related, way is articulated in the *Guanzi*: "Yin and Yang are the great principles of Heaven and Earth." (陰陽者，天地之大理也。)[14] "Principle" (理) is an interesting term that originally described the patterns in jade, but evolved to include more regulated patterns and the abstract ideas of "organization" and "reason."[15] Elsewhere in the *Guanzi* it is used both as a verb and an adjective, meaning "to regulate/regulated"[16] or "to order/ordered," so these concepts should be considered when elaborating the implications of "(regulating/ordering) principle." I see no serious discrepancy between "aspect" and "principle" in the descriptions of Yin and Yang here.

---

13. *Laozi* ch. 42. Also, *Laozi* ch. 28 begins with the gender-inclusive: "Know [when to use] the male but preserve the female." (知其雄，守其雌。)

14. *Guanzi* 管子 ch. 39 (水地); cf. W. Allyn Rickett, *Guanzi: Political, Economic, and Philosophical Essays from Early China* (Princeton: Princeton University Press, 1985, 1998), 2:111.

15. Willard Peterson proposed "coherence" as a better translation of *li* 理 in 1986, which Brook Ziporyn takes up, along with other candidates like "intelligibility," in his *Ironies of Oneness and Difference: Coherence in Early Chinese Thought; Prologomena to the Study of* Li 理 (Albany: State University of New York, 2012) and *Beyond Oneness and Difference*: Li 理 *in Chinese Buddhist Thought and Its Antecedents* (Albany: State University of New York Press, 2013).

16. *Guanzi* ch. 35 (侈靡): "Sages regulate [their] Yin and Yang." (聖人者，陰陽理。) *Guanzi* ch. 49 (內業): "When the mind is tranquil and *qi*-substance regulated, the Way can then be made to stay." (心靜氣理，道乃可止。) cf. Rickett, *Guanzi*, 2:312, 41.

I should note that while Yin and Yang are certainly the two primary aspects (or principles) of *qi*-substance, they also have earlier and later meanings. Originally, Yin and Yang referred to geographical locations. Yin was the northern (shadier, cooler) side of a mountain or a southern (shadier, cooler) riverbank, while Yang characterized the southern (sunnier, warmer) side of a mountain or a northern (sunnier, warmer) riverbank. (This is, of course, only true in the northern hemisphere.) This is how they came to stand for "cold" and "hot" respectively. The *Zuozhuan* says: "The six *qi*-substances [of Heaven] are Yin, Yang, wind, rain, darkness, and brightness." (六氣曰陰、陽、風、雨、晦、明也。)¹⁷ But Yin and Yang here simply refer to cold and hot, and not to Yin and Yang as the primary aspects of *qi*-substance, as the passage goes on to say that "excess" (淫) in any of these six atmospheric conditions will lead to different kinds of sickness. Furthermore, a subsequent list of six human emotions says they are produced from six kinds of *qi*-substance, which are the six atmospheric conditions mentioned above.¹⁸ So it is good to remember that Yin-Yang, while emphasized in this book as the two primary aspects of *qi*-substance, do have larger semantic parameters.

Similarly, the first step in this creation story—the arising of *qi*-substance with its two complementary aspects—is not uncontested. One creation story begins with the Way instead of *qi*-substance, and then interposes another step between the Way and Yin-Yang. This story, in the *Lüshi chunqiu*, says: "The Great One brought forth two norms; the two norms brought forth Yin and Yang." (太一出兩儀，兩儀出陰陽。)¹⁹ "The Great One" is explained a few lines later as another name for the Way.²⁰ The "two norms" are not explained and appear nowhere else in the text, but I take them to be

---

17. *Zuozhuan* 左傳 (昭公 1); cf. Stephen Durrant, Wai-yee Li, David Schaberg, *Zuozhuan: Commentary on the "Spring and Autumn Annals"* (Seattle: University of Washington Press, 2016), 3:1331.

18. *Zuozhuan* (昭公 25): "The people have likes and dislikes, delight and anger, sadness and happiness, derived from the six [atmospheric] *qi*-substances." (民有好惡、喜怒、哀樂，生於六氣。) cf. Durrant, Li, Schaberg, Zuozhuan, 3:1639.

19. *Lüshi chunqiu* 呂氏春秋 ch. 5.2 (大樂); cf. John Knoblock and Jeffrey Riegel, *The Annals of Lü Buwei* (Stanford: Stanford University Press, 2000), 136.

20. "The Way is ultimate essence, cannot become a form, and cannot be named; forced to articulate it, [I] would call it the Great One." (道也者，至精也，不可為形，不可為名；彊為之謂之太一。) Some scholars identify the Great One with the Pole Star; see David Pankenier, *Astrology and Cosmology in Early China: Conforming Earth to Heaven* (Cambridge: Cambridge University Press, 2013), 88–92. Others explain it as a "nature

"normative tendencies" that consequently result in full-fledged Yin and Yang. Elsewhere in the same text, *qi*-substance and the Way are both omitted (or assumed), and Yin-Yang are said to be created by Heaven: "As a general rule, [all] humans and things are [produced by] the developments of Yin and Yang. Yin and Yang are created and completed by Heaven." (凡人物者，陰陽之化也。陰陽者，造乎天而成者也。)[21] This account has Heaven preceding Yin and Yang, even though in the "standard" account that I argue for, based on the *Hengxian* and the *Shuowen jiezi* quotes above, it is Yin and Yang that precede Heaven and Earth. One possible way to resolve this difference is to presume that Yin and Yang here simply mean dark and light, not unlike their use as cold and hot in the *Zuozhuan* quote above. This explanation is bolstered by a sentence elsewhere in the *Lüshi chunqiu* itself: "Heaven produces Yin, Yang, cold, heat, wet, and dry; the changes of the four seasons; and the transformations of the myriad things." (天生陰陽寒暑燥溼，四時之化，萬物之變。)[22] In the *Zuozhuan*, Yin and Yang were used for cold and hot; here, since cold and hot are already articulated, they cannot denote these two. But there are again six items, with light and dark not specifically articulated, and since Yin and Yang originally denoted the darker and lighter sides of a mountain, it seems likely that they are standing in for light and dark here. (This explanation is the "principle of charity" at work.)

Another creation account has two spirits (神) preceding Heaven and Earth, all four of which somehow preceding Yin-Yang, with the appearance of *qi*-substance left unclear. The *Huainanzi* says:

> Anciently, in the time before there was Heaven and Earth, there was only semblance but no form. Obscure and dark, vague and unclear, shapeless and formless: no one knew its gateway. There were two spirits, born in murkiness, that established Heaven and constructed Earth. So vast: no one knows where they ultimately end. So broad: no one knows where they finally stop. Thereupon

---

deity." See Lai Guolong, *Excavating the Afterlife: The Archaeology of Early Chinese Religion* (Seattle: University of Washington Press, 2015), 30, 35; for an interesting analysis of what some scholars take to be an early image of the Great One, pp. 131–34. It is likely that, as with other "ultimate entities" in other cultures, some saw it as anthropomorphic and others as an abstract idea or principle.

21. *Lüshi chunqiu* ch. 20.3 (知分); cf. Knoblock and Riegel, *Lü Buwei*, 519.
22. *Lüshi chunqiu* ch. 3.2 (盡數); cf. Knoblock and Riegel, *Lü Buwei*, 99.

they separated into Yin and Yang, and differentiated into the eight cardinal directions. The firm and yielding formed correspondingly to each other; the myriad things thereupon took shape. Turbid *qi*-substance made creatures, while essential *qi*-substance made humans. This is why the essential spirit belongs to Heaven, while the skeletal system belongs to Earth.

(古未有天地之時，惟像無形，窈窈冥冥，芒芠漠閔，澒濛鴻洞：莫知其門。有二神混生，經天營地。孔乎：莫知其所終極。滔乎：莫知其所止息。於是乃別為陰陽，離為八極。剛柔相成，萬物乃形。煩氣為蟲，精氣為人。是故精神，天之有也；而骨骸者，地之有也。)[23]

Several questions arise when we compare this passage with the "standard account" described above. First, what is the "semblance" (像) in the first sentence, so obscure and vague? The first chapter of the *Huainanzi* refers to the Way as a "formless semblance" (無形之像), so the Way is probably the unspoken referent here too.[24] Second, what are these "two spirits" (二神) that the Way produced? The text does not say, and the term "two spirits" appears nowhere else in the book.[25] I will argue below that "spirit" here in fact refers to a "creative edge" of *qi*-substance and is in fact quite similar to the "essence" (精) used in adjectival form in the last two sentences of the

---

23. *Huainanzi* 淮南子 ch. 7 (精神); cf. John Major, Sarah Queen, Andrew Meyer, and Harold Roth, *The Huainanzi: A Guide to the Theory and Practice of Government in Early Han China* (New York: Columbia University Press, 2010), 240–41.

24. *Huainanzi* ch. 1 (原道). Major, Queen, Meyer, and Roth, *Huainanzi*, 54. It may be relevant to note that in the "Xici zhuan" 繫辭傳 commentary on the *Yijing* 易經, "semblances" refer to heavenly asterisms, the various configurations of the sixty-four hexagrams, as well as abstractions like "loss" and "gain" that are indicated by a particular hexagram. For more on this imaginative term, see Cai Zong-qi, "The *Yi-Xiang-Yan* Paradigm and Early Chinese Theories of Literary Creation," in *The Rhetoric of Hiddenness in Traditional Chinese Culture*, ed. Paula Varsano (Albany: State University of New York Press, 2016), 333–57.

25. *Huainanzi* ch. 1 (原道) has another creation story that begins with the Way and gives the Way credit for the way Heaven and Earth and the myriad things are, without explaining how they came about. Then the narrative introduces "two august [ones]" (二皇), and shortly thereafter mentions the activities of "spirit/spirits/spiritousness" (神), which some scholars take to be the spirits *of* the "two august [ones]." Others, including myself, do not read it this way. Alternatively, Mark Lewis suggests the two spirits might be Fuxi 伏羲 and Nüwa 女媧, two of several mythopoetic figures from *Huainanzi* ch. 6 (覽冥), but while this is possible, I find the evidence too scant to be persuasive. See Mark Lewis, *Writing and Authority in Early China* (Albany: State University of New York Press, 1999), 203.

quote above. A third problem is that after these spirits create Heaven and Earth, the narrative continues with "Thereupon they separated into Yin and Yang," but does the "they" refer to Heaven and Earth or to the two spirits? Grammatically, either is possible, but since it doesn't make sense to me that Heaven and Earth could precede Yin and Yang, I think "they" refers to the two spirits. This reading would thus equate the "two spirits" here with the "two norms" (兩儀) in the *Lüshi chunqiu* passage in the previous paragraph. In both cases, I think the two proclivities, spirit or norm, refer to incipient aspects of *qi*-substance in an undifferentiated state, prior to separating into active Yang and passive Yin. Fourth, *qi*-substance appears late in the paragraph, but does the author nevertheless assume that it is ontologically prior? I think so, not least because this would bring the passage in line with the "standard model" that I am proposing.[26] This leads to a final question on the "turbid" and "essential" *qi*-substances in the penultimate sentence. Should they be understood as identical to the two creative spirits, as things directed by them, as identical to Yin and Yang, or as something different altogether? I suspect they are the same as Yin and Yang, with the caveat that the sentence is hyperbole: all physical objects are composed of turbid *qi*-substance, while all living things—not just animals and not just humans—have essential *qi*-substance as well.[27] Humans simply have more of it and can do more with it, especially if one practices self-cultivation.

---

26. Harold Roth and John Major seem to agree with this assessment in their preface to their translation of this chapter, where they say of this creation story: "everything in the world is made of *qi*. . . . *Shen* [spirit] can be thought of as composed of the most highly rarified and purified kind of *qi*. . . ." Major, Queen, Meyer, and Roth, *Huainanzi* (2010), 234. *Heguanzi* 鶡冠子 ch. 8 (度萬) might provide counterevidence when it says "*Qi*-substance is produced from spirit; the Way is completed by spirit." (氣由神生，道由神成。) cf. Carine Defoort, *The Pheasant Cap Master: A Rhetorical Reading* (Albany: State University of New York Press, 1997), 201. Though the context is not clear, I think the *qi*-substance and the spirit here are not primordial *qi*-substance and spirit(s). Rather, I think this passage is saying that the *human* spirit is able to produce certain kinds of *qi*-substance for physical health as well as to complete, or complement, the Way for mental health.
27. Even some non-living things are said to have essential *qi*-substance in them. *Lüshi chunqiu* ch. 3.2 (盡數): "For essential *qi*-substance to gather, there must be something [for it] to enter into. [If it] gathers in feathered birds, with it they are made to fly and soar. [If it] gathers in footed animals, with it they are made to wander and walk. [If it] gathers in pearls and jade, with it they are made translucent and luminous. [If it] gathers in trees and shrubs, with it they are made lush and full. [If it] gathers in sagely people, with it they are made broad and percipient." (精氣之集也，必有入也。集於羽鳥與為飛揚，集於走獸與為流行，集於珠玉與為精朗，集於樹木與為茂長，集於聖人與為敻明。) cf. Knoblock and Riegel, *Lü Buwei*, 99–100.

The most famous early Chinese story of cultivating one's *qi*-substance is probably one told by Mengzi about his own practice. In it, Mengzi's student is conversing with his teacher:

> [Gongsun Chou:] "I venture to ask what you are most developed in?" [Mengzi] replied: "I understand rhetoric, and I am competent at nourishing my flood-like *qi*-substance." [Gongsun Chou:] "I venture to ask what you mean by flood-like *qi*-substance?" [Mengzi] replied: "It is difficult to explain. This *qi*-substance is extremely vast and extremely strong. [If you] use uprightness to nourish it and do not harm it, then it can fill the space between Heaven and Earth. This *qi*-substance complements propriety and the way; without them, it is starved. It is what *accumulated* propriety produces; it is not that propriety can get it indiscriminately. [If your] actions are deficient in your mind [i.e., doing the right thing but for the wrong reasons], then it will starve."

> (「敢問夫子惡乎長？」曰：「我知言，我善養吾浩然之氣。」「敢問何謂浩然之氣？」曰：「難言也。其為氣也，至大至剛。以直養而無害，則塞於天地之間。其為氣也，配義與道；無是，餒矣。是集義所生者；非義襲而取之也。行有不慊於心，則餒矣。」)[28]

Clearly, this "*qi*-substance," produced by the virtue of propriety, is not the *qi*-substance of which all things are made. Mengzi must either be describing a particular kind of *qi*-substance—on which, more in a moment—or he is using "*qi*-substance" metaphorically, to describe his feeling of moral exuberance and a kind of "oneness" with the cosmos. I think he is actually doing both, with a bit of hyperbole thrown in for rhetorical flourish. That it seems to be a particular type of *qi*-substance is indicated by the modifier "this," as in "this [particular type of] *qi*-substance."[29] That he is using

---

28. *Mengzi* 孟子 ch. 2A2 (公孫丑上); cf. Bryan Van Norden, *Mengzi: With Selections from Traditional Commentaries* (Indianapolis: Hackett, 2008), 38–39. To "nourish" (養) is nearly synonymous with "cultivate" (修); the former is an animal husbandry metaphor while the latter is an agricultural metaphor. Readers paying special attention to the one should probably pay attention to both.

29. The grammar is actually slightly more opaque than this. *Qi wei qi ye* 其為氣也 is something like "This *qua qi*-substance . . ." where "*qua*" means "acting in the character of." The "this" refers to the object of the previous sentence: "flood-like *qi*-substance," so "this [i.e., flood-like *qi*-substance] acting in the character of [regular, ontological] *qi*-substance" suggests that

"*qi*-substance" metaphorically is indicated by its somewhat unusual use in the context of cultivating virtuosity. By framing moral cultivation as a kind of psychic expansiveness, Mengzi succeeds in creating a memorable poetic image that reminds the reader of the nondual ontology underlying things as disparate as human bodies and human virtues. The hyperbole comes when he says that "it can fill the space between Heaven and Earth." One explanation of this expression is that it is meant to convey a kind of unity with the cosmos, one dependent on (cultivated) virtuosity.

Another explanation returns us to metaphor: perhaps "filling the space between Heaven and Earth" is a metaphor for the idea of "as above, so below." That is, if Mengzi cultivates his bodily *qi*-substance, this could bring him closer to understanding the activities of (the *qi*-substance of) Heaven. A century or so after Mengzi, Lu Jia wrote: "Thus, if (human) nature is kept safely in humans, then (our) *qi*-substance will reach to Heaven. The minutely small and the vastly great: the study of what is below [leads to] the apprehension of what is above." (故性藏於人，則氣達於天。纖微浩大：下學上達。)[30] We should read "kept safely" as a matter of self-cultivation, with "reach" (達) also translatable as "apprehend," as it is at the end of the sentence.[31] I translate the two differently only to show the poetic ambiguity.[32] But the underlying meaning is clear.

So, *qi*-substance as the "stuff of the cosmos" has two aspects, Yang and Yin, which separate to form Heaven and Earth, but it also has wider implications, both literal and metaphorical. Just as one may differentiate "matter" into specific kinds, the same is true of *qi*-substance. "Generally speaking, life is not from the development of a single *qi*-substance, growth is not from the efforts of one thing, and completion is not from the achievements

---

"flood-like *qi*-substance" is somehow *like qi*-substance, but in fact is *not qi*-substance. So, what is he referring to? Since Mengzi's "flood-like *qi*-substance" is produced by accumulated propriety, a cardinal virtue, we should probably construe it as "flood-like virtuosity."

30. *Xinyu* 新語 ch. 2 (術事); cf. Ku Mei-kao, *A Chinese Mirror for Magistrates* (Canberra: Australian National University, 1988), 77. The final statement, "the study of what is below . . ." is a reference to *Lunyu* 14.35. A reverse, but complementary, thought is found in the *Yucong, yi* 語叢一: "Examine the way of Heaven in order to develop the people's *qi*-substance." (察天道以化民氣。) cf. Scott Cook, *The Bamboo Texts of Guodian* (Cornell: Cornell University East Asia Program, 2012), 2:829.

31. To "apprehend" a thing denotes a more tenuous understanding than to "comprehend" it.

32. Another connection obscured by the translation is that the word for "flood-like" (浩) in *Mengzi* is the same word as the "vastly" in the *Xinyu*. I translate them differently because "flood-like" is already well-established for Mengzi, while "flood-like great" for Lu Jia would be clumsy in English.

of one form." (凡生非一氣之化也，長非一物之任也，成非一形之功也。)³³ Later in the same chapter, after briefly describing clouds, the sun, the moon, and various celestial bodies, it details various kinds of *qi*-substance: "Of the *qi*-substances, there are [those that] ascend but do not reach to Heaven, [those that] descend but do not reach to Earth, [those that] are abundant above but sparse below, (those that) are like waves on water, [and those that] are like fluttering leaves on trees: yellow in spring, black in summer, blue-green in autumn, red in winter." (其氣有上不屬天，下不屬地，有豐上殺下，有若水之波，有若山之楫：春則黃，夏則黑，秋則蒼，冬則赤。)³⁴ Despite the *Lüshi chunqiu* being something of an encyclopedic work,³⁵ this description seems rather terse, and almost arbitrary. It is unclear, for example, if the four colors at the end of this passage describe four distinct types of *qi*-substance, or if they are just examples of the changing colors of tree leaves and are simply meant to imply that there are many types of *qi*-substance, just as there are many shades of leaves. Nevertheless, it gives a good sense of the possible variety of *qi*-substances in the world.

Moving from cosmology to anthropology, Mozi writes of the effect of food on one's *qi*-substance(s), recalling the invention of agriculture and the effect this had on health. "When ancient people did not yet know how to make beverages or food, [they ate] simple food and [the sexes] lived separately. Therefore sagely people arose to instruct [them], [teaching] men the arts of plowing, sowing, and planting, in order to have the people eat. This way of eating was quite sufficient to increase *qi*-substance, fill emptiness, strengthen bodies, and satisfy bellies." (古之民未知為飲食時，素食而分處。故聖人作誨，男耕稼樹藝，以為民食。其為食也，足以增氣充虛，彊體適腹而已矣。)³⁶ The *Guiguzi*, meanwhile, says that human development depends

---

33. *Lüshi chunqiu* ch. 6.5 (明理); cf. Knoblock and Riegel, *Lü Buwei*, 167. The final two phrases are slightly off-topic, but they mean that your body does not grow just from the efforts of, say, your bones: other bodily components "grow" your body too. Likewise, you cannot realize your "completion" just from, say, bodily accomplishments, your mind also has to accomplish things in order for you to be completed. We are complex biomes, not simple organisms.

34. *Lüshi chunqiu* ch. 6.5 (明理); cf. Knoblock and Riegel, *Lü Buwei*, 169. I follow Gao You 高誘 in reading *shu* 屬 (belong to) as *zhi* 至 (reach), even though "belong to" makes sense too, and follow Chen Qiyou 陳奇猷 in amending *shan zhi ji* 山之楫 ("mountain oars") to *mu zhi she* 木之檨 ("fluttering leaves on trees"). See Chen Qiyou 陳奇猷, Lü shi chunqiu *jiaoshi* 呂氏春秋校釋, 2 vols., (1984; rpt. 臺北: 華正書局, 1988) 1:368–69, n. 45.

35. Mark Lewis describes it as such in his *Writing and Authority in Early China* (Albany: State University of New York Press, 1999), 302–08.

primarily on five kinds of *qi*-substances: those of spirit, mind, virtuosity, will, and thought (神心德志思).[37] These kinds of things—virtuosity, will, and thought in particular—are now usually thought to be non-material, so it is interesting to note that here they are in some sense composed of, or at least influenced by, *qi*-substance. Xunzi is probably also referring to psychological impulses when he remarks on "perverse" and "accordant" *qi*-substances (逆氣 and 順氣) that may arise in humans as a result of listening to different kinds of music.[38] *Qi*-substance, therefore, is every bit as vague as "matter," and the various kinds introduced here are certainly not exhaustive. But lying, in a sense, "between" generic *qi*-substance and its various kinds (both cosmological and anthropological) are two particularly creative styles of *qi*-substance that we have already encountered: essence and spirit.

I argue that "essence" and "spirit" are similar, but with considerable semantic overlap. Both are creative (or, perhaps, are creativity itself), but essence has acted upon non-living things and has acted upon *and* is still acting within living things, while spirit is active in living and conscious things. Specifically, things like rocks and streams, while the product *of* essence, probably do not have essence *in* them,[39] nor do they have spirit (though an independent nature spirit may reside *in* them). Meanwhile, things like trees have essence, but probably not spirit; while sentient animals have both essence and spirit. If this seems imprecise or sprawling, it may help to consider the wide range of activities and habitats that *kami* 神 in Japanese Shinto are involved in, or even the wide range of meanings that "spirit" has in contemporary English discourse.

Now that we have explored the role of *qi*-substance in the unfolding of creation down to humans, let us return to cosmology to examine its relationship to essence. If Yin, for example, is an *aspect* of *qi*-substance, and "ascending" and "compliant" are *characteristics* of *qi*-substances, then essence is a discrete *type* of some, but not all, *qi*-substances. I should

---

36. *Mozi* 墨子 ch. 6 (辭過); cf. John Knoblock and Jeffrey Riegel, *Mozi: A Study and Translation of the Ethical and Political Writings* (Berkeley: University of California, Berkeley, 2013), 71–72.

37. *Guiguzi* 鬼谷子 ch. 15 (本經陰符七術篇); cf. Thomas Cleary, *Thunder in the Sky* (Boston: Shambhala, 1994), 57–58.

38. *Xunzi* ch. 20 (樂論); cf. Hutton, *Xunzi*, 220.

39. With the possible exception of things like translucent and luminous pearls and jade; cf. note 27 above.

point out that "aspect," "characteristic," and "type" are all words that I am imposing on the narrative. The *Guanzi*, sidestepping this analytical problem, says only that "Essence is the essence of *qi*-substance." (精也者，氣之精者也。)[40] Nevertheless, as such, the reason why essence has its particular value lies in its ability to create and transform things. On the most basic level, "essential *qi*-substance makes things" (精氣為物);[41] that is, it causes them to be. Further, it causes developmental changes in them: "[That which] is one with *qi*-substance and is able to transform [it] is called 'essence.'" (一氣能變曰精。)[42] Finally, essence creates life, among other things. "As a general rule, for the essences of things: these then create life. Below, [they] produce the five grains, and above [they] create the arrayed stars." (凡物之精，此則為生。下生五穀，上為列星。)[43] The early Chinese may well have thought that at least some stars were, in a sense, alive, and even sentient; perhaps as manifestations of royal ancestors.[44] In any case, the creative activity of essential *qi*-substance is a spontaneous affair, just as the original arising of *qi*-substance was in the *Hengxian*. This makes it a precious commodity. For humans, "[when] essence is preserved [within], life is produced of itself" (精存自生).[45] Essence, then, is shorthand for essential *qi*-substance, which operates both on cosmic and human scales. It creates, transforms, and instills life, spontaneously. Some living things have, in addition to life, sentience, and this is where spirit comes most clearly into play.

Let us close this section on cosmology with another creation story; for contrast and variety, this one has no mention of the creative effects of *qi*-substance, essence, Yin-Yang, or Heaven and Earth. It is clearly more anthropocentric, and focused on human virtuosity.

---

40. *Guanzi* ch. 49 (內業); cf. Rickett, *Guanzi*, 2:43.

41. *Yijing* 易經, "Xici zhuan I" 繫辭上傳; cf. Richard Lynn, *The Classic of Changes: A New Translation of the* I Ching *as Interpreted by Wang Bi* (New York: Columbia University Press, 1994), 52.

42. *Guanzi* ch. 37 (心術下); cf. Rickett, Guanzi, 3:60. Although the verb "transform" does not have an object here, given the parallel in the following line, the "[it]" supplied here probably refers back to "*qi*-substance" itself.

43. *Guanzi* ch. 49 (內業); cf. Rickett, *Guanzi*, 2:39.

44. See Sarah Allan, "On the Identity of Shang Di 上帝 and the Origin of the Concept of a Celestial Mandate (*Tian Ming* 天命)," *Early China* 31 (2007): 1–46.

45. *Guanzi* ch. 49 (內業); cf. Rickett, *Guanzi*, 2:47.

BODY (體)   49

In the great beginning there was formlessness, without form and without names, and it was that from which the one thing arose: there was the one, but without shape. [When] things get [it] in order to live, [we] call this [their] "virtuosity." [When things] are still shapeless, yet have allotments that continue uninterruptedly, [we] call this [their] "fate." Through rest and movement, things were produced; as things were completed, patterns were produced: [we] call this [their] "body." Bodied entities protecting spirits [within], each with [their][46] own norms and rules, [we] call this [their] "nature." [Inner] nature that is cultivated to return to virtuosity [achieves] virtuosity that is full and equal to that of the beginning. Equal to [that] and thus open-minded; open-minded and thus great. [When they can] harmonize with the chirping of birds, and the chirping of birds harmonize [with them], [then they can] harmonize with Heaven and Earth. This harmony is obscure, [and they may] seem foolish or dim: [we] call this [their] "mysterious virtuosity," which is equal to great accordance [with the "one thing," the Way].

(泰初有無，無有無名；一之所起：有一而未形。物得以生，謂之德。未形者有分，且然無閒，謂之命。留動而生物，物成生理，謂之形。形體保神，各有儀則，謂之性。性修反德，德至同於初。同乃虛，虛乃大。合喙鳴；喙鳴合，與天地為合。其合緡緡，若愚若昏，是謂玄德，同乎大順。)[47]

Given the source of this passage, the "one" is probably the Way, but it could also be read, without much difficulty, as a reference to undifferen-

---

46. "Each" (各) could refer either to each "bodied entity" (形體) or to "entities" (體) and "spirits" (神). If the former, then "each" entity probably refers to different kinds of animals, including humans, since it was generally thought that all humans share a single nature (though it is not impossible that this passage is an exception). If the latter, then it is interesting to note that our bodies and our spirits have different sets of norms and rules. Cheng Xuanying 成玄英 (fl. 631–652) thinks this means that some bodies are ugly while others beautiful, and some spirits are stupid while others are wise.

47. *Zhuangzi* 莊子 ch. 12 (天地); cf. Burton Watson, *The Complete Works of Zhuangzi* (New York: Columbia University Press, 1968; 2013), 88–89. For another use of "great compliance," see *Laozi* ch. 65.

tiated *qi*-substance. "Rest and movement" seem implicitly to point to Yin and Yang. As for Heaven and Earth, though they do not appear here as explicitly creative agents, it is not unreasonable to suggest that they are the agents behind the "completion" that follows the "production" of bodies. The cultivation of (inner, human) nature and the role of open-mindedness will be discussed in later chapters Finally, the "harmonizing with the chirping of birds" line is typical of Zhuangzi's writing style, and points to a state where humans are harmonized with nature. It is a poetic way of describing what Xunzi, above, called creating "a triad with Heaven and Earth." Thus, though this creation account reads, on the surface, quite differently from that of the *Hengxian* account, they nevertheless are quite compatible.

In this section on cosmology, we saw that there are a number of cosmogonies that are generally congruous, even while displaying considerable differences at first glance. The story begins with uncreated *qi*-substance that spontaneously separates into Yin-Yang aspects, which take their positions vis-à-vis our planet in the Heaven-Earth dyad. The spontaneous production of living things is attributed to essential *qi*-substance, while the spontaneous production of sentient things is attributed to spiritous *qi*-substance. Other types of *qi*-substances fill out the complexity of our reality. All of these cosmological ingredients are foundational to our own anthropology, to which we shall now turn.

Living Humans (生者)

The appearance of humans in the unfolding cosmological scheme is first a matter of *qi*-substances. That is, human anthropogony is described thus: "Human life is a convergence of *qi*-substances: when they converge there is life; when they scatter there is death." (人之生，氣之聚也；聚則為生，散則為死。)[48] Since essence is the creative type of *qi*-substance, it is therefore possible to understand the previous sentence substituting "essence" for

---

48. *Zhuangzi* ch. 22 (知北遊); cf. Watson, *Zhuangzi*, 177. *Hanshi waizhuan* 韓詩外傳 ch. 8.2 says much the same thing: "Of our bodies, what is most valuable? Nothing is more valuable than *qi*-substance/s. When humans obtain *qi*-substance/s they live, and when they lose them they die." (然身何貴也？莫貴於氣。人得氣則生，失氣則死。) cf. James Hightower, *Han Shih Wai Chuan: Han Ying's Illustrations of the Didactic Application of the Classic of Songs* (Cambridge: Harvard University Press, 1952), 253.

"*qi*-substance." "As a general rule, for human life, Heaven gives forth its essence and Earth gives forth its form: harmonize these in order to create a human. With [such] harmony there is life, without [such] harmony there is no life." (凡人之生也,天出其精,地出其形:合此以為人。和乃生,不和不生。)[49] Where the first author uses a "convergence" and "scattering" of *qi*-substance to describe life and death, the second author uses "harmony" and a lack of harmony of essence (i.e., essential *qi*-substance) to describe them.

At a "higher" level, there is spirit (i.e., spiritous *qi*-substance). I have said that essence and spirit are very much akin, except that spirit is something like a more sentient version of essence. The essential, "creative edge" of *qi*-substance is responsible for the creation of all things, and spirit is a particular, more ethereal, subset of it. From *Guanzi* chapter 37 we learned, above, that "[That which] is one with *qi*-substance and is able to transform [it] is called 'essence.'" (一氣能變曰精。) In chapter 49 it says, similarly, "[That which] is one with things and able to develop [them] is called 'spirit.'" (一物能化謂之神。)[50] The verbs "transform" and "develop" indicate their creativity, which is borne out in people. Humans have both a physical "essence," in the form of reproductive fluids,[51] and a mental "essence," in the form of a spirit.

The human spirit resides in the human body, but is not restricted to staying there, even while one is alive. It can leave when one is dreaming, or sick, or even if one lives a particularly disordered life. The *Guanzi*, which has much to say about the human spirit, says "There is a spirit that [may] spontaneously reside in the body, but no one can [fully] apprehend its coming and going: lose it and [you] will certainly be disordered; obtain it and [you] will certainly be ordered. Respectfully clean its lodging place, and this essence will spontaneously arrive. With essential [i.e., creative] thinking apprehend it; with calm reflection order it." (有神自在身,一往一來,莫之能思:失之必亂,得之必治。敬除其舍,精將自來。精想思之,寧念治之。)[52] This passage contains a lot of information but also raises many

---

49. *Guanzi* ch. 49 (內業); cf. Rickett, *Guanzi*, 2:52.
50. *Guanzi* ch. 49 (內業); cf. Rickett, *Guanzi*, 2:44.
51. *Guanzi* ch. 39 (水地): "Humans are fluid. When the essential *qi*-substances of male and female unite, fluid flows [between them] and assumes form." (人,水也。男女精氣合,而水流形。) cf. Rickett, *Guanzi*, 2:103.
52. *Guanzi* ch. 49 (內業); cf. Rickett, *Guanzi*, 2:45.

questions. We do not know the comings and goings of the spirit: does this mean humans do not know precisely when a spirit first arrives in the body of a baby, nor precisely when it departs at death? Or does it refer to more frequent comings and goings: when dreaming, sick, or disordered? Or does it imply both, meaning simply that the spirit is invisible? The connection between one's spirit and the states of order and disorder, which are central to early Chinese thought, raises the question: what exactly does it mean to be ordered and disordered? Do these terms refer to relative mental "normalcy" and some kind of psychosis? Or should we read them more prosaically, and read them as pointing to more subtle and ordinary states of mind? That is, if one feels frazzled after a demanding day at the office, can the "distraction" that results be considered a loss of spirit? Respect, as noted in the introduction, is a key early Chinese virtue, and its use here should bring to mind this important cultural undercurrent. The "lodging place"[53] of the spirit could refer to the entire body or to the mind; I would assume both. If this is the case, then how to "clean its lodging place" is precisely the topic of this book.

Perhaps the most unexpected item in this passage is that if one does successfully "clean its lodging place," the result is that one will be rewarded with more essence. Since humans have both physical and mental essences, should this be read as referring to both? Ambiguity is often a wonderful thing—just not in academic analyses. However this phrase should be read, it is certainly noteworthy that once an extra dose of essence has arrived, courtesy of a cleanly-situated spirit, we are asked to use "essential" thinking to apprehend that spirit. What is "essential" thinking? Given that essence is defined by its creativity, I suggest that it is in fact creative thinking. Recall the "open-mindedness" in the creation story that closed the last section: harmonizing with the chirping of birds, whatever that connotes, would surely take a bit of creative thinking. Finally, with calm reflection, we find ourselves in a position to "order" the spirit—the very thing we must have in order to be ordered ourselves. It is a neat prescription: though we are all already born with essence and spirit, we need a cleanly-situated spirit

---

53. Though the text does not define or explicitly locate the spirit's "lodging place," it does recommend a way of creating one: "Only after [you] are able to rectify and make tranquil [your person], may it become settled, and [only] with a settled mind within, and eyes and ears clear and sharp, and the four limbs firm and steadfast, can [you] make a lodging place for essence." (能正能靜，然後能定。定心在中，耳目聰明，四枝堅固，可以為精舍。) *Guanzi* ch. 49 (內業); cf. Rickett, *Guanzi*, 2:43.

to get the extra essence necessary for the kind of thinking and reflection capable of controlling the spirit.

Taking care of the spirit, then, brings clear mental benefits in the form of extra "essence" for "essential thinking." But it is also good for the body. Zhuangzi says "embrace the spirit with tranquility and the body will rectify itself" (抱神以靜，形將自正).[54] And the extra essence has other advantages. Recall Mengzi's cultivated, flood-like *qi*-substance that "filled the space between Heaven and Earth" and Lu Jia's *qi*-substance that reached to Heaven. Given that essence is a creative type of *qi*-substance, we might also expect to find that it is involved with a creative cosmos. Thus: "[When] essence is added to essence, then [one can] connect with Heaven." (精有精乃通於天。)[55] We saw above that we can add extra essence to our existing essence by "cleaning" the body and/or the mind. And, as with the "reach/apprehend" (*da* 達) verb in the Lu Jia quote above, so *tong* 通 here can also be read as a literal "connect" or as an abstract "understand." (Such are the joys of text criticism.)

The human spirit and human mind thus enjoy a remarkable coexistence, given that spirit is the spiritous *qi*-substance responsible for sentience. Thus, another passage from the *Guanzi* says "Pure spirit produced the mind." (清神生心。)[56] Given the spirit's creative capacity, its relationship to sentience, its separability from the body, and the fact that it can cause extra essence to appear in us, which can then be used to influence our thinking, this claim is unsurprising. Yet the mind is nevertheless said to control the spirit, as we have just seen. Xunzi, in fact, goes so far as to say "The mind is the ruler of the body and the master of spiritous percipience. [It] issues commands but does not receive commands." (心者，形之君也，而神明之主也。出令而無所受令。)[57] So, the spirit is instrumental for the creation of the mind, the optimal use of the mind, the health of the body, and the mind's ordering of that selfsame spirit. Such interconnectedness within the body is also

---

54. *Zhuangzi* ch. 11 (在宥); cf. Watson, *Zhuangzi*, 77. Furthermore, if we do not "embrace the spirit with tranquility," we can actually hurt it: "Those who [excessively] express their emotions [can] harm their spirit." (信其情者傷其神。) *Guanzi* ch. 35 (侈靡); cf. Rickett, *Guanzi*, 2:312.

55. *Lüshi chunqiu* ch. 18.8 (具備); cf. Knoblock and Riegel, *Lü Buwei*, 472. Note: 有 = 又.

56. *Guanzi* ch. 85 (輕重己); cf. Rickett, *Guanzi*, 2:510. Most commentators say that "pure" (清) should actually be "essential" (精).

57. *Xunzi* ch. 21 (解蔽); cf. Hutton, *Xunzi*, 229.

reflected in its relationship with the outer environment. The larger theme, again, is our coming from the cosmos and, in some sense, returning to it:

> [When one's] Heavenly [endowment] is kept intact, then the spirit is harmonious, the eyes clear, the ears sharp, the nose discerning, the mouth sensitive, and the three hundred and sixty joints [of the body] all move fluently. Such people are trusted without even speaking, act appropriately without even planning, and obtain things without even pondering: their essence can connect to [or "understand"] Heaven, and their spirit can cover the cosmos. These people toward all things: there is nothing they do not accept, nothing they do not embrace—[they] are like Heaven and Earth in this way.
>
> (天全則神和矣，目明矣，耳聰矣，鼻臭矣，口敏矣，三百六十節皆通利矣。若此人者：不言而信，不謀而當，不慮而得；精通乎天地，神覆乎宇宙。其於物：無不受也，無不裹也，若天地然。)[58]

In addition to a spirit, humans also have souls. Souls come in two varieties: Yin and Yang. A Yin soul is called a *po*-soul (魄) and a Yang soul is called a *hun*-soul (魂).[59] One early Chinese intellectual defined them as "the mind's essential vigor" and, like the spirit, it seems they can leave and return to the body, but if they leave for too long, death will ensue.[60] They are thus something like an animating "life-force" in animals. These two souls are, in a sense, more "biological" than the spirit which, while a material entity, is somehow more ethereal and elusive and, in a literary sense, imaginative. The souls, despite sometimes being defined in terms of cognitive "vigor," do not seem to actually affect cognitive function much. For this reason, they do not turn up in the literature very often, except when the topic is death. That is, the precise function of the *hun*- and *po*-souls while one is

---

58. *Lüshi chunqiu* ch. 1.2 (本生); cf. Knoblock and Riegel, *Lü Buwei*, 66.

59. *Huainanzi* ch. 9 (主術): "Heavenly *qi*-substance constitutes the *hun*-soul and Earthly *qi*-substance constitutes the *po*-soul." (天氣為魂，地氣為魄。) cf. Major, Queen, Meyer, and Roth, *Huainanzi* (2010), 296.

60. *Zuozhuan* (昭公 25): "The mind's essential vigor: this is called the *hun*- and *po*-souls. If the *hun*- and *po*-souls leave one, how could one last for long?" (心之精爽，是謂魂魄。魂魄去之，何以能久？) cf. Durrant, Li, Schaberg, *Zuozhuan*, 3:1635.

alive is not articulated; they are simply what account for the difference, in sentient animals, between being alive and dead.⁶¹ Most references to these souls are in stories about death, a subject to which we shall turn shortly.

A living human body was not considered to be very much different from that of other living animals. Mengzi said, rather famously, "That by which humans differ from domesticated and wild animals is quite small. Most people throw it away, but noble people preserve it." (人之所以異於禽獸者幾希：庶民去之，君子存之。)⁶² This "small" difference has nothing to do with spirits or souls, which all animals have: it is virtuosity that can, *potentially*, set humans apart.⁶³ This is where self-cultivation comes into play. But the human person consists just of the elements we have mentioned: *qi*-substance, essence, spirit, and *hun*- and *po*-souls, which constitute the body, with its mind, nature, emotions, intentions, and all the rest. Just like any other animal, only with a greater potential for creativity and for practicing virtuosity. As for any kind of religious or philosophical "I" behind it all, Zhuangzi, like some Buddhists on the other side of the Himalayas, doubted if any such entity existed (or, at least, persisted through time).⁶⁴ Instead, we are enjoined to treat our bodies with care: "[One] must be tranquil, [one] must be pure; without belaboring your body, and without convulsing your essence: then [you] can live long." (必靜必清，無勞汝形，無搖汝精，乃可以長生。)⁶⁵ The "tranquility" might refer both to simple rest and sleep, or to some kind of early introspection practice. The "purity" can refer both to what you physically eat, or to how you ethically act. The early Chinese were keen on exercise, so "belaboring" must refer to what we would call

---

61. It is a historical curiosity that West Asian—that is, Greek and Christian—ideas of the spirit and soul are precisely the opposite: spirit (*pneuma*) is the "breath of life," while "soul" (*psyche*) has more cognitive (and eschatological) responsibilities. This is not to imply that these two terms were used with much more clarity in ancient times than in the modern, English-speaking world.

62. *Mengzi* ch. 4B19 (離婁下); cf. Van Norden, *Mengzi*, 107.

63. Although virtuosity was extremely important to early Chinese authors, it was often portrayed as a small but important thing, like a hinge or a linchpin: little things upon which much depends. The *Shijing* has an old saying: "Virtuosity is as light as a feather, but few people are able to lift it." (德輶如毛、民鮮克舉之。) *Shijing* 詩經 #260 (烝民); cf. Arthur Waley, *The Book of Songs: The Ancient Chinese Classic of Poetry* (1937; edited with additional translations by Joseph Allen; New York: Grove Press, 1996), 276.

64. See *Zhuangzi* chs. 1, 2, 4, and 6.

65. *Zhuangzi* ch. 11 (在宥); cf. Watson, *Zhuangzi*, 78.

"over-exertion."⁶⁶ The text does not specify what "convulsing" the essence refers to—perhaps it is just a restatement of the previous phrase—but just as not "belaboring" recalls being "tranquil," so not "convulsing" may refer back to being "pure," in both body and mind. These are the ideas that underlie the cultivation of life.

Dead Humans (逝者)

Death in early China was certainly seen as a natural process, but it was not conceived as an event as simple and quick as turning off a light switch. When a person dies, the *qi*-substance dissipates, but different parts of the person do so at different rates of speed. The heavier physical body decomposes at one rate (though bones of course last longer than flesh), while the more rarefied souls last some years longer. The texts are not clear about the fate of the spirit, though it too will eventually evaporate, as nothing was thought to last forever. But it seems that the spirits of some people do persist after death, while those of others do not. Likewise, some people have ghosts while others do not. The process, understandably, is as murky as it is in the West. Even Kongzi either did not know, or did not want to speculate on it.

> Zigong asked of Kongzi saying: "Do the dead have consciousness? Or do they not?" The scholar replied: "Were I to say the dead *do* have consciousness, then I fear filial children and obedient grandchildren would harm the living in having them accompany the dead. And were I to say the dead *do not* have consciousness, then I fear filial children would abandon their parents' [bodies] and not [bother to] bury them. You want to know if the dead have consciousness or not, but this is not important right now: later [i.e., when you die], you will know this yourself."

> (子貢問於孔子曰：「死者有知乎？將無知乎？」子曰：「吾欲言死之有知，將恐孝子順孫妨生以送死；吾欲言死之無知，將

---

66. One piece of evidence for this claim is the exercise chart of different stretching poses found in 1973, in a tomb that was closed in 168 BCE, at Mawangdui 馬王堆. See Donald Harper, *Early Chinese Medical Literature: The Mawangdui Medical Manuscripts* (New York: Kegan Paul International, 1998), 310–27.

恐不孝之子棄其親而不葬。賜欲知死者有知與無知，非今之急，後自知之。」)⁶⁷

Zhuangzi was more willing to discuss the matter. Two of his anecdotes are particularly relevant here. In the first, his wife has just died, and he has this to say, of both her birth and death: "In the midst of vagueness, there was a transformation and then there was *qi*-substance; the *qi*-substance transformed and then there was a form; the form transformed and then there was life. Now there has been another transformation and there was death. It is like the progression of the four seasons: spring, autumn, winter, summer." (雜乎芒芴之間，變而有氣；氣變而有形，形變而有生。今又變而之死：是相與為春秋冬夏四時行也。)⁶⁸ Like Kongzi, he does not address the question of post-mortem consciousness here; the point is only that death is simply a matter of transformation, as are so many other things.

In another story from Zhuangzi, there were four friends, one of whom was on his deathbed. One of the friends came to visit, and at the bedside wondered aloud about what was going to happen to his sick friend: "Great is creative development! What will it make of you? Where will it send you? Will you become a rat's liver? Will you become a bug's arm?" (偉哉造化！又將奚以汝為？將奚以汝適？以汝為鼠肝乎？以汝為蟲臂乎？)⁶⁹ This is not a story about reincarnation. (That might have been the case if this story were told in India, but this is from early China.) It should not be taken to imply that the sick person's consciousness would be transferred into that of a rat or bug. Rather, it is simply an amplification of the theme of transformation in the previous story. The *qi*-substance that makes up your entire person will dissolve and become re-formed into other entities. The rat's liver and bug's arm may not even be mutually exclusive, for in an earlier part of the story another friend speculated that different body parts may transform

---

67. *Kongzi jiayu* 孔子家語 ch. 8 (致思); cf. Robert Kramers, *K'ung Tzu Chia Yü: The School Sayings of Confucius* (Leiden: E.J. Brill, 1949), 238. There were many scholars in early China, but "the scholar" in dialogues like this always refers to Kongzi. Having living people "accompany the dead" was an ancient practice of killing the servants of powerful people and burying them together, so that the former may continue to serve the latter in the afterlife. Kongzi was famously against this, and the practice, already declining in his lifetime, seemed to have died out within a few centuries. See Lai, *Excavating the Afterlife*, 109.

68. *Zhuangzi* ch. 18 (至樂); cf. Watson, *Zhuangzi*, 141.

69. *Zhuangzi* ch. 6 (大宗師); cf. Watson, *Zhuangzi*, 48.

into different things, with his spirit potentially turning into a horse. The subsequent entities do not even need to be other sentient animals. This latter story suggests that perhaps one arm may turn into a crossbow bolt and the buttocks may turn into a wheel. In yet another story, a dead person reveals to his brother (in a dream) that he has been turned into the berries of a cypress tree.[70] In fact, there need not even be a specific subsequent entity, as Zhuangzi also describes the after-death possibility of "roaming between Heaven and Earth as a unified *qi*-substance" (遊乎天地之一氣).[71] So perhaps you will turn into a cloud when you die. No mention is made in these anecdotes of what becomes of the *hun*- and *po*-souls. Fortunately, this is specified in other sources.

The *Liji* records a father's pronouncement over the grave of his eldest son: "The bones and flesh returning to earth is fate. But perhaps the *hun*-soul will have nowhere that it cannot go." (骨肉歸復於土，命也。若魂則無不之也。)[72] The "perhaps" sounds poignant, and maybe a little wistful. Yet other passages bear this hope out. In a later description of a prototypical funeral, the author states unequivocally: "[They] looked toward Heaven and buried [the body] in the Earth: the body's *po*-soul then descended and the conscious *qi*-substance ascended." (天望而地藏也，體魄則降，知氣在上。)[73] The first passage does not mention the *po*-soul by name, nor does the second passage mention the *hun*-soul by name, but together they are rather clear. The lighter, Yang, *hun*-soul goes up and can travel around, while the heavier, Yin, *po*-soul stays in (or near) the tomb. The former may be amenable to prayerful entreaties for help of various kinds, while the latter is the recipient of grave-side offerings and commemoration.

But sometimes people die unhappily and come back to haunt the living as ghosts.[74] These ghosts are somehow derived primarily from *po*-souls who are not content with their afterlife existence, but insist upon bringing

---

70. *Zhuangzi* ch. 32 (列禦寇); cf. Watson, *Zhuangzi*, 280.

71. *Zhuangzi* ch. 6 (大宗師); cf. Watson, *Zhuangzi*, 50.

72. *Liji* 禮記 ch. 4 (檀弓下); cf. James Legge, *Li Chi: Book of Rites* (1885; rpt. New York: University Books, 1967), 1:193.

73. *Liji* ch. 9 (禮運); cf. Legge, *Li Chi*, 1:369.

74. For a good introduction to ghosts in early China, see Poo Mu-chou, "The Concept of Ghost in Ancient Chinese Religion," in *Religion and Chinese Society, Volume I: Ancient and Medieval China*, ed. John Lagerwey (Hong Kong: The Chinese University of Hong Kong Press, 2004), 173–91.

bother to others, especially those who caused them to die unhappily. (It appears that *hun*-souls can also become ghosts, but this is less likely.) It seems that a ghost is simply a postmortem soul gone rogue. There are many ghost stories in early Chinese literature, but two stand out for our purposes here, and both come from authoritative figures. In the first, a man named Boyou had recently died, and when the noted minister and intellectual Zichan visited his state, someone asked him about Boyou.

> When Zichan went to the state of Jin, Zhao Jingzi asked of him, saying, "Is it possible for Boyou to still become a ghost?" Zichan replied: "It is possible. When people are born, a beginning development [within one] is called a *po*-soul. When the *po*-soul has already been produced, its Yang [part] is called the *hun*-soul. Using things [for food] increases essence [within one], thus the *hun*-soul and *po*-soul get stronger. They are that by which the essence is invigorated, and can [even] be full of spiritous percipience. When an ordinary man or woman violently dies, their *hun*-soul and/or *po*-soul can still oppress people, by becoming a malevolent wraith."
>
> (及子產適晉，趙景子問焉，曰：「伯有猶能為鬼乎？」子產曰：「能。人生始化曰魄，既生魄，陽曰魂。用物精多，則魂魄強。是以有精爽，至於神明。匹夫匹婦強死，其魂魄猶能馮依於人，以為淫厲。」)[75]

This story should not be taken to suggest that Zhao Jingzi was uncertain about the existence of ghosts, rather, he was uncertain about whether or not this *particular* person would become one. This implies that not everyone turns into a ghost. Also, Zhao Jingzi asked if Boyou could still become a "ghost" (鬼), and Zichan replied that he may have become a "malevolent wraith" (淫厲), which implies that the latter is a subset of the former. (There were many kinds of ghosts in early China.) Later in the passage, Zichan does say that because Boyou "had died a violent death, so he was able to become a ghost" (強死，能為鬼). We also learn that the Yin *po*-soul (temporally) precedes the Yang *hun*-soul and, although the wording is not clear enough for us to be certain, the latter seems originally to have been part of the former, and subsequently

---

75. *Zuozhuan* (昭公 7); cf. Durrant, Li, Schaberg, *Zuozhuan*, 3:1427.

separated off. The main question that I have with this story is: since there is no conjunction between the *hun-* and *po*-souls in the Chinese, should it be read as saying the *hun*-soul *and* the *po*-soul, together, turned into the ghost, or should it be *either* the *hun*-soul *or* the *po*-soul turned into the ghost? This question seems to be addressed in the following story.

Zichan (d. 522) was a few decades older than Kongzi (d. 479), and Kongzi held him in high esteem.[76] In this next story, Kongzi gives his own take on the afterlife, told in the context of how people came to venerate the spirits of the deceased.

> Zai Wo said, "I have heard the names 'ghost' and 'spirit,' but I do not know what they mean." The scholar said, "*Qi*-substance flourishes as spirits, and *po*-souls flourish as ghosts: harmonizing with ghosts and spirits is the epitome of teaching. All of the living must die, and the dead must return to the ground: [some of] these are called ghosts. Bones and flesh rot below, and their Yin-substance become the ground of fields. [But] the *qi*-substance that issues forth and ascends on high becomes visible percipients, with odors given off, and sadness [felt]: this is the essence of many things, a manifestation of spirit. Based on the essence of things, established as its culmination, and clearly named 'ghost' and 'spirit,' [they] became the first principles for the masses. The masses are in awe of them and the people venerate them."
>
> (宰我曰:「吾聞鬼神之名,不知其所謂。」子曰:「氣也者,神之盛也;魄也者,鬼之盛也:合鬼與神,教之至也。眾生必死,死必歸土,此之謂鬼。骨肉斃於下,陰為野土。其氣發揚於上,為昭明,焄蒿,淒愴:此百物之精也,神之著也。因物之精,制為之極,明命鬼神,以為黔首則。百眾以畏,萬民以服。」)[77]

Several questions arise from reading this passage. First, to say that "*po*-souls flourish as ghosts" indicates that ghosts are more active than *po*-souls. Perhaps this is because they are more restless due to their unjust deaths. Second, only *po*-souls are mentioned as "flourishing as ghosts," so does that mean that *hun*-souls cannot become ghosts, as was (potentially) implied in the previous story? To harmonize these two stories, we must conclude that

---

76. See *Lunyu* 論語 5.16; cf. Edward Slingerland, *Confucius: Analects, with Selections from Traditional Commentaries* (Indianapolis: Hackett, 2003), 46.

77. *Liji* ch. 24 (祭義); cf. Legge, *Li Chi*, 2:220–21.

either *hun*- or *po*-souls *can* become ghosts, but it is more *likely* that ghosts derive from *po*-souls. Third, although Kongzi above declined to speculate on whether or not the dead were conscious, here it is clear that living humans should nevertheless "harmonize" with them. This certainly fits into the general pattern of ancestor veneration in early China. Fourth, the "many living things" sentence implies that living things, and not just people, may have ghosts. It is unclear if, or how, the "*po*-souls flourish as ghosts" line should modify this claim. I am not sure about the percipients and odors in the air above a gravesite (maybe the "percipient" here is a clever ghost?), but people have been known to report many unusual things around cemeteries. Certainly, people typically do feel sadness around the dead.

Fifth, "the *qi*-substance that issues forth and ascends on high" we would expect to be the *hun*-soul, but the word "*hun*-soul" does not appear in this passage, and the end of the sentence identifies it as spirit. In another text, Kongzi does say that, at death, "The bodily form descends, and the *hun*-soul *qi*-substance ascends." (形體則降，魂氣則上。)[78] And, elsewhere in the *Liji*, though not in a saying of Kongzi, it does say that "*Hun*-soul *qi*-substance returns to Heaven, bodily *po*-soul returns to Earth." (魂氣歸於天，形魄歸於地。)[79] So why would Kongzi leave the *hun*-soul out of this account? It is perhaps worth noting that the terms "*hun*-soul" and "*po*-soul" do not appear in Kongzi's most authoritative sayings, the *Lunyu*. But he does, three times in that text, reference "ghosts and spirits." This leads me to speculate that, for whatever reason, Kongzi was simply more comfortable with the phrase "ghosts and spirits" than with "*hun*- and *po*-souls." (It is not impossible that "ghosts and spirits" should sometimes be understood as "ghostly spirits" where "ghostly" simply means "uncanny.") If this was the case, then his identification of the *qi*-substance that "ascends on high" after death as a "spirit," is technically incorrect, and is just a manner of speaking.[80] But the ultimate import of the passage is clear: ghosts and spirits are proper objects of human awe and veneration.

---

78. *Kongzi jiayu* ch. 6 (問禮); cf. Kramers, *K'ung Tzu Chia Yü*, 222.

79. *Liji* ch. 11 (效特牲); cf. Legge, *Li Chi*, 1:444.

80. That Kongzi meant "*hun*-soul" by his use of "spirit" here is an explanation used by Wei Litong 魏荔彤 (1670–?) in his *Da Yi tongjie* 大易通解 ch. 13. A second possibility is that Kongzi considered *hun*-souls to be a subset of spirits. Thus, though Chinese does not have definite or indefinite articles, the "a manifestation of spirit" could mean "one of the [possible] manifestations of spirit." As I have described them, both are Yang *qi*-substance essences, which I differentiate by saying the *hun*-soul is more biological and the spirit is more psychological, but this may have been a difference without distinction to Kongzi. In the end, I still prefer the loose "manner of speaking" explanation.

It is possible to read the passage above as saying that ghosts do not derive exclusively from humans, but this is a contested claim. On the one hand, one text seems to differentiate humans from other creatures. "When the myriad creature die, they are all said to disintegrate, when people die, they [can be] called ghosts." (萬物死,皆曰折;人死,曰鬼。)[81] On the other, another text categorizes three different kinds of ghosts. "There are Heavenly ghosts, there likewise are the ghosts and spirits of mountains and rivers, and there also are people who have died and become ghosts." (有天鬼,亦有山水鬼神者,亦有人死而為鬼者。)[82] It is not clear if these other non-human ghosts are the ghosts of other animals, or if they always were ghosts. I suspect that, as with the Kongzi quote above, sometimes people did not write as carefully as modern academics. Imagine that.

Precisely what ghosts do is, naturally, a bit mysterious, given that we cannot usually see or hear them.[83] Mainly they seem to punish bad people and reward good people. Mozi, though he was probably the leading ancient Chinese cheerleader for the belief in ghosts (he thought the fear of them would be good for social order), is probably representative of his age when he says we should "Assume that ghosts and spirits are able to reward the worthy and punish the wicked." (嘗若鬼神之能賞賢如罰暴也。)[84] This idea accounts for most of the appearances that ghosts make in the literature. Related to these duties, there are two specific functions that I would like to highlight: haunting (one kind of punishing) and helping (one kind of rewarding).

We saw above that an angry ghost can "oppress" (憑依) people, which has the effect of frightening them. But a ghost can also up the ante and "haunt" (祟) people, which can have more serious consequences. One text explains:

> As a general rule, for those who are said to be "haunted," [their] *hun-* and *po-*souls have left [them] and their essence and spirit are disordered. [Since their] essence and spirit are disordered,

---

81. *Liji* ch. 23 (祭法); cf. Legge, *Li Chi*, 2:203.
82. *Mozi* ch. 31 (明鬼下); cf. Knoblock and Riegel, *Mozi*, 271.
83. Kongzi said, of both ghosts and spirits: "Look for them but [you] will not see [them], listen for them but [you] will not hear [them]." (視之而弗見,聽之而弗聞。) *Liji* ch. 31 (中庸); cf. Legge, *Li Chi*, 2:307.
84. *Mozi* ch. 31 (明鬼下); cf. Knoblock and Riegel, *Mozi*, 267.

[they] thus are without virtuosity. If ghosts would not haunt people, then their *hun*- and *po*-souls would not leave [them], and if the *hun*- and *po*-souls are not gone, then the essence and spirit would not be disordered, and having essence and spirit that are not disordered is called having virtuosity.

(凡所謂祟者，魂魄去而精神亂，精神亂則無德。鬼不祟人則魂魄不去，魂魄不去而精神不亂，精神不亂之謂有德。)[85]

For this author, the effect of losing one's souls (due to being frightened by being haunted by a ghost) leads to moral decline; any cognitive effect goes unremarked. But we learned above that the *hun*- and *po*-souls are also defined as "the mind's essential vigor," so losing them will at least entail losing mental vigor as well as virtuosity.

Ghosts in early China, however, can reward as well as punish. The *Guanzi* gives an example of how they can help us in this next passage, where "it" does not refer to any specific thing, but instead indicates whatever goal you might have in mind: "Think about it, [and if you] think about it but do not obtain it, ghosts and spirits may teach you. This is not [due to] the strength of ghosts and spirits, [but rather it is due to] their exceptional essential *qi*-substance." (思之，思之不得，鬼神教之。非鬼神之力也，其精氣之極也。)[86] The text does not imply that we need specifically to ask ghosts and spirits to teach us, but only that they may, assuming they are inclined to so reward us. The last sentence provides some insight into how they might accomplish this teaching. It seems they do not simply and directly impart knowledge by fiat, but rather they help us with their own extraordinary essence. I suspect that they do not directly "give" us some of their essence, in something like an act of Buddhist or Christian grace, but rather that their very presence, essence-filled as it is, somehow "inspires" us. Recall that spirit is associated primarily with creativity, which seems to always manifest mysteriously.

Given that ghosts and spirits can either reward or punish us, what is the best way for us to deal with them? There are two answers to this, one

---

85. *Hanfeizi* 韓非子 ch. 20 (解老); cf. Liao Wengui, *The Complete Works of Han Fei Tzu* (London: Arthur Probsthain, 1939, 1959), 1:186–87. "Essence and spirit" could alternatively be read as "essential spirit/ousness."

86. *Guanzi* ch. 37 (心術下); cf. Rickett, *Guanzi*, 2:60.

formal and religious and the other informal and philosophical. The first may be summarized thus: "[If one] presents respect at the ancestral temple, ghosts and spirits will manifest." (宗廟致敬，鬼神著矣。)[87] The context of this passage is advice to the king, who certainly would have had an ancestral temple in which to present respect. But whether at an ancestral temple, a smaller family temple, a gravesite, or even a household memorial, the important thing is to show respect to one's ancestors, for this is the kind of virtuosity to which ghosts and spirits respond. Ancient Chinese ideas of family, filiality, ancestor veneration, and morality are closely related and were extremely important. Nevertheless, these ideas existed side by side, in the same culture, with a markedly different attitude.

The more "philosophical" response to ghosts and spirits is decidedly more languid and, curiously, comes primarily from early China's archetypal conservative, Kongzi. We learned above that Kongzi declined to speculate on whether or not the dead retained consciousness. Here, despite the prominence of correct mortuary protocol in his teaching, he reiterates his ultimate focus on this world. "Jilu asked about devotion to ghosts and spirits. The scholar replied: '[You] are not yet able to be devoted to people, so how will you be able to be devoted to ghosts?' [Jilu then said: 'I] would like to ask about death.' [Kongzi] replied: '[You] do not yet know about life, so why should you know about death?'" (季路問事鬼神。子曰：「未能事人，焉能事鬼？」「敢問死？」曰：「未知生，焉知死？」)[88] This is a surprising exchange in the context of early China as a whole but is quite in keeping with the teachings of Kongzi. It is one of the things that make him stand out among his peers as much as he does. In another passage, he gives his signature pronouncement on the issue. "Fan Chi asked about wisdom. The scholar said: 'Attending to the propriety of the people, and respecting the ghosts and spirits while yet keeping them at a distance, can be called wisdom.'" (樊遲問知。子曰：「務民之義，敬鬼神而遠之，可謂知矣。」)[89] Why should we keep at a distance entities that can help us learn? I have two speculations (aside from concluding that the two authors simply disagreed with each other). One is that Kongzi was just a more cautious person and had something of a "don't play with

---

87. *Xiaojing* 孝經 ch. 16 (感應); cf. Henry Rosemont, Jr. and Roger Ames, *The Chinese Classic of Family Reverence: A Philosophical Translation of the* Xiaojing (Honolulu: University of Hawaii Press, 2009), 115.

88. *Lunyu* 11.12; cf. Slingerland, *Analects*, 115.

89. *Lunyu* 6.22; cf. Slingerland, *Analects*, 60.

fire" attitude, for even if said fire was potentially beneficial, it was also potentially quite harmful. The other is that the *Guanzi* author, who said "ghosts and spirits may teach you," was speaking metaphorically. Perhaps the "ghosts and spirits" that can teach us with their exceptionally creative essence are just poetic anthropomorphisms of fundamentally inscrutable human creativity.

Returning to our anthropological survey of dead people: at death the body rots, the *hun*-soul goes up, the *po*-soul goes down, and an unhappy *po*-soul (or maybe *hun*-soul) may or may not turn into a ghost. The fate of the human spirit after death is less clear. There are spirits "between Heaven and Earth," and they probably did not all derive from dead humans because, as we learned above, spirits preceded humans in the unfolding of creation. But are *some* of them from dead humans? If so, under what circumstances does a human spirit persist after death? And for how long? I do not know of any early Chinese authors that address these questions clearly.

Some spirits, however, are said to persist after death, for a time, and thereby may come to inhabit the space between Heaven and Earth. Such disembodied spirits naturally play a significant role in religion. But unlike the traditionally Christian and Islamic societies of West Asia, where the activities of dead ancestors (prior to "Judgment Day") remain a hazy and seldom-discussed topic, early Chinese society often articulated the endeavors of postmortem relatives. The *Shijing* contains an ode that reads like a general benediction, with a benevolent Heaven and benevolent spirits, noting that "The spirits' kindness bestows upon you many blessings." (神之弔矣，詒爾多福。)⁹⁰ Another ode describes a funeral, wherein a priest-like "incantor" and a young relative "representing" the deceased both play central roles. After the funeral service is finished, the ode describes its denouement: "The rites of protocol have been completed; the bells and drums have ceased their summons. The filial heirs have gone to their places; the skilled incantor has relayed the announcement: 'the spirits are all drunk.' The esteemed representative of the dead thereupon rises. The drums and bells send off the representative of the dead; the spirit protectors thereupon return." (禮儀既備，鍾鼓既戒。孝孫徂位，工祝致告：「神具醉止」。皇尸載起。鼓鍾送尸，神保聿歸。)⁹¹ This passage, though it does not end here, does not specify exactly where the spirit protectors return to, whether they return to a single place or many different places, how long they persist after death

---

90. *Shijing* #166 (天保); cf. Waley, *The Book of Songs*, 139.
91. *Shijing* #209 (楚茨); cf. Waley, *The Book of Songs*, 195.

(assuming they were once human), or give us much information about their existence. But they are around, in the space between Heaven and Earth, and they can bless humans, and withhold blessings too.

Perhaps it is the case that humans do not "have" spirits, but rather, we sometimes just play host to one. The sentence above translated as "There is a spirit may spontaneously reside in the body . . ." (有神自在身) could have been translated more definitively as "There is a spirit that spontaneously resides in the body."[92] Ancient Chinese grammar is sufficiently imprecise to allow either reading. But the more equivocal translation also makes better sense of the rest of that line: "but no one can [fully] apprehend its coming and going" (一往一來，莫之能思。) Such an interpretation has the further advantage of fitting well with the metaphorical reading just mentioned. I realize that playing the metaphor card is an easy out, analytically speaking, but I would argue that texts that deal with supernatural entities have a long history, globally, of being read in just this way.

Bodily Self-Cultivation (治氣)

Cosmology and anthropology are the context and constituent of bodily self-cultivation. The primary goal of bodily self-cultivation is a smooth operation or flow of *qi*-substances. Since the body is made entirely of *qi*-substances, the "flow" must refer to those parts of the body that can, in fact, flow: blood and breath chief among the literal parts, with essence and spirit as likely candidates for metaphorical "flow."

> Generally speaking, people have three hundred and sixty joints, nine orifices, five major organs, and six minor organs. The skin should be smooth, the blood vessels should be free-flowing, the sinews and bones should be firm, the mind and will should be harmonious, and the essential *qi*-substance should circulate. If they are like this, then sickness will have no place to stay and corruption no means to grow. Sickness remains and corruption grows when essential *qi*-substance is sluggish. Thus, when waterways are sluggish they become fetid; when trees are too dense they become bug-infested; when plants are too dense they become withered.

---

92. *Guanzi* ch. 49 (內業). Previously quoted at n. 52 above.

(凡人三百六十節，九竅五藏六府。肌膚欲其比也，血脈欲其通也，筋骨欲其固也，心志欲其和也，精氣欲其行也。若此則病無所居而惡無由生矣。病之留、惡之生也，精氣鬱也。故水鬱則為污，樹鬱則為蠹，草鬱則為蕢。)[93]

This passage implicates both bodily health and mental harmony, while the word "corruption" (惡) could refer to body, mind, or even morality. Zhuangzi describes a different kind of impediment to this flow, which is when anger makes one's *qi*-substance "overwrought" (茀然). If this situation escalates, then we get both short-tempered *and* become morally unworthy.[94]

We therefore should avoid "sluggish" and "overwrought" *qi*-substances,[95] but the texts also offer the positive advice to circulate and regulate them. The following passage describes an ideal civil servant, but it is not difficult to extrapolate to our own circumstances. Zichan, whom we met above, is diagnosing a sick local ruler.

> I have heard noble people have four times: mornings are for listening to government affairs, afternoons for asking questions, evenings for improving laws, and nights for relaxing themselves. Accordingly, they regulate and circulate their *qi*-substances, not allowing there to be a place for them to be blocked or quagmired, which would weaken their limbs. This [kind of] mind would not be vigorous, but rather confused and disordered in a hundred [different] ways. Now, [in your case,] it is doubtless that exclusively doing one thing [of the four just mentioned] has produced sickness.

> (僑聞之，君子有四時：朝以聽政，晝以訪問，夕以修令，夜以安身。於是乎節宣其氣，勿使有所壅閉湫底，以露其體。茲心不爽，而昏亂百度。今無乃壹之，則生疾矣。)[96]

The benefits of having a schedule are clear to anyone who juggles a number of commitments. This four-part system, by no means unmodifiable, may

---

93. *Lüshi chunqiu* ch. 20.5 (達鬱); cf. Knoblock and Riegel, *Lü Buwei*, 527.
94. *Zhuangzi* ch. 4 (人間世); cf. Watson, *Zhuangzi*, 28.
95. The former being excessively Yin and the latter excessively Yang.
96. *Zuozhuan* (昭公 1); cf. Durrant, Li, Schaberg, *Zuozhuan*, 3:1327.

in fact fit well with academics: mornings for research, early afternoons for the classroom, late afternoons for committee work, and evenings, ostensibly, for oneself and family. In any case, we are instructed to "regulate" (節) and "circulate" (宣) our *qi*-substances, which is an indication to regularly alternate between more settled times of regulated breathing and blood-flow, and more animated times, when breath and sweat are dispersed from the body.

There are many other things, in addition to scheduling our time, that we can do for the benefit of our *qi*-substance. What we eat, where we live, and our daily habits are three things that are explicitly mentioned in our sources as things that need our attention. We noted above that food can increase one's *qi*-substance, but food consumption has a variety of effects in our bodies.

> Eating and drinking should be moderated for the organs; tastes and flavors should be moderated for the *qi*-substances; work and rest should be moderated for the sinews and bones; hot and cold should be moderated for the skin: thereafter the *qi*-substances and the organs will be equanimous, the mind's procedures will be ordered; thoughtful consideration will be successful; delight and anger will be timely. Activity and rest will be happy; activities will be timely and [the things one] uses will be sufficient. Those who do these are said to be able to nourish themselves.
>
> (飲食適乎藏，滋味適乎氣，勞佚適乎筋骨，寒煖適乎肌膚：然後氣藏平，心術治，思慮得，喜怒時，起居而遊樂，事時而用足。夫是之謂能自養者也。)[97]

Different individuals will have different requirements and tolerances when it comes to diet (spices in particular), activity level, and external temperature. Therefore, "moderation" is both a key term and a problem in need of solving.

Moderation is usually good advice, especially when it comes to consumption, but sometimes an author will venture into (a little) more specificity. Here is one example: "To often consume sweet things is beneficial to

---

97. *Hanshi waizhuan* ch. 3.20; cf. Hightower, *Han Shih Wai Chuan*, 98. *Guanzi* ch. 49 (內業) uses a different term for "moderation," but the import seems to be the same: "Between gorging and abstention: this is called moderation." (充攝之間：此謂和成。) cf. Rickett, *Guanzi*, 2:53.

muscle but not good for bones. To often consume bitter things is beneficial to bones but not good for joints. To often consume savory things is beneficial to joints but not good for *qi*-substance." (多食甘者，有益於肉而骨不利；多食苦者，有益於骨而筋不利；多食辛者，有益於筋而氣不利。)⁹⁸ The text does not give any reasons for these opinions, and this sort of advice takes us out of the realm of philosophy and into the realm of medicine.

The constructed environment in which we live—our housing—was also considered to be an important ingredient in self-cultivation. Moderation is similarly an issue here: "Moderation in eating and drinking, housing and residence, results in the nine orifices, hundred joints, and thousand blood vessels all functioning correctly." (飲食居處適則九竅百節千脈皆通利矣。)⁹⁹ Although unstated, moderation may be the motivation behind observations like this one: "High rooms have excessive Yang, and big rooms have excessive Yin, therefore neither should be lived in." (高室多陽，大室多陰，故皆不居。)¹⁰⁰ A later text repeats this warning, then continues with comments on the food and clothes of the good kings of old:

> [Their] flavors were not [too] heavy or exotic, and [their] clothes were not [too] thick or hot. If [clothes are too] thick or hot then the conduits will get congested, and if the conduits are congested, then the *qi*-substances will not flow. If flavors are [too] heavy or exotic, then the stomach will be gorged, and if the stomach is gorged then the innards will get distended, and if the innards are distended, then the *qi*-substances will not flow. With these conditions, would long life be attainable?
>
> (味不眾珍，衣不燀熱。燀熱則理塞，理塞則氣不達。味眾珍則胃充，胃充則中大鞔；中大鞔而氣不達。以此長生可得乎？)¹⁰¹

The general advice for moderation and simplicity is well-taken. Most commentators take the "conduits" as referring to veins, even though blood is

---

98. *Gongsun Nizi* 公孫尼子 fragment #7, in Ma Guohan 馬國翰, *Yuhan shanfang ji yi shu* 玉函山房輯佚書 (c. 1855; rpt. in 5 vols. 揚州：廣陵書社, 2004), 4:2506.
99. *Lüshi chunqiu* ch. 21.1 (開春); cf. Knoblock and Riegel, *Lü Buwei*, 548.
100. *Shizi* 尸子 fragment 114; cf. Paul Fischer, *Shizi: China's First Syncretist* (New York: Columbia University Press, 2012), 155.
101. *Lüshi chunqiu* ch. 1.3 (重己); cf. Knoblock and Riegel, *Lü Buwei*, 69.

not mentioned. Although morality is always implicit when referring to the rulers of antiquity, the goal here is unambiguously health and long life.

Another external factor that influences the flow of *qi*-substance is our everyday habits, the protocol with which we interact with others: family, neighbors, colleagues, and people in positions of power.[102] Such civilizing and socializing protocol was the central concern for Xunzi: "As a general rule, for the arts of ordering [one's] *qi*-substances and nourishing the mind, nothing is more direct than following protocol, nothing is more important than finding a teacher, nothing is more spiritous than having focused interest." (凡治氣養心之術，莫徑由禮，莫要得師，莫神一好。)[103] Xunzi had great faith in character-building through culture and education, which explains his emphasis on protocol and teachers. And, as a teacher himself, he knew the salubrious effects of mental concentration, which can open up ordinary attention to uncommon insight.

External engagements like time-management, food, housing, and habits are not the only things to consider. Internal factors are important too. We will consider four: age, breathing, emotional calm and, once again, mental focus. For age, Kongzi had a simple tripartite plan: "Kongzi said, 'Noble people have three cautions: when young, the blood and *qi*-substances are not settled, [so they] are cautious about sex. Coming to their prime, the blood and *qi*-substances are adamant, [so they] are cautious about fighting. Coming to their old age, the blood and *qi*-substances have declined, [so they] are cautious about accumulating [things].'" (孔子曰：「君子有三戒：少之時，血氣未定，戒之在色。及其壯也，血氣方剛，戒之在鬥。及其老也，血氣既衰，戒之在得。」)[104] Sensuality, contentiousness, and acquisitiveness are certainly important considerations on the path of self-cultivation. Kongzi gives no advice about these things other than to say that we should be cautious about them.

Breathing deeply is often correlated with calmness. In the next passage, the aspirational character is called a "genuine" person, whose example is only magnified by the fact that they lived in the romanticized "olden days." Zhuangzi says: "The 'genuine people' of old: they slept without dreaming, and awakened without worries; they ate simply and breathed deeply. 'Gen-

---

102. For more on how the environment was conceived, see Mark Lewis, *The Construction of Space in Early China* (Albany: State University of New York Press, 2006).
103. *Xunzi* ch. 2 (修身); cf. Hutton, *Xunzi*, 12.
104. *Lunyu* 16.7; cf. Slingerland, *Analects*, 195. It is possible that it should be read "blood *qi*-substance" rather than "blood and *qi*-substances."

uine people' breathe from their heels, while the masses breathe from their throats." (古之真人：其寢不夢，其覺無憂，其食不甘，其息深深。真人之息以踵，眾人之息以喉。)[105] Whether deep breathing should be construed as a cause or an effect of self-cultivation is unclear. But as a potential method of self-cultivation, we may assume the former.[106] For unlike dreamless sleeping, which must remain an effect, we can do something about how we breathe. That we cannot, in fact, breathe from "the heels," highlights the metaphor.

Emotional calm is an unambiguous goal in many early Chinese texts. In one sense, calm comes from avoiding extremes and seeking what is appropriate. In this passage, some examples of which extremes to avoid are given.

> Heaven produces Yin and Yang, cold and heat, wet and dry, the changes of the four seasons, and the transformations of the myriad things. All can cause benefit, and all can cause harm. Sagely people examine what is appropriate to Yin and Yang, and discern what is beneficial among the myriad things in order to improve life. Thus, if essence and spirit are secure in [your] body, then [your] lifespan will achieve longevity with them. Longevity is not taking what is short and lengthening it, [but rather it is] fulfilling one's years. The task of fulfilling one's years entails getting rid of the harmful. What does it mean to get rid of the harmful? Excessive sweetness, sourness, bitterness, savoriness, and saltiness: if these five fill the body, then life will be harmed. Excessive delight, anger, anxiety, fear, and sadness: if these five adhere to the spirit, then life will be harmed. Excessive cold, heat, aridity, humidity, wind, rain, or fog: if these seven disturb the essence, then life will be harmed. Therefore, as a general rule, in nourishing life, nothing is as good as knowing the origins [i.e., causes]. If [you] know the origins, then sickness will have nowhere from which to arrive.

> (天生陰陽寒暑燥溼，四時之化，萬物之變，莫不為利，莫不為害。聖人察陰陽之宜，辨萬物之利以便生。故精神安乎形，而年壽得長焉。長也者，非短而續之也，畢其數也。畢數之務，

---

105. *Zhuangzi* ch. 6 (大宗師); cf. Watson, *Zhuangzi*, 42.

106. *Zhuangzi* ch. 15 (刻意) explicitly refers to breathing and stretching as forms of bodily cultivation that lead to long life, but it is a rather opaque passage; cf. Watson, *Zhuangzi*, 119.

在乎去害。何謂去害？大甘、大酸、大苦、大辛、大鹹，五者充形則生害矣。大喜、大怒、大憂、大恐、大哀，五者接神則生害矣。大寒、大熱、大燥、大溼、大風、大霖、大霧，七者動精則生害矣。故凡養生，莫若知本，知本則疾無由至矣。）107

The body is impaired by an unbalanced diet, the spirit is impaired by unbalanced emotions, and the essence is impaired by exposure to inclement weather. This passage specifies what we should avoid, and I suppose no one would disagree with the things it enumerates. For the emotions, positive advice elsewhere entails being "centered" and "harmonious." A mostly long-lost text specifically on cultivating *qi*-substance exists in fragmented form. One of the fragments says that "When noble people get angry they return to centeredness and gladden themselves with harmoniousness; when delighted they return to centeredness and collect themselves with correctness; when anxious they return to centeredness and comfort themselves with attentiveness; when fearful they return to centeredness and fill themselves with essence." (君子怒則反中，而自說以和；喜則反中，而收之以正；憂則反中，而舒之以意；懼則反中，而實之以精。）108

The goal is centeredness, and there are four means for achieving it. Harmonious thoughts when angry seems like good advice. "Correctness" is an important and central term in early Chinese texts, but it is a little vague, though I suppose no more vague than "harmony." Here, it means "what is acceptable in a given situation." Delight in itself is not bad, rather, as with all these emotions, excess—the opposite of centeredness—is the problem. Anxiety, or concern, also has its place, and it seems that in this case the worry is about decision-making. Finally, fear is remedied with essence. We learned above that essence will come if we "respectfully clean its lodging place." Whatever mental exercise this involves, calmness would certainly seem to be requisite, and essence is a harbinger of creativity. If you find yourself in a fearful situation, a cool head and a good idea may well be the best ways to resolve it.

Focus is akin to attentiveness, but describes something more like an attitude, or a habit, than a single event. Mengzi reminds us that, although our minds are in charge, we sometimes can run on "auto-pilot" or, alternatively, can be swept along by the situation. "If [your] will is unified then it will move [your] *qi*-substance [i.e., attention], but if [your] *qi*-substance is

---

107. *Lüshi chunqiu* ch. 3.2 (盡數); cf. Knoblock and Riegel, *Lü Buwei*, 99.
108. *Gongsun Nizi* fragment #13, in Ma, *Yuhan shanfang ji yi shu*, 4:2506.

unified, then it will move [your] will. Now say there is one who stumbles or one who rushes around: this is [due to their] *qi*-substance, which has turned back to move the mind." (志壹則動氣，氣壹則動志也。今有蹶者趨者，是氣也，而反動其心。)[109] The "stumbling" and the "rushing around" have been variously interpreted, but in any case, they point to situations where the mind is not quite in charge and is either inattentive (as when we stumble) or is being led by circumstance (as when we rush around needlessly or ineffectively). What should we focus on? Whatever requires our attention at the moment, is one answer. Another, more general answer popular in early Chinese texts is that we should focus on the underlying principles of how the world works. "[That when noble people] are settled and relaxed yet [their] blood and *qi*-substance are not debilitated, is [because they] grasp the principles [of things]." (安燕而血氣不衰，柬理也。)[110] This is because their inner mental focus keeps their body alert and sharp. This brings us to a consideration of the physical benefits of self-cultivation.

There are several potential results from smoothly-flowing *qi*-substance in the body. Perhaps the most obvious is that we will avoid getting sick.

> When exasperated and pent-up *qi*-substance is [suddenly] dispersed but does not return, then it becomes insufficient. If it ascends and does not re-descend, then it causes people to become irritable. If it descends and does not re-ascend, then it causes people to become forgetful. If it neither ascends nor descends, staying in the middle of the body around the heart, then you will get sick.
>
> (夫忿滀之氣，散而不反，則為不足。上而不下，則使人善怒。下而不上，則使人善忘。不上不下，中身當心，則為病。)[111]

This advice was given to someone who had gotten sick after seeing a ghost, so the "sudden dispersal" of *qi*-substance probably refers to being scared silly. The remainder of the passage, however, seems simply to be describing what

---

109. *Mengzi* 2A2 (公孫丑上); cf. Van Norden, *Mengzi*, 38.
110. *Xunzi* ch. 2 (修身); cf. Hutton, *Xunzi*, 15. "Principles" is unmodified here, so presumably it refers to the generic "principles of things." But a few sentences prior, there is a reference to "the [human] way's principles" (道理), so is it possible to read it this way too. Practically speaking, there is no difference in meaning.
111. *Zhuangzi* ch. 19 (達生); cf. Watson, *Zhuangzi*, 150.

happens when *qi*-substance does not circulate freely. "Getting the blood flowing" like this is the reason why so many people in China, even today, go outside in the morning and evening to exercise in groups.

Free-flowing *qi*-substance will also calm you, which, then as now, is taken to be a good thing.

> Expand [your] mind and let go, broaden [your] *qi*-substance and relax, then [your] body will be at ease and not fidgety, and [you] will be able to maintain focus and eliminate a myriad annoyances. Then, on seeing benefit [you] will not be enticed, and on seeing harm [you] will not be afraid. Relaxed and leisurely yet good, detachedly happy in your person: this is called "cloud[-like]" *qi*-substance, [with which your] intentions and actions will be like Heaven.
>
> (大心而敢，寬氣而廣，其形安而不移，能守一而棄萬苛。見利不誘，見害不懼。寬舒而仁，獨樂其身，是謂雲氣，意行似天。)[112]

The use of "expand" and "broaden" here are both metaphors for "letting go" and "relaxing," so for the first sentence, to avoid tautology, we must take *qi*-substance as mental *qi*-substance, otherwise the sentence would be claiming that "if you relax then you will be relaxed." Rather, it is saying that if you relax your mind then your body will follow. Calmness allows for focus and imperturbability, which is exemplified in the two examples of "seeing benefit" and "harm." "Good" here is ethical goodness, without which one could not really be happy. The "cloud[-like]" *qi*-substance has several explanations. It could refer to the smooth movement of a cloud, or the expansiveness of large clouds; other commentators read *yun* 運 (to move) for *yun* 雲 (cloud) and thus read it as "flowing *qi*-substance." The first and third of these explanations are nearly the same, but I like the "cloud" image because it calls to mind effortless movement, which surely was the author's intention.

Avoiding sickness and achieving calmness will have the effect, as you might suspect, of increasing one's chances for a long life. In the passage that follows, Peng Zu is China's paradigmatic long-lived person, much as the

---

112. *Guanzi* ch. 49 (內業); cf. Rickett, *Guanzi*, 2:54. The original term for "let go" is *gan* 敢 (to venture [to do something]), which I amend to *fang* 放 (to release, let go). Another possibility that has been suggested is *chang* 敞 (to make spacious).

biblical "Methuselah" might be in the West; Yao and Yu are famous sage-kings (think Marcus Aurelius or Abraham Lincoln); and the "competence" here refers primarily to the virtues of protocol and trustworthiness. "The measure for extensive competence: use [it] to order [your] *qi*-substance and nourish [your] life, then [you] will outlive Peng Zu; and use [it] to cultivate your person and make a name for yourself, then [you] will match Yao and Yu." (扁善之度：以治氣養生，則後彭祖；以修身自名，則配堯禹。)[113] The goals of self-cultivation here are explicitly long life and the kind of fame that comes with being an ethical exemplar. "Making a name" for oneself does not necessarily imply the level of fame of a sage-ruler; your reputation might only be among your family or friends.

Finally, flowing *qi*-substance facilitates skillfulness. Zhuangzi is particularly famous for such skill stories, so it is appropriate to quote him here. This is the story of a woodworker.

> Woodworker Qing was carving wood to make a bell-stand. When the bell-stand was completed, those who saw it were astonished, [and thought it was as well-made] as if [it had been made by] a ghost or spirit. The Lu Marklord saw it and asked of him, saying: "What art do you have that you could make this?" [Qing] replied: "I am a craftsman; what 'art' would I have? Nevertheless, there is one thing to it. When I am about to make a bell-stand, I never allow it to consume my [mental] *qi*-substance, but always fast in order to quiet my mind. After fasting for three days, I no longer presume to care about acclaim or reward, rank or salary. After fasting for five days, I no longer presume to care about censure or praise, craftiness or clumsiness. After fasting for seven days, I always forget that I have a four-limbed body. Right at this time, [for me, it is as if] there is no royal court; my skill is focused and the outside [world] has slipped away. After this I go into a mountain forest, and observe the Heavenly nature [of the trees, to see which has] the perfect shape. After this I see the completed bell-stand [in my imagination], and after this, I put my hand to it; otherwise, I leave it alone. In this way the Heavenly is matched with the Heavenly. Utensils that are suspected of being the result of spirits are due to this!"

---

113. *Xunzi* ch. 2 (修身); cf. Hutton, *Xunzi*, 10.

(梓慶削木為鐻，鐻成，見者驚猶鬼神。魯侯見而問焉，曰：「子何術以為焉？」對曰：「臣工人，何術之有？雖然，有一焉。臣將為鐻，未嘗敢以耗氣也，必齊以靜心。齊三日，而不敢懷慶賞爵祿。齊五日，不敢懷非譽巧拙。齊七日，輒然忘吾有四枝形體也。當是時也，無公朝，其巧專而外骨消。然後入山林，觀天性，形軀至矣。然後成見鐻，然後加手焉；不然則已。則以天合天。器之所以疑神者，其是與！」)[114]

Woodworker Qing is reluctant to call his skill an "art" because it does not derive solely from practice. Practice is certainly necessary, but there is also something else, the "one thing," that he feels is particularly important. Typically, fasting would involve not eating, and not eating, as we learned above, ought to deplete one's *qi*-substance. So it is probable that he is here referring to a kind of fasting called "mind-fasting," which we shall discuss in chapter 3. But whether the author is referring to dietary fasting or mind fasting, in keeping with what we have learned above, it would entail a mental focus that can keep one's otherwise undernourished person from becoming sluggish. In this way, his skill becomes focused and his powers of creative observation become sharpened. This is a state that he calls "Heavenly," which we might call "inspired." Thus, when he says that "the Heavenly is matched with the Heavenly," he means that his "Heavenly" state—a state in which he is at his mental peak—matches with the natural condition of a tree that has grown in such a way as to make a perfect bell-stand, or at least matches the particular bell-stand that he has envisioned. But all this is dependent on the first prerequisite: not allowing his (mental) *qi*-substance to be depleted by his work. This kind of bodily self-cultivation is the basis for all the other kinds of self-cultivation we will discuss in this book.

---

114. *Zhuangzi* ch. 19 (達生); cf. Watson, *Zhuangzi*, 152–53.

Chapter 2

Nature (性)

"By nature [people] are similar; it is by practice that they become different."

—*Lunyu* 17.2

性相近也,習相遠也。《論語．陽貨》

Various Aspects of Human Nature

"Human nature" is an idea that is both fractured and contested. It is fractured because the word, in both Chinese and English, can refer to several different things. Chief among them is one's persona(s), personality, character, disposition, inclinations, or an eponymous nature. As I use these terms, your "persona" refers to particular aspects of yourself; people often present different personas to different people. Consider the differences in how you act around your parents, your friends, your colleagues. Your "personality" may be said to be the amalgamation of your various personas, how one assimilates various aspects into a whole. Your "character" refers to what you have made of yourself, which is why we say certain experiences "build character." Your "disposition," on the other hand, may be thought of as genetic, something like a family trait. (We might say that someone has a "happy" or "angry" disposition and compare this to that of their parents.) Your "inclinations" refer to the fact that humans have similar emotions and desires; they are somewhat more articulatable versions of the instincts we may share with our mute animal relatives. Finally, human "nature" is a fuzzy concept, more theoretical than "inclinations," and said to inform all humans. Take, for example, the declarative sentence: "He is, by nature, reasonable." This could refer to many things. That he is reasonable in certain environments, but not others (say, at work but not at home), suggests a reasonable persona. If he seems to be reasonable across a variety of social settings, then perhaps he has a reasonable personality. If his reasonableness is the result of his own effort, then we may say he has "matured" or "evolved" into a person with a reasonable character. If his parents are considered reasonable people too, then we might say he has a reasonable disposition. If his reason seems to have the upper hand with his emotions and desires, then we may say he is "reasonably inclined." And if we presume all humans to be "rational animals," then to say he has a reasonable nature may refer to that presumption. We *can* make these distinctions, but we often do not.[1] As to why "human nature" is a contested idea, some people deny that all humans even share a common nature, and therefore take the term to be vacuous and of no use.[2] Hence the semantic parameters of human "nature" are rather broad.

Early Chinese authors often used the term "nature" (性), and many thought it was an intangible something that could and should be cultivated. The cultivation of human nature has several potential avenues that may involve how others see you, how you see yourself, who you think you can be, your family traits, or how you think humans are as a species. And it is likely that these will not be clearly delineated, though often much can be gleaned from context. We will not be dealing with persona, personality, and character, because they do not play a significant role, related to this topic, in our sources. One's inherited disposition, translated below as "native substance" (質) plays only a minor role. Emotional health, however, plays a crucial role, as a subset of one's "inclinations" (情). In fact, the two ideas of "inclinations" (情) and "nature" (性) are closely related, linguistically and conceptually, in the literature. One wrinkle in their relationship is the

---

1. This is also the case in modern Chinese, where one can make these distinctions, but they are not widely utilized in everyday speech. Consider the semantic overlap among persona (角色), personality (人格), character (品格), disposition (品質)—similar to temperament (氣質)—inclinations (情趣), and human nature (人性).

2. This is the view of the Existentialists, and is argued, for example, by Jose Ortega y Gasset, in his *Toward a Philosophy of History*, trans. Helene Weyl, Eleanor Clark, and William Atkinson (New York: W.W. Norton, 1941).

evolution of the term *qing* 情 from an earlier meaning of "actual" or "true," in the sense of "the real or inherent situation," to a more specific human "inclinations," which takes place over the course of the time period under consideration here.

Kongzi, despite his pronouncement that "by nature people are similar," at the head of this chapter, was reluctant to speak further about human nature.[3] He did, however, account for some differences among humans by pointing to them having different "native substance," much as we may say that certain people have "the right stuff." He never elaborated on what this "native substance" was, so it remains an interesting but mostly unarticulated aspect of his teachings. In any case, Kongzi thought it fundamental, saying "When native substance overcomes cultural refinement, the result is a rustic. And when cultural refinement overcomes native substance, the result is a pedant. Only when cultural refinement and native substance are balanced can the result be a noble person." (質勝文則野，文勝質則史。文質彬彬，然後君子。)[4] This "native substance" is doubtless the same as what we might now call "disposition." And as for *qing* 情 (inclinations), the *Lunyu* only uses the word twice, both times in the earlier sense of "truth."[5]

Human Nature Comes from Heaven and Earth

The nature of humans ultimately derives from Heaven and Earth, just as our bodies do:

> Heaven and Earth's mainstays: the people truly follow them. [We] follow the bright [lights] of Heaven, rely on the [fecund] nature of Earth, are born with their six *qi*-substances, and make use of their five phases. The *qi*-substances inform the five flavors, manifest as the five colors, are revealed in the five tones: [but human] excess leads to ignorance [of this relationship] and to disorder, [whereupon] the people lose their nature.

---

3. See *Lunyu* 論語 5.13; cf. Edward Slingerland, *Confucius: Analects with Selections from Traditional Commentaries* (Indianapolis: Hackett, 2003), 44.

4. *Lunyu* 6.18; cf. Slingerland, *Analects*, 59. Another passage about the importance of both "native substance" and "cultural refinement" is at *Lunyu* 12.8.

5. *Lunyu* 13.4 and 19.19.

(天地之經,而民實則之。則天之明,因地之性,生其六氣,用其五行。氣為五味,發為五色,章為五聲:淫則昏亂,民失其性。)[6]

The "bright [lights]" of Heaven refer, of course, to the sun, moon, and stars, which herald the seasons, while the "[fecund] nature" of Earth is its productivity. The six *qi*-substances, we learned last chapter, are Yin, Yang, wind, rain, darkness, and brightness. The "five phases" are an early "periodic table" like that learned in chemistry class; this early iteration includes water, fire, earth, wood, and metal.[7] These five were thought to set the pattern for many other things, including the flavors, colors, and musical tones referenced here. But the last line reveals two key ideas: that our human nature can, in fact, be lost, and that "excess" is to blame. Would a human who has lost their human nature still be human? There is a good reason why we call people who have gone beyond the pale "animals."

Precisely what kind of "excess" is not specified, but the usual suspects are emotion or desire. We will deal more with desire in the following chapter; here it is important to note that human nature precedes both the emotions and the desires that make up (part of) our inclinations.

> [Human] nature is an accomplishment of Heaven. [Human] inclinations are the substance of [human] nature. Desires are the responses of the inclinations. The inclinations certainly cannot avoid seeking that which is desired and can be obtained. It is wisdom that must carry out [only] that which *should* be done. Thus, even a gatekeeper cannot eliminate desires, [as they] are the instruments of [human] nature.

(性者,天之就也;情者,性之質也;欲者,情之應也。以所欲為可得而求之,情之所必不免也。以為可而道之,知所必出也。故雖為守門,欲不可去,性之具也。)[8]

---

6. *Zuozhuan* 左傳 (昭公 25); cf. Stephen Durrant, Wai-yee Li, David Schaberg, *Zuozhuan: Commentary on the "Spring and Autumn Annals"* (Seattle: University of Washington Press, 2016), 3:1637.

7. They are referred to as "phases" rather than "elements" because they were thought to coexist in mutually interacting cycles.

8. *Xunzi* 荀子 ch. 22 (正名); cf. Eric Hutton, *Xunzi: The Complete Text* (Princeton: Princeton University Press, 2014), 244. Gatekeepers, presumably, had a reputation for

Human nature is something rather ephemeral, not least because, as we saw above, it is possible to lose it. Its slightly more concrete, more "substantial," instantiation lies in our shared inclinations, which manifest themselves in response to the physical world. Specifically, *how* we interact with the world and the things in it is revealed by our desires. It is worth noting that being completely rid of our desires is not a possibility that is ever seriously entertained. (Even the advent of Buddhism in China, centuries later, would not change this, at least not among those we might call "classical" Chinese authors.) Human nature, as an "accomplishment of Heaven," is more of a (potential) guiding force, subsequently made manifest in our human inclinations, which in turn respond to the world via our desires. This is how desires are the "instruments" of human nature. But wisdom, as the putative ruler of the body, has the responsibility to moderate the desires. Heavenly "bright[ness]" and human wisdom are thereby analogous.

Human Nature is Universal

Kongzi did not say much about human nature, except to say that it was "similar" (近) among humans, and Laozi never used the word, nor is it found in the first, earliest, seven chapters of the *Zhuangzi*, but this might be explained by the word "nature" being in flux at that time. Nevertheless, that human nature is universal is a claim often seen in early China. A text called *Xingzi mingchu*, or *[Human] Nature Derives from [Heaven's] Mandate*, has perhaps the most straightforward pronouncement on this matter: "Within the four seas, their natures are the same; their use of their minds such that each is different, [however,] is caused by education." (四海之內，其性一也，其用心各異，教使然也。)⁹ "Within the four seas" is an ancient reference to the whole world, "they" refers to people in general, and the importance of education in East Asia clearly has ancient roots.

Claiming that all humans have the same nature was one thing, but a question that nevertheless arose in early China was whether or not there

---

being rather emotionless, perhaps because, if they wanted to keep their jobs, they had to refuse to open the gates (after gate-closing time)—even for their friends who had been out late partying.

9. *Xingzi mingchu* 性自命出 is an excavated text from Guodian acquired by the Shanghai Museum in 1993; cf. Scott Cook, *The Bamboo Texts of Guodian* (Ithaca, NY: Cornell University East Asia Program, 2012), 2:705.

were outliers: specifically, is the nature of a "sage" the same as that of regular folk? Both Mengzi and Xunzi agree that it is. Mengzi said: "Sagely people and we are of the same kind." (聖人與我同類者。)[10] Xunzi, though he disagreed with Mengzi on whether this nature was good or bad (i.e., selfless or selfish), concurred: "The nature of noble people is the same as that of petty people." (君子之與小人，其性一也。)[11] A clear extrapolation is that if even sages and the rest of us share one kind of nature, it is certainly justifiable to call such a nature "universal."[12]

Human Nature: Good or Bad?

A more pointed question in early Chinese intellectual history was whether our human nature was good or bad. Two authors who paid close attention to this question were Mengzi and Xunzi, both of whom claimed to be carrying on the work and ideas of Kongzi, who was famously reticent on the matter.

---

10. *Mengzi* 孟子 ch. 6A7 (告子上); cf. Bryan Van Norden, *Mengzi: With Selections from Traditional Commentaries* (Indianapolis: Hackett, 2008), 150. The connection between the "kind" of creature a thing is and its "nature" is made clear at *Guanzi* 管子 ch. 11 (宙合): "Sagely people understand that the *nature* of a thing definitely comes from the *kind* of thing it is." (聖人明乎物之性者必以其類來也。) *Guanzi* ch. 35 (侈靡), moreover, explicitly refers to a "human nature" (人性), which is what we are interested in here; cf. W. Allyn Rickett, *Guanzi: Political, Economic, and Philosophical Essays from Early China* (Princeton: Princeton University Press, 1985, 1998), 1:214 and 2:305.

11. *Xunzi* ch. 23 (性惡); cf. Hutton, *Xunzi*, 253.

12. There is some counterevidence to this claim. *Hanfeizi* 韓非子 ch. 50 (顯學): "Wisdom is [a matter of] nature, and long life is [a matter of] fate." (夫智，性也；壽，命也。) cf. Burton Watson, *The Basic Writings of Han Fei Tzu* (New York: Columbia University Press, 1964), 126. Since wisdom obviously differs from person to person, this implies that nature does too. The evidence from the *Zhuangzi* is mixed. Ch. 8 (駢拇) says: "Amalgamated toes and appended fingers [may] come from [one's inner] nature, but are superfluous to [one's] virtuosity." (駢拇枝指，出乎性哉，而侈於德。) If such unusual features come from one's nature, then we humans must have different natures. But it is possible that the author is here using "nature" to mean "that which we were individually born with" and not as "human nature" as a universal principle. In any case, ch. 9 (馬蹄) talks about the "genuine nature" (真性) of things like horses, clay, and wood, which implies that humans, too, have a "genuine nature." Ch. 9 also refers to "people's nature" (民性), and chs. 13 (天道) and 29 (盜跖) to "the nature of people" (人之性) as if it were universal. But ch. 12 (天地), contrary to Mengzi and Xunzi, says that a sage named Nie Que 齧缺 had a nature that surpassed other people's (其性過人). Ultimately, I think the evidence in the *Zhuangzi* is contradictory and cancels itself out.

Mengzi claimed that human nature was good. He said, "People all have hearts that do not tolerate [the suffering] of others." (人皆有不忍人之心。)[13] He illustrated this claim with an anecdote that is now quite famous:

> Suppose some people suddenly see a child about to fall in a well. They will all have worry and compassion in their minds: *not* because they want to establish good relations with the child's parents; *not* because they want to seek praise from among their village groups and friends; and *not* because they hate the sounds it will make. Looking at it this way, those without compassion in their minds are not human, those without shame in their minds are not human, those without deference in their minds are not human, and those without [ethical] judgment in their minds are not human. A mind with compassion has the beginning of goodness. A mind with shame has the beginning of propriety. A mind with deference has the beginning of protocol. A mind with [ethical] judgment has the beginning of wisdom. People [all] have these four "sprouts" like they [all] have four limbs.
>
> (今人乍見孺子將入於井，皆有怵惕惻隱之心；非所以內交於孺子之父母也，非所以要譽於鄉黨朋友也，非惡其聲而然也。由是觀之，無惻隱之心，非人也；無羞惡之心，非人也；無辭讓之心，非人也；無是非之心，非人也。惻隱之心，仁之端也；羞惡之心，義之端也；辭讓之心，禮之端也；是非之心，智之端也。人之有是四端也，猶其有四體也。)[14]

We should note first that "all" (皆) is rhetorical, and does not include one hundred percent of all humans. A better translation would be "[almost] all," but this would deprive the narrative of its pointedness. He is referring to "regular" people, not sociopaths and psychopaths. Second, he claims only that people will *feel* this way, not that they will necessarily *act* on those feelings. Finally, his "four sprouts" theory is not unlike a more articulated version

---

13. *Mengzi* ch. 2A6 (公孫丑上); cf. Van Norden, *Mengzi*, 45.
14. *Mengzi* ch. 2A6 (公孫丑上); cf. Van Norden, *Mengzi*, 46. The third phrase in the second sentence, "and not because [they] hate the sounds it will make" could also be understood as "and not because [they] hate the reputation [this would get them]." This interpretation is more congruous with the preceding two phrases, but it would also be slightly redundant.

of the Western theory that we are (almost) all born with a "conscience."[15] Mengzi specifies four parts to such a conscience, and the term "sprouts" is well-chosen, for just as a sprout is a delicate thing that can easily wilt on its own or be trampled by outside forces, so these "four sprouts" are precarious and in need of cultivation.

Without cultivation, our "four sprouts," which have the *potential* of *eventually* growing into human goodness, propriety, protocol, and wisdom (仁, 義, 禮, 智), will die. This is why many people are, in practice, not good. Mengzi, in fact, specifies two threats to our "sprouts": other, bad people and our own lack of self-cultivation.[16] He only hints at the influence of other people, in a second famous anecdote, that of "Ox Mountain." Here, he continues with the agricultural metaphor of "sprouts" with the trees that may or may not eventually grow from them.

> The trees on Ox Mountain were once beautiful, but because of its proximity to a large state, axes cut them down: can it now be considered beautiful? [Alternatively, even] with respite provided day and night, and the watering of rain and dew, it is not that there is no growth of sprouts on it [due to humans and their axes], but [rather that] oxen and sheep came along afterwards and grazed on it, and because of this it is barren like that. People see its barrenness and think it has never been wooded. But how could such [barrenness] be in the nature of a mountain?
>
> Even when it comes to what exists in people, how could they lack a mind with goodness and propriety? That by which they let go of their [originally] conscientious minds is just like the axes in relation to the trees. If every morning it is cut at, can it remain beautiful? If, with the respite provided day and night, and the equanimous morning *qi*-substance [i.e., air], with their preferences and aversions similar to those of other people, with only slight variation, then it is what they do during the day that

---

15. The idea of a (nearly) universal human conscience seems to be a part of Western culture. It may or may not stem from "Jeremiah" 31.33, which has the deity say, "I will put my law within them, and I will write it on their hearts." The "them/their" refers only to Jews, not all humans, but I have anecdotally heard this extended to all humans.

16. I use "bad people" *not* to refer to people who are intrinsically bad, but rather as shorthand for "(otherwise—perhaps even originally—good) people who habitually do bad things" (however one wishes to define such actions).

shackles and kills it. If this shackling is repeated over and over, then [even] the night air will not be enough to preserve it. If the night air is not enough to preserve it, then such [people] will not be much different from animals. When others see them as animals, they will [wrongly] assume that they are people who never [even] had the capacity in them [to begin with]. But how could this be, [given our common] human inclinations? Thus, if they just get nourishment, all (of these) things will develop, and if they just lose their nourishment, all (of these) things will disintegrate.

(牛山之木嘗美矣；以其郊於大國也，斧斤伐之，可以為美乎？是其日夜之所息，雨露之所潤，非無萌蘖之生焉；牛羊又從而牧之，是以若彼濯濯也。人見其濯濯也，以為未嘗有材焉。此豈山之性也哉？

雖存乎人者，豈無仁義之心哉？其所以放其良心者，亦猶斧斤之於木也。旦旦而伐之，可以為美乎？其日夜之所息，平旦之氣，其好惡與人相近也者幾希；則其旦晝之所為，有梏亡之矣。梏之反覆，則其夜氣不足以存。夜氣不足以存，則其違禽獸不遠矣。人見其禽獸也，而以為未嘗有才者；是豈人之情也哉？故苟得其養，無物不長；苟失其養，無物不消。)[17]

In the parable of Ox Mountain, the main culprits are the "axes," which Mengzi equates with people who "let go of" (放) their "conscientious minds" (良心). Secondary culprits are the "oxen and sheep" that graze on the remaining sprouts of the axe-denuded landscape. Mengzi does not specify how these creatures figure into his analogy, but I suspect they represent other people who are bad influences upon oneself. I think this because the very next story in the text is about a king who fails to attain wisdom precisely because he is surrounded by people who are a bad influence. In this next story, Mengzi compares such people to a "frost" that withers the king's "sprouts," and not to oxen and sheep, but the point of the story is that other people can exert an unfavorable influence on our incipient good nature. Therefore, whether or not Mengzi had other people in mind as the referent for the oxen and sheep in the story above, they are certainly part of the story of why humans can and do fail to successfully cultivate their natural sprouts of goodness.

---

17. *Mengzi* ch. 6A8 (告子上); cf. Van Norden, *Mengzi*, 151–52.

The main fault for our moral condition unambiguously lies with ourselves. We ourselves are the "axes" that cut down our own naturally growing "trees" of personal and social competence. Mengzi pinpoints a single, simple reason for our self-neglect: we fail to "think about" (思) it.

> Goodness, propriety, protocol, and wisdom are not welded onto us from the outside; we originally have them, it's just that we [often] do not think about [them]. Thus [I] say, "If you seek [them], you will get them; if you abandon [them] you will lose them." Some people are twice, or five times, or [even] countless times [worse] than others; this is because they have been unable to fully use their capacities.
>
> (仁、義、禮、智，非由外鑠我也，我固有之也，弗思耳矣。故曰：「求則得之，舍則失之。」或相倍蓰而無算者，不能盡其才者也。)[18]

The "inability" to use one's inherent, natural "capacities" (才) is due to our own failure to think sufficiently about the situation. There is no talk about a failure of "will" (志), or of an excess of "desire" (欲) in these sentences, though both of these issues arise in the following passages. We shall deal with them in the next chapter.

Xunzi, conversely, thought human nature was bad. Both of the words "good" and "bad" are ambiguous in English, insofar as they may or may not refer to morality. One can say that "he is a good person" and "he is a good plumber" with moral overtones for the first statement and not for the second. It is better to say that Mengzi and Xunzi disagreed over whether or not human nature was "competent or incompetent," rather than "good or bad," except that the former locution is a little awkward. In any case, this disagreement should not be construed in terms of "good and evil," and should not be conflated with the debate in the West, with its implications of "sin," "original" or otherwise. But it is interesting to note that, whereas the idea of an "evil" human nature has been prevalent in the West since Augustine, Mengzi's idea of a good human nature eventually won out in East Asia.

---

18. *Mengzi* ch. 6A6 (告子上); cf. Van Norden, *Mengzi*, 149. Ch. 6A15 reiterates the importance of thinking.

NATURE (性)

Xunzi thought human nature was "bad," as in "incompetent," as in "a selfish mess." He does not tell parables the way Mengzi did, but his diagnosis is clear.

> Human nature is bad; its goodness [i.e., competence] is contrived. Now human nature is born with a love of profit in it, [and if you] go along with this, then contention and conflict arise, while deference and the ability to yield to others vanish in it. [It is also] born with jealousy and hate in it, [and if you] go along with these, then injury and theft arise, while loyalty and fidelity vanish in it. [It is also] born with sensual desires, with preferring certain sounds and colors in it, [and if you] go along with these, then excess and disorder arise, while protocol, propriety, civility, and principle vanish in it. In these ways, to follow human nature, to accord with human inclinations, will certainly result in contention and conflict, will endorse the rejection of allotments and the disordering of principles, and [will end with] a return to brutality. Thus it is necessary to have the development from teachers and norms, and the ways of protocol and propriety, and only then will the result be deference and the ability to yield to others, endorsement of civility and principle, and a return to order. Looking at it this way, it is clear that human nature is bad, and that its goodness is contrived.
>
> (人之性惡，其善者偽也。今人之性，生而有好利焉，順是，故爭奪生而辭讓亡焉。生而有疾惡焉，順是，故殘賊生而忠信亡焉。生而有耳目之欲，有好聲色焉，順是，故淫亂生而禮義文理亡焉。然則從人之性，順人之情，必出於爭奪，合於犯分亂理，而歸於暴。故必將有師法之化，禮義之道，然後出於辭讓，合於文理，而歸於治。用此觀之，人之性惡明矣，其善者偽也。)[19]

For Xunzi, then, we are all born selfish, jealous, and desirous. I suppose pretty much anyone who has babysat will confirm this. And these natural tendencies result in social disharmony and violence. The crux of the matter for Mengzi was "thinking" about the issue; for Xunzi, we are to seek out

---

19. *Xunzi* ch. 23 (性惡); cf. Hutton, *Xunzi*, 248. Note: 疾 = 嫉. Our "allotments" (分) are the (various) "roles" we play in life: some that we were born into, others that were given to us. "Contrivance" for some authors is seen as a bad thing, but for Xunzi it is definitely good.

the development brought by (good) teachers and (good) norms. "Norms" (法) is an expansive term that can refer to role models, or anything that models good behavior, and may even include state-sponsored laws. We are, therefore, like unruly children who need to be socialized, or enculturated. Returning to Mengzi's "child on the well" scenario, it is interesting that Xunzi asks us to consider universal human nature by looking at the selfish and oblivious child, while Mengzi asks us to identify with the nearby adult who is concerned for said child.

Furthermore, Xunzi notably does not employ Mengzi's agricultural metaphor of "sprouts," but instead uses the mechanical metaphors of "warped wood" and "dull blades" in need of straightening and sharpening. The very next sentence after the passage above reads: "Thus, warped wood must await the straightening tool, and only after using the straightening tool is it straight; and blunt metal must await grinding, and only after grinding is it sharp. Now human nature is bad [i.e., incompetent], and must await teachers and norms, and only afterwards is it correct; it must acquire protocol and propriety, and only afterwards is it ordered." (故枸木必將待檃栝，烝矯然後直；鈍金必將待礱厲然後利。今人之性惡，必將待師法然後正，得禮義然後治。)[20] Our "straightening tools" and "grinders" are our cultural teachers and our social norms. In the case of early China, such teachers are often the sage-kings of old, and such norms are the cultural norms of exterior protocol and interior propriety. "Protocol" encompasses many things that we may take for granted; for example, saying "please" and "thank you," or waiting in line. "Propriety," too, is an expansive ideal that includes things like the feeling of deference one might have to allow an elderly or injured person to cut in line in front of you.

Human Nature Needs Cultivation

Perhaps unsurprisingly, both Mengzi and Xunzi agree that self-cultivation is necessary, even though they disagreed on the underlying nature upon which such cultivation acts. For Mengzi, who, as we saw above, emphasized "thinking" (思), it should not be surprising to learn that he focuses on our minds: "Those who make full use of their mind will understand their nature, and if they understand their nature they will understand Heaven.

---

20. *Xunzi* ch. 23 (性惡); cf. Hutton, *Xunzi*, 248.

Preserving one's mind and nourishing one's nature is how to serve Heaven. Not feeling conflicted by [the prospect of] early death or long life, but cultivating oneself in order to await it, is how to establish one's destiny." (盡其心者，知其性也；知其性，則知天矣。存其心，養其性，所以事天也。殀壽不貳，修身以俟之，所以立命也。)[21] Using our minds to think about our natures connects us to Heaven. Not worrying about our unavoidable fates but rather being concerned with living up to the potential that is our destiny is a fundamental aspect of self-cultivation. Self-cultivation is a prerequisite for being connected to Heaven.

Xunzi, who emphasizes cultural "teachers and norms," naturally begins with enculturation, which includes both mental and physical repetition. We saw in chapter 1 that "Concentration and habituation are the means by which we develop our nature." (注錯習俗，所以化性也。)[22] But Xunzi uses another key term to denote the means by which "teachers and norms" function: "contrivance" (偽). "Contrivance," despite its slightly negative connotation in English, for Xunzi is unambiguously a good thing: human effort creating ingenious methods for social harmony. "[Human] nature is the root beginning and raw material; [but human] contrivance brings civility, principle, excellence, and fullness. Without [human] nature, [human] contrivance would have nothing to act upon, and without [human] contrivance, [human] nature would be unable to beautify itself." (性者、本始材朴也；偽者、文理隆盛也。無性則偽之無所加，無偽則性不能自美。)[23] The use of "beautify" here is more appropriate and poetic in Chinese, because the "bad" (惡) in Xunzi's theory of bad human nature also means "ugly."

These two authors are not the only ones to articulate the need for the cultivation of human nature. Another author writes: "Now the nature of water is to be clear, but dirt can muddy it, which is why it can then lose clarity. The nature of humans is to be long-lived, but things can 'muddy' it, which is why it can then lose longevity. Things [ought to] be for the nourishing of [your] nature, and [ought] not be what nature is nourished for." (夫水之性清，土者抇之，故不得清。人之性壽，物者抇之，故不得壽。

---

21. *Mengzi* ch. 7A1 (盡心上); cf. Van Norden, *Mengzi*, 171. I suppose that "destiny" may sound corny or grandiloquent to some readers, but I don't know of a better word for it. It will be explained more in chapter 9.
22. *Xunzi* ch. 8 (儒效); cf. Hutton, *Xunzi*, 65. Previously quoted at chap. 1, n. 2.
23. *Xunzi* ch. 19 (禮論); cf. Hutton, *Xunzi*, 210.

物也者,所以養性也,非所以性養也。)²⁴ He goes on to say that we need to prioritize activities in our lives such that important endeavors are recognized as such and given their due. This is a program of self-cultivation via filtering.

A fourth author also sees "things" as affecting human nature, but he sees them as only one of many possible influences: "As a general rule, [external] things *move* [human] nature, [but internal] pleasures *anticipate* [human] nature; customs *facilitate* [human] nature, propriety *sharpens* [human] nature, circumstances *allow expression of* [human] nature, practice *nourishes* [human] nature, and the [human] way *develops* [human] nature." (凡動性者,物也;逆性者,悅也;交性者,故也;屬性者,義也;出性者,勢也;養性者,習也;長性者,道也。)²⁵ Some of these things we should welcome—the sharpening, nurturing, and developing—but with others we should exercise some care or, as Mengzi would say, some thought.

A final author argued for something more specific than just "thought." He thought that there must be "honesty" (誠),²⁶ for both the student and teacher in Xunzi's theory, to facilitate the successful completion of one's nature.

> [Human] nature involves [a kind of] percipience that comes from honesty, while teaching involves [a kind of] honesty that comes from percipience. [Thus, for students] honesty leads to percipience, and [for teachers] percipience leads to honesty. In this world, only those with full honesty are able to completely use *their* natures; [only they] . . . are able to induce *others* to completely use their natures; [only they] . . . are able to induce other *things* to completely use their natures; [only they] . . . can then participate in the development and nurturing of Heaven and Earth; and [only they] . . . can form a triad with Heaven and Earth.
>
> (自誠明,謂之性;自明誠,謂之教。誠則明矣,明則誠矣。唯天下至誠,為能盡其性;能盡其性,則能盡人之性;能盡人之性,

---

24. *Lüshi chunqiu* 呂氏春秋 ch. 1.2 (本生); cf. John Knoblock and Jeffrey Riegel, *The Annals of Lü Buwei* (Stanford: Stanford University Press, 2000), 65.

25. *Xingzi mingchu*; cf. Cook, *The Bamboo Texts of Guodian*, 2:706–07.

26. This important concept is also sometimes translated as "sincerity," but Roger Ames translates it as "creativity." See Roger Ames, *Confucian Role Ethics: A Vocabulary* (Honolulu: University of Hawaii Press, 2011), 67.

則能盡物之性；能盡物之性，則可以贊天地之化育；可以贊天地之化育，則可以與天地參矣。)²⁷

This passage begins with our human nature, which it associates with a kind of perceptivity. This is not the cognitive perceptivity of Mengzi nor the cultural perceptivity of Xunzi, but rather it refers to what we now call "emotional intelligence." This kind of intelligence can only derive from our own honesty, and primarily from honesty with the various facets of our own selves. An experienced teacher, conversely, brings their emotional intelligence to bear on the kind of honesty most suitable to a particular student. Brutal honesty is not appropriate for every student. After this tête-à-tête, the author goes on to ground the whole sagely enterprise in human nature—from the student working on themself, to the teacher working on others, to the noble person or sage (i.e., "those with full honesty") working even on other living things, and finally to the sage or some other aspirational figure (i.e., those who can "participate in the development and nurturing of Heaven and Earth") who can form a triad with Heaven and Earth. According to these various narratives, we are born with the necessities; it remains up to us, to our thinking, our culture, and our own honesty, to undertake the self-cultivation requisite for realizing the potential harmony with the cosmic dyad.

Emotions Derive from Inclinations, which Derive from Human Nature

Honesty with oneself can produce a kind of emotional intelligence because we are, by nature, emotional. Early Chinese texts are generally positive, though with a degree of caution, towards the emotions. Our authors vary on this, but the classical articulation of emotions lists seven: "What are human inclinations? The ability [to feel], without learning, these seven: delight, anger, sadness, fear, love, hate, and desire." (何謂人情？喜怒哀懼愛惡欲七者，弗學而能。)²⁸ Other authors, such as Xunzi, proffer lists that are similar, shorter, and more symmetrical; for example: "Likes and dislikes, delight and anger, sadness and happiness are stored within, and these are

---

27. *Liji* 禮記 ch. 31 (中庸); cf. James Legge, *Li Chi: Book of Rites* (1885; rpt. New York: University Books, 1967), 2:318–19. The ellipses are only for avoiding repetition.
28. *Liji* ch. 9 (禮運); cf. Legge, *Li Chi*, 1:379.

called the Heavenly inclinations." (好惡喜怒哀樂臧焉，夫是之謂天情。)[29] Recall that for Xunzi, "Heavenly" means "natural." These emotional "inclinations" are elsewhere referred to as the "transformations of life" (生之變).[30] Another author refers to them as types of *qi*-substance:

> In general, although people have a nature, their minds do not have fixed intentions; [rather, they] encounter things and only then are aroused, encounter pleasures and only then act, encounter practice and only then become settled. [Human] nature consists of the *qi*-substances of delight and anger, sadness and grief. As for their exterior manifestation, it is the case that things draw them out. [Human] nature comes forth from the mandate, and the mandate is sent down from Heaven. The [human] way begins from [human] inclinations, and [human] inclinations are produced from [human] nature. At the beginning [of one's life or learning], one is nearer to the inclinations, while at the end [of one's life or learning] one is nearer to propriety. Those who understand their inclinations are able to express it [i.e., propriety] [properly], while those who understand propriety are able to rein them [i.e., inclinations] in [properly]. Likes and dislikes are [human] nature; that which one likes and dislikes are things. Competence and incompetence are [also human] nature. That in which one is competent or incompetent is the situation.
>
> (凡人雖有性，心亡奠志，待物而後作，待悅而後行，待習而後奠。喜怒哀悲之氣，性也。及其見於外，則物取之也。性自命出，命自天降。道始於情，情生於性。始者近情，終者近義。知[情者能]出之，知義者能納之。好惡，性也。所好所惡，物也。善不[善，性也]。所善所不善，勢也。)[31]

This is a dynamic, complex, and interrelated account of human nature. Intentionality, desire, "practice" (which could refer to either unconscious

---

29. *Xunzi* ch. 17 (天論); cf. Hutton, *Xunzi*, 176.
30. *Guanzi* ch. 26 (戒); cf. Rickett, *Guanzi*, 1:379.
31. *Xingzi mingchu*; cf. Cook, *The Bamboo Texts of Guodian*, 2:700. The graphs in brackets are missing in the original, due to the imperfect physical condition of the excavated texts, and were added by modern scholars.

socialization or conscious self-cultivation), and emotions are all portrayed as attributes in flux. The emotions—for which there was, at the time, no specific Chinese term—are referred to as "*qi*-substances" and, unlike in the two quotes just above, are equated with our nature, rather than our inclinations. This may simply be an instance of "cutting out the middle-man," since Xunzi, above, said that our inclinations are the "substance" of our nature, and he—as well as other authors—states quite plainly that "[human] inclinations are produced from [human] nature" (情生於性).[32] The "mandate" is here simply an extension of Heaven, which is why it did not play a major role in chapter 1, but we shall return to it in chapters 8 and 9, where "mandate" and "Heaven" manifest as "fate" and "destiny."

The "[human] way" that we choose is implicitly a path of self-cultivation. We start with our untutored inclinations and, after practice, end up nearer the goal of propriety, creating something like an inner "moral compass." Of course, our inclinations can never go away, so our cultivated propriety and our genetic inclinations work complementarily (or, at least, in tandem). This balance is, precisely, the "way" we are to follow.

The passage ends with two final thoughts, both potentially confusing. First, that all humans have a certain set of emotions seems rather uncontroversial, but our "likes and dislikes" and our "competence and incompetence" might seem more person-specific. On such a reading, they should not be equated with "nature" or "inclinations," but rather with something more variable: our "native substance" (質), say, or our "capacities" (才), which are similar to the "disposition" described at the beginning of this chapter. But the author said above that human nature is universal, therefore these final issues must also be taken as universal. Therefore, our "likes and dislikes" and our "competence and incompetence" must be interpreted as *human* likes and dislikes, competence and incompetence, as opposed to the likes and competencies of other animals.[33]

The second and final point is that both likes and competencies should also be contextualized with regard to the *things* we like and dislike, and the *situations* in which we perform competent or incompetent acts. Just as

---

32. *Xunzi* ch. 8, cited above in n. 8. Also in the *Yucong, er* 語叢二; cf. Cook, *The Bamboo Texts of Guodian*, 2:850.

33. For example, the (general) human dislike of putrid smells (which other animals may find interesting), and the (general) human competence at walking upright (which other quadrupeds may be able to do, but not as well).

with our emotions: our human competencies and incompetencies derive from Heaven, via human nature, via human inclinations, but they manifest differently with different things, in different contexts, which both serve to draw them out differently.

How to Deal with Emotions

Early Chinese authors agree that there are right ways and wrong ways to deal with our emotions. For example, "for happiness, there is singing and dancing" (樂有歌舞).[34] These are "appropriate" (宜) ways of expressing this emotion, and when one expresses emotions appropriately, then we "are able to harmonize with the natures of Heaven and Earth" (乃能協於天地之性): our human nature in sync with the natures of the cosmos.[35] For us to express ourselves appropriately, there must be a degree of self-regulation. Hence: "That people are born tranquil is [due to] their Heavenly nature. . . . [But when] likes and dislikes are unregulated within, and [our] knowing is enticed from without, [then we] are unable to return to our own selves, and the principles of Heaven [within us] are destroyed." (人生而靜，天之性也. . . . 好惡無節於內，知誘於外，不能反躬，天理滅矣。)[36] Thus, we must "regulate" (節) ourselves in order to express ourselves appropriately. And to do this, we must "return to our own selves" from the inexorable pull exerted by the (shiny) things of the world. To be sure, there is nothing wrong with the things of the world: we should certainly interact with them, explicitly to gain knowledge of them (this is specified in a section I did not quote), but we should also regularly look within for self-cultivation. Otherwise, while the "principles of Heaven" will continue to operate all around us, they will be "destroyed" within us.

This synchronicity between the macrocosm outside us and the microcosm within us is a common theme in early China. The correlations are no doubt sometimes overstated for a modern audience, but the general principle that our own bodily biome is a reflection of the larger environmental biome is still worth contemplating.

---

34. *Zuozhuan* (昭公 25); cf. Durrant, Li, Schaberg, *Zuozhuan*, 3:1639.
35. *Ibid.*
36. *Liji* ch. 19 (樂記); cf. Legge, *Li Chi*, 1:96. A very similar passage is also at *Huainanzi* ch. 1 (原道).

[If I] wish to care for my self, first [I should] know my inclinations, everywhere observing [the things within] the six directions, in order to consider what is within my self. Knowing the appearances [of things] like this, then [I can] know how to express [my] inclinations. Once [I] know how to express my inclinations, then [I] will know how to nourish [my] life.

(欲愛吾身，先知吾情，君親六合，以考內身。以此知象，乃知行情。既知行情，乃知養生。)[37]

That such caring is dependent upon knowing, and such knowing is dependent upon observing is perhaps uncontroversial. But it is interesting that we are enjoined to observe the world *in order to* know what is within ourselves. Given the interrelatedness between our outer and inner worlds described in the previous section, it is not surprising that we are asked to know about the things in this world so that we can understand how and *why* we respond to them the way we do. Dancing may be an appropriate way to express happiness, but it may also be the case that the happiness was *caused* by seeing others dance. The final sentence clearly connects our emotional expressiveness to self-cultivation, at least in theory: knowledge of the one leads to knowledge of the other.

Desire is addressed in the next chapter, but because desire and emotion are both said to derive from our natures, and because our natures are causally influenced by the natures of other things, it is appropriate to recall the correlative aspect of the context of our natures and desires, our intrinsic and mutual place in the natural order. "Ordering the desires is not a matter of the desires but of natures. Natures are the roots of the myriad things, and cannot be increased or decreased, [because they] rely upon that which is certainly so to be as they are. They are calibrations of Heaven and Earth." (治欲者不於欲於性。性者萬物之本也，不可長，不可短，因其固然而然之。此天地之數也。)[38] Heaven and Earth conspire to bestow on us our (specifically calibrated) natures, and our (probably less calibrated) desires stem from our natures. So if we want to work on our potentially unruly desires, just

---

37. *Guanzi* ch. 35 (侈靡); cf. Rickett, *Guanzi*, 2:96. Note: 君親 = 遍視 or 周視. The "six directions" are the usual cardinal four, plus up and down.

38. *Lüshi chunqiu* ch. 24.6 (貴當); cf. Knoblock and Riegel, *The Annals of Lü Buwei*, 620.

as with our potentially unruly emotions, we should do so in the context of working on the larger (inner) environment of our own human natures.

The Role of Concern (憂)

The emotion that the English word "concern" evokes is a particularly tricky emotion. On the one hand, "anxiety" is definitely something that no one wants; "worry" and "apprehension" are usually seen as unwelcome, unless there is something to be "legitimately" worried about; and "concern" can be used in negative, neutral, and positive ways. For example, an "overly-concerned" helicopter parent may be frowned upon; concern about the weather seems neutral; while a "concerned citizen" may well be construed as a good thing. But all of these refer to the same basic type of emotion and we usually choose our descriptor based on whether or not we find the emotion appropriate to the situation. Other times, however, we resort to generic terms like "concern" or "worry" even when the person being described would admit to neither; therein lies potential miscommunication. It can be annoying for another to tell us "don't worry about it" when, in fact, we feel not the slightest bit of worry, even if we might admit to some concern.

The *locus classicus* for "concern" in early China is this passage from Mengzi: "Noble people have lifelong concern, [though] they do not worry for [even] one morning." (君子有終身之憂，無一朝之患也。)[39] It might appear that this is quite clear: "concern" (憂) is good, while "worry" (患) is bad. But the record is not so clear. Kongzi said: "Do not worry that you are not known to other people, rather worry that you do not know other people." (不患人之不己知，患不知人也。)[40] In fact, to use the "principle of charity," one should translate the two terms in reversed ways for these two authors, given that Kongzi uses *huan* 患 most often in a positive sense and *you* 憂 in a negative sense, while Mengzi does the reverse.[41] This reversal

---

39. *Mengzi* ch. 4B28 (離婁下); cf. Van Norden, *Mengzi*, 112.
40. *Lunyu* 1.16; cf. Slingerland, *Analects*, 7.
41. Kongzi, in the *Lunyu*, uses *you* 憂 (worry; concern) fifteen times, usually with a negative connotation (exceptions are at 7.3 and 15.32), and *huan* 患 (concern; worry) thirteen times, usually with a neutral or positive connotation (12.5 may be an exception). Mengzi uses *you* 憂 thirty times but, contra Kongzi's use, usually with a positive or neutral connotation, and uses *huan* 患 fifteen times, sometimes as "harm" and sometimes as "worry" with a negative or neutral connotation. Mengzi 6B15 seems to use *huan* 患 in the same sentence with both a negative and positive connotation.

makes these ideas rather difficult to interrogate. I have argued elsewhere that these two passages do not mean that we should live lives of continuous concern or worry, but rather that, as in English, sometimes authors engage in hyperbole.[42] In the two quotes above, I contend, both authors are being a little hyperbolic, that Kongzi and Mengzi did not literally mean us to be concerned, continuously, for our entire lives. Both authors probably meant us to be "mindful" of things. One piece of evidence for this claim is that elsewhere in the same text, Kongzi clearly implies that concern is not a state of mind to be pursued, inasmuch as the "good" (仁) person and the "noble person" are both unconcerned (不憂).[43]

It is worth noting that Mengzi's "frenemy" Xunzi, unsurprisingly, had a very different take on the "lifelong concern" that Mengzi appears to advocate. His rejoinder borrows the same locution of pairing "lifelong" with "[even] one morning," but comes to a decidedly different conclusion:

> Zilu asked of Kongzi: "Do noble people have concerns?" Kongzi replied: "Noble people, *before* becoming successful, are happy in their intentions, and *after* having become successful, are happy in their orderliness: these are those by which they have lifelong happiness, and are without [even] one morning's concern."
>
> (子路問於孔子曰：「君子亦有憂乎？」孔子曰：「君子，其未得也，則樂其意，既已得之，又樂其治：是以有終身之樂，無一日之憂。」)[44]

Here, happiness trumps even a single morning of "concern." Nevertheless, as in English, "concern" seems to have a limited place in the ideal life.

Tranquility (靜) is the Goal

While the role of "concern" is not entirely clear or consistent in our sources, its opposite, "tranquility," is broadly lauded. We saw above that "people are born tranquil" (人生而靜) but that this tranquility is disturbed by our

---

42. Fang Po 方破, "儒家憂與靜矛盾的分析,"《簡帛》第十輯 (2015): 37–49.
43. *Lunyu* 9.29 and 14.28: "Good people are not concerned" (仁者不憂); *Lunyu* 12.4: "Noble people are not concerned" (君子不憂); cf. Slingerland, *Analects*, 96, 165, 126.
44. *Xunzi* ch. 29 (子道); cf. Hutton, *Xunzi*, 328–29.

natural desires. And, as with "concern," there is more than one word used to express the general idea of "tranquility."

> As a general rule, people in their lives certainly make use of correctness and equanimity, and that by which they are lost is certainly via delight, happiness, sadness, and anger. For regulating [the potential excesses of] anger, nothing is better than music; and for regulating [the potential excesses of] music, nothing is better than protocol. For preserving [appropriate] protocol, nothing is better than [an underlying attitude of] respect. Those who are outwardly respectful and inwardly tranquil will certainly [be able to] return to their natures.
>
> (凡民之生也，必以正平，所以失之者，必以喜樂哀怒。節怒莫若樂，節樂莫若禮。守禮莫若敬。外敬而內靜者，必反其性。)[45]

"Equanimity" (平) and "tranquility" (靜) refer to similar mental states here. "Respect," which is arguably the earliest of early China's important virtues, is key to the socialization, via protocol, that serves to "return" our emotions to their original state.

Another term similar to "tranquility" is "centeredness" (中), which plays a key role in the following pericope.

> That which Heaven mandates is called [human] nature. That which follows [human] nature is called the [human] way. That which cultivates the way is called the teaching. The way should not for an instant be departed from; [that which] may be departed from is not the way. This is why noble people are on guard and cautious [even] where they cannot be seen, are fearful and apprehensive [even] where they cannot be heard, [even if] no one reveals [what they have] hidden and no one makes manifest [what they have] obscured. Therefore noble people are cautious in their solitude. When delight, anger, sadness, and happiness are not [yet] expressed, [we] call this centeredness. [When they] are expressed but are all centered and regulated, [we] call this harmony. Centeredness is the great root of the world; harmony is the connective way of the world. Extend [your] centeredness

---

45. *Guanzi* ch. 37 (心術下); cf. Rickett, *Guanzi*, 2:63.

and harmony, [because even] Heaven and Earth are situated in them, and the myriad creatures are nurtured by them.

(天命之謂性。率性之謂道。修道之謂教。道也者，不可須臾離也；可離非道也。是故君子戒慎乎其所不睹，恐懼乎其所不聞；莫見乎隱，莫顯乎微。故君子慎其獨也。喜怒哀樂之未發謂之中。發而皆中節謂之和。中也者天下之大本也；和也者天下之達道也。致中和，天地位焉，萬物育焉。)[46]

It is an apparent contradiction that noble people are described both as "fearful and apprehensive" and yet "centered" and "harmonious." As with the consideration of "concern" in the previous section, the only way to reconcile these contentions is to assume that the former is hyperbolic, an exaggerated way of saying we should be "mindful" while still being centered and harmonious. Assuming this to be the case, then, it is clear that a state of emotional tranquility is being recommended. This tranquility does not reject the emotions, but only seeks to "center" and "harmonize" them.

What, precisely, does it mean to be centered? The text does not define the term, but a thousand years later Zhu Xi did define it, saying "'Centeredness' is to be not biased or partial; it refers to being neither excessive nor insufficient." (中者，不偏不倚、無過不及之名。)[47] Thus, "centering" involves not over-reacting: a centered emotion is one that is felt, yet it may or may not be expressed. The next line in the extract above raises the question: what is the difference between being "centered" and being "regulated," given that the combination of these two results in being "harmonious"? The answer lies in the following sentence: being "centered" is an internal state, while being "regulated" manifests in a social context. Thus, "harmony" is the result of internal emotional moderation *and* external emotional moderation. The following line identifies "centeredness" as the original "root" of things—that is, each individual thing—which is its inner, natural, and naturally good state. "Harmony," meanwhile, is this inner centeredness plus the "connective way." We touched upon "connective" (達) in chapter 1, where I translated

---

46. *Liji* ch. 31 (中庸); cf. Legge, *Li Chi*, 2:300–01. The first four sentences were quoted in the introduction, n. 65.

47. Zhu Xi 朱熹 (1130–1200), *Zhongyong zhangzhu* 中庸章句 in the Sibu beiyao 四部備要 edition of the *Sishu jizhu* 四書集注, (1927–35; rpt. 台北: 中華書局, 1984), 1a; cf. Daniel Gardner, *The Four Books* (Indianapolis: Hackett, 2007), 107.

it as "reach" and "apprehend," as well as "flow." Here, it modifies the "way" in which things properly interact with each other; how things ideally reach each other, apprehend each other, and flow among each other.

The final sentence only makes sense in the context of humans being able to "form a triad" with Heaven and Earth. Proper human action, action that extends our emotional centeredness and harmony, operates in the same cosmic milieu as Heaven and Earth. Heaven and Earth may not have human emotions, but they nevertheless are "centered" and "harmonious" insofar as they are sufficient and measured and orderly, both in themselves and in their interactions with each other.

Chapter 3

Mind (心)

"There is no sadness greater than the death of the mind."

—*Zhuangzi* ch. 21

夫哀莫大於心死。《莊子。田子方》

Cultivate Your Mind (修心)

Cultivation of the mind results in mental harmony and intelligence. Even the oldest works of Chinese intellectual history enjoin us to think about our thoughts with the aim of improving them. The *Shujing* notes that intelligence is a matter of effort: "Even the sagely, [if they] do not reflect, may become foolish; and even the foolish, [if they] are able to reflect, may become sagely." (惟聖罔念作狂，惟狂克念作聖。)[1] This may not be as easy as it sounds, however, given the complexity of the human mind: "In general, the human mind is more perilous than mountains and rivers, and more difficult to understand than Heaven." (凡人心險於山川，難於知天。)[2] Heaven, even given its "creator" capacity, is notable precisely for its regularity and predictability. Nevertheless, Heaven, like nature in general—even today—connotes mystery. The coming of spring may be quite predictable, while the coming of the next tornado decidedly is not. Likewise,

---

1. *Shujing* 書經 ch. 46 (多方); cf. James Legge, *The Chinese Classics, Vol. 3: The Shoo King* (1865; 2nd ed., 1894; rpt. Hong Kong: Hong Kong University Press, 1960), 500.
2. *Zhuangzi* 莊子 ch. 32 (列禦寇); cf. Burton Watson, *The Complete Works of Zhuangzi* (New York: Columbia University Press, 1968; 2013), 283.

while other cultures may put something like the "soul" at the top of the interior human hierarchy, the mind unambiguously holds this position in early China. "The mind within the body holds the position of ruler." (心之在體，君之位也。)³ So the mind is in charge, but it is, or at least can be, a "perilous" and difficult thing to understand. Were this not the case, this chapter would probably be much shorter.

One aspect of the "difficult to understand" allegation is the multifariousness of the mind. In the preceding pages we have already encountered its capacities for willing (志), intending (意), knowing (知), imagining or apprehending (思), thinking (想), reflecting (念), and pondering, considering, or deliberating (慮). A complete taxonomy, in Chinese or English, would probably be futile. This multifariousness, however, is related to the prior allegation of the mind being "perilous," insofar as keeping on top of a variety of mental operations that function simultaneously greatly increases the potential for doubt and the necessity of inquiry. One ramification of having a "perilous" mind, then, is the concomitant need for ongoing cultivation. "When noble people doubt, then they do not speak [about it; i.e., the thing about which they have doubts]; if they have not yet inquired, then they will not speak [about it]: though their way is long, they daily improve." (君子疑則不言，未問則不言：道遠日益矣。)⁴ Not speaking about a doubtful point does not mean that they do not ask questions about it, but only that they don't speak as if they knew what they do not, in fact, know. That one's way is long is not meant to be discouraging, just realistic. On the other hand, the way is not without signposts. As we read in the introduction, if we "cultivate the mind, make tranquil the intention, then the Way can be obtained."⁵ When that happens, you will notice it. And one sign of having obtained the Way is having an open mind.

An Open Mind (虛心) . . .

An open mind is critical to the pedagogical holy grail of "critical thinking." "Critical thinking" means different things to different people, but for some

---

3. *Guanzi* 管子 ch. 36 (心術上); cf. W. Allyn Rickett, *Guanzi: Political, Economic, and Philosophical Essays from Early China* (Princeton: Princeton University Press, 1985, 1998), 2:71. *Xunzi* ch. 21 (解蔽) makes the same claim.

4. *Xunzi* 荀子 ch. 27 (大略); cf. Eric Hutton, *Xunzi: The Complete Text* (Princeton: Princeton University Press, 2014), 310.

5. *Guanzi* ch. 49 (內業); cf. Rickett, *Guanzi*, 2:42. Previously quoted in the introduction, n. 74.

it refers to the mental paradigm that often rejects the attitude of "claim X is either true or false" in favor of the more nuanced "claim X may be considered true *to the degree that there is persuasive evidence to support it.*" This means being able to live with varying degrees of certainty, which is more difficult than simply sorting claims into the easy categories of "fact" or "fiction." This kind of ambivalent objectivity is advised not only for rulers, who need to have honest people to whom they can delegate responsibility, but also to the rest of us. "Words [should] have things [to back them up] and actions [should] have investigations [to back them up]. . . . Thus noble people listen much, but substantiate [it before] accepting it; aspire to much, but substantiate [it before] embracing it; and essentially understand [a thing before] attempting to put it into action." (言有物而行有格也. . . . 故君子多聞，質而守之；多志，質而親之；精知，略而行之。)[6] Indeed, the "investigation of things" (格物) is an important theme to which we shall return in chapter 6.

The quintessential metaphor for an objective mindset is reflected in the "mind as mirror" trope. "Just be open-minded. Fulfilled people use their minds like a mirror, neither seeing [things] off, nor welcoming them: responding but not storing." (虛而已。至人之用心若鏡，不將不迎：應而不藏。)[7] The "not storing" part of the last phrase does not mean we should immediately forget things we have witnessed or learned—for one thing, we don't have that ability—but rather that we should not cling to what we think we have witnessed or learned, as we could be mistaken: "storing" does not equate to "remembering," but rather to "place in an unassailable position." It is remarkable to find this "Enlightenment value" in early China. But our sources are quick to point out several varieties of "dust" that can settle on such a mirror, causing otherwise objective observation to become distorted.

> Break through the confusions of conviction, disentangle the entanglements of the mind. . . . Honors and wealth, prominence and prestige, fame and profit: these six [can] confuse the intentions. Appearance and deportment, attractiveness and externalities, passions and convictions: these six [can] entangle the mind. . . . If correct, then tranquil; if tranquil then clear and percipient; if clear and percipient then open-minded; if

---

6. *Liji* 禮記 ch. 33 (緇衣); cf. James Legge, *Li Chi: Book of Rites* (1885; rpt. New York: University Books, 1967), 2:360–61.

7. *Zhuangzi* ch. 7 (應帝王); cf. Watson, *Zhuangzi*, 59. To "see something off" is a polite way of saying that you reject it.

open-minded, then [you can] act uncontrivedly, yet nothing will be left undone.

(通意之悖，解心之繆. . . . 貴富顯嚴名利六者，悖意者也。容動色理氣意六者，繆心者也. . . . 正則靜，靜則清明，清明則虛，虛則無為而無不為也。)[8]

These "confusions" and "entanglements" can thwart our intentions not because they are necessarily bad in themselves, but because they should, ideally, be the natural consequences of a life well-lived, and should not be our primary goals. A well-lived life might fairly be described as one in which "nothing is left undone," wherein one's potential, one's destiny, is completely fulfilled. According to this author, such a life is realized by acting uncontrivedly, which is a consequence of open-mindedness, which in turn is achieved by being clear and intelligent, which can only obtain in the tranquility with which we concluded the previous chapter. Nevertheless, before moving on to uncontrived action, we should linger a moment longer with tranquility.

The archetypal pairing of "open-mindedness" and "tranquility" may be traced back to descriptions of the cosmic dyad of Heaven and Earth which, as we saw in the introduction, were described as "open"—as in "open-ended" (i.e., vast) and "full of mysterious potential"—and "tranquil," respectively.[9] The ideal ruler, too, is said to possess these two qualities which, it was hoped, would lead to both objectivity and appropriate ruling techniques. "Because [they] are open-minded [they can] know the inclinations of reality, and because [they] are tranquil [they can] know correct action." (虛則知實之情，靜則知動者正。)[10] But our primary concern here is with regular people, not rulers *per se*. In the following passage, open-mindedness and tranquility are joined with the practical activity of focus.

> How do people know the way? [I] say it is with the mind. How does the mind know it? [I] say it is through open-mindedness,

---

8. *Lüshi chunqiu* 呂氏春秋 ch. 25.3 (有度); cf. John Knoblock and Jeffrey Riegel, *The Annals of Lü Buwei* (Stanford: Stanford University Press, 2000), 632. A similar passage is at *Zhuangzi* ch. 23.9 (庚桑楚); cf. Watson, *Zhuangzi*, 197.
9. *Guanzi* ch. 36 (心術上). Previously quoted in the introduction, n. 28.
10. *Hanfeizi* 韓非子 ch. 5 (主道); cf. Burton Watson, *The Basic Writings of Han Fei Tzu* (New York: Columbia University Press, 1964), 16.

focus, and tranquility. The mind is always storing; nevertheless, it can have what is called open-mindedness. The mind is always distracted; nevertheless, it can have what is called focus. The mind never stops moving; nevertheless, it can have that which is called tranquility. When people are born they have consciousness, and with consciousness there is the will, and what is willed is what is stored [in the mind]. Nevertheless, [the mind] can have what is called open-mindedness. *Not to let that which is already stored harm that which is being received is called open-mindedness.*

(人何以知道？曰：心。心何以知？曰：虛壹而靜。心未嘗不臧也，然而有所謂虛；心未嘗不兩也，然而有所謂壹；心未嘗不動也，然而有所謂靜。人生而有知，知而有志，志也者，臧也。然而有所謂虛：不以所已臧害所將受謂之虛。)[11]

This definition of the rather abstract concept of open-mindedness is readily familiar. Although our minds continually store perceptions and ideas, the final line of the passage points out that we can still be open-minded as long as we do not allow what we already know to "harm" the new perceptions and ideas that we receive (and conceive).

In chapter 1 we read of Woodworker Qing, the bell-stand maker who was tranquil and focused. That story does not employ the term "open-minded," but he did "forget" about external pressures and even his own person before undertaking his task, which may be construed as a form of open-mindedness. In that story, Woodworker Qing said that he "fasted" in order to quiet, or make tranquil, his mind. Elsewhere in that text the idea of "mind-fasting" (心齋) is specifically described. When asked to define it, a scholar replied:

Focus your will. Do not listen with your ears but listen with your mind. [Even better:] do not listen with your mind but listen with your *qi*-substance. Listening stops at the ears, and the mind stops at making a tally [of what has been heard]. As for *qi*-substance, by being open it awaits things. The Way can only collect in open-mindedness. Mind-fasting is open-mindedness.

---

11. *Xunzi* ch. 21 (解蔽); cf. Hutton, *Xunzi*, 228.

(若一志。無聽之以耳而聽之以心。無聽之以心而聽之以氣。聽止於耳，心止於符。氣也者，虛而待物者也。唯道集虛。虛者，心齋也。)[12]

To "listen with your *qi*-substance" is similar to what we might call "following your gut." It is to suspend disbelief long enough to gain potential insight. It is an antidote to confirmation bias, which is due to the preconceived notions denoted by the "tallies" that the mind makes of its apperceptions. *Qi*-substance is here described as being "open" rather than "open-minded" only because it would sound peculiar to describe *qi*-substance as "open-minded," but the word (in Chinese) is the same, and the intent of the sentence is clear. An open-minded person "awaits things" in the same way that the above-mentioned mirror objectively reflects things. Such a person does not chase after things, nor does he reject them, but rather allows perceptions and ideas to enter freely. "Mind-fasting" and "open-mindedness" are both metaphors that refer to the same phenomenon, only the former is in the active voice ("fast"), with a verb, and the latter is in the passive voice, as an adjective ("open").

Broadmindedness is similar to open-mindedness, though it speaks more to the *range* of things that we allow ourselves to be open to, rather than the *attitude* of being open. Here, the "frog in a well" metaphor finds a ready expression.

> [If you] look at stars from the inside a well, only a few stars will be visible. [But if you] look [at them] from a hilltop, then [you will not only] see those beginning to emerge, but will also see those setting. This is not [due to any] increased brightness, [but rather your] position makes it so. Being selfish-minded is [like] being in a well, while being broadminded is [like] being on a hilltop. Thus wisdom conveyed in selfishness knows but little, while [wisdom] conveyed in broadmindedness knows much.

(因井中視星，所視不過數星。自邱上以視，則見其始出，又見其入。非明益也，勢使然也。夫私心，井中也；公心，邱上也。故智載於私則所知少，載於公則所知多矣。)[13]

---

12. *Zhuangzi* ch. 4 (人間世); cf. Watson, *Zhuangzi*, 25.
13. *Shizi* 尸子 ch. 10 (廣); cf. Paul Fischer, *Shizi: China's First Syncretist* (New York: Columbia University Press, 2012), 100.

The chapter that this passage comes from goes on to extol the virtue of impartiality, and indeed claims that a number of early Chinese scholars did in fact extol open-mindedness, even if they each used their own terminology.

. . . Leads to Non-Contrivance (無為) . . .

Open-mindedness has several aspects and several outcomes, but one outcome notable in our sources is the attainment of an unforced and graceful way of being and behaving. Although there is no single word for it in English, this way can be seen in any number of skill-acquisition stories that culminate in a performance that is, by the performer's own account, unaccountably agile and elegant. Such performances are sometimes described as "effortless" or "spontaneous" or "flowing" but, while the smooth "flow" may be undeniable, the hours of practice that made such performances possible are attenuated by the poetic descriptors "effortless" and "spontaneous." The hours of practice, however, are, by themselves, insufficient to deliver such performances which, by all accounts, also demand a kind of mental receptivity—an open-mindedness—to be realized. The Chinese term for this kind of apparently "effortless" action is *wu wei* 無為, translated here as "non-contrivance."[14]

> Open-mindedness, tranquility [of emotions], serenity [of desires], quietude [in speech], and non-contrivance [in action] are the equanimity of Heaven and Earth, the fulfillment of the Way and virtuosity. Therefore the thearch-kings and sagely people relaxed in them. With *relaxation* comes open-mindedness, and with open-mindedness comes veracity, and with veracity comes fulfillment. With *open-mindedness* comes tranquility, and with tranquility comes [proper] action, and with [proper] action comes success. With *tranquility* comes non-contrivance, and with non-contrivance, those who are in charge of affairs fulfill their

---

14. This translation stems from the opinion that *wu wei* 無為 ("without doing") is another way of writing *wu wei* 無偽 ("without contrivance"), insofar as the former, read literally, in context, is clearly *not* the intended meaning. I do, however, suppose that there was (and is) a poetic resonance between the (ostensibly) unmoving North Star that can be described as literally "doing nothing" (無為) and human "non-contrivance" (無偽) that is "unmoved" by other people's expectations of us.

duties. With *non-contrivance* comes placidity, and in those who are placid, worry and anxiety do not dwell, and their years are long.

(夫虛、靜、恬淡、寂漠、無為者，天地之平而道德之至，故帝王聖人休焉。休則虛，虛則實，實者備矣。虛則靜，靜則動，動則得矣。靜則無為，無為也則任事者責矣。無為則俞俞，俞俞者憂患不能處，年壽長矣。)[15]

The connection between open-mindedness and the eventual achievement of non-contrivance is clear, as are the ultimate goals of avoiding anxiety and living a long life. Relaxation is a physical and emotional state while open-mindedness is a mental state, but the latter does seem dependent on the former, insofar as it is difficult to be open-minded when physically or emotionally tense. The "flow" of non-contrivance also presupposes a kind of bodily looseness. "Veracity" means things as they actually are, rather than as we would like them to be, and "fulfillment" means to be complete, as well as to be fully prepared for things, as one will be if one has a grasp of things as they really are.

Part of non-contrivance is knowing when not to force things. There is a fine line between the placidity that delivers us from anxiety, and laziness or lack of any ambition to improve things. We saw above that our "*qi*-substance, by being open it awaits things." This "awaiting," or rather, knowing when to wait and when to act, is fundamental to the skill of non-contrivance, and one of the more difficult-to-attain fruits of experience. "[When things] get confusing such that they appear disordered, be tranquil with them and they [may] order themselves. Forcing the issue will not always right it; wisdom cannot always plan for it." (紛乎其若亂，靜之而自治。強不能遍立，智不能盡謀。)[16] The mind, and its thinking, are crucial to self-cultivation in early China. But thinking alone cannot solve all problems. Sometimes there are issues with one's genetic disposition, other times with excessive emotions, and sometimes these issues will prove amenable to being fixed by *thinking* of solutions. Other times they simply will not. "For inflexible and aggressive blood and *qi*-substance, make them flexible with integrative harmony. For saturating and immersive conscious pondering, focus it with easy good-naturedness." (血氣剛強，則柔之以調和。知慮漸深，則一之以易良。)[17] "Inflexible and aggressive blood

---

15. *Zhuangzi* ch. 13 (天道); cf. Watson, *Zhuangzi*, 98.
16. *Guanzi* ch. 36 (心術上); cf. Rickett, *Guanzi*, 2:73.
17. *Xunzi* ch. 2 (修身); cf. Hutton, *Xunzi*, 11.

and *qi*-substance" has a modern analogue in the Britishism "bloody-minded." Then, as now, a bit of flexibility in one's thinking can help with this malady. "Saturating and immersive" are accurate, if not mellifluous, translations, but the former means "to become absorbed" in or by something, here to an excessive degree, while the latter means "deep" to the point of being in over one's head. "Easy good-naturedness" is not a common phrase in early China, where it is mostly used to describe music or musicians and is contrasted with "extravagance" (奢); here it connotes moderation, even in pondering.

Those who extolled the efficacy of non-contrivance were sometimes overcome by awe and resorted to hyperbole. Zhuangzi was especially fond of this device. In an effort to describe how you might "get out of your own way" or "get out of your own head," in order to tap into a creative flow, he described an aspirational model as having a body "like dried wood" (如槁木) and a mind "like dead ashes" (如死灰).[18] Elsewhere, he describes a practice, not unlike "mind-fasting," called "sitting and forgetting." The primary goal is to forget oneself, or at least one's thoughts about oneself. "To break apart the limbs and torso, dismiss discriminating percipience, take leave of [one's] form, get rid of consciousness, and merge with the 'great thoroughfare': this is called 'sitting and forgetting.'" (墮肢體，黜聰明，離形去知，同於大通：此謂坐忘。)[19] There was, of course, no physical mutilation involved in this practice, and this is only a poetic way of saying that the creative flow—the "great thoroughfare"—becomes accessible to us only after a kind of "letting go."

Just what to "let go" of will change from person to person, and even from situation to situation, but one inclusive referent is the "self." The person with a mind "like dead ashes" described himself in that situation, saying, "I have lost myself" (吾喪我). Selflessness, in early China or modern English, is a phrase that lends itself to various kinds of exegesis: is it an ontological claim, such as the Buddhists make, or is it an ethical claim, as is common in English? I suspect it is here more of a psychological claim, as we shall see. In any case, for early Chinese authors, it certainly at least includes open-mindedness, and also invites poetic rhapsodizing. The following passage is about open-mindedness and non-contrivance in the workplace, where a flexible attitude can go far.

---

18. *Zhuangzi* ch. 2 (齊物論); cf. Watson, *Zhuangzi*, 7.
19. *Zhuangzi* ch. 6 (大宗師); cf. Watson, *Zhuangzi*, 53.

Without [caring about] praise or blame, now a [lofty] dragon, now a [lowly] snake, fully developing with the times, and unwilling to be bound to a single course of action; now [employed in] a superior position, now in an inferior position, taking harmony as the measure. Floating and wandering with the ancestor of the myriad things, treating [specific] things as [specific] things, but not being treated as a [specific] thing by other things. If it were thus, how could one be caught and entangled?

(無譽無訾，一龍一蛇，與時俱化，而無肯專為；一上一下，以和為量。浮遊乎萬物之祖，物物而不物於物：則胡可得而累邪？)[20]

The first sentence is about working effortlessly and harmoniously—selflessly—no matter what sort of workplace you find yourself in. But the second sentence is more specifically psychological, insofar as it has to do with self-perception. To be "selfless" in this manner means that you are not locked into a particular conception of yourself. Other people may want you to treat them in a certain way that accords with their identity, with how they perceive themselves, but the aspirational figure here has no such identity, no such self, and therefore has chameleon-like flexibility. In this way he is not "entangled," either in a particular role that he has defined for himself or in a role that others may want to impose. It is another level of open-mindedness.

This flexibility extends all the way to the top, so to speak, and though the Way does not literally speak, one may still posit: "That which the Way speaks of is one, but the ways of using it vary." (道之所言者一也，而用之者異。)[21] The recognition of this naturally leads to a respect for education, the proper pursuit of which should always include an inquiry into history and should always lead to a more open mind. "Noble people . . . follow the path of asking and learning . . . cherishing the old yet knowing the new." (君子 . . . 道問學 . . . 溫故而知新。)[22] Selflessness, then, makes way for gaining the knowledge that somehow, mysteriously, informs uncontrived action that is nevertheless suitable to the occasion.

---

20. *Zhuangzi* ch. 20 (山木); cf. Watson, *Zhuangzi*, 156–57.
21. *Guanzi* ch. 2 (形勢); cf. Rickett, *Guanzi*, 1:80.
22. *Liji* ch. 31 (中庸); cf. Legge, *Li Chi*, 2:323.

. . . and Creativity

Human creativity is difficult to analyze. Artists of all kinds are nearly unanimous in claiming to be unable to control it. Even today, when no one follows the Greek deities, we still speak of the "muses" that may or may not visit us with their gifts. This inscrutability forces authors to resort to unconventional language. Consider the following three sayings of Laozi. He said that "for the mind, competence lies in depth" (心善淵); that if we "grasp the ancient Way," we will be able to "use it to ride the forms of today" (執古之道，以御今之有); and that those who "abide in formlessness" (常無) will be able to "observe the mysteries" (觀其妙) of the Way.[23]

All of these claims refer to creativity, even though the term "creativity" (造) is not employed in any of them. "Depth" is a metaphor that conveys having a variety of levels (i.e., possibilities) to draw upon, and being open to those possibilities facilitates creativity. The "form" and "formlessness" of the next two passages are ontological terms that designate "things" and "potentiality" respectively. "Ride" literally means "to drive a chariot" and, by extension, "to manage," so "to ride the forms of today" is a visual metaphor for being able to handle a situation. As in the last indented passage quoted in the section just above, this ideally requires a degree of flexibility, which is necessary for creativity. Finally, "formlessness" or "potentiality" is an ontological term that stands in for the psychological term "open-mindedness." To "abide in formlessness" is a poetic and rather Zen way of saying we should be open-minded. If we can manage that, then we put ourselves in a position to observe the mystery of creativity.

One example of such creativity is Woodworker Qing in chapter 1. A more earthy example may be found in a story about Yanzi, a court advisor celebrated for his cleverness. One day while walking to work he passed three famous warriors (and bullies) who also worked for the same duke as he. Though he was senior in rank to them, they did not respectfully rise as he passed, and this breach of protocol Yanzi thought was bad for morale. He mentioned the incident to the duke, but the duke said they were too strong and fierce for anyone to arrest them. So Yanzi went to them with two peaches and suggested that the bravest two should each have one. The three of them argued over who was the bravest. When the first two had

---

23. *Laozi* chs. 8, 14, and 1.

told their stories of bravado and subsequently taken a peach, they heard the third man tell his tale, felt inferior to him, returned their peaches, and committed suicide. When the third man saw this, he felt ashamed for causing two great warriors to commit suicide and committed suicide himself.[24] Though neither the story of Woodworker Qing nor the story of Yanzi uses the terms "open-minded" or "creative," they are each good examples of these mental qualities.

. . . and Honesty (誠)

There is a selflessness that underlies non-contrivance, which in turn leads to creativity, but this selflessness also results, ideally, in the important virtue of honesty. "Honesty is the way of Heaven. Becoming honest is the way of people. The honest person is centered without forcing [himself], is successful without imagining [success], is centered in the way and follows it tolerantly: a sage. One who is honest is one who chooses competence and firmly holds to it." (誠者，天之道也；誠之者，人之道也。誠者不勉而中，不思而得，從容中道，聖人也。誠之者，擇善而固執之者也。)[25] This author does not take Heaven to be an anthropomorphic entity (as we saw in the introduction that some earlier authors did); nevertheless, it may sound odd to say that Heaven can be "honest." Here it should be taken to mean "dependable," not capricious, and, so to speak, "transparent" about what it is doing. "Centeredness" was discussed in the previous chapter, where it described an emotional equanimity. It seems uncontroversial to say that honesty—a lack of duplicity—would lead to such a state. The following idea, that the honest person "is successful without imagining [success]" is less obvious. This seems directly contrary to the "visualization" techniques used in recent decades as part of programs like the "prosperity gospel" popular in America. This author, in contrast, advises us *not* to imagine some future success, but rather, in some sense, to "trust" (the way of) Heaven. If we follow it "tolerantly"—which is to say, fully and agreeably—then success will happen organically. An honest person, then, does not seek clever, duplicitous, short-cuts, but rather chooses solid "competence" instead.

---

24. *Yanzi chunqiu* 晏子春秋 ch. 2.24; cf. Olivia Milburn, The *Spring and Autumn Annals of Master Yan* (Leiden: Brill, 2016), 234–36.

25. *Liji* ch. 31 (中庸); cf. Legge, *Li Chi*, 2:317–18.

A commitment to competence will entail work. Hence the passage above continues (with "it" referring to "honesty"): "Extensively learn it, critically inquire after it, carefully apprehend it, perceptively discern it, earnestly practice it." (博學之，審問之，慎思之，明辨之，篤行之。)[26] Learn about honesty from books, ask about it from people you trust, try to apprehend what it entails from your environment, discern real honesty from half-truths and self-serving logical fallacies in your own mind, and finally, once you understand it, practice it with your whole person.

Pursuing honesty in this way will not only lead to us "completing" ourselves as individuals but will also lead us back to the holy grail of becoming a "triad" with Heaven and Earth: of humans taking responsibility not just for themselves, but for their communities as well. "Honesty [can] complete you, and the way [of honesty can] guide you. Honesty is the beginning and end of things: without honesty there would be nothing [to the cosmic and social orders as we now know them]. This is why noble people take being honest as honorable. But honest people do not merely complete themselves, [they are also] those who complete others. To complete oneself results in goodness; to complete others results in wisdom." (誠者自成也，而道自道也。誠者物之終始，不誠無物。是故君子誠之為貴。誠者非自成己而已也，所以成物也。成己，仁也；成物，知也。)[27]

That honesty might be a road to success (that is, to "completion") and that it might serve as a central virtue is not surprising. The second sentence of this quote, however, sounds a bit more extraordinary in its scope. As above, "honesty" here should be taken as referring to the "dependability" or "transparency" of the cosmos: if Heaven were like a capricious deity, then the world would appear haphazard—a chaos, not a cosmos—and the world as we know it would not be here. The same insight applies to the social order: without honesty, the "social contract" that binds communities together would not be possible. But there is another layer to this. Again, that we might "complete" ourselves with "honesty" and thereby become "good" is perhaps uncontroversial, but we are also said to be able to complete other things (including other people), and thereby gain wisdom. The human potential to "form a triad with Heaven and Earth," cited in the previous chapter, is just a few sentences prior to this passage.

---

26. *Ibid.*

27. *Liji* ch. 31 (中庸); cf. Legge, *Li Chi*, 2:321–22.

With this analytic lens, humans may be seen as "completing" other things by "improving" them. In the social realm, an honest person may be said to "improve" a dishonest person by inspiring them to be more honest. In the nonhuman environment, humans honestly working for the betterment of human society may be said to "improve" the raw materials that Heaven and Earth have provided us: for example, by making houses from trees, by domesticating both plants and animals for human consumption, and by working with the "transparently" cyclical seasons to create a dependable agricultural calendar. With this rather expansive idea of "honesty," humans can complete themselves, other humans, and the resources of the environment, simultaneously gaining knowledge of all three. Indeed, "For noble people, in nourishing their minds, nothing is more excellent than honesty." (君子養心莫善於誠。)²⁸

But: Follow (Natural) Principles (理)

Honesty is an interior commitment, and in the early Chinese paradigm, its exterior counterpart lies in the order of the cosmos. We saw in chapter 1 that "Yin and Yang are the great principles of Heaven and Earth" (陰陽者，天地之大理也); the sentence continues, saying "the four seasons are the great mainstays of Yin and Yang" (四時者，陰陽之大經也).²⁹ In one respect, these principles are inescapable, but in another, they can be ignored, even if doing so may make life more difficult. Following the twists and turns of natural principles, determinedly yet gracefully, is compared with the flow of water. "Water moves according to principle, not losing [it for even] the smallest moment: this is also the case with wise people." (夫水者緣理而行，不遺小間：似有智者。)³⁰ It is the wise that pay particular attention to natural principles. One such principle is the four seasons; two more are, essentially, "what goes up will come down" and "whatever lives will die."³¹

---

28. *Xunzi* ch. 3 (不苟); cf. Hutton, *Xunzi*, 19. I typically translate the key word *shan* 善 as "competence," but here that would be awkward, so I use "excellent" instead.

29. *Guanzi* ch. 39 (水地); cf. Rickett, *Guanzi*, 2:111. Previously quoted at chap. 1, n. 14.

30. *Hanshi waizhuan* 韓詩外傳 ch. 3.25; cf. James Hightower, *Han Shih Wai Chuan: Han Ying's Illustrations of the Didactic Application of the Classic of Songs* (Cambridge: Harvard University Press, 1952), 106.

31. *Yanzi chunqiu* ch. 7.2: "That which waxes will also wane; that which lives will also die: [these] are Heaven's allotments. That things have certain outcomes and matters have certain regularities is the ancient Way." (夫盛之有衰，生之有死，天之分也。物有必至，事有常然，古之道也。) cf. Milburn, *Master Yan*, 370–71.

Such principles can inform both practical and moral issues. "Thus, discerning without the appropriate principle can result in contrivance, and knowing without the appropriate principle can result in deception. . . . Principles are the ancestors of right and wrong." (故辨而不當理則偽，知而不當理則詐. . . . 理也者，是非之宗也。)[32]

For better or worse, no early Chinese author undertook the task of writing up a comprehensive list of "principles" for us to consult; nothing corresponds to the lists of "commandments" or "rules" found in some religions. On the contrary, it was noted that such an undertaking would be impossible.

> In general, the use of consciousness is [a part of] human nature, and that which can be known are the principles of things. [If you] take the use of consciousness in human nature to seek the principles of that which can be known about things, there will be no certain endpoint. Thus, [even] to the end of [your] life and the completion of [your] years, [you] will be unable to [know] them all. Even if these principles were gathered together, though millions and millions, it would still be insufficient to [know] all the changes of the myriad things, and you would be about the same as a fool.
>
> (凡以知，人之性也；可以知，物之理也。以可以知人之性，求可以知物之理，而無所疑止之。則沒世窮年不能徧也。其所以貫理焉雖億萬，已不足浹萬物之變，與愚者若一。)[33]

So, apprehending natural principles is important, but complicated.

Some passages on the advisability of humans apprehending natural principles sound positively scientific. There is no need to be anachronistic about such passages, and we should certainly not read into them more than what is there, but what they plainly say is quite striking. Consider the claim: "In general, spoken words must be thoroughly assessed, and when they have to do with people, then they must be checked against [natural] principles." (凡聞言必熟論，其於人必驗之以理。)[34] The "[natural] principles" in this case are exemplified in two hearsay claims that had been misconstrued, but for

---

32. *Lüshi chunqiu* ch. 18.4 (離謂); cf. Knoblock and Riegel, *The Annals of Lü Buwei*, 453.
33. *Xunzi* ch. 21 (解蔽); cf. Hutton, *Xunzi*, 233.
34. *Lüshi chunqiu* ch. 22.6 (察傳); cf. Knoblock and Riegel, *The Annals of Lü Buwei*, 583.

which reasonable explanations were later found.³⁵ This is similar to trying to work backwards from the final iteration of a repeatedly whispered sentence in the children's game of "telephone," to work out what was originally said. "[Natural] principles" (理) here are like the "internal logic" of a situation, or the "inherent reasonableness" of the cosmos: they are principles that humans have to figure out, using what we would now call "reason" or "logic." But the emphasis here is on the principles in the world, rather than a human mental capacity, though the two do correlate as we might expect.

Natural principles are knowable and when we apprehend their cause-and-effect workings, we perceive the "reasons" (故) for things being as they are. These reasons are not incidental, but necessary:

> In general, there must be reasons for why things are as they are. If you do not know these reasons, then it will be the same no matter if you act appropriately or not: there will certainly be problems. That by which former kings, famous officials, and perceptive teachers surpassed ordinary people was in their knowing [these reasons]. That rivers depart from mountains and travel to the sea is not because rivers hate mountains and desire the sea, but rather because [the difference between] high and low cause them to do this.
>
> (凡物之然也，必有故。而不知其故，雖當與不知同：其卒必困。先王名士達師之所以過俗者，以其知也。水出於山而走於海，水非惡山而欲海也，高下使之然也。)³⁶

This focus on the comprehensibility of the world—its natural principles and inherent reasonability—implies a concomitant aversion to unfounded preconceptions. In fact, we do find in the literature that "noble people" avoid such preconceptions, and seem to be aware of what we now call "confirmation bias." In the following passage, the author is explaining

---

35. The first claim was that someone had only "one foot" when in fact what was meant was that his "one [way] was sufficient"; both claims can be written with the same graphs (i.e., 一足, in which 足 means both "foot" and "sufficient"). The second claim was that someone "had found a person *in* a well," whereas what was meant was that he "had found a person *for* [digging] a well" (i.e., 穿井得一人). Again, prepositions, even implied ones, matter.

36. *Lüshi chunqiu* ch. 9.4 (審己); cf. Knoblock and Riegel, *The Annals of Lü Buwei*, 216.

himself, and the opening quote is something he previously said. "Their" refers to "noble people."

> "Their responses [to things] are without assumptions and their interactions [with things] are without preferences." This is called "accordance." Those who are accordant take things, rather than themselves, as the rule. To sense [a particular thing] and *then* to respond is to be "without assumptions." To act following [natural] principles is to be "without preferences." Mistakes are due to using your own [assumptions], and faults are due to changing [preferences]. If you use your own [assumptions] then you are not open-minded, and [if you] are not open-minded, then you will be contrary to things. If you change [preferences] then contrivance is born, and when contrivance is born, then there is disorder.
>
> (「其應非所設也,其動非所取也」。此言因也,因也者,舍己而以物為法者也。感而後應,非所設也,緣理而動,非所。取也。過在自用,罪在變化。自用則不虛,不虛則仵於物矣。變化則為生,為生則亂矣。)³⁷

There are three technical terms in this passage: assumptions (設), preferences (取), and accordance (因). "Assumptions" are what we work from when we do not work from our senses; that is, preconceptions. "Preferences" influence our actions when we do not follow the natural principles of things: they place subjectivity over objectivity. We might call them "biases." And "accordance" is to rely on the objective world, not the subjective world of opinion. Such subjectivity is explicitly opposed to open-mindedness.

Along with the advice to follow natural principles rather than our own opinions, we are also reminded that such a path is never ending. "Accord with the way of Heaven, return to the principles of things: investigate, examine, and study them, and when you finish, then start again." (因天之道,反形之理,督參鞠之,終則有始。)³⁸ Perseverance in the pursuit of natural principles is a virtue.

---

37. *Guanzi* ch. 36 (心術上); cf. Rickett, *Guanzi*, 2:80.
38. *Hanfeizi* ch. 8 (揚權); cf. Watson, *Han Fei Tzu*, 36. Note: 有 = 又. Previously quoted in the introduction, n. 49.

Detachment (無執 / 處超然 / 獨 / 遊心)

In the previous chapter we saw that human *emotions* derive from human inclinations (情) which in turn derive from human nature (性), and that we should deal with them by expressing them appropriately (宜), which is accomplished by regulating (節) them. We also saw that human *desires* (欲) are the instruments (具) of human nature, and the responses (應) of our inclinations. Desire is a slippery topic with little overt consensus about the best way to deal with it in a program of self-cultivation. One reason for this is that to "want" something—a rather common human activity—and to "desire" something are denoted by the same word in Chinese. Therefore, it must be made clear from context whether the "desire" in question is mundane, good, or excessive. Nevertheless, in this section I argue that detachment is the most fundamental—or at least, most nuanced—attitude towards desire in our sources.

Desire, like emotion, is certainly seen as natural. Here, it is paired with its opposite, aversion: "Human inclination desires longevity and is averse to dying young, desires security and is averse to danger, desires glory and is averse to disgrace, desires ease and is averse to toil. If the [former] four are obtained, and the [latter] four are avoided, then the mind will be moderated. Obtaining the [former] four lies in success with [natural] principles." (人之情，欲壽而惡夭，欲安而惡危，欲榮而惡辱，欲逸而惡勞。四欲得，四惡除，則心適矣。四欲之得也，在於勝理。)[39] These desires are mundane, and perhaps even universal. But desire can also be cast as malicious. "Nourishing of the will is for when the thoughts of the mind's *qi*-substance are not thoroughgoing [i.e., when the mind is "scattered" from chasing various whims]. When there is desire, the will dwells [on its object] and imagines it. *The will is the agent of desire.* If desires are many, then the mind will be scattered; and if the mind is scattered, then the will deteriorates; and if the will is deteriorated, then thinking will not be thoroughgoing." (養志者，心氣之思不達也。有所欲，志存而思之。志者，欲之使也。欲多則心散，心散則志衰，志衰則思不達。)[40] Here the problem arises when desires are too many; it is not located in desire itself. In this way, where excess is the

---

39. *Lüshi chunqiu* ch. 5.4 (適音); cf. Knoblock and Riegel, *The Annals of Lü Buwei*, 143.
40. *Guiguzi* 鬼谷子 ch. 15 (本經陰符七術篇); cf. Thomas Cleary, *Thunder in the Sky* (Boston: Shambhala, 1994), 58–59.

problem, desire is similar to emotion. And indeed, some would prescribe the same approach to it: regulating it until it is appropriate.[41]

Sometimes authors, no doubt in an attempt to catch the reader's eye, will wax hyperbolic about desire and omit any modifier, though a close reading always seems to reveal that a modifier is implied. The *Guanzi* advises the reader to "empty your desires" (虛其欲) and to "be rid of desires" (去欲).[42] But just a few sentences prior to the first claim, the author more clearly identifies the problem not simply as "desires" but as "cravings and desires that fill [the mind] to overflowing" (嗜欲充益). And two sentences after it, the author notes that "all people desire wisdom" (人皆欲智). So it seems clear that *some* desires are good, and that the problem is, as above, one of excess. Thus, a careful translation may add the implied adjective: be "empty of your [excessive] desires" and "be rid of [excessive] desires."

Similarly, the *Laozi* repeatedly advises us to be "without desire" (無欲).[43] Yet we read elsewhere in that text that we should only "decrease desire" (寡欲) and, in an obvious play on words, that "sages desire to not desire" (聖人欲不欲).[44] The text also often uses the word "desire" in the mundane, value-neutral sense of "want;" for example: "sages, [if they] desire to lead people, are always conciliatory towards them in speech" (聖人欲上民，必以言下之).[45] For the *Laozi*, however, the problem is not so much "excessive" desire as "contrived" desire, but this adjective too must be inferred from context.

Xunzi may have read the *Guanzi* and *Laozi* and may have been unhappy with the opacity of their hyperbole: "All those who say that orderliness must await the elimination of desires are those who lack the means to guide desire and are troubled with even *having* desires. [Likewise,] all those who

---

41. *Xunzi* ch. 22 (正名): "Although desires cannot be completely fulfilled, [you] can come close to fulfilling them. Although desires cannot be completely eliminated, [you] can seek to regulate them. Though desires cannot be completely fulfilled, seeking can come close to fulfilling them. Though desires cannot be completely eliminated, and [one] will not always get what [one] seeks, those who reflect will want to regulate what [they] seek." (欲雖不可盡，可以近盡也；欲雖不可去，求可節也。所欲雖不可盡，求者猶近盡；欲雖不可去，所求不得，慮者欲節求也。) cf. Hutton, *Xunzi*, 244.

42. *Guanzi* ch. 36 (心術上); cf. Rickett, *Guanzi*, 2:72, 76.

43. *Laozi* chs. 3, 34, 37, and 57.

44. *Laozi* chs. 19 and 64; *Zhuangzi* ch. 20 (山木) and *Mengzi* ch. 7B (盡心下) agree with *Laozi* ch. 19 in its advice to "decrease desire" (寡欲).

45. *Laozi* ch. 66, but for similar uses, see also chs. 29, 36, 39, and 61.

say that orderliness must await the decrease of desires are people who lack the means to regulate desires and are troubled with having *too many* desires. [Those] with and without desires are of different categories: [namely,] the living and the dead." (凡語治而待去欲者，無以道欲而困於有欲者也。凡語治而待寡欲者，無以節欲而困於多欲者也。有欲無欲，異類也，生死也。)[46] His sarcasm is nearly palpable.

The *Lunyu* also uses "desire" in a mundane sense. For example, "The noble person desires to be slow to speak, but quick to act." (君子欲訥於言，而敏於行。)[47] This text also twice repeats the phrase "Do not impose upon others that which you yourself do not desire." (己所不欲，勿施於人。)[48] In contrast to these decidedly banal uses, "desire" is also sometimes disparaged in this text. In one passage, Kongzi describes the "complete person" (成人) to a student by combining the virtues of four different people, one of whom was said to simply "not desire" (不欲).[49] Still, given the counterexamples that we just considered, it seems reasonable to infer that the "complete person" does not desire *excessively*. In another passage, "desire" is listed with some vices: "combativeness, boastfulness, resentment, and desire" (克、伐、怨、欲),[50] which gives it an unmistakably negative connotation. But one might yet argue, as most commentators do, that the intention was of excessive or unruly desire. This interpretation is made explicit only once in the text, where Kongzi, in listing the "five merits" (五美) of noble people, explains one by saying they "desire, but are not greedy" (欲而不貪).[51] This is echoed in what may be the world's most famous one-sentence autobiography, where Kongzi says: "At fifteen I set my mind upon learning; at thirty I took my place [in society]; at forty I became free from doubts; at fifty I understood Heaven's mandate; at sixty my ear was accordant [to it]; and at seventy I could follow my mind's desires without overstepping the bounds." (吾十有五而志於學，三十而立，四十而不惑，五十而知天命，六十而耳順，七十而從心所欲，不踰矩。)[52] The epitome of his lifelong evolution is that he follows his desires, but not excessively.

---

46. *Xunzi* ch. 22 (正名); cf. Hutton, *Xunzi*, 243.
47. *Lunyu* 論語 4.24; cf. Edward Slingerland, *Confucius: Analects with Selections from Traditional Commentaries* (Indianapolis: Hackett, 2003), 37.
48. *Lunyu* 12.2, 15.24; cf. Slingerland, *Analects*, 126, 183.
49. *Lunyu* 14.12; cf. Slingerland, *Analects*, 158.
50. *Lunyu* 14.1; cf. Slingerland, *Analects*, 153.
51. *Lunyu* 20.2; cf. Slingerland, *Analects*, 233.
52. *Lunyu* 2.4; cf. Slingerland, *Analects*, 9.

There is, however, another idea about how to handle desires, excessive or not, and that is through the attitude of detachment. To be detached is to observe your own desires without being controlled, overwhelmed, or unduly influenced by them. It is to privilege the rational part of the mind over the human "inclinations" (情) from which desire derives, and with which we are all born. A desire arises, you assess it, and decide whether or not to act on it. This is possible for our authors because, as we saw above, "The mind within the body holds the position of ruler."

The idea of detachment does not have a single, technical term to signify it in early China, which is why there are four parenthetical terms in the header of this section. Perhaps the clearest is "non-attachment" (無執), which appears in the *Laozi* in the injunction "Those who act contrivedly, fail; those who are attached [to things], lose [those] things. This is why sages are uncontrived and thus do not fail; do not get attached [to things] and thus do not lose [them]." (為者敗之，執者失之。是以聖人無為，故無敗；無執，故無失。)[53] Laozi elsewhere describes the sage thus: "Even when there are glorious sights to behold, [they] calmly dwell detachedly." (雖有榮觀，燕處超然。)[54] "Detachedly" (超然), here, is literally "above/beyond it all."

The *Guanzi* author sometimes borrows the word "alone" (獨) to signify detachment: "If [people] get rid of [excessive] desire, then they will be opened; if opened, then [they can be] tranquil; if tranquil, then [they can be] essential; if essential then [they can be] detached; if detached, then [they can be] percipient; if percipient, then [they can be] spiritous." (去欲則宣，宣則靜矣，靜則精，精則獨立矣，獨則明，明則神矣。)[55] As we saw in chapter 1, "essential" and "spiritous" refer to physical creativity and cognitive creativity, respectively. Thus, this passage is saying that if we can reduce desire, then we will "create space" for other mental operations,

---

53. *Laozi* ch. 64. The first sentence also appears in ch. 29.

54. *Laozi* ch. 26. The phrase also appears in the *Chuci* 楚辭 ch. 6 (卜居) and *Huainanzi* 淮南子 ch. 19 (脩務); cf. David Hawkes, *Ch'u Tz'u: The Songs of the South* (1959; rpt. Boston: Beacon Press, 1962), 89; and John Major, Sarah Queen, Andrew Meyer, and Harold Roth, *The Huainanzi: A Guide to the Theory and Practice of Government in Early Han China* (New York: Columbia University Press, 2010), 779.

55. *Guanzi* ch. 36 (心術上); cf. Rickett, *Guanzi*, 2:76. Most commentators gloss *xuan* 宣 (declare) as *tong* 通 (clear through), *kong* 空 (empty), or *gua* 寡 (uncluttered), which I elide with "opened"; cf. Rickett, *Guanzi*, 2:76. I think Zhuangzi also uses the term "alone/detached" (獨) with the latter meaning in an enigmatic passage in ch. 6 (大宗師); cf. Watson, *Zhuangzi*, 46–47. While I am not ready to endorse such a reading yet, it is an interesting thought experiment to read the word, typically translated as "alone," as "detachedly" in *Laozi* chs. 20 and 25 (the only chapters in which this term appears in this text).

including tranquility; tranquility is often requisite for a creative "flow," and this "flow" can carry us out of emotional ruts; being freed from emotional ruts can allow for new ways of seeing things, and those new ways of seeing things might foster cognitive creativity.

Desires are typically for external things that may be possessed or consumed, and while an ordinary mind is pushed and pulled by these desires, the detached mind remains unmoved until a decision has been made. Zhuangzi uses the phrase "wandering mind" (遊心) to describe this state, using "wandering" in the sense of "freely roaming" (and *not* in the sense of "unable to focus"). He explains such "wandering" as being "without both that which draws [you] out or invites [you] in" (無有所將，無有所迎).[56] That is, to hold fast to the imperturbable "mirror mind" and not get pulled into states of mind that compromise one's objectivity. But, as with the emotions, where to be dispassionate is not to not be devoid of passion, but rather to not be too attached to the passions one feels, so it is with desires. He suggests precisely this when he says in the following sentence that we should be able to "change externally but not change internally" (外化而內不化).[57] If we were impervious to interacting with the world, then we would never change; in Zhuangzi's scenario, we do indeed change, but only while holding to our unchanging attitude of (aspirational) objectivity. It is rather like being both a flexible person while at the same time being someone "with a backbone." The two metaphors are literally at odds, but it is certainly possible to be simultaneously inwardly resolute while outwardly adaptable.

Nevertheless, sometimes "detachment" is mistakenly taken to mean a rejection of the world, just as sometimes people mistakenly take "dispassion" for emotional coldness. Zhuangzi tells the story of Yao, who did not want "that which [all] people desire" (人之所欲), namely, "long life, wealth, and many sons" (壽、富、多男子).[58] He did not want them, he said, because they were worldly hassles and would not help with his project of "nourishing virtuosity" (養德). But Yao had mistaken detachment for outright disconnection, and he was upbraided for completely rejecting that which one should properly only be detached from. One can be engaged with the

---

56. *Zhuangzi* ch. 22 (知北遊); cf. Watson, *Zhuangzi*, 186.
57. *Ibid.* Zhuangzi also described detachment without any technical or poetic term denoting it. See, for example, the last anecdote in ch. 23 (庚桑楚); cf. Watson, *Zhuangzi*, 198.
58. *Zhuangzi* ch. 12 (天地); cf. Watson, *Zhuangzi*, 87.

world and still detached from it. His interlocutor said: "The sage resides as [carefree as] a quail, eats as [unfussily as] fledglings, and leaves no trace, like a flying bird." (聖人：鶉居而鷇食，鳥行而無彰。)[59] You can desire what others desire, and you can act upon those desires too, but you should nevertheless not be attached to those things to the point of jeopardizing the equanimity of your mind. Above we were told to "ride the forms of today" in order to be creative; similarly, Zhuangzi says that "to 'ride things' with a 'wandering mind,' and to consign [oneself] to the inevitable for the nourishing of what is central, is fulfilling." (乘物以遊心，託不得已以養中，至矣。)[60] If desires are inevitable, as Xunzi says they are, and not to be avoided, as Yao's interlocutor says, then to "consign" oneself to them means to experience them as they come, yet not at the expense of what is "central," which can only be the Way or your fate or destiny.

Detachment works with both desires and emotions. Zhuangzi elsewhere explains attaining a "wandering mind" as attaining "fulfilling beauty and fulfilling happiness, and those who attain fulfilling beauty and wander in fulfilling happiness are called fulfilled people (至美至樂也，得至美而遊乎至樂，謂之至人).[61] Beauty resides in exterior objects of desire, while happiness is an (interior) emotion: both are to be navigated with a wandering mind, itself another metaphor for an open mind. A third sort of detachment, from one's self-identity, may be detected in the butterfly story, where Zhuangzi, upon awaking from a dream in which he was a butterfly, could not clearly discern if he was a person who had dreamt he was a butterfly, or was in fact a butterfly who was now dreaming it was a person.[62] Not being too attached to who you think you are allows for greater latitude in self-discovery, and may change both how one perceives beauty and experiences happiness, making it a felicitous milestone of self-cultivation.

In theory, we may be able to subsume the ideas of being rid of, or reducing, desires, into the process of detachment, insofar as it rids one of, or reduces, the pernicious *effects* of desire, even though it does not claim to reduce or get rid of desires themselves. It is impossible to know if the advocates of reducing desires would assent to the paradigm of detachment, but it seems likely that they would at least accept it as a first step, if not

---

59. *Ibid*. This is reminiscent of Jesus' words at "Matthew" 6.25–26.
60. *Zhuangzi* ch. 4 (人間世); cf. Watson, *Zhuangzi*, 28.
61. *Zhuangzi* ch. 21 (田子方); cf. Watson, *Zhuangzi*, 170.
62. *Zhuangzi* ch. 2 (齊物論); cf. Watson, *Zhuangzi*, 18.

as a more nuanced way of articulating the exact same program. In any case, they would agree that violence stemming from desire is to be avoided, and that the gracefulness of detachment should be embraced. "Fulfilled people," according to Zhuangzi, "do not fight with people or things for the sake of profit or loss . . . they innocently arrive and freely go." (至人者 . . . 不以人物利害相攖 . . . 儵然而往，侗然而來。)[63] Profit and loss invite human desire; in dealing with desire when one has an attitude of detachment, our focus is on a larger picture—the community or the cosmos—and not exclusively on the self.

Contentment (知足) and Humility (謙遜)

The attitude of detachment brings with it a sense of contentment. But the goal of contentment involves a subtle distinction that is crucial for an important balance between pragmatism and idealism. On the one hand, a perfectly content person—or perhaps we should say, a complacent person—might seek no changes in themselves or the world, which would undermine the lofty goal of creating a fair society and the more immediate goal of self-cultivation. On the other hand, a person who is never satisfied will never know peace or happiness. When it is said, then, that "those who know contentment are rich" (知足者富), or that "no misfortune is greater than not knowing contentment" (禍莫大於不知足), the author is not asking us to give up all efforts at improving a situation, but rather not to be avaricious.[64] It can be seen as a matter of judging which desires are excessive. One author sets the bar rather low, saying that we can be content if we simply do not crave useless things, though the judgment of what is and is not "useless" is surely a subjective one.[65] Another says it is a matter of not having "selfish" desires.[66] Knowing contentment is to desire what equanimity is to emotion;

---

63. *Zhuangzi* ch. 23 (庚桑楚); cf. Watson, *Zhuangzi*, 193.

64. *Laozi* ch. 33; *Laozi* ch. 46; several examples of the last point are explicitly adduced in *Hanfeizi* ch. 21 (喻老).

65. *Huainanzi* ch. 14 (詮言): "If [you] do not covet what is useless, then [your] desires will not harm your nature, and if [your] desires are not immoderate, then [you can] nourish life and know contentment." (不貪無用，即不以欲害性；欲不過節，及養生知足。) cf. Major, Queen, Meyer, and Roth, *Huainanzi*, 540.

66. *Zhuangzi* ch. 28 (讓王): "Those who know contentment are not entangled by selfish gain." (知足者不以利自累也。) cf. Watson, *Zhuangzi*, 246.

both are matters of self-regulation. In the end, not much more may be said, other than: "Those who know how to regulate what to take for one's person thereby know contentment." (知以身取節者，則知足矣。)[67]

The attitude of humility derives from the knowledge that knowledge is infinite. It is a natural correlative of open-mindedness and a cousin to contentment. "To know [when you] do not know is best" (知不知：上)[68] is probably a claim that few would disagree with. Looking within, the guiding principle of humility should be, quite simply: "Examine what you know *and* examine what you do not know." (察所知，察所不知。)[69] Looking outward, of course, we should pay attention to natural principles and remember to combat confirmation bias to, in this sense, be selfless: "How can we be selfless? By imitating the main precept(s) of Heaven and Earth."[70] Contentment and humility are both mental attitudes that can be cultivated, but they can also be the byproducts of open-mindedness.

Focus, on the other hand, is not a byproduct but, like open-mindedness, it is amenable to effort and willpower. We saw in chapter 1 that "Focusing on one thing and not two may result in a connection with spiritous intelligence, and the creation of a triad with Heaven and Earth," and how Woodworker Qing created marvelous bell-stands by, in part, "focusing [his] skill" (巧專).[71] These are interesting and noteworthy goals, both made possible by the increased productivity and creativity that focus can bring. There is nothing magical about mental focus, of course: it works by changing one's perspective. "Unify [your] intention and focus [your] mind, and [your] ears and eyes will not be profligate, and though [a thing or event] be distant, it will appear as if it were near." (一意摶心，耳目不

---

67. *Kongcongzi* 孔叢子 ch. 7 (居衛); cf. Yoav Ariel, *K'ung-tsung-tzu: The K'ung Family Masters' Anthology* (Princeton: Princeton University Press, 1989), 108. This text is of especially uncertain provenance, possibly dating to c. 200 CE, but ch. 7 might have been part of an earlier work, now lost, called the *Zisizi* 子思子, named after Kongzi's grandson.

68. *Laozi* ch. 71. This is similar to *Zhuangzi* ch. 2 (齊物論): "Knowledge that rests in that which it does not know is best." (知止其所不知，至矣。) cf. Watson, *Zhuangzi*, 14. Both of these narratives seem to predict what is now known as the Dunning-Kruger effect; see chap. 6, n. 8.

69. *Yucong, yi* 語叢一; cf. Scott Cook, *The Bamboo Texts of Guodian* (Cornell: Cornell University East Asia Program, 2012), 2:830.

70. *Guanzi* ch. 38 (白心). Quoted in the introduction, n. 32.

71. *Xunzi* ch. 8 (儒效); cf. Hutton, *Xunzi*, 65. *Zhuangzi* ch. 19 (達生); cf. Watson, *Zhuangzi*, 152–53. These quotes appeared in chap. 1, nn. 2 and 114.

淫,雖遠若近。)⁷² Repeatedly performing a task in which one is focused will eventually result in acquiring skill at that task. In addition to creating bell-stands, Zhuangzi also describes the skills of catching cicadas, swimming, archery, sailing, and drawing.⁷³

Laozi situates "focus" second in a list of six suggestions: (1) embrace the "One" (抱一); (2) focus your *qi*-substance (專氣); (3) polish your "mysterious mirror" (滌除玄鑒); (4) love the people (愛民); (5) be "feminine" (為雌); (6) be uncontrived (無為).⁷⁴ The "One" is another name for the cosmic Way. It comes first because it creates context for what follows. (Even if a reader did not subscribe to the cosmic Way, they could still read the "One" as the human way that we should follow.) "*Qi*-substance" here refers to our mental energies, inasmuch as it is the only kind of *qi*-substance that we are able to focus. The "mirror" as a metaphor for the mind we have already met, and being "feminine" is a metaphor for flexibility and adaptability. The first three items refer to interior self-cultivation goals, while the second three describe exterior actions that follow; all six unfold logically. First one should recognize the inherent order of the cosmos as something that should be understood, as living in harmony with it is the point of self-cultivation. To learn about this order takes mental focus, as there are many other things that distract us from it. As we focus, we should also be careful to maintain objectivity; mirrors reflect what they "see" without bias. If we can do these three things, then we are ready for social interaction. Love for others is a good foundation for this, and flexibility in dealing with others is a *sine qua non* for a functioning community. To do all five of these things effortlessly and unselfconsciously is the final objective.

Zhuangzi tells a cautionary tale about what happens when one focuses on one thing to the exclusion of all else. In it, he was wandering in a park when a "peculiar magpie" (異鵲) flew by and brushed his forehead before settling in a tree. He thought the bird peculiar because, while it had unusually large wings and eyes, it was neither flying well nor seeing clearly. Zhuangzi surmised that it was evidently distracted by something, but he did not know what. In the bird's line of sight, he saw a cicada, and behind that cicada was a praying mantis about to pounce on the cicada. He looked up and saw that the magpie was in fact eyeing the praying mantis—this is

---

72. *Guanzi* ch. 49 (內業); cf. Rickett, *Guanzi*, 2:51.
73. *Zhuangzi* ch. 19 (達生).
74. *Laozi* ch. 10.

what had distracted it such that it had brushed against his forehead on the way to the tree—and that Zhuangzi himself was just another link in this chain of distractedness. Even the cicada might have had its eyes on something that was distracting *it* from the praying mantis, and so on down the food chain. This living metaphor spooked Zhuangzi, who then realized he himself was about to be caught by a park ranger who would have arrested him for poaching in the park had he not run away.[75] This was his "road to Damascus" story, and the moral is clear. Although focus is good, and a necessary part of mental self-cultivation, one should never forget one's surroundings. Context is always important.

Mental focus can be related to percipience (明).[76] The first paragraph of the opening chapter of the *Xunzi* concludes: "Noble people learn broadly but [also] thrice daily examine themselves; thus their knowing is percipient and their actions are not excessive." (君子博學而日參省乎己，則知明而行無過矣。)[77] To "examine" is a kind of "focus" and, along with a broad education, leads to percipience. The author later adds another qualifier, saying "Impartiality produces percipience; bias produces ignorance." (公生明，偏生闇。)[78] Today, such an observation is unremarkable. In early China, though, percipience was contextualized with Heaven and its natural principles. Indeed, we find them linked. "To follow the indications of Heaven, [your] actions must be percipient." (從天之指者，動必明。)[79] And: "Wise people understand calculations, perceive [natural] principles, and cannot be fooled by dishonesty." (智者達於數、明於理，不可欺以不誠。)[80] The "calculations" and "[natural] principles" that wise people understand have only multiplied since those words were written. In modern times, focus has become even more important, as the demand on our attention—a precious resource—has also increased, to the point where we now must "filter" the entities competing for our attention. Such filtering is a kind of

---

75. *Zhuangzi* ch. 20 (山木); cf. Watson, *Zhuangzi*, 164–65.

76. The term "percipience" (明) here refers to mental acuity, lucidity, or perspicacity and not to any innate ability. The root meanings of this graph are "brightness" and "good vision."

77. *Xunzi* ch. 1 (勸學); cf. Hutton, *Xunzi*, 1.

78. *Xunzi* ch. 3 (不苟); cf. Hutton, *Xunzi*, 22.

79. *Guanzi* ch. 35 (侈靡); cf. Rickett, *Guanzi*, 2:313.

80. *Guiguzi* ch. 10 (謀篇); cf. Cleary, *Thunder in the Sky*, 46. "Calculations" (數) is a broad term that includes mathematics and calendrics.

focus or, more accurately, a kind of triage that must be performed before we *can* focus.

Embrace the Unified Cosmos (抱一) and Know Yourself (自知)

We saw above, in Laozi's six suggestions, that the first idea was to "embrace the One." In the context of the *Laozi*, the "One" probably refers to the cosmic Way, but within the larger context of early Chinese intellectual history, this "One" may also be construed as a unified cosmos. To be sure, this could be a distinction without a difference: one the one hand, the cosmic Way is what unifies the cosmos; on the other, the cosmos simply *is* unified on its own, with or without a thing that unifies it. To say that the cosmos is "unified" means that it is interrelated and that we, as with everything else, are part of it. If this claim seems unexceptional, consider the ideologies that say we do not really belong here; that our "true home" is elsewhere (e.g., in "heaven"). In early China, such ideologies came into focus in the Han dynasty (202 BCE–220 CE), most prominently with the introduction of Buddhism from India. But for the scholars of pre-Han China, a complex, dynamic, integrated cosmos, within which humans sought to articulate their proper place and function, was the norm.

A unified cosmos of which humans are a part can be construed as a progenitor of the most fundamental kind. Given the ancient cultural practice of honoring ancestors, this makes it extremely venerable. Thus: "The One is that which all things most value; no one knows its origin or first appearance, no one knows its beginning or end, yet the myriad things take it to be their ancestor." (一也齊至貴；莫知其原，莫知其端；莫知其始，莫知其終，而萬物以為宗。)[81] The mystery of the cosmos, coupled with its comprehensibility (discussed above), make it singularly compelling. Humans have the mental capacity to analyze their environment and can therefore see its unity as well as its diversity. The dynamic aspect of this unity may be seen in the fact that, when conceived on the largest, cosmic scale, it is translated as "Way," but when conceived from a more modest, human point

---

81. *Lüshi chunqiu* ch. 3.5 (圜道); cf. Knoblock and Riegel, *The Annals of Lü Buwei*, 111.

of view, it is translated as "way."[82] Xunzi is referring to the latter here, albeit in maximal form: "The myriad things are but one facet of the [human] way, as each thing is but one facet of the myriad things. Foolish people take each thing as a [separable] facet, and thereby assume they know the way: this is to lack wisdom." (萬物為道一偏，一物為萬物一偏。愚者為一物一偏，而自以為知道，無知也。)[83] He goes on to adduce the "ways" of several scholars, lamenting the lack of unity across various human ideologies, and implicitly putting forth his own way as "*the* way" to unite them all. As the many human "ways" ideally might be combined into "the" way, so the innumerable, particular things may be conceived collectively as "the myriad things," which is to say, the unified cosmos. To have unbiased knowledge, then, is to "investigate things" in the context of theorizing that those things are all related, indeed, are all facets of a unified cosmos.[84]

This outlook is easily lost in the mix of human emotion and cognition. Zhuangzi characterizes this as a loss of objectivity due to preferences. For humans to prefer one thing over another is inevitable but, as with confirmation bias, it is still an inclination that can be consciously fought. "The myriad things are one: this is to take that which is beautiful as spiritous and wonderful, and that which is ugly as foul and rotten, as the foul and

---

82. As mentioned in the introduction, this is an English construct imposed on the Chinese, which makes no *explicit* distinction between "way" and "Way;" nevertheless, I find this distinction, derived from the context, to be a useful one, especially for non-specialists. Though I avoid such classifications in this book, generally speaking, Ruists (Confucians) focused on the human point of view (i.e., "way") and Daoists focused on the cosmic point of view (i.e., "Way").

83. *Xunzi* ch. 17 (天論); cf. Hutton, *Xunzi*, 181. Xunzi used this statement to preface a complaint about rival thinkers, whom he characterized as one-sided, and whom he wanted to corral into a comprehensive "way of [former] kings." But the statement, as a much larger claim, still stands, particularly in relation to the sentences that precede it. "The myriad things are but one facet of the [human] way," in context, means that the human way makes use of both the exterior, material world *as well as* interior, non-material things like protocol, sagely example, outer flexibility combined with inner fortitude, competence, and the inclinations of things.

84. This may be the meaning of the passage from the excavated *Liude* 六德: "The noble person not only perceives the incipient subtleties [of things] but also thereby knows their unity." (君子不啻明乎萌微而已，又以知其一矣。) cf. Cook, *The Bamboo Texts of Guodian*, 2:795.

rotten will [eventually] turn and develop into the spiritous and wonderful, while the spiritous and wonderful will [eventually] turn and develop into the foul and rotten. Thus [I] say: 'Simply merge with [or, understand] the world's unified *qi*-substance.' Sages therefore value [cosmic] unity." (萬物一也：是其所美者為神奇，其所惡者為臭腐；臭腐復化為神奇，神奇復化為臭腐。故曰「通天下一氣耳。」聖人故貴一。)[85]

The caveat here is three-fold. First, things change, so a beautiful flower today may be a moldy lump tomorrow. Second, our perceptions of things change, so a kind of flower we once thought beautiful we may no longer find attractive now. Third, perceptions change from person to person, so one person's beautiful flower is another person's ugly weed. This kind of relativism, or perspectivism, is one of Zhuangzi's major themes, one that is also found in the *Laozi*, which says, additionally, that the unity underlying the multiplicity can act as a model for a comprehensive, selfless attitude.[86] This attitude, according to Mengzi, will also bring happiness and goodness. "The myriad things are all complete in us. Honest self-inquiry: nothing brings more happiness than this. Practicing diligent considerateness: nothing is closer to seeking goodness than this." (萬物皆備於我矣。反身而誠：樂莫大焉。強恕而行：求仁莫近焉。)[87] That everything is "complete" in us is not a mystical claim, but rather a claim that we each belong to, and are part of, this world.[88] Self-inquiry, by itself, may or may not reveal our contexualization, but *honest* self-inquiry, according to this narrative, will.[89] "Considerateness" is the external manifestation of honest self-inquiry.[90]

Mengzi elsewhere says that "honest self-inquiry" consists of "perceiving [our own] competencies" (明乎善),[91] which is to say, realizing our

---

85. *Zhuangzi* ch. 22 (知北遊); cf. Watson, *Zhuangzi*, 177.

86. *Laozi* ch. 22: "Bent then whole, crooked then straight; empty then full, worn-out then new; without then with, abundant then uncertain. With this [i.e., this principle of change] the sage embraces the One to become a model for the world." (曲則全，枉則直；窪則盈，敝則新；少則得，多則惑。是以聖人抱一為天下式。)

87. *Mengzi* 孟子 ch. 7A4 (盡心上); cf. Bryan Van Norden, *Mengzi: With Selections from Traditional Commentaries* (Indianapolis: Hackett, 2008), 172.

88. The preposition "in" in the quote may thus be read in the sense of "with."

89. *Mengzi* ch. 4A12 (離婁上): "Honesty is the way of Heaven; thinking about [how to be] honest is the way of humans." (誠者，天之道也。思誠者，人之道也。) cf. Van Norden, *Mengzi*, 95.

90. Similarly, Buddhists claim that insight (*prajna*) and compassion (*karuna*) are necessarily related.

91. *Mengzi* ch. 4A12 (離婁上); cf. Van Norden, *Mengzi*, 95.

individual destinies (a topic that we shall discuss in chapter 9). But he does not say how this is to be done. Other authors say that self-inquiry may be facilitated by quiet introspection. Laozi seems to be describing something like meditation when he says that "those who know" (知者): "Block the openings, close the doors, blunt the sharpness, untangle the knots, soften the glare, and merge with the dust: this is called mysterious unity." (塞其兌，閉其門，挫其銳，解其紛，和其光，同其塵：是謂玄同。)[92] Zhuangzi's description is even more imaginative. In describing "mind nourishment" (心養) he says: "You need only abide in non-contrivance and things will develop themselves. Let your form and body fall away, release your senses, forget your relationships and [all] things, merge with the watery depths, relax your mind and unbind your spirit, empty and *hun*-soulless." (汝徒處無為，而物自化。墮爾形體，吐爾聰明，倫與物忘；大同乎涬溟，解心釋神，莫然無魂。)[93] These "watery depths" are, of course, not a physical place, but an imaginative space, a relaxed and open and formless state of mind. You may recall from chapter 1 that the "*hun*-soul" is the active soul; I doubt that to be "*hun*-soulless" literally means to be rid of it, but rather means to put the (over-) active mind into abeyance, the better to facilitate introspective self-inquiry.

Zhuangzi also depicted the embrace of the unified cosmos in colorful language. In one place he describes an aspirational figure as someone who "sometimes thinks he is a horse and sometimes thinks he is an ox" (一以己為馬，一以己為牛),[94] This is open-mindedness and merging with one's environment taken to a playful (and hyperbolic) extreme. Elsewhere he describes a sage in more expansive terms:

> The evidence that one is holding steadfastly to the beginning is real fearlessness. One brave officer will heroically enter [a battle with] nine divisions, but it is his seeking fame that enables him to want to do this. If is it like this, how much more so for one who takes Heaven and Earth as his office and the myriad things as his storehouse, who takes his body simply as a lodging place and sense-impressions as [mere] semblances: knowledge of unity is what he knows, and his mind never experiences death!

---

92. *Laozi* ch. 56.
93. *Zhuangzi* ch. 11 (在宥); cf. Watson, *Zhuangzi*, 81. "Senses" is, literally, "hearing and sight."
94. *Zhuangzi* ch. 7 (應帝王); cf. Watson, *Zhuangzi*, 55.

(夫保始之徵,不懼之實。勇士一人,雄入於九軍,將求名而能自要者。而猶若是,而況官天地,府萬物,直寓六骸,象耳目:一知之所知,而心未嘗死者乎!)⁹⁵

The "beginning" refers to cosmic unity, which was also just described above as the "One" (一) and as "unified *qi*-substance" (一氣); with introspection we can realize a "mysterious unity" (玄同) with it, dwelling, as it were, in its "watery depths" (滓溟). To "return" to such a state for temporary respite is one kind of advice; to drolly "lose yourself" among a herd of horses and oxen is another; but to actually identify with the cosmic unity is a decidedly more radical suggestion. That "his mind never experiences death" does not refer to some kind of post-mortem existence, but rather, for those who identify not with their particular bodies but with the unified cosmos as a whole, the death of the former in no way implies the death of the latter. Individual self-identification is common in the modern West; to identify primarily with the family lineage was common in premodern East Asia; some authors suggested we identify primarily with our human family, and others with our human community; but Zhuangzi asks us to consider identifying with the entire cosmos.

Self-inquiry that undertakes quiet introspection, that "blocks the openings and closes the doors," that "relaxes the mind and unbinds the spirit," and that, in some sense, "takes knowledge of unity" as what should be known, must include a rather esoteric state of mind. Imagine a (temporary) state of mind where the senses are curtailed and thinking is quieted, where you apprehend what is in your field of vision without identifying the individual items in it. One author reifies this perspective as a "mind within the mind." He writes: "Within the mind is another mind. Awareness precedes words; after awareness there is form; after form there is thought; after thought there is knowledge." (心之中又有心。意以先言,意然後形,形然後思,思然後知。)⁹⁶ The "form" that follows awareness and precedes thought refers to an unarticulated image, the apprehension that X differs from Y, but not yet the thought—which uses words—that specifies that difference. The author does not say if the "inner" mind includes only wordless awareness, or if it includes awareness plus the apprehension of form, with the "outer" mind

---

95. *Zhuangzi* ch. 5 (德充符); cf. Watson, *Zhuangzi*, 35.
96. *Guanzi* ch. 37 (心術下); cf. Rickett, *Guanzi*, 2:63. The first sentence also appears in *Guanzi* ch. 49 (內業); cf. Rickett, *Guanzi*, 2:47.

as the space for articulated thoughts and knowledge. But the spatial metaphors are just that, and ultimately the location of the division is irrelevant.

Self-inquiry that involves this kind of introspection achieves both self-knowledge as well as knowledge of the unified cosmos.

> What does it mean to inquire after it in oneself? It is to moderate the senses and regulate the desires, to be free of "wise" stratagems and be rid of scheming rationalizations, in order to let awareness roam in the temporary lodging of the limitless and engage the mind on the path of spontaneity. If one is like this then there will be nothing to harm one's Heavenly [allotment]. If there is nothing to harm one's Heavenly [allotment], then one will know the essence, and if one knows the essence, then one will know the spirit, and to know the spirit means to attain "the One."

> (何謂反諸己也？適耳目，節嗜欲，釋智謀，去巧故，而游意乎無窮之次，事心乎自然之塗。若此則無以害其天矣。無以害其天則知精，知精則知神，知神之謂得一。)[97]

One's "Heavenly [allotment]" is one's destiny, to which we shall return in chapter 9. It stands to reason that self-inquiry would facilitate realizing one's destiny. Knowing one's "essence" and "spirit" are, as discussed in chapter 1, matters of creativity. The former refers to creativity on a biological level, while the latter refers to it on a psychological level. Creativity requires open-mindedness, and to self-identify with the unified cosmos would require, to say the least, a great deal of open-mindedness.

Sagely People (聖人)

Sages are perhaps the quintessential aspirational figures for open-mindedness. The foundation for this lies in their relationship with Heaven and Earth.

---

97. *Lüshi chunqiu* ch. 3.4 (論人); cf. Knoblock and Riegel, *The Annals of Lü Buwei*, 106. The "it" that one is inquiring after in the first sentence is the "ruling way" (主道), which is mentioned in a previous passage. But the advice is not restricted to rulers. Also, the "wise" here may be sarcastic (it is difficult to tell when authors are joking), or it may be that the author is saying even truly wise stratagems should sometimes be temporarily abandoned, for the sake of experiencing unity with the unified cosmos.

We have already encountered the idea of "forming a triad with Heaven and Earth," and the sage indeed does this.[98] Sometimes this relationship is articulated in physical terms, other times in psychological terms. Physically, this can be expressed via the concepts of Yin and Yang: "The lives of sages are a Heavenly process, their death a transformation of things. In tranquility, their virtuosity is unified with Yin; in activity, their flow is unified with Yang." (聖人之生也天行，其死也物化；靜而與陰同德，動而與陽同波。)[99] It can also be described in terms of "essence," in that sages store it within themselves.[100] But sages are also thought of as cognitively self-cultivated and mentally astute. We saw above that "fulfilled people" (至人) use their minds objectively, like a mirror; the same is also true of sagely people.[101] One author compares the sage with the "genuine" person (to be discussed in chapter 8), claiming the former goes beyond the latter in word and deed: "Genuine people are one with Heaven. But those that inwardly cultivate and train [themselves] and know this [oneness] are called sages." (真人者，與天為一。內修練而知之，謂之聖人。)[102] In this passage, it is specifically the unified cosmos, inclusive of humans, that is the object of the sage's knowledge.

Being aware of, or embracing, the unified cosmos can, generally speaking, be done in two ways. One way is the quiet, introspective reflection of the "block the openings and close the doors" sort, whereby one might actually *feel*, in some deep way, that one is part of this unity. But it would be impractical to block one's senses all, or even much, of the time. Thus, the second way is just going about one's life with the background knowledge that we are inseparable from our larger environment. In everyday life, then, it is the natural principles that the sage follows.[103] These two ways are articulated in the opening chapter of the *Laozi*, where it describes two ways of experiencing the cosmic Way, also known as the "One," and

---

98. *Liji* 禮記 ch. 9 (禮運): "Sagely people form a triad with Heaven and Earth." (聖人參於天地。) cf. James Legge, *Li Chi: Book of Rites* (1885; rpt. New York: University Books, 1967), 1:37.

99. *Zhuangzi* ch. 15 (刻意); cf. Watson, *Zhuangzi*, 120.

100. *Guanzi* ch. 49 (內業): "In general, it is the essence of things by which they gain life. . . . [Those who] store it up within the breast are called sages." (凡物之精，此則為生。. . . 藏於胸中，謂之聖人。) cf. Rickett, *Guanzi*, 2:39.

101. *Zhuangzi* ch. 13 (天道): "The sage's mind in tranquility is a mirror of Heaven and Earth, a reflection of the myriad things." (聖人之心靜乎：天地之鑑也，萬物之鏡也。) cf. Watson, *Zhuangzi*, 98.

102. *Guiguzi* ch. 15 (本經陰符七術); cf. Cleary, *Thunder in the Sky*, 57.

103. *Zhuangzi* ch. 15 (刻意): "Sages . . . follow along with the [natural] principles of Heaven." (聖人 . . . 循天之理。) cf. Watson, *Zhuangzi*, 120.

here, referred to as "it": "[If you] abide in formlessness you may thereby observe its wonders, and [if you] abide in form you may thereby observe its manifestations." (常無，欲以觀其妙；常有，欲以觀其徼。)[104] Experiencing formlessness refers to apprehending the unified cosmos during introspective reflection, while experiencing form refers to the "investigation of things" by means of discovering, and making use of, natural principles.

Though natural principles inform all things, sages are partial to *living* things. We saw in chapter 1 that "Sagely people examine what is appropriate to Yin and Yang, and discern what is beneficial among the myriad things in order to improve life."[105] Elsewhere, it says quite plainly: "Sagely people deeply contemplated the world [and found] nothing more valuable than life." (聖人深慮天下，莫貴於生。)[106] Living things, of course, may thereby observe the sages themselves. We read in chapter 1 about the role of "essence," the creative edge of matter, which in humans might be construed generally as "health." If we preserve it, then:

> one's appearance will have a composed glow; stored within, it becomes a wellspring: floodlike, yet harmonious and equanimous, creating a deep pool of *qi*-substance. If this pool does not dry up, the [body's] four limbs will be firm; if this wellspring is not exhausted, the [body's] nine openings will remain clear. Then [you] will be able to explore all of Heaven and Earth and encounter [all within] the four seas [thus]: within, no delusions; without, no calamities; within, the mind will be complete; without, the body will be complete. Encountering neither Heaven's calamities nor human harm: [we] call them sagely people.
>
> (其外安榮，內藏以為泉原，浩然和平，以為氣淵。淵之不涸，四體乃固，泉之不竭，九竅遂通，乃能窮天地，被四海：中無惑意，外無邪菑。心全於中；形全於外。不逢天菑，不遇人害，謂之聖人。)[107]

---

104. *Laozi* ch. 1. Scholars disagree on the punctuation and interpretation of this famous passage; I follow the argument by Anthony Yu, "Reading the *Daodejing*: Ethics and Politics of Rhetoric," *Chinese Literature: Essays Articles Reviews* 25 (Dec. 2003): 165–87.
105. *Lüshi chunqiu* ch. 3.2 (盡數); see chap. 1, n. 107.
106. *Lüshi chunqiu* ch. 2.2 (貴生); cf. Knoblock and Riegel, *The Annals of Lü Buwei*, 80.
107. *Guanzi* ch. 49 (內業); cf. Rickett, *Guanzi*, 2:47–48. A passage similar to this in spirit, but quite different in wording, is in *Lüshi chunqiu* ch. 1.2 (本生); cf. Knoblock and Riegel, *The Annals of Lü Buwei*, 66.

Health, in both body and mind, is thus a central factor in the description of a sage. How one looks, how one feels, and how one's sense organs function all conspire to create a foundation for the task of successfully exploring the world.

One reason sages are successful in exploring the world is their willingness to help others. We saw in chapter 1 that "sagely people arose to instruct [them], [teaching] men the arts of plowing, sowing, and planting, in order to have the people eat."[108] Sometimes this beneficial activity of the sage is called "completing" others.[109] These sages "complete" others by helping them with new technologies (in our sources, these are things such as plows); by helping them to make their own inclinations and natures harmonious,[110] both within the individual and among individuals in a community; and even by helping them become more intelligent. In a conversation about some famous sages of old, Mengzi notes: "Heaven, in producing the people, causes those who *understand* things first, to awaken those who would understand things later; and causes those who *awaken* first, to awaken those who would awaken later." (天之生此民也，使先知覺後知，使先覺覺後覺也。)[111] Mengzi was something of a centrist when it came to the question of just how anthropomorphic Heaven is, but we do not need to mirror his ambivalence, and can take it as the creative aspect of the natural order. Looking at it this way, sages are, by nature, explorers, inventors, and teachers (though the obverse, of course, does not necessarily follow).

But sages, despite their considerable accomplishments, are not perfect, either by birth or by education. We saw in chapter 2 that several authors thought that sages and regular humans were of the same kind, with the same human nature. And when Mengzi was asked "Do even sages make mistakes?" (聖人且有過與？), he replied that they "do make mistakes, *but* then they rectify them" (過則改之).[112] Of course, their mistakes must first be

---

108. *Mozi* ch. 6 (辭過); see chap. 1, n. 36.

109. *Xunzi* ch. 10 (富國): "Heaven and Earth produce them [i.e., the people], but sagely people complete them." (天地生之，聖人成之。) cf. Hutton, *Xunzi*, 87.

110. *Kongzi jiayu* 孔子家語 ch. 7 (儀解) "Those who are called sages . . . complete the inclinations and natures [of other people and possibly other things]." (所謂聖者 . . . 成情性。) cf. Robert Kramers, *K'ung Tzu Chia Yü: The School Sayings of Confucius* (Leiden: E.J. Brill, 1949), 225.

111. *Mengzi* 5A7 (萬章上); cf. Van Norden, *Mengzi*, 127. Mengzi goes on to say that he is one of those to have awakened first.

112. *Mengzi* ch. 2B9 (公孫丑下); cf. Van Norden, *Mengzi*, 57.

brought to light, either by themselves or others, before they can be rectified. But the implication is that there is no shame in making mistakes, only in persisting in them once they have been discovered.

A few more observations may be made about sagely people. Unsurprisingly, they limit their desires.[113] We saw in the introduction that they "are not of two minds,"[114] which means they are focused. They are, of course, intelligent too, but their intelligence derives from both self-control and objectivity. Consider the following passage on sages, worth quoting in full:

> Actions follow the mind and the mind follows desires. For those whose desires lack moderation, their minds will [also] lack moderation, and for those whose minds lack moderation, then that which they would do cannot be known [because it will be chaotic]. Human minds are concealed and difficult to see; they are deep and difficult to gauge. Therefore sagely people observe the intentions in them [i.e., human minds]. That by which sagely people surpass other people is by foresight. Foresight always comes from the examination of evidence or indications, and without evidence or indications, then [although there may be] the desire for foresight, [even the sages] Yao and Shun would be the same as regular people. No matter whether evidence is easy [to find] or indications are difficult [to discern], sagely people will not rush, whereas the masses have no way [even] to arrive at them [i.e., evidence and indications]. Without a way to arrive [at them], they take [foresight] to be the work of spirits or [just] good luck. But it is neither the work of spirits nor good luck: this technique is indispensable.

> (事隨心，心隨欲。欲無度者，其心無度；心無度者，則其所為不可知矣。人之心隱匿難見，淵深難測，故聖人於事志焉。聖人之所以過人以先知。先知必審徵表，無徵表而欲先知，堯、舜與眾人同等。徵雖易，表雖難，聖人則不可以飄矣，眾人則無道至焉。無道至則以為神，以為幸。非神非幸：其數不得不然。)[115]

---

113. *Lüshi chunqiu* ch. 2.3 (情欲): "Sagely people cultivate and regulate [themselves] in order to restrain desires, which is why their actions do not exceed their inclinations." (聖人修節以止欲，故不過行其情也。) cf. Knoblock and Riegel, *The Annals of Lü Buwei*, 84.

114. *Xunzi* ch. 21 (解蔽); see introduction, n. 61.

115. *Lüshi chunqiu* ch. 20.5 (觀表); cf. Knoblock and Riegel, *The Annals of Lü Buwei*, 540–41. Note: 事 = 觀.

People are sometimes inscrutable, but human motivation often exhibits telltale signs that may be read by careful observation. The "foresight" that sagely people engage is seen in the passage above to consist precisely of this kind of observation. When trying to divine another person's hidden intentions, sages look for these telltale signs. In the example story that follows this passage, a sagely government envoy ingeniously "reads" the mind of a neighboring ruler by deduction worthy of Sherlock Holmes. He infers impending political chaos in that neighboring state by the less-than-joyful music played for him and by the expensive jade piece gifted to him. (The former reflected the ruler's general anxiety, and the latter suggested that he was distributing his treasures for safe-keeping.) The chapter concludes by saying that many situations—both personal and political—will have telltale signs that should be investigated before action is taken.[116]

While analyzing nonverbal evidence is crucial to sagely action, in a literate society, it may be more often the case that it is other people's verbal claims that need verifying. Our sources note: "Statements that are thought to be wrong often are right, and those that seem right are often wrong." (辭多類非而是，多類是而非。)[117] This observation has stood the test of time. The sagely approach to this problem, as we have seen, is to remain objective, to look for the "inclinations" (情) of the situation, which should exhibit "evidence" (徵) or "indications" (表) that are the signs of underlying "[natural] principles" (理).

This impartial approach to life results in a kind of freedom, which might be thought of as a kind of freedom both from uncertainty about how to act in the world and from unexamined subjectivity. The confusion stems from intemperate emotions and unbridled desires, particularly those for fame and power. Thus one author says that sagely people "are not perturbed by things" (不以物惑),[118] and another that "Sagely people are not mired in things, and so are able to change as the world changes." (聖人不凝滯於物，而能與世推移。)[119] Objectivity thereby abets flexibility; no one wants to be stuck. Yet, while sagely judgments about things change with new evidence and information, there remains an underlying commitment

---

116. Nowadays, this "foresight" is sometimes called "thin-slicing."
117. *Lüshi chunqiu* ch. 22.6 (察傳); cf. Knoblock and Riegel, *The Annals of Lü Buwei*, 584.
118. *Guanzi* ch. 26 (戒); cf. Rickett, *Guanzi*, 1:379.
119. *Chuci* 楚辭 ch. 7 (漁父); cf. David Hawkes, *Ch'u Tz'u: The Songs of the South* (1959; rpt. Boston: Beacon Press, 1962), 90.

to truth. "Sagely people pattern themselves on Heaven and venerate genuineness and thus are not constrained by tradition." (聖人法天貴真，不拘於俗。)[120] "Genuineness" (真) and "inclinations" (情) are abstractions, and understandings of them cannot but be contingent, not only on the things that we perceive, but also on the way in which we perceive them. Mental self-cultivation addresses this.

---

120. *Zhuangzi* ch. 31 (漁父); cf. Watson, *Zhuangzi*, 276.

PART II

ENVIRONMENT (地)

Chapter 4

Virtuosity (德)

"Set your heart on the way, rely on virtuosity, lean on goodness, and explore the arts."

—*Lunyu* 7.6

志於道,據於德,依於仁,游於藝。《論語。述而》

Introduction

Virtuosity (德) in early Chinese texts is usually social, functioning for the sake of communal harmony and political unity, but it also affects personal character growth and even physical grace. The meaning of the word evolved, in the time under consideration here, from the charisma of a popular leader to something much broader, referring to the "peak performance" of a given thing. (This is why it is sometimes translated as "power.") Thus, the "virtuosity" of water lies in its flexibility, and the "virtuosity" of humans lies in their ability to balance pursuing personal development with coexisting harmoniously in society. But virtuosity is conceived not only as an aspect of specific things, particularly humans: the cosmos also has its virtuosities. We saw them articulated in the introduction: "Heaven covers [all] without partiality; Earth bears [all] without partiality, the sun and moon shine [on all] without partiality, the four seasons proceed without partiality. [They] proceed with their virtuosities and the myriad things obtain consequent maturation with them."¹ Virtuosity is also sometimes paired with the cosmic Way, where it might play the active Yang role to the more fundamental Yin role. "The Way is open and formless, while virtuosity develops and nurtures the myriad things." (虛無無形謂之道，化育萬物謂之德。)² The two are connected—as Yin and Yang must be—shortly thereafter: "Virtuosity is the embodiment of the Way; things obtain it to live." (德者道之舍，物得以生。)³ This, then, is the broadest conception of virtuosity: making use of raw potential to create something concrete and specifically appropriate to the individual.

Virtuosity is aspirational and integral to self-cultivation. The *Shijing* notes its aspirational quality thus: "Virtuosity is as light as a feather, but few people are able to lift it." (德輶如毛，民鮮克舉之。)⁴ This is not because virtuosity is thought to be *only* aspirational or that the source of virtuosity is somewhere far off and all but unattainable.⁵ Virtuosity comes from within: "Noble people attend to the roots: when the roots are firmly established then the way will grow [from them]." (君子務本，本立而道生。)⁶ The way of virtuosity is, furthermore, not always unambiguous. The cosmic Way may not waver, but the way of humans is anything but set in stone. At the very least, we must carefully consider the options, for "Conduct that is not debated within oneself will not become established." (行莫辯於身者不立。)⁷ Finally, virtuosity in early Chinese texts is for naught if it is not put into practice. With just a hint of sarcasm, one author notes that "There are those who sit and discuss the way, and there are others who

---

1. *Lüshi chunqiu* 呂氏春秋 ch. 1.5 (去私); see introduction, n. 31.

2. *Guanzi* 管子 ch. 36 (心術上); cf. W. Allyn Rickett, *Guanzi: Political, Economic, and Philosophical Essays from Early China* (Princeton: Princeton University Press, 1985, 1998), 2:72.

3. *Guanzi* ch. 36 (心術上); cf. Rickett, *Guanzi*, 2:77.

4. *Shijing* 詩經 #260 (烝民); cf. Arthur Waley, *The Book of Songs: The Ancient Chinese Classic of Poetry* (1937; edited with additional translations by Joseph Allen; New York: Grove Press, 1996), 276.

5. As might be said, for example, of the Christian saying: "Be perfect, therefore, as your heavenly father is perfect." (Matthew 5:48)

6. *Lunyu* 論語 1.2; cf. Edward Slingerland, *Confucius: Analects with Selections from Traditional Commentaries* (Indianapolis: Hackett, 2003), 1.

7. *Mozi* 墨子 ch. 2.4 (修身); cf. John Knoblock and Jeffrey Riegel, *Mozi: A Study and Translation of the Ethical and Political Writings* (Berkeley: University of California, Berkeley, 2013), 50.

take action to put it into practice." (或坐而論道，或作而行之。)[8] Kongzi is well-known for his determination to make virtuosity a part of everyday life. He remarked upon his own practice that "To *not* cultivate virtuosity, to *not* expand upon what I have learned, to *not* follow what I have heard to be proper, and to *not* reform my incompetent ways: these are my concerns." (德之不修，學之不講，聞義不能徒，不善不能改：是吾憂也。)[9]

Fifteen Virtuosities (敬公讓忠勇，禮義孝仁智，慎柔恕誠和)

Virtuosity is also spoken of as having discrete components, particularly those relating to humans. There is no definitive list of virtues in our sources, but there are a few differing lists nevertheless. In fact, one of the classics—possibly the earliest—opens with one: "It is said that if [we] examine antiquity the Thearch Yao, [who was also] called Fangxun, was reverential, percipient, cultured, thoughtful, calmly steady, sincerely courteous, and capable of yielding." (曰若稽古帝堯，曰放勳：欽、明、文、思、安安、允恭、克讓。)[10] That this ruler was "yielding" does not mean he was spineless, but rather that he was amenable to persuasion: "yielding" is the opposite of "stubborn." A later chapter of the same text describes a list of "nine virtuosities" (九德) as juxtaposed sets of two: "generous yet careful, flexible yet grounded, sincere yet courteous, regulating yet respectful, easy-going yet resolute, upright yet warm, imposing yet modest, tough yet just, strong yet proper." (寬而栗、柔而立、愿而恭、亂而敬、擾而毅、直而溫、簡而廉、剛而塞、彊而義。)[11] Another classic advises us to "take precautions against the unforeseen, be cautious in your utterances, respectfully observe dignified ritual, be always flexible and good-tempered" (用戒不虞、慎爾出話、敬爾威儀、無不柔嘉); it then goes on to note that people have a tendency to remember injudicious remarks: "A flaw in a white jade tablet can still be polished away, but a defect in one's speech cannot be undone." (白圭之玷、尚可磨也，斯言之玷、不可為也。)[12] The implication is that virtuosity is, like Mengzi's sprouts

---

8. *Zhouli* 周禮 ch. 6 (考工記). The context for this quote deals with royal artisans, but I am confident that the observation would be considered widely applicable.

9. *Lunyu* 7.3; cf. Slingerland, *Analects*, 64.

10. *Shujing* 書經 ch. 1 (堯典); cf. James Legge, *The Shoo King*, 2nd ed. (1894; rpt. Hong Kong: Hong Kong University Press, 1960), 15.

11. *Shujing* ch. 4 (皋陶謨); cf. Legge, *Shoo King*, 71.

12. *Shijing* #256 (抑); cf. Waley, *The Book of Songs*, 264.

in chapter 2, something that must be worked at with continual vigilance. Underscoring the fragility and importance of virtuosity, Zhou King Mu (r. 956–918) is said to have carved in stone a list of nine virtuosities that he had inherited from his royal ancestors.[13]

Later lists exhibit more overlap with one another. One that purports to come from 609 BCE says "Filiality, respect, loyalty, and trustworthiness are good virtuosities, while robbery, rebellion, conspiracy, and betrayal are bad virtuosities." (孝敬忠信為吉德，盜賊藏姦為凶德。)[14] Kongzi apparently had a short list that was important enough to make it into the *Lunyu* twice: "The wise are not confused, the good are not anxious, the courageous are not afraid." (知者不惑；仁者不憂；勇者不懼。)[15] Texts ascribed to other scholars have other lists that are just as succinct. The *Guanzi* has protocol, propriety, candor, and a sense of shame (禮義廉恥), but another chapter lists the "nine virtuosities" as goodness, wisdom, propriety, good conduct, purity, bravery, integrity, tolerance, and eloquence (仁知義行潔勇精容辭).[16] The *Shizi* has goodness, propriety, loyalty, and trustworthiness (仁義忠信).[17] The *Wuxing*, excavated at Guodian, has goodness, propriety, protocol, wisdom, and sagacity (仁義禮智聖).[18] Another text excavated at Guodian, the *Liude*, or *Six Virtuosities*, has four of the five from the *Wuxing*, but pegs its six virtuosities to three relationships: wisdom and trustworthiness (智信) mark the husband-wife relationship, sagacity and goodness (聖仁) characterize the father-son relationship, while propriety and loyalty (義忠) are attributed

---

13. This, at any rate, is the interpretation of Guo Pu 郭璞 (276–324) on the first line of the sixth chapter of the *Mu tianzi zhuan* 穆天子傳. A translator of this text believes that this list survives in the c. 100 CE *Da Dai Li ji* 大戴禮記 ch. 72 (文王官人). See Cheng Te-k'un, "The Travels of Emperor Mu," *Journal of the North China Branch of the Royal Asiatic Society* 65 (1934): 141.

14. *Zuozhuan* 左傳 (文公 18); cf. Stephen Durrant, Wai-yee Li, David Schaberg, *Zuozhuan: Commentary on the 'Spring and Autumn Annals'* (Seattle: University of Washington Press, 2016), 1:573.

15. *Lunyu* 9.29 and 14.28; cf. Slingerland, *Analects*, 96 and 165.

16. *Guanzi* ch. 1 (牧民); cf. Rickett, *Guanzi*, 1:53; *Guanzi* ch. 39 (水地); cf. Rickett, *Guanzi*, 2:102. These nine are used to describe the virtuosities of jade.

17. *Shizi* 尸子 ch. 3 (四儀); cf. Paul Fischer, *Shizi: China's First Syncretist* (New York: Columbia University Press, 2012), 70.

18. *Wuxing* 五行; cf. Scott Cook, *The Bamboo Texts of Guodian* (Cornell: Cornell University East Asia Program, 2012), 1:486–87.

to the ruler-subject relationship.[19] The *Xunzi* tweaks this list slightly in its definition of the human "way" as "protocol, propriety, deference, the ability to yield, loyalty, and trustworthiness" (禮義辭讓忠信).[20] These later lists are both shorter and exhibit more reduplication among them than the earlier lists. Perhaps the authors were influenced by one another, or perhaps society as a whole was coming to define its virtuosities more specifically. In any case, we will proceed here by looking at fifteen virtuosities that were particularly important in our sources. Most, but not all, are mentioned in the lists above. It is necessary to have this many because the role of virtue in early Chinese intellectual history and early Chinese self-cultivation really cannot be over-emphasized.

The first early Chinese virtuosity really has to be (1) **respect** (敬). Even back when "virtuosity" referred primarily to the charisma of a leader, it was said that "respect brightens their virtuosity" (敬明其德).[21] Another meaning of the word translated here as "brighten" (明) is "percipient," so respect could also be understood here as making virtuosity more perceptive, in the sense of taking native charisma and socializing it to make it more useful and beneficial. Similarly, an early commentary on the *Yijing* notes that "noble people are respectful in order to be straight on the inside" (君子敬以直內) and that establishing respect (and propriety) results in "virtuosity that is not 'orphaned'" (德不孤).[22] "Brightening" and "straightening" are both metaphors for improving whatever degree of virtuosity one was born with. Shifting the metaphor yet again, "orphaned" virtuosity would surely be less effective than virtuosity informed by related virtuosities like respect. The *Zuozhuan* also says that respect is a kind of enhancement of generic virtuosity: "Respect is an accumulation of virtuosity. [If you] are able to be respectful, then [you] certainly [already] have virtuosity." (敬，德之聚也。能

---

19. *Liude* 六德; cf. Cook, *Bamboo Texts of Guodian*, 2:751–52. There are many things that I find admirable about early Chinese thought but, even while making allowances for the realities of the time, attributing wisdom to the husband and trustworthiness to the wife (even while noting that trustworthiness does *not* denote sexual fidelity) is not one of them.

20. *Xunzi* 荀子 ch. 16 (彊國); cf. Eric Hutton, *Xunzi: The Complete Text* (Princeton: Princeton University Press, 2014), 168.

21. *Shijing* #299 (泮水); cf. Waley, *The Book of Songs*, 311. The "their" refers to Lu Duke Xi 魯僖公 (r. 659–627).

22. *Yijing* 易經 #2 (坤), "Wen yan" (文言) commentary on line two; cf. Richard Lynn, *The Classic of Changes: A New Translation of the* I Ching *as Interpreted by Wang Bi* (New York: Columbia University Press, 1994), 147.

敬必有德。)²³ Given that respect is necessarily directed towards others, it may seem odd that, as the *Yijing* quote notes, it is good for one's interior, but respect must begin within one's person. Thus, another early text says that "As [a guide for] action, nothing is better than respect." (動莫若敬。)²⁴ Action is exterior movement, but it begins with interior intention. Respect, then, is a foundational virtuosity that, like all the virtuosities discussed here, involves both the inner and the outer, Yin *and* Yang.

That we should respect everyone may seem a modern notion, but our ancient sources concur. Xunzi said: "Respecting others has a [proper] way: if [they are] worthy people, then honor and respect them, and if [they are] unworthy then be apprehensive but [still] respect them; if [they are] worthy people then treat them like family and respect them, and if [they are] unworthy, then distance yourself from them but [still] respect them. In [both of] these cases the respect is the same, but the circumstances are different." (敬人有道：賢者則貴而敬之，不肖者則畏而敬之；賢者則親而敬之，不肖者則疏而敬之。其敬一也，其情二也。)²⁵ The context for this claim is not anything like the "inherent worth" of all people, entailing that everyone "deserves" respect, rather, it is simply what the good person (仁者) does.

Respect for others implies, at the very least, that our interactions with others begin in a manner that is fundamentally (2) **impartial** (公). This was seen as elementary in the political arena: "Anciently, when prior sage-kings ruled the world, [they] invariably began with impartiality, for if [they] were impartial, then the world would be equanimous. Equanimity is attained with impartiality." (昔先聖王之治天下也，必先公，公則天下平矣。平得於公。)²⁶ The text goes on to quote the advice of the *Shujing* to "not be partial and not be partisan" (無偏無黨)。²⁷ But impartiality was not just for rulers; it was seen as integral to the human "way." One text declares

---

23. *Zuozhuan* (僖公 33); cf. Durrant, Li, Schaberg, *Zuozhuan*, 1:453. As a slight rejoinder to my comment in note 19 above, the respect mentioned in this passage is in the context of a man who respected his wife so much that a passing official noticed it and recommended the man to his duke. (Who, coincidentally, was the Lu Duke Xi mentioned in note 21 above.)

24. *Guoyu* 國語 ch. 3 (周語下).

25. *Xunzi* ch. 13 (臣道); cf. Hutton, *Xunzi*, 139.

26. *Lüshi chunqiu* 呂氏春秋 ch. 1.4 (貴公); cf. John Knoblock and Jeffrey Riegel, *The Annals of Lü Buwei* (Stanford: Stanford University Press, 2000), 70.

27. *Shujing* ch. 32 (鴻範); cf. Legge, *Shoo King*, 331. *Zhuangzi* ch. 33 (天下) praises three early Chinese scholars, Peng Meng 彭蒙, Tian Pian 田駢, and Shen Dao 慎到, for being "impartial and nonpartisan" (公而不當).

that if "the great [human] way is followed, [the people of] the world will be impartial." (大道之行也，天下為公).²⁸ This was exemplified by treating people unrelated to you as family, and by caring for widows, orphans, and the disabled. In this way, impartiality was seen to underlie social justice generally. People respond well to being treated fairly, and society functions better with the kindness of strangers, but another reason for the importance of impartiality is that it increases one's own wisdom. Another text compares selfishness—that is, being partial to your own interests, which is the opposite of impartiality—to having tunnel-vision: "Being selfish-minded is [like] being in a well, while being broadminded [i.e., impartial-minded] is [like] being on a hilltop." (夫私心，井中也；公心，邱上也。)²⁹ Much more useful information is available to those who are impartial, making this virtuosity, too, beneficial for others as well as oneself.

The ability to (3) **yield to others** (讓) is the opposite of stubbornness, just as impartiality is the opposite of selfishness. It is a form of humility (謙), but it appears more often in our sources than does humility.³⁰ Perhaps the most conspicuous trait of the ancient sage-kings—who were the most prominent aspirational figures in our sources—was their celebrated penchant for yielding the throne to the most virtuous person rather than via a patrilineal line. The incongruity of this ideal with the actual practice of rulers keeping their power in their bloodline has always been a little comical.³¹ But we are concerned here with regular people and not just rulers. One early source claims: "The ability to yield is the mainstay of virtuosity, and is called 'excellent virtuosity.'" (讓，德之主也，謂懿德。)³² Another says "As

---

28. *Liji* 禮記 ch. 9 (禮運); cf. James Legge, *Li Chi: Book of Rites* (1885; rpt. New York: University Books, 1967), 1:364.

29. *Shizi* ch. 10 (廣); cf. Fischer, *Shizi*, 100. Quoted with fuller context in chap. 3, n. 13. I use "broadminded" in this quote rather than "impartial-minded" only because it fits the metaphor of "being on a hilltop" better.

30. *Yijing* #15 (謙) is a notable exception.

31. One possible exception was when Yan King Kuai 燕王噲 (r. 320–312) yielded the throne to the worthy Zi Zhi 子之, but the king's show of sagely virtuosity was promptly brought to an end when Qi King Xuan 齊宣王 (r. 319–301), spooked by this display of abdication, invaded Yan and restored the royal bloodline to the throne. See *Mengzi* 孟子 ch. 2B8–10 (公孫丑下) or *Hanfeizi* 韓非子 ch. 35 (外儲説右下). For a detailed analysis of this "incongruity," see Sarah Allan, *Buried Ideas: Legends of Abdication and Ideal Government in Early Chinese Bamboo-Slip Manuscripts* (Albany: State University of New York Press, 2015).

32. *Zuozhuan* (昭公 10); cf. Durrant, Li, Schaberg, *Zuozhuan*, 3:1455.

[a guide for] virtuosity, nothing is better than the ability to yield to others." (德莫若讓。)³³ Other texts provide fuller descriptions. "Noble people exalt others and diminish themselves, put others first and themselves last: thus the people come to exhibit the ability to yield." (君子貴人而賤己，先人而後己，則民作讓。)³⁴

We saw in chapter 2 that one of Mengzi's "four sprouts" within human nature was "deference" (辭讓) that may, with care, grow into protocol (禮). "Deference" is translated here from a compound word that contains both "deference" (辭) and "the ability to yield to others" (讓). Xunzi famously asserted that both of these virtuosities would, in a state of nature without socialization or education, vanish due to what he conceived as our innate desire for profit. But regardless of whether or not we perceive the ability to yield to be natural or not, it is important to remember that it is an *ability* to yield that is under consideration, and not an *imperative* to yield. Kongzi is China's archetypal teacher, yet even he said: "When it comes to being good, do not yield [to others, even] to your teacher." (當仁，不讓於師。)³⁵ Children should "defer" to adults, and subordinates should defer to their superiors, but any person, in any social position, should "yield," when practicable, to those more *competent* than themselves. Knowing when someone else is more competent than you is a matter of broad-mindedness (to be discussed below).

(4) **Loyalty** (忠) is an obvious social asset, even though the vagaries of exactly when to withdraw loyalty are typically uncertain. Loyalty is also not a one-way street, something that inferiors owe to superiors. The *Zuozhuan* defines loyalty six times, and the first explicitly says loyalty can be something that rulers display to their subjects: "Superiors thinking about how to benefit the people is loyalty." (上思利民，忠也。)³⁶ Admittedly, the loyalty that subjects give to their rulers is couched in more extensive terms: "To know that which benefits the lord's household, and doing anything [for it], is loyalty." (公家之利，知無不為，忠也。)³⁷ Seen from both the perspective of ruler and ruled, then, it is fair to say that "Loyalty is the guarantor of the

---

33. *Guoyu* ch. 3 (周語下).
34. *Liji* ch. 30 (坊記); cf. Legge, *Li Chi*, 2:287.
35. *Lunyu* 15.36; cf. Slingerland, *Analects*, 188.
36. *Zuozhuan* (桓公 6); cf. Durrant, Li, Schaberg, *Zuozhuan*, 1:97.
37. *Zuozhuan* (僖公 9); cf. Durrant, Li, Schaberg, *Zuozhuan*, 1:295.

state" (忠，社稷之固也) and "Loyalty is to not forget the state when faced with trouble." (臨患不忘國，忠也。)³⁸ A couple of broader definitions are that "Loyalty is the correctness of virtuosity" (忠，德之正也) and "loyalty is to not be selfish." (無私，忠也)³⁹ These last two definitions, when brought back to the political arena of ruler and ruled, provide the basis for what loyalty ideally looks like.

Early China has a long tradition of advisors to the king speaking honest words of advice and getting punished, and sometimes killed, for it. Thus one source says: "Perfect loyalty is contrary to the ear and inverts the mind: who but a worthy ruler is able to listen to it?" (至忠逆於耳、倒於心: 非賢主其孰能聽之？)⁴⁰ Another asks, rhetorically, "[If you] are loyal to someone [in a position above you], can [you really] *not* instruct them?" (忠焉，能勿誨乎？)⁴¹ The answer, of course, is that real loyalty will necessarily include honest feedback. A good ruler, moreover, must not only listen to good advice (though not necessarily follow it), he must treat his advisors with respect.⁴² It should be noted that while "loyalty" generally refers to the political arena, it does have a broader semantic range. One text says we should "loyally advise and competently guide" (忠告而善道) our friends.⁴³ Another says that "parents [should] act with loyal affection" (忠愛，父母之行也).⁴⁴ Therefore, while "loyalty" typically refers to an unequal political or economic relationship, it is also possible to be a loyal friend and a loyal family member.

Here, "loyalty" overlaps with "trustworthiness" (信), a virtuosity often paired with loyalty that primarily refers to being "as good as one's word." Zengzi famously said: "Every day I examine myself in three ways: Have I

---

38. *Zuozhuan* (成公 2); cf. Durrant, Li, Schaberg, *Zuozhuan*, 2:729. *Zuozhuan* (昭公 1); cf. Durrant, Li, Schaberg, *Zuozhuan*, 3:1309. *She ji* 社稷 refer to the altars to the spirits of the land and grain, which were maintained by the state.
39. *Zuozhuan* (文公 1); cf. Durrant, Li, Schaberg, *Zuozhuan*, 1:467; *Zuozhuan* (成公 9); cf. Durrant, Li, Schaberg, *Zuozhuan*, 2:781.
40. *Lüshi chunqiu* ch. 11.2 (至忠); cf. Knoblock and Riegel, *The Annals of Lü Buwei*, 244.
41. *Lunyu* 14.7; cf. Slingerland, *Analects*, 156.
42. *Lüshi chunqiu* ch. 14.2 (本味); cf. Knoblock and Riegel, *The Annals of Lü Buwei*, 308.
43. *Lunyu* 12.23; cf. Slingerland, *Analects*, 136.
44. *Shizi* ch. 8 (治天下); cf. Fischer, *Shizi*, 95.

been disloyal in making plans with others? Have I been untrustworthy in communicating with friends and acquaintances? Have I not put into practice [the lessons that I] have been taught?" (吾日三省吾身：為人謀而不忠乎？與朋友交而不信乎？傳不習乎？)[45] That is a telling checklist from one of Kongzi's most illustrious students. A short text excavated from Guodian, entitled *Zhongxin zhidao*, or *The Way of Loyalty and Trustworthiness*, echoes his perspective. It opens with the sentence: "To neither mislead nor conceal is the height of loyalty; to not deceive the uninformed is the height of trustworthiness." (不訛不慆，忠之至也；不欺弗智，信之至也。)[46] These two virtuosities, then, are closely related, but given the political bent of so many of our sources, loyalty claims a more prominent position within them.

Loyalty in early China typically involves someone in a lower and vulnerable position giving honest advice to someone in a higher and more powerful position. It therefore requires a degree of (5) **courage** (勇), a virtuosity that is desirable on the battlefield as well as in life in general. It is defined in terms of decisiveness: "To confront matters with habitual decisiveness is called courage." (臨事而屢斷，勇也。)[47] It is also defined as an ability to be fearless.[48] As in English, "courage" naturally conjures images of the battlefield. "In warfare, although noble people may have troops [to command, they know that] it is courage that is fundamental to them i.e., the troops]." (君子戰雖有陳，而勇為本焉。)[49] As we might expect, this kind of courage is described in martial terms: "To know that death [is imminent] and yet to not avoid it is courage." (知死不辟，勇也。)[50] A description of the "courage" of jade may also be extended back to the soldier: "To break without bending is courage." (折而不撓，勇也。)[51] Such a maxim would be counterintuitive in every other human situation, but the battlefield is a peculiar place.

The peculiarity of warfare, and of the courage necessary to it, is evident in this passage:

---

45. *Lunyu* 1.4; cf. Slingerland, *Analects*, 2.
46. *Zhongxin zhidao* 忠信之道; cf. Cook, *Bamboo Texts of Guodian*, 1:577.
47. *Liji* ch. 19 (樂記); cf. Legge, *Li Chi*, 2:130.
48. *Mengzi* 孟子 ch. 2A2 (公孫丑上); cf. Bryan Van Norden, *Mengzi: With Selections from Traditional Commentaries* (Indianapolis: Hackett, 2008), 36.
49. *Mozi* ch. 2 (修身); cf. Knoblock and Riegel, *Mozi*, 48.
50. *Zuozhuan* (昭公 20); cf. Durrant, Li, Schaberg, *Zuozhuan*, 3:1571.
51. *Guanzi* ch. 39 (水地); cf. Rickett, *Guanzi*, 2:102.

In general, weapons are the most perilous of instruments, and courage is the most perilous of virtuosities. [One should] raise a perilous instrument or act with perilous virtuosity only when it is unavoidable. [One should] raise a perilous instrument when it is necessary to kill, and killing should be for the sake of the lives [of others]. [One should] act with perilous virtuosity when it is necessary to be forceful, and forcefulness should be for the sake of intimidating [others]. When the enemy is intimidated and the people live: this is why proper soldiers are honored.

(凡兵，天下之凶器也；勇，天下之凶德也。舉凶器，行凶德，猶不得已也。舉凶器必殺；殺，所以生之也。行凶德必威；威，所以懼之也。敵懼民生：此義兵之所以隆也。)⁵²

But the battlefield is not the only place where courage is requisite. The virtuosities that make one fit for battle also equip one for civil service: "Those who are courageous, daring, and strong: when there are no matters [of war] in the realm, then [one] employs them for [matters of] protocol and propriety; and when there *are* matters [of war] in the realm, then [one] employs them for warfare and victory." (故勇敢強有力者，天下無事，則用之於禮義；天下有事，則用之於戰勝。)⁵³ Therefore, whether at war or during peacetime, a noble person always "enacts the principles of the [human] way with courage" (行道理也勇).⁵⁴

The efficacy of courage depends, in part, on temperance. Xunzi says, in two separate places, that courage must be balanced with apprehension (憚) or diffidence (怯) in order to function properly.⁵⁵ Other authors maintain that courage must be integrated with other virtuosities such as protocol (禮) or propriety (義), both of which will be discussed below.⁵⁶ Courage can thus be seen as important, but something that should be handled with care. It is also a virtuosity that can be applicable in a number of situations.

---

52. *Lüshi chunqiu* ch. 8.2 (論威); cf. Knoblock and Riegel, *The Annals of Lü Buwei*, 194. For more specific battlefield guidelines, see *Xunzi* ch. 15 (議兵).
53. *Liji* ch. 48 (聘義); cf. Legge, *Li Chi*, 2:463.
54. *Xunzi* ch. 2 (修身); cf. Hutton, *Xunzi*, 15.
55. *Xunzi* ch. 6 (非十二子) and ch. 28 (宥坐); cf. Hutton, *Xunzi*, 43 and 318.
56. See *Liji* ch. 28 (仲尼燕居) and *Lunyu* 2.24, 17.23; cf. Legge, *Li Chi*, 2:270 and Slingerland, *Analects*, 16, 210–11.

Zhuangzi describes the courage of fishermen, hunters, warriors, and sages, each of whom have their own difficulties to confront.[57]

Courage is also depicted as something that may not always be available to one, even if it is desired. Shizi gave several examples of "courageous people who [sometimes] also acted with diffidence" (勇而能怯者).[58] One source locates the reason for this variation in one's physical health: "People are neither constantly courageous nor constantly diffident. If [they] have [sufficient] *qi*-substance, then [they] will be replete, which [may] lead to courage, and if [they] lack [sufficient] *qi*-substance, then [they] will be depleted, which [may] lead to diffidence." (夫民無常勇，亦無常怯。有氣則實，實則勇；無氣則虛，虛則怯。)[59] The author goes on to admit that the causes for this fluctuation in *qi*-substance are "very subtle" and that only sages can understand them. This, unfortunately, leaves the reader with little practical advice, but "*qi*-substance" here may well refer to something more metaphorical than literal. That is, whatever the "spirit" in the English phrase "fighting spirit" may refer to, it likely is also what is being referred to with "*qi*-substance" in this passage. In any case, understanding that courage is a virtuosity requiring balance should lead one to a greater appreciation of the balance required to navigate the cultural norms of protocol.

The importance of (6) **protocol** (禮) in early Chinese culture was enormous, as it articulated how people should ideally interact with one another in a wide variety of situations. Protocol includes all the actions we do for social cohesion and harmony: greeting others with "good morning," stopping at red lights, standing in line at the checkout. We saw above that Mengzi claimed that protocol was the result of the nurturing of an innate sense of "deference" (辭讓). Others defined protocol in terms of "respect" (敬), implying that protocol is an external manifestation of this internal attitude.[60] The *Liji*, or *Protocol Records*, as its name implies, is singularly interested in this topic and conceives this virtuosity in even broader terms. In one chapter, it says that protocol "is simply the ordering of affairs" (即事之治也); in another, it notes that "worthy people" (賢者), "[in matters

---

57. *Zhuangzi* 莊子 ch. 17 (秋水); cf. Burton Watson, *The Complete Works of Zhuangzi* (New York: Columbia University Press, 1968; 2013), 134.
58. *Shizi* ch. 15 (君治); cf. Fischer, *Shizi*, 117.
59. *Lüshi chunqiu* ch. 8.4 (決勝); cf. Knoblock and Riegel, *The Annals of Lü Buwei*, 200.
60. *Mozi* 墨子 ch. 40 (經上); cf. Ian Johnston, *The Mozi: A Complete Translation* (New York: Columbia University Press, 2010), 380. Mengzi too, in ch. 4B28 (離婁下), says "the person who acts with protocol respects others" (有禮者敬人); cf. Van Norden, *Mengzi*, 111.

of] protocol, follow what is appropriate" (禮從宜).⁶¹ It further says that the cultivation of protocol is the means by which we should pursue external self-cultivation.⁶² Xunzi, the early Chinese scholar who emphasized protocol the most, tweaks this claim only slightly when he says that it is the means by which we can "correct our persons."⁶³ He also defines protocol more generally, as simple "orderliness" (節).⁶⁴ Another author avers that "Protocol is for the [correct] expression of [one's] inclinations, [just as] culture is for the [correct] embellishment of [one's] substance." (禮為情貌者也，文為質飾者也。)⁶⁵ Ideally, protocol just makes social life easier and more elegant.

Protocol is not the same as ritual or ceremony (儀), though their meanings overlap. One story in the *Zuozhuan* differentiates the two, describing courteous activities such as "saluting" (揖) as ritual or ceremony, but describes protocol in much broader terms: "Protocol is the mainstay of Heaven and the propriety of Earth, and is how people [should] conduct themselves." (夫禮：天之經也，地之義也，民之行也。)⁶⁶ If we recall from chapter 1 that humans are inescapably contextualized within the natural world, this claim makes more sense. Both the *Liji* and the *Xunzi* also contextualize human protocol in this way. The former says "In general, protocol's greatest expressions are expressions of Heaven and Earth, modelled on the four seasons, regulated by Yin-Yang, and in accord with human inclinations." (凡禮之大體，體天地，法四時，則陰陽，順人情。)⁶⁷ The latter, meanwhile, says "Protocol has three roots: Heaven and Earth are the roots of life; predecessors and ancestors are the roots of one's kind; leaders and teachers are the roots of social order." (禮有三本：天地者，生之本也；先祖者，類之本也；君師者，治之本也。)⁶⁸ While these accounts provide us with a wider scope, protocol is also said to have its origins in the individual.

---

61. *Liji* chs. 28 (仲尼燕居) and 1 (曲禮上); cf. Legge, *Li Chi*, 2:272 and 1:63.
62. *Liji* ch. 8 (文王世子): "Protocol is the means for cultivating [one's] exterior." (禮：所以修外也); cf. Legge, *Li Chi*, 1:349.
63. *Xunzi* ch. 2 (修身): "Protocol is the means for correcting the self" (禮者：所以正身也); cf. Hutton, *Xunzi*, 14.
64. *Xunzi* ch. 27 (大略): "Protocol is orderliness" (禮：節也); cf. Hutton, *Xunzi*, 292.
65. *Hanfeizi* ch. 20 (解老); cf. Liao Wengui, *The Complete Works of Han Fei Tzu* (London: Arthur Probsthain, 1939, 1959), 1:173.
66. *Zuozhuan* (昭公 25); cf. Durrant, Li, Schaberg, *Zuozhuan*, 3:1637.
67. *Liji* ch. 49 (喪服四制); cf. Legge, *Li Chi*, 2:465. The Guodian text *Xingzi mingchu* 性自命出 also connects protocol with human inclinations: "Protocol arose from human inclinations, but it also elevates them." (禮作於情，又興之也。) cf. Cook, *Bamboo Texts of Guodian*, 2:714.
68. *Xunzi* ch. 19 (禮論); cf. Hutton, *Xunzi*, 202.

Xunzi elsewhere describes protocol in strictly human terms.

> How did protocol come about? [I] say: People are born with desires, and if desires are not fulfilled, then they cannot do other than seek [fulfillment]. If this seeking is without measure or boundaries, then they cannot do other than fight [with one another]. Fighting brings disorder, which brings hardship. Former kings hated this disorder, and therefore created the allocations of protocol and propriety, in order to [properly] nourish human desire and [properly] fulfill human seeking. [They] made it so that desire would not exhaust resources and resources would not be depleted by desire, so that these two would both work together and flourish. This is how protocol came about.
>
> (禮起於何也？曰：人生而有欲，欲而不得，則不能無求。求而無度量分界，則不能不爭；爭則亂，亂則窮。先王惡其亂也，故制禮義以分之，以養人之欲，給人之求。使欲必不窮於物，物必不屈於欲，兩者相持而長。是禮之所起也。)[69]

The manner in which protocol is related to social harmony, broadly speaking, as well as to other virtues, is also remarked upon in our sources. The *Shijing* asks, rhetorically and rather baldly: "People who do not act with protocol: why don't they just quickly die?" (人而無禮，胡不遄死？)[70] It is unclear if the author is suggesting that discourteous people go and end their lives for the sake of social harmony, or if he is observing that discourteous people will likely not last long in societies that value harmony (as all, to some extent, surely do). As colorful as the first interpretation may be, the latter is supported by Xunzi's claim that protocol—that is, orderliness on cosmic, social, and individual scales—is necessary for harmony and health. He predicates protocol as the smooth functioning of things as disparate as the movement of the stars in the sky to the flow of blood in our veins.

Other authors note that protocol is necessarily involved in the efficacious functioning of different virtuosities. Kongzi is on record making such connections twice. In one, he says "Protocol that does not have respect at its core will be called uncouth; protocol that does not have courtesy at its core will be called glib; protocol that does not have courage at its core will be called disingenuous." (敬而不中禮，謂之野；恭而不中禮，謂之給；勇而不中禮，

---

69. *Xunzi* ch. 19 (禮論); cf. Hutton, *Xunzi*, 201.
70. *Shijing* #52 (相鼠); cf. Waley, *The Book of Songs*, 43.

VIRTUOSITY (德)

謂之逆。)[71] In another, he says that "Courtesy without protocol is tiresome; prudence without protocol is timid; courage without protocol is reckless, frankness without protocol is impatient." (恭而無禮則勞；慎而無禮則葸；勇而無禮則亂；直而無禮則絞。)[72] From both of these pronouncements, we can see that protocol is the proper exteriorization of a variety of internal attitudes. This goes some ways to account for its versatility and breadth of application.

The first chapter of the *Liji* describes the scope of protocol thus:

> Protocol is that which defines [how one acts toward] near and distant relatives, decides [how to deal with] suspicious or doubtful [matters], discriminates [what makes matters] similar or different, and clarifies right and wrong. With protocol, [one] does not recklessly [try to] please others, and does not waste words. With protocol, [one] does not exceed what is proper: [one] does not encroach upon or insult [others], nor curry favor [with them]. Self-cultivation and keeping one's word are known as competent behaviors. Conduct that is cultivated and words that are [in accord with] the [human] way are the substance of protocol.
>
> (夫禮者所以定親疏，決嫌疑，別同異，明是非也。禮，不妄說人，不辭費。禮，不逾節，不侵侮，不好狎。修身踐言，謂之善行。行修言道，禮之質也。)[73]

But other authors acknowledge that the range of human activities to which protocol might reasonably apply is almost limitless. Some note that the social rules of protocol can and should be adapted to the situation at hand; others note that we essentially create our own protocols through our particular actions.[74] Given the fluid environment of the creation and

---

71. *Liji* ch. 28 (仲尼燕居); cf. Legge, *Li Chi*, 2:270.
72. *Lunyu* 8.2; cf. Slingerland, *Analects*, 78.
73. *Liji* ch. 1 (曲禮上); cf. Legge, *Li Chi*, 1:63. However, much of the *Liji* is actually dedicated to protocol associated with six ceremonies: capping (i.e., coming of age), marriage, funerals, sacrifices, feasts, and interviews (冠、昏、喪、祭、鄉、相見).
74. For the former, see *Hanshi waizhuan* 韓詩外傳 ch. 4.12; cf. James Hightower, *Han Shih Wai Chuan: Han Ying's Illustrations of the Didactic Application of the Classic of Songs* (Cambridge: Harvard University Press, 1952), 137. For the latter, see *Hanfeizi* ch. 20 (解老): "In general, when people respond to external things, they do not know they are enacting their personal protocols." (凡人之為外物動也，不知其為身之禮也。) cf. Liao, *Han Fei Tzu*, 1:172.

evolution of protocol on both the social and individual scales, it is clear that we should pay attention to our context. Rather than passively accept the protocol to which we are exposed while growing up, we should think about ourselves and our place in the wider community. One author says "Only after you know yourself will you know others, only after you know others will you know protocol, and only after you know protocol will you know how to act." (知己而後知人，知人而後知禮，知禮而後知行。)[75] The motivation to know protocol is perpetuated by an inner sense of wanting to do the right thing. It is to this virtuosity that we turn next.

(7) **Propriety** (義) is the internal side of the coin to external protocol; it is the desire to live a healthy life in a harmonious society.[76] The *Liji* says that protocol is the "realization" (實) and "bringing forth" (達) of inner propriety.[77] Other authors aver that protocol is the "embodiment" (體) and the "civilized display" (文) of propriety.[78] One origination story goes like this: "When father and son are affectionate, then propriety is born. Once propriety has been born, then protocol arises. Once protocol has arisen, then the myriad things will be stable. To be without distinctions [i.e., between Heaven and Earth, father and son, etc.] and without propriety is the way of animals." (父子親，然後義生。義生，然後禮作。禮作，然後萬物安。無別無義，禽獸之道也。)[79] Xunzi agreed with the last statement and gave a slightly more detailed taxonomy: "Water and fire have *qi*-substance but are without life. Grasses and trees have life but are without awareness. Birds and beasts have awareness but are without propriety. People have *qi*-substance, life, awareness, and also propriety, which is why they are the most honorable in all the world." (水火有氣而無生，草木有生而無知，禽獸有知而無義，人有氣、有生、有知，亦且有義，故最為天下貴也。)[80] Like protocol, propriety is predicated on that which is appropriate:

---

75. Guodian *Yucong, yi* 語叢一; cf. Cook, *Bamboo Texts of Guodian*, 2:831.

76. Propriety is also a vague term in a similar sense to the English idea that one may want to do what is "proper" or "right." This vagueness is complicated both by the semantic range of the word which, among other things, includes "meaning," as well as its interchangeability, in some contexts, with the word *yi* 儀 (ritual or ceremony).

77. *Liji* ch. 9 (禮運); cf. Legge, *Li Chi*, 1:390, 1:393.

78. *Huainanzi* 淮南子 ch. 11 (齊俗); cf. John Major, Sarah Queen, Andrew Meyer, and Harold Roth, *The Huainanzi: A Guide to the Theory and Practice of Government in Early Han China* (New York: Columbia University Press, 2010), 409. *Hanfeizi* ch. 20 (解老); cf. Liao, *Han Fei Tzu*, 1:171.

79. *Liji* ch. 11 (效特牲); cf. Legge, *Li Chi*, 1:440.

80. *Xunzi* ch. 9 (王制); cf. Hutton, *Xunzi*, 76.

Propriety is that which is appropriate to each situation. Protocol [both] relies upon human inclinations and follows along with the principles of propriety, as well as being that which regulates [the inclinations] and patterns [the principles]. Thus, protocol is said to have principles, and these principles clarify allocations in order to articulate the meaning of propriety. Thus, protocol grows out of propriety, propriety grows out of principles, and principles rely on that which is appropriate.

(義者，謂各處其宜也。禮者，因人之情，緣義之理，而為之節文者也。故禮者謂有理也，理也者，明分以諭義之意也。故禮出乎義，義出乎理，理因乎宜者也。)[81]

We saw in chapter 2 that Mengzi was of the opinion that propriety was a mature virtuosity that grew out of an inborn sense of shame that required cultivation. Xunzi, on the other hand, felt that propriety was invented by sages to be instilled in us by socialization and education.[82] It is, however, not too difficult to agree with both of these positions, that humans have some innate sense of right and wrong that is thereby amplified by our respective cultures. A separate question is: is our sense of propriety—our "conscience" or "proto-conscience"—the same for everyone? The answer seems to be: usually no, but sometimes yes; that is, it is different for everyone except for those who know the human way or cosmic Way, in which case their senses of propriety *will* be the same.[83] Such people can then go on to "use propriety to change and respond [to various situations]" (以義變應).[84] These various situations can be both interior and exterior. On the one hand, "Noble people are able to use impartiality and propriety to overcome selfish desires." (君子之能以公義勝私欲也。)[85] On the other, exterior "laws are produced

---

81. *Guanzi* ch. 36 (心術上); cf. Rickett, *Guanzi*, 2:77.
82. *Xunzi* ch. 23 (性惡): "In general, protocol and propriety are created by the contrivance of sages." (凡禮義者，是生於聖人之偽。) cf. Hutton, *Xunzi*, 250.
83. *Mozi* ch. 12 (尚同中): "People of the world [all] have different proprieties." (天下之人異義。), cf. Knoblock and Riegel, *Mozi*, 117. He goes on to say that ancient sage-kings unified the various senses of propriety into one. *Hanfeizi* ch. 14 (姦劫弒臣): "Those who know [the Way and virtuosity] agree in propriety but differ in customs." (知之者，同於義而異於俗。) cf. Liao, *Han Fei Tzu*, 1:125.
84. *Xunzi* ch. 3 (不苟); cf. Hutton, *Xunzi*, 18.
85. *Xunzi* ch. 2 (修身); cf. Hutton, *Xunzi*, 15.

from propriety" (法生於義).[86] Kongzi expressed the foundational aspect of propriety when he said: "Noble people take propriety as their substance, protocol as its vehicle, modesty as its expression, and trustworthiness as its completion." (君子義以為質，禮以行之，孫以出之，信以成之。)[87] In this way, it is a basic building block of virtuosity.

But while propriety is basic to early Chinese self-cultivation, its more advanced form remains aspirational. "Principled propriety is in short supply in the world, while reckless negligence is abundant." (世之所不足者，理義也；所有餘者，妄苟也。)[88] We saw above that propriety grows out of principles, so all propriety is, in some sense, "principled propriety," but this author is certainly referring to a kind of propriety that has more fully realized its roots. Similarly, Xunzi said "If [you] practice propriety with an honest mind, then [you] will be principled, and if principled, then [you] will be percipient." (誠心行義則理，理則明。)[89] One of our earliest sources puts the responsibility for such propriety squarely on ourselves: "When Heaven looks down upon the people below, it measures their propriety, and sends down years that are either long-lasting or not long-lasting. It is not that Heaven causes people to die prematurely, [but rather that] people cut short their own destinies." (惟天監下民，典厥義，降年有永有不永。非天夭民，民中絕命。)[90] However, while propriety thus plays an important role in self-cultivation, informing protocol in particular but also influencing social interactions in general, it additionally influences how we experience the small, individual pleasures in life. Kongzi famously noted: "Eating plain food and drinking [plain] water, with a bent arm as a pillow: happiness may be found even in this. To be rich and honored but without propriety is to me [as ephemeral and pointless] as floating clouds." (飯疏食飲水，曲肱而枕之，樂亦在其中矣。不義而富且貴，於我如浮雲。)[91] This sentiment brings us back to the very basics of how to live the good life.

---

86. *Huainanzi* ch. 9 (主術); cf. Major, Queen, Meyer, and Roth, *Huainanzi*, 320.
87. *Lunyu* 15.18; cf. Slingerland, *Analects*, 181.
88. *Lüshi chunqiu* ch. 19.1 (離俗); cf. Knoblock and Riegel, *The Annals of Lü Buwei*, 474.
89. *Xunzi* ch. 3 (不苟); cf. Hutton, *Xunzi*, 19–20.
90. *Shujing* ch. 24 (高宗肜日); cf. Legge, *Shoo King*, 264–66. This quote was also used in the introduction, n. 34. The *Zuozhuan* (隱公 1) concurs, without mentioning any actions of Heaven: "Often doing what is not proper will certainly result in your own death." (多行不義，必自斃。) cf. Durrant, Li, Schaberg, *Zuozhuan*, 1:9.
91. *Lunyu* 7.16; cf. Slingerland, *Analects*, 69.

Early Chinese authors located the root of several important virtuosities within the first human interactions: that of a child with its parents. The general feeling of "looking up to" one's parents is called (8) **filiality** (孝). As with protocol, filiality has its own eponymous classic, and the *Xiaojing*, or *Filiality Classic* begins, perhaps unsurprisingly, by saying that filiality is the "root" (本) of all virtuosity. It continues with a fundamental Chinese idea: "The body, [even down to the] hair and skin, were received from one's father and mother, and [therefore we] do not risk harm or injury [to it]: this is the *beginning* of filiality. Establishing ourselves and walking the [proper human] way, elevating the family name for posterity in order to extol our parents: this is the *completion* of filiality." (身體髮膚，受之父母，不敢毀傷，孝之始也。立身行道，揚名於後世，以顯父母，孝之終也。)[92] We ought not "risk harm or injury" to ourselves because we should be healthy in order to take care of our parents when they are old, just as they took care of us when we were young. An earlier classic, the *Shijing*, implies that we should be "always filial and thoughtful" (永言孝思), a phrase that remained important enough that it was later quoted by both Mengzi and Xunzi.[93]

Filiality, however, is not simply a matter of looking up to, caring for, or obedience to one's parents. Kongzi noted that even dogs and horses care for their parents; human filiality must be accompanied by respect (敬).[94] This is echoed by a later author, who defines filiality in terms of nourishing, respecting, and providing security, adding that these need to be done to the very end.[95] But even respect can be grudging. This is why Zhuangzi said that "It is easier to be filial out of respect, but harder to be filial out of love." (以敬孝易，以愛孝難。)[96] Ultimately, as with all virtuosity, filiality must not be contrived, but must be performed sincerely, from the heart.[97]

---

92. *Xiaojing* 孝經 ch. 1 (開宗明義); cf. Henry Rosemont, Jr. and Roger Ames, *The Chinese Classic of Family Reverence: A Philosophical Translation of the* Xiaojing (Honolulu: University of Hawaii Press, 2009), 105. Though the *Xiaojing* has the word "classic" (*jing*) in its title, it was not considered one of *the* classics, of which there were only six (in our time period).

93. *Shijing* #243 (下武); cf. Waley, *The Book of Songs*, 240–41. *Mengzi* ch. 5A4 (萬章上); cf. Van Norden, *Mengzi*, 122. *Xunzi* ch. 7 (仲尼); cf. Hutton, *Xunzi*, 50.

94. *Lunyu* 2.7; cf. Slingerland, *Analects*, 10.

95. *Lüshi chunqiu* ch. 14.1 (孝行); cf. Knoblock and Riegel, *The Annals of Lü Buwei*, 306.

96. *Zhuangzi* ch. 14 (天運); cf. Watson, *Zhuangzi*, 109.

97. *Yu cong yi*: "Contrived filiality: this is not filiality." (為孝，此非孝也。) cf. Cook, *Bamboo Texts of Guodian*, 2:828.

Some authors go on to specify various ways that we should be filial. One details several activities and proclivities that could potentially harm filiality: being lazy, playing too many games, drinking too much alcohol, or being greedy, selfish, indulgent, or contentious.⁹⁸ One ingenious author argued that being filial entailed "impartial love" (兼愛) for everyone in one's community, if not the whole world. His reasoning was that children who wanted to care for their parents would logically want others in their community to look after their parents too, should the children be out of town or otherwise indisposed. "Surely, were I to first deal with matters by loving and benefitting other people's parents, then later other people would respond to me by loving and benefitting *my* parents." (即必吾先從事乎愛利人之親，然後人報我以愛利吾親也。)⁹⁹ Other than on the practical grounds of there not being enough hours in the day to pursue this plan, it is hard to gainsay the logic of this assertion. Nevertheless, some did criticize it for being "unnatural" to love other people's parents as one's own. Yet "impartial" here might be construed as "extending to everyone" but not necessarily "extending to everyone *to the same exact degree*." It is also not impossible to read "impartial" as slight hyperbole. Were this to be the case, one might strive for a practically-graded love based on things like geographical proximity, but still aim for inclusiveness. This would be not unlike the once-popular slogan: "Think globally, act locally."

But what if your parents are Nazis? Should you still obey them? Kongzi once remarked that a truly "upright" (直) son whose father had stolen a sheep would cover up his father's crime and not report it.¹⁰⁰ Should this be taken to imply that filiality trumps the common good? While the import of this anecdote seems clear, the record is not, and other authors clearly disagreed. What I mean by "the record is not" is that this story appears in a longer form in other texts with differing "morals." In one, the son turned his father in and then asked to be punished instead of his father, but the ruler was impressed by the son's trustworthiness and exonerated them both. The point of this iteration is that the "upright" son gained a reputation for being "trustworthy" (信) at the expense of his father's reputation, and in this version Kongzi counters that it would be better to be untrustworthy than to gain a reputation for trustworthiness at the expense of his father's.¹⁰¹

---

98. *Mengzi* 4B30 (離婁下); cf. Van Norden, *Mengzi*, 113.
99. *Mozi* ch. 16 (兼愛下); cf. Knoblock and Riegel, *Mozi*, 166.
100. *Lunyu* 13.18; cf. Slingerland, *Analects*, 147.
101. *Lüshi chunqiu* ch. 11.4 (當務); cf. Knoblock and Riegel, *The Annals of Lü Buwei*, 251–52.

This later account could be an embellishment of the earlier narrative or the earlier story could be a garbled and truncated version of the later one. A third author signaled his ambivalence towards this topic by concluding that a son who turned in his father would indeed be "upright" (直) and "trustworthy" (信), but not "honorable" (貴).[102] The moral of the story here seems to be that sometimes it is difficult to know which virtuosity should take precedence. Finally, in a fourth telling of this story, the son reports his father and the ruler executes the son for being unfilial even though he was a good citizen. The moral of this story taken by itself is unclear, but within the larger context of the book in which it appears, it is clear the author prioritizes the good citizen above the filial son and this story serves as an unfortunate counterexample.[103]

This well-known story, then, caused some consternation among the authors of our sources, but two other authors addressed this general situation and came out on the side of the community over the family. Xunzi claimed that an "old saying" went: "Follow the [human] way and not your ruler [if the two conflict]; follow propriety and not your father [if the two conflict]." (從道不從君，從義不從父。)[104] Interestingly, the anecdote in which this saying appears is followed by an anecdote in which Kongzi complexifies what he said in the example above with the son of the father who stole a sheep. Here, Kongzi says: "A son who [simply] follows [whatever his] father [says], how can that son be [truly] filial?" (子從父，奚子孝？) This implies that courage is necessary for true filiality. The moral of the story lies in the advice Kongzi concludes with: "Carefully examining the *reasons* why one follows may be called [true] filiality." (審其所以從之之謂孝。)[105] This position is reinforced by Zhuangzi, who says "Filial sons do not flatter their parents. . . . [Those who] follow everything that their parents say and approve of everything they do will be regarded by everyone as bad children." (孝子不諛其親. . . . 親之所言而然，所行而善，則世俗謂之不肖子。)[106] Note that neither of these injunctions—to carefully examine the reasons for following a parent, and to not unquestionably do everything a parent says—does not unambiguously repudiate the idea that a filial child should not turn in their

---

102. *Huainanzi* ch. 13 (氾論); cf. Major, Queen, Meyer, and Roth, *Huainanzi*, 506.
103. In *Hanfeizi* ch. 49 (五蠹); cf. Burton Watson, *The Basic Writings of Han Fei Tzu* (New York: Columbia University Press, 1964), 105–06.
104. *Xunzi* ch. 29 (子道); cf. Hutton, *Xunzi*, 325.
105. *Xunzi* ch. 29 (子道); cf. Hutton, *Xunzi*, 325–26.
106. *Zhuangzi* ch. 12 (天地); cf. Watson, *Zhuangzi*, 94–95.

sheep-stealing parent. After all, in the story, the father did not ask the son to conceal his crime. Given all the evidence above, it seems justifiable to say that, despite the famous story of the son with a sheep-stealing father in the *Lunyu*, filiality did not necessarily trump propriety in early China. Listening to our parents may be a good first instinct, but as we grow older, we learn that parents are not always sages, and the advice to "carefully examine" what is asked of us seems prudent. Propriety, after all, is not the same as mere custom or even law, both of which may contravene a sagely conception of propriety. But filiality did hold a very high position in the thought of our sources because it was the *first* virtuosity that a child could reasonably be expected to learn, and in this sense, was the root of all the rest.

Though respect comes first among all virtuosities in the historical record, and filiality is the first virtuosity we learn as children, it is nevertheless the case that (9) **goodness** (仁) ranks first as the most important virtuosity in classical China. Goodness is widely defined as simply loving others.[107] Upon this foundation some authors added other elements. One said we should also benefit things (利物), and another specified that this benefit should be with our own material assets (財), while a third averred that materially benefitting others was not a matter of goodness, but of a closely related virtue, conscientiousness (良).[108] Another author defined goodness in terms of love and civility (文), while others thought it a matter of respect (敬) or benevolence (恩) or caring kindness (慈惠), or accordance (順).[109] Goodness, here and now, as then and there, is an important but multifaceted thing.

---

107. *Lunyu* 12.22: "Fan Chi asked about goodness. The scholar replied: '[It is] to love others.'" (樊遲問「仁」。子曰：「愛人。」); *Mozi* ch. 40 (經上): "Goodness is to embody love." (仁：體愛也。); *Mengzi* ch. 7A46 (盡心上): "Good people have no one they do not love." (仁者無不愛也。); *Xunzi* chs. 15 (議兵) and 29 (子道): "Good people love others." (仁者愛人。); also, *Xunzi* ch. 27 (大略): "Goodness is love." (仁，愛也。); *Shizi* ch. 5 (分): "Love that fulfills its allocation is called goodness." (愛得分曰仁。); *Hanfeizi* ch. 20 (解老): "Of those who are good, it is said their inner hearts gladly love people." (仁者，謂其中心欣然愛人也。); *Huainanzi* ch. 20 (泰族): "There is no greater goodness than to love others." (仁莫大於愛人。)

108. *Zhuangzi* ch. 12 (天地): "To love others and benefit things is to be good." (愛人利物之謂仁。) cf. Watson, *Zhuangzi*, 85; *Shizi* ch. 2 (貴言): "To benefit the world with [your] material assets is to be good." (益天下以財為仁。) cf. Fischer, *Shizi*, 69; *Guanzi* ch. 26 (戒): "To give others [of your] virtuosity is called goodness; to give others [of your] material assets is called conscientiousness." (以德予人者，謂之仁；以財予人者，謂之良。) cf. Rickett, *Guanzi*, 1:383.

109. *Guoyu* ch. 3 (周語下): "Goodness is civilized love." (仁，文之愛也。); *Xunzi* ch. 13 (臣道): "Good people always respect others." (仁者必敬人。) cf. Hutton, *Xunzi*, 138;

Goodness is described as "the luminosity of virtuosity" (德之光) and as the result of when "virtuosity embraces everything" (德無不容).[110] The most famous, sentence-long definition of goodness is what is known in the West as "the Golden Rule." One of its several formulations in our sources is: "Do not impose upon others that which you yourself do not desire."[111] Another potentially familiar explanation holds that "To repay enmity with virtuosity is goodness that expands one's person." (以德報怨，則寬身之仁也。)[112] All of these sayings sum up goodness pretty well; nevertheless, a longer exposition runs: "Warm conscientiousness is the *root* of goodness; respectful caution is the *ground* of goodness; broad generosity is the *activity* of goodness; modest receptivity is the *ability* of goodness; proper orderliness is the *outward aspect* of goodness; verbal discussion is the *civility* of goodness; singing and music are the *harmony* of goodness; allocative [i.e., proportionate] sharing is the *practice* of goodness." (溫良者，仁之本也；敬慎者，仁之地也；寬裕者，仁之作也；孫接者，仁之能也；禮節者，仁之貌也；言談者，仁之文也；歌樂者，仁之和也；分散者，仁之施也。)[113]

We saw in the previous chapter that Mengzi thought that goodness was innate as a potentiality in humans, that we were born with a sense of compassion that might, with sufficient cultivation, mature into goodness.[114] Whether or not that was a widely-held assumption, goodness is certainly an interior virtuosity. Another well-known explanation says of goodness: "By restraining oneself and returning to protocol [one may] become good. . . .

Huainanzi ch. 11 (齊俗): "Goodness is the result of benevolence." (仁者，恩之效也。) cf. Major, Queen, Meyer, and Roth, *Huainanzi*, 408; *Hanfeizi* ch. 47 (八說): "Good people are those who are caring and kind and look lightly upon wealth." (仁者，慈惠而輕財者也。) cf. Liao, *Han Fei Tzu*, 2:254–55; *Liji* ch. 9 (禮運): "Goodness is the root of propriety, the embodiment of accordance." (仁者，義之本也，順之體也。) cf. Legge, *Li Chi*, 1:390.

110. *Hanfeizi* ch. 20 (解老); cf. Liao, *Han Fei Tzu*, 1:173; *Zhuangzi* ch. 16 (繕性); cf. Watson, *Zhuangzi*, 122.

111. *Lunyu* 12.2, 15.24. Quoted above at chap. 3, n. 48. Similarly, *Guanzi* ch. 51 (小問): "Goodness is to not do unto others that which you do not desire." (非其所欲，勿施於人，仁也。) cf. Rickett, *Guanzi*, 2:190.

112. *Liji* ch. 32 (表記); cf. Legge, *Li Chi*, 2:332.

113. *Liji* ch. 41 (儒行); cf. Legge, *Li Chi*, 2:409.

114. *Huainanzi* ch. 20 (泰族) may or may not be in agreement with Mengzi on this point when it says: "Human nature has the material for goodness and propriety. . . ." (人之性有仁義之資。. . .) cf. Major, Queen, Meyer, and Roth, *Huainanzi*, 804.

being good comes from oneself: how could it [possibly] come from others?" (克己復禮，為仁. . . . 為仁由己，而由人乎哉？)[115] This brings us back to the topic of self-cultivation.

Kongzi was clear that goodness, while aspirational, was not a far-away goal. He said: "Merely set your mind on goodness and you will be without badness." (苟志於仁矣，無惡也。)[116] He implicitly elaborates upon that "merely" a few chapters later, when he asks, rhetorically: "Is goodness [really] far away? When I desire goodness, then goodness is here." (仁遠乎哉？我欲仁，斯仁至矣。)[117] Be this as it may, surely some effort is required to realize such goodness. Another author says that we should "Cultivate our persons with the [human] way, and cultivate the [human] way with goodness." (修身以道，修道以仁。)[118] Shortly thereafter, he says that "Goodness is what completes the self." (成己，仁也。)[119] Such cultivation no doubt runs the full gamut of the virtuosities that we are considering here. In addition to virtuosity, it likely also involves more formal study. In fact, Kongzi's student remarked, "Broad learning with sincere purposefulness, incisive questioning with thinking about what is near to hand: goodness is [precisely] in these." (博學而篤志，切問而近思: 仁在其中矣。)[120] Just what is involved in "learning" is discussed in chapter 6.

In addition to being integral to self-cultivation, goodness also has practical applications. For statecraft, it is said that "Noble people who embody goodness are sufficient to be leaders." (君子體仁，足以長人。)[121] Another text avers, "[Those who have] great virtuosity but lack full goodness should not be given control of the state." (大德不至仁，不可以授國柄。)[122] Speaking more broadly, Mengzi says that "Good people have no enemies in the whole world." (仁人無敵於天下。)[123] Indeed, on a more positive note, another author says that "Good people are able to save [others] from contention." (仁者所以救爭也。)[124] This would be quite a useful gift.

---

115. *Lunyu* 12.1; cf. Slingerland, *Analects*, 125.
116. *Lunyu* 4.4; cf. Slingerland, *Analects*, 30.
117. *Lunyu* 7.30; cf. Slingerland, *Analects*, 74.
118. *Liji* ch. 31 (中庸); cf. Legge, *Li Chi*, 2:312.
119. *Liji* ch. 31 (中庸); cf. Legge, *Li Chi*, 2:321.
120. *Lunyu* 19.6; cf. Slingerland, *Analects*, 223.
121. *Yijing* #1 (乾), "Wen yan" (文言) commentary; cf. Lynn, *The Classic of Changes*, 130.
122. *Guanzi* ch. 4 (立政); cf. Rickett, *Guanzi*, 1:102.
123. *Mengzi* ch. 7B3 (盡心下); cf. Van Norden, *Mengzi*, 185.
124. *Huainanzi* ch. 8 (本經); cf. Major, Queen, Meyer, and Roth, *Huainanzi*, 272.

The importance of goodness may be seen in Kongzi's pronouncement that "There are only two [human] ways: being good and not being good." (道二：仁與不仁而已矣。)[125] This declaration, combined with what Kongzi said above about goodness being available to those who desire it, identifies those who are interested in pursuing goodness and those who are not. For those who are interested, it is relevant that the culture-specific *way* of goodness is propriety, which is why goodness and propriety are often paired in the literature. A representative example highlights their relative differences: "Goodness is the right hand and the [human] way is the left hand. Goodness is for humanity and the way is for propriety. [If one] has abundant goodness but insufficient propriety then [they] will be treated with affection but not honored, and [if one] has abundant propriety but insufficient goodness then [they] will be honored but not treated with affection." (仁者右也，道者左也。仁者人也，道者義也。厚於仁者薄於義，親而不尊；厚於義者薄於仁，尊而不親。)[126] That goodness is important if you want to be liked in your community may not be a surprising conclusion; Mengzi, however, thinks it significantly more important than that, insinuating that a lack of it may even be cause for an early death: "If one does not set one's heart upon goodness, then until the end of your life you will have anxiety and shame, until you [finally] sink into death." (苟不志於仁，終身憂辱，以陷於死亡。)[127] In a complicated and evolving society, however, it may take more than good intentions and cultural norms to escape such a fate.

(10) **Wisdom** (智) is the virtuosity of discernment, and is sometimes comprehensively paired with goodness. One author opined: "[You] must consider [your] actions, but do not [always] allow others to know them: certainly be prepared for the unexpected. Those who trust others are good, and those who cannot be deceived are wise: to be both wise *and* good is to be a complete person." (動作必思之，無令人識之：卒來者必備之。信之者仁也，不可欺者智也：既智且仁，是謂成人。)[128] Another characterized these two as the very roots of virtuosity: "In general, in human nature, nothing is more honorable than goodness, but nothing is more critical than wisdom. Take goodness to be [your] substance, but use wisdom to actualize it." (凡人之性，莫貴於仁，莫急於智。仁以為質，智以行之。)[129] Without these two anchoring them, other virtuosities will not result in a harmonious society.

---

125. *Mengzi* ch. 4A2 (離婁上); cf. Van Norden, *Mengzi*, 90.
126. *Liji* ch. 32 (表記); cf. Legge, *Li Chi*, 2:332.
127. *Mengzi* ch. 4A9 (離婁上); cf. Van Norden, *Mengzi*, 94.
128. *Guanzi* ch. 12 (樞言); cf. Rickett, *Guanzi*, 1:221.
129. *Huainanzi* ch. 9 (主術); cf. Major, Queen, Meyer, and Roth, *Huainanzi*, 338.

Kongzi famously said that "The wise are not confused, the good are not anxious, and the courageous are not afraid."[130] His framing of wisdom as a matter of decisiveness, albeit vague, fits with what Mengzi said in the previous chapter, which is that we are born with a rudimentary conscience, a basic knowing of right from wrong, that must be cultivated if wisdom is ever to be obtained. Others frame wisdom as more contemplative of the world, a characterization that may yet be construed as building upon deciding between right and wrong. One said that "Wise people investigate principles and ponder things at length." (智者究理而長慮。)[131] This "investigating" and "pondering" logically precede the subsequent decisiveness. Some ramifications of this process include far-sightedness and timeliness.[132] These abilities, in turn, result in better predictive capabilities and preparing for the unexpected.[133]

That wisdom is said to derive, at least partially, from study and learning, is precisely why an entire chapter of this book is devoted to the place of learning in self-cultivation. One source says that "To learn without tiring is wisdom." (學不厭，智也。)[134] I do not know if this should be taken in some proto-Zen way, where the path *is* the goal, or if the verb "is" is just a poetic way of saying "will result in," but I suspect it is the latter.[135] We saw in the previous paragraph that "investigating" and "pondering" were requisite, and the emphasis on learning in this paragraph may be understood as informing both of them. Pondering, by itself, however, was not thought to be sufficient, as Kongzi makes clear: "I once spent an entire day without eating and an entire night without sleeping, in thought, but it was without

---

130. *Lunyu* 9.29 and 14.28; see note 15 above.

131. *Guanzi* ch. 18 (大匡); cf. Rickett, *Guanzi*, 1:287.

132. *Lüshi chunqiu* ch. 11.5 (長見): "Differences in wisdom lie in its [relative] far-sightedness and short-sightedness." (智所以相過，以其長見與短見也。) And ch. 15.6 (不廣): "When wise people begin a project, they always rely on timeliness." (智者之舉事必因時。) cf. Knoblock and Riegel, *The Annals of Lü Buwei*, 253 and 360.

133. *Lüshi chunqiu* ch. 23.3 (知化): "In general, the value of wisdom is its valuing knowledge of development." (凡智之貴也，貴知化也。) cf. Knoblock and Riegel, *The Annals of Lü Buwei*, 593; *Huainanzi* ch. 9 (主術): "Wise people fully prepare for those things that can be prepared for." (物之可備者，智者盡備之。) cf. Major, Queen, Meyer, and Roth, *Huainanzi*, 337.

134. *Mengzi* ch. 2A2 (公孫丑上); cf. Van Norden, *Mengzi*, 94.

135. Likewise, *Liji* ch. 31 (中庸) says: "To enjoy learning is to be close to wisdom" (好學近乎知), where "to *be* close to" (近) might also be understood as "to *bring* one close to"; cf. Legge, *Li Chi*, 2:314.

gain: it is better to learn." (吾嘗終日不食,終夜不寢,以思;無益,不如學也。)¹³⁶ Both are necessary, of course, but first things first.

"Know thyself" is one of 147 maxims carved on the Temple of Apollo in Delphi by the early Greeks. Our sources include one that is similar: "Those who know others are wise; those who know themselves are percipient." (知人者智,自知者明。)¹³⁷ In a related story, Kongzi asks three of his students to define wisdom and goodness, and he ranks the three replies in ascending order. The first (i.e., lowest), probably with a mind to the political arena, says wisdom is getting others to know you and goodness is getting them to love you. This is good advice if you are looking for a career in government, for if you do not succeed in getting others to know and love you, you will not succeed in getting into office. The second student says wisdom lies in knowing others and goodness lies in loving them. This is the standard line for our sources, as we have seen in the foregoing. The last student, however, says that wisdom lies in knowing yourself and goodness lies in loving yourself, and he wins the prize.¹³⁸ The moral of the story is that all three are right, but, just as filiality is said to be the beginning of virtuosity, insofar as we learn it as children, so knowing and loving ourselves is, practically-speaking, prior to knowing and loving others or getting others to know and love you.¹³⁹

There is another anecdotal similarity with early Greek philosophy, which is also connected with the oracle at Delphi. The oracle said that there was no one wiser than Socrates. Perplexed by this claim at first, upon reflection Socrates admitted that he *was* wise to the extent "that I do not think that I know what I do not know."¹⁴⁰ Kongzi (551–479), a generation before Socrates (c. 470–399), said "To take that which [you] know as that which [you] know, and to take that which [you] do not know as that which [you] do not know: this is wisdom." (知之為知之,不知為不知,是知也。)¹⁴¹ Kongzi, furthermore, also seems to have invented the "Socratic method"

---

136. *Lunyu* 15.31; cf. Slingerland, *Analects*, 186.

137. *Laozi* 老子 ch. 33.

138. *Xunzi* ch. 29 (子道); cf. Hutton, *Xunzi*, 328.

139. Our sources are not to be blamed if this observation has now attained the status of cliché.

140. Plato, *Apology* 21a-d, translated by Hugh Tredennick in *Plato: The Collected Dialogues*, eds. Edith Hamilton and Huntington Cairns (Princeton: Princeton University Press, 1961), 8.

141. *Lunyu* 2.17; cf. Slingerland, *Analects*, 13.

of asking questions with an interlocutor until a resolution is arrived at. He said: "Do I have wisdom? [No, I] do not have wisdom. [Even] a bumpkin can ask a question of me, [and my mind may] draw a blank, [but then] I inquire about it from beginning to end, and [finally] resolve it with him." (吾有知乎哉？無知也。有鄙夫問於我，空空如也；我叩其兩端而竭焉。)[142]

Wisdom, then, begins with the humility of knowing what it is that you do not know, studying up on the question or asking questions with your interlocutor, pondering what you have learned, and then drawing a (tentative) conclusion. However, sometimes even this process will prove insufficient: "[When things] get confusing such that they appear disordered, be tranquil with them and they [may] order themselves [in your mind]. Forcing the issue will not always right it; wisdom cannot always make plans [to resolve it]." (紛乎其若亂，靜之而自治。強不能遍立，智不能盡謀。)[143] This methodological humility and uncertainty is grounded in our next virtuosity.

When the first ruler of China's first dynasty asked his most trusted advisor how to improve his virtuosity, the advisor said: "Be cautious in your person and cultivate your thoughts ceaselessly." (慎厥身，修思永。)[144] Later in this same ancient text, the first two rulers of the Zhou dynasty—the dynasty that is the primary temporal focus of this book—are said to have "cautiously made bright (their) virtuosity" (慎明德).[145] From this, we can see that (11) **caution** (慎) is a foundational virtuosity in our sources. One author says that "Being respectfully cautious and without excessiveness will daily renew your virtuosity." (敬慎無忒，日新其德。)[146] And we saw above that "respectful caution is the ground of goodness."[147]

One popular aphorism in our sources is formulated thus: "If [you] are as cautious at the end as at the beginning, then there will be no failure in [your] affairs." (慎終如始，則無敗事。)[148] This indicates that caution is an abiding concern. Another common saying notes that "Noble people are

---

142. *Lunyu* 9.8; cf. Slingerland, *Analects*, 89.
143. *Guanzi* ch. 36 (心術上); cf. Rickett, *Guanzi*, 2:73.
144. *Shujing* ch. 4 (皋陶謨); cf. Legge, *Shoo King*, 69.
145. *Shujing* ch. 56 (文侯之命); cf. Legge, *Shoo King*, 613.
146. *Guanzi* ch. 49 (內業); cf. Rickett, *Guanzi*, 2:48.
147. *Liji* ch.41 (儒行). See above, note 113.
148. *Laozi* ch. 64. Similar statements are found in *Shujing* ch. 16 (太甲下), *Zuozhuan* (襄 25), *Liji* ch. 8 (文王世子), and *Xunzi* chs. 15 (議兵) and 19 (禮論).

cautious [even] in their solitude." (君子慎其獨也。)[149] One's thoughts and actions are important to self-cultivation, even—and perhaps, especially—when they are *not* scrutinized by others. This idea is related to the "first, love yourself" idea four paragraphs back. Of course, it is also the case that "Noble people are cautious in their interactions with others." (君子慎其所以與人者。)[150] Navigating social relationships, as we have seen, is an important part of all of the virtuosities we have touched upon so far (with the possible exception of wisdom, which might be acquired even on a proverbial desert island).

The *Yijing* is a storehouse of aphorisms, and it too notes that "[If you] are cautious, there will be no harm." (慎不害也。)[151] A somewhat longer explanation comes from a later text: "Sagely people respect the small and are cautious with the subtle. In action [they] do not neglect timing; in all preparations [they] emphasize precautions, and calamity therefore never arises. When planning, [they cautiously] *under*estimate [the chances of] a fortunate outcome, and when considering what to do, [they cautiously] *over*estimate [the chances of] an unfortunate outcome." (聖人敬小慎微。動不失時，百射重戒，禍乃不滋。計福勿及，慮禍過之。)[152] This kind of prudence is wittily summarized in the adage: "Be cautious day by day, [because] people never stumble over mountains, but rather stumble over anthills." (日慎一日：人莫躓於山，而躓於蛭。)[153] Because events do not always transpire as expected, a wise and cautious person will sometimes have to change tack. The degree to which one is able to change with the circumstances is the degree to which one may be said to have the next virtuosity.

(12) **Flexibility** (柔) is a slippery, but important, virtuosity. As half of a flexible-inflexible (柔剛) duality, it is sometimes just another name for the Yin in Yin-Yang.[154] In this sense, Yang-Heaven is inflexible, insofar as the

---

149. *Liji* chs. 10 (禮器), 31 (中庸), 42 (大學); *Xunzi* ch. 3 (不苟); *Huainanzi* ch. 10 (繆稱); cf. Legge, *Li Chi*, 1:402, 2:300, 2:413; Hutton, *Xunzi*, 20; Major, Queen, Meyer, and Roth, *Huainanzi*, 338.
150. *Liji* ch. 10 (禮器); cf. Legge, *Li Chi*, 1:411.
151. *Yijing* #2 (坤), "Xiang" (象) commentary; cf. Lynn, *The Classic of Changes*, 148.
152. *Huainanzi* ch. 18 (人間); cf. Major, Queen, Meyer, and Roth, *Huainanzi*, 739. Note: 射 = 預.
153. *Huainanzi* ch. 18 (人間); cf. Major, Queen, Meyer, and Roth, *Huainanzi*, 721.
154. One early example of this is in the *Yijing*, which often uses the term "flexible" to refer to the broken, Yin lines.

objects in it move in dependable orbits beyond the influence of humans, while Yin-Earth is subject to change from both natural events and human efforts. Thus, one who recognizes a cosmic Way may say "The Way I know can be supple or stiff, flexible or inflexible, Yin or Yang, dark or bright, and can encompass Heaven and Earth." (吾知道之可以弱可以強，可以柔可以剛，可以陰可以陽，可以窈可以明，可以包裹天地。)[155]

In this paradigm, balance is the goal. "Sagely people properly abide between inflexibility and flexibility and thereby attain the root of the Way." (聖人正在剛柔之間，乃得道之本。)[156] But even this general goal of balance has two caveats. One is that different external situations may call for an increase in either flexibility or inflexibility. We saw above, with the virtuosity of being able to yield to others, that having the humility to know that one's opinion may not always be correct, combined with the wisdom to see the superiority of other opinions, should, at least occasionally, result in yielding to others. At other times, however, a backbone in standing up to others will be required. But flexibility differs from the ability to yield in that its focus is primarily directed inward, whereas the ability to yield is, by definition, a social skill. The second caveat, then, is that internal changes may require us to make compensatory internal adjustments. In this way, increased flexibility may be required to offset an increase in inflexibility which, in one's mental life, may include the vexation of stubbornness. This is what one author had in mind when he advised, "For inflexible and aggressive blood and *qi*-substance, make them flexible with integrative harmony."[157] Again, knowing when one is being stubborn and when one is taking a principled stand is a matter of wisdom.

Flexibility can also be construed negatively. The term appears only once in the *Lunyu*, where it refers to a flexibility that manifests as being two-faced, which I therefore translate as "hypocritical." "Kongzi said: 'There are three kinds of beneficial friends and three kinds of harmful friends. Friendship with the straightforward, the trustworthy, and the broadly learned are beneficial. Friendship with the devious, the hypocritical, and the ingratiating are harmful.'" (孔子曰：「益者三友，損者三友。友直，友諒，友多聞：益矣。友便辟，友善柔，友便佞：損矣。」)[158] Here, "hypocritical" might

---

155. *Huainanzi* ch. 12 (道應); cf. Major, Queen, Meyer, and Roth, *Huainanzi*, 439.
156. *Huainanzi* ch. 13 (氾論); cf. Major, Queen, Meyer, and Roth, *Huainanzi*, 498.
157. *Xunzi* ch. 2 (修身). Quoted at greater length in chap. 3, n. 17.
158. *Lunyu* 16.4; cf. Slingerland, *Analects*, 194.

literally be translated "competent at being flexible," but the implication is definitely negative. But this negative and relatively rare use of the term is not in my purview here, except as an example of excess.

Flexibility that is not merely one half of a Yin-Yang balance, but is something that may be said to be inherently (albeit only slightly) superior to inflexibility, is an idea that primarily derives from one author. Laozi unequivocally says "The flexible and supple defeat the inflexible and stiff" (柔弱勝剛強), and "The most flexible things in the world run circles around the most rigid things in the world" (天下之至柔，馳騁天下之至堅).[159] Even though he is a proponent of a Yin-Yang balance, he can still say this because Yin, in a practical sense, is prior to Yang. One way to think about this is to consider the human sleep-waking cycle: all (Yang) action depends on sufficient (Yin) sleep, but sleep depends on no action, only the passage of time. Laozi compares physically flexible babies with the relatively stiff and inflexible aged.[160] In fact, he sees this in all of nature: "People in life are flexible and supple, in death they are rigid and stiff. The myriad things, including plants and trees, in life are flexible and tender, in death they are wilted and withered. Thus, the rigid and stiff are 'disciples of death' and the flexible and supple are 'disciples of life.' This is why when armies are stiff they do not succeed, and when trees are stiff they get the axe. [Thus,] the stiff and mighty [should] abide below [in conciliation], while the flexible and supple [should] abide above [in leadership]." (人之生也柔弱，其死也堅強。萬物草木之生也柔脆，其死也枯槁。故堅強者死之徒，柔弱者生之徒。是以兵強則不勝，木強則折。強大處下，柔弱處上。)[161] In this way, flexibility correlates with life but, as the reference to "stiff" armies makes clear—if we infer that he is not talking about soldiers with aching joints but rather soldiers who are set in their ways of thinking—it also correlates with open-mindedness.

While Laozi is our primary champion of this intriguing idea, others shared it too. Another author, describing the virtues of water, said: "In being flexible yet able to attack, supple yet able to conquer, [it is like] courage." (柔而能犯，弱而能勝，勇也。)[162] A third adduces the necessity of

---

159. *Laozi* chs. 36 and 43. See also ch. 78: "The supple defeats the stiff; the flexible defeats the inflexible." (弱之勝強，柔之勝剛。)
160. See *Laozi* ch. 10 for this metaphor.
161. *Laozi* ch. 76.
162. *Shizi* ch. 15 (君治); cf. Fischer, *Shizi*, 119.

flexibility for things like trees in a storm or leather used by humans. In the case of mental flexibility, "inflexible" may be construed as "certainty." He notes: "Those who want certainty must maintain it with flexibility." (欲剛者必以柔守之。)[163] The ostensible Yin-Yang balance is further undermined when he says "Strength can overcome that which is less than itself: when it encounters its equal, there will be a tie. Flexibility can overcome that which is greater than itself: its power is immeasurable." (強勝不若己者：至於若己者而同。柔勝出於己者：其力不可量。)[164] Not only is flexibility here considered superior, it also confers a sense of equanimity. Sagely people, it is said, are "flexible and supple in tranquility; relaxed and calm in security" (柔弱以靜，舒安以定)。[165]

Mental flexibility overlapping with calm open-mindedness is emblematic of what we now might call a "scientific" mindset. With this attitude, confidence and doubt coincide: we may be confident that our theory accounts for the known evidence, but still doubt that we have in fact been able to analyze, or even gather, all relevant evidence. Such a flexible mindset allows science to progress by continuously replacing old theories with new ones, going wherever the accumulated evidence suggests.[166] This paradox of being simultaneously certain (of one's analysis) and uncertain (that one has considered *all* potential evidence) allows Laozi to claim, counterintuitively, that "protecting flexibility is called strength" (守柔曰強)。[167] Compare the following description of "noble people" with your mental image of the ideal scientist: "Noble people are generous but not lax, candid but not cutting, amenable to debate but not argumentative, analytical but not provocative, straightforward but not domineering, strong but not overbearing, flexible but not passive, respectful and cautious yet tolerant." (君子寬而不僈，廉而不劌，辯而不爭，察而不激，直立而不勝，堅強而不暴，柔從而不流，恭敬謹慎而容。)[168] The correspondence, however unintentional, is, to me, striking. A final image for the simultaneous comportment of confidence and doubt

---

163. *Huainanzi* ch. 1 (原道); cf. Major, Queen, Meyer, and Roth, *Huainanzi*, 60. The word here translated as "certainty" was translated as "inflexible" above.
164. *Huainanzi* ch. 1 (原道); cf. Major, Queen, Meyer, and Roth, *Huainanzi*, 60.
165. *Huainanzi* ch. 1 (原道); cf. Major, Queen, Meyer, and Roth, *Huainanzi*, 62.
166. This attitude, called "fallibilism" by the physicist David Deutsch, is discussed at length in David Deutsch, *The Beginning of Infinity* (New York: Penguin Books, 2011).
167. *Laozi* ch. 52.
168. *Xunzi* ch. 3 (不苟); cf. Hutton, *Xunzi*, 17.

comes from Zhuangzi. Perceiving that ostensibly "complete" (成) theories will likely nevertheless carry some "deficiencies" (虧), he recommends that we conduct ourselves with a "torch of slippery doubt" (滑疑之耀).[169]

Human interaction guided by a "torch of doubt" will involve being (13) **considerate** (恕) because a considerate attitude begins with the premise that we cannot always generalize from our own situation to that of others. Considerate people certainly do try to understand other people's situations, but the effort to understand begins from a place of doubting that you already know what that situation is. Even starting with this fundamental doubt, however, it is still the case that the first practice of considerateness is to extrapolate from oneself. Thus, a common definition of considerateness is also its most well-known rule of thumb: "Do not impose upon others that which you yourself do not desire." No less an authority than Kongzi himself said that this single virtuosity, defined in this way, could serve as "a lifelong guide" (終身行).[170]

Other authors connected considerateness with propriety and goodness. One said: "To act with considerateness is the rule of virtuosity and the mainstay of protocol." (恕而行之，德之則也，禮之經也。)[171] Another noted that "Nothing is nearer to the seeking of goodness than the diligent practice of considerateness." (強恕而行，求仁莫近焉。)[172] The highest praise, however, comes from a second-generation student of Kongzi, who remarked: "[Out of] merit that extends to children and grandchildren, brilliance that shines over a hundred generations, and the virtuosity of sagely people: nothing is finer than considerateness." (功及子孫，光輝百世，聖人之德：莫美於恕)[173] Returning to the topic of self-cultivation, the virtuosity of considerateness may also be used for self-inquiry. Even while it is primarily directed towards others, the "Do not impose upon others" maxim is nevertheless rooted in self-understanding. Thus, within the context of interpersonal reciprocity,

---

169. *Zhuangzi* ch. 2 (齊物論); cf. Watson, *Zhuangzi*, 12.

170. *Lunyu* 12.2, 15.24; cf. Slingerland, *Analects*, 183. We have already met this quote at ch. 3 n. 48 and above at n. 111. The 'lifelong guide' is at 15.24. Other formulations of this maxim are at *Lunyu* 5.12; *Liji* ch. 31 (中庸); *Guanzi* chs. 51 (小問), 66 (版法解); *Shizi* ch. 7 (恕); *Huainanzi* ch. 9 (主術).

171. *Zuozhuan* (隱公 11); cf. Durrant, Li, Schaberg, *Zuozhuan*, 1:65.

172. *Mengzi* ch. 7A4 (盡心上); cf. Van Norden, *Mengzi*, 172.

173. Shizi 世子 (c. 450 BCE) quoted in the *Chunqiu fanlu* 春秋繁露 ch. 17 (俞序), a c. 110 BCE text; cf. Sarah Queen and John Major, *Luxuriant Gems of the Spring and Autumn* (New York: Columbia University Press, 2016), 182.

one author can claim: "If you hate it in other people then rid it from yourself. If you desire it in other people then seek it in yourself: *this* is to be considerate." (惡諸人，則去諸己；欲諸人，則求諸己：此恕也。)[174] In this sense, everyone you encounter is a kind of teacher.

(14) **Honesty** (誠) was discussed in the previous chapter, but it is too important a virtuosity to not be included here. One inward-looking definition says: "What is meant by 'making your thoughts honest' is not allowing self-deception." (所謂誠其意者，毋自欺也。)[175] But honesty is typically portrayed as an outward-extending activity. Thus, we are told that "Sagely people . . . protect genuineness, embrace virtuosity, and project honesty." (聖人 . . . 保真、抱德、推誠。)[176] But honesty in early China was also conceived as a kind of interaction with the environment, both natural and social. Zhuangzi said: "Cultivate honesty in your heart in order to respond to the inclinations of Heaven and Earth." (修胸中之誠，以應天地之情。)[177] The "inclination" under examination in the context of this passage may be paraphrased as "pride goes before a fall," which the reader is invited to consider as a kind of natural truth. But the implications of the sentence quoted are much broader, and other passages posit that the cosmos itself has a kind of honesty. "Heaven and Earth are great, but without honesty they would be unable to develop the myriad things. Sagely people are wise, but without honesty they would be unable to develop the myriad people." (天地為大矣，不誠則不能化萬物；聖人為知矣，不誠則不能化萬民。)[178] This stretches the parameters of the English term "honesty," but not, I think, past the breaking point. (Though perhaps "integrity" might serve as a better translation in this particular context.) However, for the purpose of speaking about this virtuosity in the human realm, "honesty" has the benefit of clarity over "integrity."

Honesty is often paired with trustworthiness, which we examined with loyalty, above. One such example is: "Worthy people are honest and trustworthy in being good, and are caring and kind in being loving." (賢者誠信以仁之，慈惠以愛之。)[179] But it also appears in wider contexts. This

---

174. *Shizi* ch. 7 (恕); cf. Fischer, *Shizi*, 92.
175. *Liji* ch. 31 (中庸); cf. Legge, *Li Chi*, 2:413.
176. *Huainanzi* ch. 9 (主術); cf. Major, Queen, Meyer, and Roth, *Huainanzi*, 299.
177. *Zhuangzi* ch. 24 (徐无鬼); cf. Watson, *Zhuangzi*, 202. "Inclination" (情) in this passage might also be translated "truth." This semantic ambivalence was noted in chapter 2.
178. *Xunzi* ch. 3 (不苟); cf. Hutton, *Xunzi*, 20.
179. *Guanzi* ch. 42 (勢); cf. Rickett, *Guanzi*, 2:133.

same source elsewhere says: "Truthfulness and honesty, generosity and charity, thoughtfulness and considerateness are called the arts of the mind." (實也誠也、厚也施也、度也恕也：謂之心術。)[180] One indicator of the importance of honesty is in who was said to practice it. The founder of China's longest dynasty was one of the top cultural heroes in early China. He was known for his compassion and his willingness to give up his kingdom rather than conscript his people to go to war with an aggressive neighboring kingdom. But his competence as a ruler was described thus: "Zhou King Wen was honest, earnest, and decisive; therefore the state was well-governed." (周文王誠莊事斷，故國治。)[181] More generally, honesty was seen as a basic virtuosity, one that was supportive of others: "Sagely people are to the Way as a sunflower is to the sun: even though they cannot begin or end with it, they face it with honesty." (聖人之於道，猶葵之與日也：雖不能與終始哉，其鄉之誠也。)[182] Since this saying is without context, we can only guess what is meant by "they cannot begin or end with it," but we might surmise that it either means a sage's relatively puny lifespan cannot compare with that of the cosmos and its Way, or that even sages begin, as children, with filiality, and end, as adults, with goodness or wisdom. The sun, in this metaphor, is the Way that "oversees" this development from beginning to end.

Honesty is a useful virtuosity. For sages intent on cultivating their minds, nothing is better than honesty.[183] Even for non-sages, self-inquiry pursued with honesty is said to result in the greatest happiness.[184] And not just happiness: honesty will actually make you smarter. "Impartiality produces percipience; bias produces ignorance. Uprightness and sincerity produce breakthroughs; deceptiveness and contrivance produce blockage. Honesty and trustworthiness produce spiritousness; exaggeration and boastfulness produce confusion." (公生明，偏生闇。端愨生通，詐偽生塞。誠信生神，夸誕生惑。)[185] "Spiritousness" is a sharpened state of mind that will be discussed in chapter 10. For now, it will suffice to say that a sharpened mind is better equipped to perceive the patterns inherent in the cosmic order. These patterns are the "[natural] principles" (理) discussed in

---

180. *Guanzi* ch. 6 (勢); cf. Rickett, *Guanzi*, 1:129.
181. *Guanzi* ch. 64 (形勢解); cf. Rickett, *Guanzi*, 1:67.
182. *Huainanzi* ch. 17 (說林); cf. Major, Queen, Meyer, and Roth, *Huainanzi*, 672.
183. *Huainanzi* ch. 20 (泰族); cf. Major, Queen, Meyer, and Roth, *Huainanzi*, 800.
184. *Mengzi* ch. 7A4 (盡心上): "Honest self-inquiry: nothing brings more happiness than this." This quote appears in chap. 3, n. 87.
185. *Xunzi* ch. 3 (不苟). The first sentence was quoted in chap. 3, n. 78.

the previous chapter. Typically used as a noun, "principle" can also be an adjective describing the ability to grasp them; as we saw above: "If [you] practice propriety with an honest mind, then [you] will be principled, and if principled, then [you] will be percipient."[186]

(15) **Harmony** (和), among people in a community, within oneself as an organism, and for integrating the latter into the former, is probably the most overarching goal in early Chinese thought. The foremost model for harmony was how Heaven and Earth seem to be separate entities, each with their own goals and rhythms, yet nevertheless are systematically coordinated. Everything benefits from the harmony between Heaven and Earth. Models of harmony that are closer at hand include harmonizing various flavors for particular dishes, various metals for particular alloys, various sounds for particular songs, various peoples in particular communities, various laws in particular governments, various members in particular families and, as we saw in chapter 1, various physical constituents for particular human bodies. The latter is the case not only for constituents like our organs and blood, but also for more subtle constituents like our human nature and our emotions.[187]

Since we need to be in a relative state of harmony in order to realize virtuosity, we might say "Harmonious joy and open-mindedness are the means by which virtuosity is nourished." (和愉虛無，所以養德也。)[188] But insofar as we aim to harmonize the various virtuosities within ourselves, and betwixt our ideals and our actions, we might say, conversely, that "Virtuosity is the cultivation of harmony that completes." (德者，成和之修也。)[189] Then again, we might conceive the various virtuosities as already coexisting harmoniously, at least in theory, and wonder if it is not possible for us to "mentally wander among the harmony of virtuosities" (遊心乎德之和).[190] In this latter, abstract sense, then, "Virtuosity *is* harmony, [just as] the Way *is* [natural] principles." (夫德，和也；道，理也。)[191] For those who think that

---

186. *Xunzi* ch. 3 (不苟). See note 89 above.

187. *Huainanzi* ch. 2 (俶真): "For sagely people of ancient times, their natures were harmoniously joyful and calmly tranquil." (古之聖人，其和愉寧靜，性也。) cf. Major, Queen, Meyer, and Roth, *Huainanzi*, 107. We saw in chapter 2 that "When delight, anger, sadness, and happiness are . . . expressed but are all centered and regulated, [we] call this harmony." *Liji* ch. 31 (中庸); see chap. 2, n. 46.

188. *Huainanzi* ch. 2 (俶真); cf. Major, Queen, Meyer, and Roth, *Huainanzi*, 103.

189. *Zhuangzi* ch. 5 (德充符); cf. Watson, *Zhuangzi*, 39.

190. *Zhuangzi* ch. 5 (德充符); cf. Watson, *Zhuangzi*, 35.

191. *Zhuangzi* ch. 16 (繕性); cf. Watson, *Zhuangzi*, 122.

humans can and should pursue the cosmic Way, that relationship is also described as one of humans harmonizing with it.[192] And if a community of people achieved harmony with the Way, then they would harmonize with each other, even while pursuing their individual destinies, just as an orchestra of different instruments playing different notes nevertheless creates a harmonious tune.

Kongzi noted that harmony was not simply a matter of verbal agreement or acquiescing to something that you may or may not actually agree with but is rather a matter of integrating disparate things into a functioning whole.[193] This requires judgment and wisdom, but results in the joy that comes with the smooth functioning of related parts. "Thus, the matter of happiness lies in a harmonious mind, and a harmonious mind lies in acting with moderation." (故樂之務在於和心，和心在於行適。)[194] Moderation is a matter of finding balance, but balance in this respect is not necessarily striving for an unvarying, fifty-fifty compromise: different situations will call for different responses. This is also the case for practicing the fifteen virtuosities outlined here: embodying one or another, or a mixture of several or all of them, will depend upon the circumstances in which you find yourself in any given moment.

The Relativity of Virtuosity

Early Chinese authors were quite consistent about the importance of the virtuosities discussed above, but agreeing on a particular virtuosity is one thing, while agreeing on exactly how that virtuosity should be translated into action in a given situation is quite another.[195] Many people in other parts

---

192. *Yijing* "Shuo gua" (說卦) commentary: "Sagely people . . . harmonize and accord with the Way and virtuosity, and [grasp] the principles of propriety; they exhaustively pursue [natural] principles and completely follow [human] nature in order to fulfill their destinies." (聖人 . . . 和順於道德而理於義，窮理盡性以至於命。) cf. Lynn, *The Classic of Changes*, 120.

193. *Lunyu* 13.23: "Noble people harmonize and do not [merely] agree; petty people agree but do not harmonize." (君子和而不同；小人同而不和。) cf. Slingerland, *Analects*, 149.

194. *Lüshi chunqiu* ch. 5.4 (適音); cf. Knoblock and Riegel, *The Annals of Lü Buwei*, 143.

195. For the specific issue of how early Ruists (Confucians) dealt with conflicting values in a particular situation, see Michael Ing, *The Vulnerability of Integrity in Early Confucian Thought* (New York: Oxford University Press, 2017).

of the world derived their morality from a deity, a deity-inspired prophet, or a deity-inspired or deity-authored book. But, depending on your conception of "deity," early Chinese culture either did not have deities or, if they did, they did not look to them as arbiters of ethics. The closest thing to a "high deity" in early China was an entity called Di 帝, translated as "thearch," sometimes called Shang Di 上帝, or "Di above"; but this entity was probably thought of as a first human ancestor that was still somehow conscious after death.[196] It is true that the *Shijing* reports: "Di said to King Wen, 'I cherish bright virtuosity.'" (帝謂文王：予懷明德。)[197] But there is no early Chinese equivalent to the "Ten Commandments," and no one looked to dead ancestors or nature spirits for moral guidance beyond correct sacrificial procedures to ensure things like a good harvest or a successful military campaign. So, how did early Chinese scholars define their ethics?

The two main answers to this are: the human way, which is to say, social traditions that may be viewed as more or less evolving and open to change; and the cosmic Way, which seeks to both challenge, and sometimes reject, traditional morality, and seeks to avoid anthropocentrism by placing the focus on larger cultural and physical environments. The cosmic Way is one of "[natural] principles" (理). In practice, ethics were probably quite often a mixture of both ways, the human and the cosmic, tradition and idealism (including proto-science).

The problem of just how to derive ethics is noted in our sources. Stated briefly, "The world has nothing to settle right and wrong." (天下是非無所定。)[198] The following exchange about Mizi, a student of Kongzi, illustrates the observation:

> Once there was a guest who introduced someone to Mizi. When the visitor left, Mizi said: "Your friend only had three faults. [He] laughed while looking at me, which is dismissive. [He] conversed without mentioning his teacher, which is contrary. [His] social interaction was shallow even while speaking about deep subjects, which is disordered." The guest responded: "To

---

196. Sarah Allan, "On the Identity of Shang Di," chap. 1, n. 44.
197. *Shijing* #241 (皇矣); cf. Waley, *The Book of Songs*, 238.
198. *Huainanzi* ch. 11 (齊俗); cf. Major, Queen, Meyer, and Roth, *Huainanzi*, 417. Mozi formulated the problem as "humans differ on propriety" (人異義), but he thought this was a problem of the past that had been solved by sage rulers. See *Mozi* ch. 11 (尚同上); cf. Knoblock and Riegel, *Mozi*, 113.

laugh while looking at you was impartiality. To converse without mentioning his teacher was straightforwardness. To interact socially while speaking about deep subjects is dedication." Thus the demeanor of the visitor was the same, but one took him to be a noble person and another took him as a petty person: this is a difference of perspective.

(故賓有見人於宓子者。賓出，宓子曰：「子之賓獨有三過：望我而笑，是攓也。談語而不稱師，是返也。交淺而言深，是亂也。」賓曰：「望君而笑，是公也。談語而不稱師，是通也。交淺而言深，是忠也。」故賓之容一體也，或以為君子，或以為小人，所自視之異也。)[199]

This may indeed be construed as a kind of "ethical relativism" that recognizes that ethics are culturally constructed, but early Chinese authors did not, thereby, shrug their collective shoulders and conclude that one ethical program was as good as another. Rather, they—as, quite probably, we do—sought to harmonize individual freedom with social concord by looking to past tradition and contemporary society on the one hand, and our own human nature and broader natural principles on the other.

The "human way" is perhaps best summed up in Kongzi's saying that "It is people that can broaden the way; it is not the way that broadens people."[200] The "people" here might be taken to mean *special* people, that is, the wise sage-kings of yore.[201] These are the culture heroes that create or inspire the memes that inform a given culture. But "people" can also be taken to mean the regular people that make up human society as a whole. The tenor of passages that support this idea seems to be: morality isn't rocket science; humans are social animals, and every human society on earth has the same basic moral code. Perhaps the most famous articulation of this

---

199. *Huainanzi* ch. 11 (齊俗); cf. Major, Queen, Meyer, and Roth, *Huainanzi*, 418.
200. *Lunyu* 15.29. This saying was also quoted in the Introduction, n. 63.
201. *Mozi* ch. 47 (貴義): "The sage kings of old wanted to transmit their way to later generations, and this is why they wrote it on bamboo and silk and engraved it on metal and stone, transmitting and bequeathing it to descendants in later generations, wanting descendants in later generations to model themselves on it." (古之聖王，欲傳其道於後世，是故書之竹帛，鏤之金石，傳遺後世子孫，欲後世子孫法之也。) cf. Knoblock and Riegel, *Mozi*, 345. Similarly, *Lunyu* 19.22 says that Kongzi followed the way of Zhou Kings Wen and Wu.

view also comes from Kongzi. He said: "The way is not far from people: if people take as a way one that is far from that of other people, then it cannot be considered *the* way. The *Shijing* says: 'Hewing axe-handles, hewing axe-handles: their standard is not far away!' Take an [existing] axe-handle in order to hew a [new] axe-handle; [only if you] squint might it seem far away. Thus, noble people take [their cues from] other people to govern the people, and once there is reform, [they] stop." (道不遠人，人之為道而遠人，不可以為道。《詩》云：「伐柯，伐柯：其則不遠。」執柯以伐柯，睨而視之，猶以為遠。故君子以人治人，改而止。)[202] The axe-handle, of course, is an arbitrary referent. Kongzi is saying that human morality is as common, and as close at hand, as any everyday object, and that if you want to carry on with the tradition—of being ethical, of using an axe in your yard—then it isn't difficult to do so: just look around you and do as others do. The last sentence might raise the question: if ethics are derived from general consensus, then why would a noble ruler need to "reform" them? But Kongzi lived in difficult times, with selfish and predatory leaders setting selfish and predatory examples for all to emulate. He no doubt felt that the populace had been led astray, and that they could and should return to their natural good selves, once they had better, nobler leaders. Or he might simply be implying that cultures and their traditions change and that the codification of those traditions will periodically change too.

While it may be true that, in general, people are good (or, at least, *want* to be good), it is probably clear to everyone that some people become famous or infamous undeservedly. The "wisdom of crowds" is a real phenomenon, but it is far from definitive on a case-by-case basis. Kongzi, again, recognized this, saying "When everyone hates someone, [we] certainly should investigate why, and when everyone likes someone, [we also] certainly should investigate why." (眾惡之，必察焉；眾好之，必察焉。)[203] This skeptical attitude suggests that we should examine all sources of ethics, but in the end the decision to follow one person or another, or to invent one's own path, lies with the individual. The ambiguity in evaluating both cultural norms and one's own freedom in accepting or rejecting them was seen above, when Kongzi (yet again) said "By restraining oneself and returning to protocol [one may] become good. . . . being good comes from oneself: how could it [possibly] come from others?"[204] The tension between socially

---

202. *Liji* ch. 31 (中庸); cf. Legge, *Li Chi*, 2:305.
203. *Lunyu* 15.28; cf. Slingerland, *Analects*, 185.
204. *Lunyu* 12.1. Quoted previously at note 115 above.

constructed "protocol" and the individual "oneself" is clear in the competing phrases "restraining oneself" (克己) and "comes from oneself" (由己). Now the rest of this passage makes clear that protocol, in fact, trumps the self, but the question returns a few chapters later when Kongzi says "Noble people seek it in themselves; petty people seek it in others." (君子求諸己；小人求諸人。)²⁰⁵ Despite these tantalizing hints of ambiguity, Kongzi and his tribe generally come down, quite clearly, on the side of following social norms and "restraining oneself." It was left to others to confront social conformity head-on.

Laozi was decidedly more skeptical of received wisdom than was Kongzi. But ambiguity over the derivation of ethics is evident in his text too. Sages are held up as exemplary figures throughout the narrative, and they are not always isolated recluses: "Sagely people are always competent at helping others, and . . . do not abandon others." (是以聖人常善救人 . . . 無棄人。)²⁰⁶ But sages are also described as taking their cues from the people: "Sages abide open-mindedly, and take the mind of the people as their mind." (聖人常無心，以百姓心為心。)²⁰⁷ In these respects, Kongzi and Laozi agree. But the rejection of traditional morality in favor of following one's own human nature, only hinted at in the sayings of Kongzi, is more explicit (sort of) in those of Laozi. One chapter says "[People of] lofty virtuosity are not virtuous: this is why [they] have virtuosity." (上德不德，是以有德。)²⁰⁸ Another says "Sagely people are not good." (聖人不仁。)²⁰⁹ To make sense of such poetic and attention-grabbing passages, the reader often has to supply missing, but implied, words. The opening sentence of the text famously says "The way that can be conveyed is not the abiding Way" (道可道非常道) but, since the rest of the text goes on precisely to convey the author's thoughts on the abiding Way, this claim only makes sense if we understand it as "The way that can be [*fully*] conveyed is not the abiding Way." In the same way,

---

205. *Lunyu* 15.21; cf. Slingerland, *Analects*, 182.

206. *Laozi* ch. 27. Sages are described as leaders of people in chs. 3, 7, 22, 28, 57, 58, 60, 66, and 79.

207. *Laozi* ch. 49. Also, though not as straightforward, the end of ch. 54 can be construed as saying that we should follow local customs: "Thus, use the person to observe the personal, use the family to observe the familial, use the community to observe the communal, use the state to observe the regional, and use the world to observe the worldly. (故以身觀身，以家觀家，以鄉觀鄉，以國觀國，以天下觀天下。)

208. *Laozi* ch. 38.

209. *Laozi* ch. 5.

the two claims above that baldly reject virtuosity and goodness only make sense if we add "contrivedly" (or "ostensibly") to them.²¹⁰ Thus: "[People of] lofty virtuosity are not [*contrivedly*] virtuous: this is why [they] have [*genuine*] virtuosity." And: "Sagely people are not [*contrivedly*] good." These additions are implied by the context of the text as a whole, which is clearly and repeatedly for acting honestly, in a "non-contrived" manner (taking 無為 as 無偽). (But once we do this, the "rejection" of certain virtuosities looks more like a modification and, moreover, one that Kongzi would have agreed with. Still, books need catchy blurbs.)

Zhuangzi elaborates on this theme. He too says things like "Great goodness is not good," (大仁不仁),²¹¹ that is, "Great goodness is not [contrivedly] good," but then goes on to explain why: "The way I see it, the beginnings of goodness and propriety, and the paths of right and wrong, are mixed up and disordered: how would I know how to distinguish between them?" (自我觀之，仁義之端，是非之塗，樊然殽亂：吾惡能知其辯？)²¹² Different sages proffer different advice; different communities have different norms: the answer to Zhuangzi's rhetorical question is threefold. First, sometimes we should just "go with the flow" because "When in Rome, do as the Romans do." But doing as Romans do while in Rome when you are not Roman may not be ostensibly good from the viewpoint of non-Roman cultures. (Should American Christians pray to Buddhist deities when they are in Japan?) Nevertheless, this advice is fine for trivial things like everyday courtesies.

For deeper problems, however, we will have to rely on our own wisdom. This is where the open-mindedness discussed in chapter 3 comes in: you cannot simultaneously "go with the flow" and "think (and act) outside of the box," but you *can* sometimes do one and sometimes the other. This is the conclusion we might draw when Laozi says, "When [everyone in] the world 'knows' the beautiful as beautiful, this [state of affairs] is just ugly; and when everyone [also] 'knows' the competent as competent, this [state of affairs] is just incompetent." (天下皆知美之為美，斯惡已；皆知善之為

---

210. Such statements not only make better sense with the addition of adjectives implied from the context when taken in isolation, they also thereby avoid contradiction with other parts of the text that explicitly praise the virtuosities in question. For example, the unemended claim that "Sagely people are not good" would contradict the claim made in ch. 8: "In interactions with others, competence lies in goodness" (與善仁), because sages are paragons of competence.

211. *Zhuangzi* ch. 2 (齊物論); cf. Watson, *Zhuangzi*, 14.

212. *Zhuangzi* ch. 2 (齊物論); cf. Watson, *Zhuangzi*, 15.

善，斯不善已。)²¹³ The implication is that, at least sometimes, we ourselves should decide what is and is not beautiful and competent; extending this to ethics is not difficult. (Well, not in theory anyway.) We will see in chapter 10 that when Butcher Ding came to a difficult spot—he was cutting up an ox, a metaphor for analyzing any given situation—he relied upon his own honed intellect (and not the suggestions of bystanders).

But the responsible individual, for Laozi and Zhuangzi, inhabits an environment that extends beyond the social. When Laozi said, above, that "sagely people are not [contrivedly] good," he went on to say that this is because they are impartial, and not just impartial to humans among humans, but impartial to humans among *all* living things. Being impartial among humans would not be surprising, but to contextualize humans within the greater natural environment was what made such sayings by Laozi and Zhuangzi so arresting, then as now. The order of the cosmos, the natural environment writ large, is the Way.²¹⁴ But the Way, despite its inviting moniker, neither advertises itself nor articulates its constituent natural principles. Still, it is there for discovering, though translating lessons from natural principles to human ethics remains a delicate enterprise. This is why it is so often described as "mysterious" and "vague."²¹⁵ Choosing to follow the Way, then, is a fourth way (after sages, tradition, and one's individual conscience) of "distinguishing between" competing ethical norms.²¹⁶

---

213. *Laozi* ch. 2.
214. *Laozi* ch. 25: "People comply with the Earth, Earth complies with Heaven, Heaven complies with the Way, and the Way complies with itself." (人法地，地法天，天法道，道法自然。) See also chs. 34, 42. Also, *Zhuangzi* ch. 16, cited above at note 191, is explicit: "the Way *is* [natural] principles."
215. *Laozi* ch. 21: "The Way, as a thing, is vague and elusive." (道之為物，惟恍惟惚。)
216. I am not a professional ethicist, but as I see it, there are eight ethical paradigms that may be categorized into three types: individual rules (with one paradigm), community rules (with four paradigms), and non-human rules (with three paradigms). The first type is natural law (i.e., follow your conscience). The set of community rules paradigms includes majoritarianism (i.e., majority rules), expert-opinion rules (e.g., Kant or Bentham), ethical pluralism (whereby a person or community derive ethics from a variety of possibly-incompatible sources), and amoralism (whereby one navigates life with familial love and community laws, avoiding judgmental morality). The set of non-human rules includes divine command (i.e., rules derived from religion), ancient ethical realism (whereby ethics are derived from nature), and modern ethical realism (whereby ethics are derived from science). Here, sages would be a type of "expert-opinion," tradition would be "majoritarianism," individual conscience is "natural law," and following the Way is a kind of "ancient ethical realism."

The cosmic "Way" actually has two referents. One is the sum of all natural principles; the other is conduct that is in harmony with those principles. This is why there is advice for living in the *Laozi* and the *Zhuangzi*, despite their occasional rejection of conventional morality. It is also why it is possible to "grasp," "abandon," "lose," "practice," "be without," and "be against" the Way.[217] None of these verbs makes much sense with a discrete cosmic Way "out there" as grammatical object, for one cannot "abandon" natural principles any more than one can "abandon" gravity. But in the derived and secondary sense of "the way of the Way," Laozi *can* say things like "When the great Way is abandoned, there is [contrived] goodness and propriety." (大道廢，有仁義。)[218] It assumes that people are naturally good (in general, but not always), and that traditions are inferior, insofar as they are ossified and therefore often inadequate to deal with cultural change. The past offers much wisdom, but not all social norms are good. This is why the advice offered in our texts is so vague: be open-minded and non-contrived, be humble and do not revel in warfare etc. . . . Only the captious or churlish would argue that advice like this could be construed, even two thousand years later, as "ossified."

These four potential sources of ethics—exemplary people, society as a whole, one's own ethical bearings, and the cosmic Way—present an interesting array of possibilities from which to choose. Different authors will at different times appeal to each of them. I suspect the consensus would be to follow all of them at one time or another. Zhuangzi seems to say as much when he says: "Do not be unified in [your] conduct, but be uneven along with the Way." (無一而行，與道參差。)[219] We might be inspired by exemplary people, guided by society as a whole, motivated by our own ethical bearings, *and* anchored by natural principles (insofar as we know them). That Kongzi and his crew wrote more about the former two and Laozi and his posse more about the latter two does not necessitate that we take sides (or even to assume that they ultimately did). Granting this, how are we to know when to follow any particular one of these sources? The answer to that lies with the aforementioned "torch of doubt." As Laozi said: "To know [when you] do not know is best, and to not know [but think that you do] know is a [kind of] sickness." (知不知：上；不知知：病。)[220] Even sages are said

---

217. *Laozi* chs. 14, 18, 38, 41, 46, and 53, respectively.
218. *Laozi* ch. 18.
219. *Zhuangzi* ch. 17 (秋水); cf. Watson, *Zhuangzi*, 131–32.
220. *Laozi* ch. 71. Partially quoted in chap. 3, n. 68.

to be fundamentally in doubt: "Sages in the world are unbiased, and on behalf of the world keep their own minds 'muddled' [i.e., doubtful]." (聖人在天下歙歙，為天下渾其心。)[221]

Noble People (君子)

In chapter 3 we looked at sagely people in connection with the mind, and here, we look at noble people in connection with virtuosity.[222] Noble people combine virtuosity with intelligence and diligence. "To listen widely and understand firmly yet [still] be able to yield to others, to act with simple competence and yet not be negligent, is to be a noble person." (博聞強識而讓，敦善行而不怠，謂之君子。)[223] These exemplary and aspirational people are generally ascribed one, some, or all of the virtuosities, but more than that, they have succeeded in taking the thoughts, feelings, and actions associated with virtuosity, not as means to an end, but as ends in themselves. This is the meaning of the claim that "Noble people take goodness as their benevolence, propriety as their principle, protocol as their behavior, and music as their harmony: they are imbued with caring goodness." (以仁為恩，以義為理，以禮為行，以樂為和：薰然慈仁；謂之君子。)[224] The virtuosities that others consciously strive for have become "imbued" in noble people to the degree that it has become second nature.

Such noble people almost unavoidably exert a positive effect on others, personally and professionally, consciously and unconsciously. "Thus the protocol of noble people results in [others being] outwardly harmonious and inwardly without animosity; this is because everyone is embraced in their goodness." (故君子有禮，則外諧而內無怨，故物無不懷仁。)[225] Goodness begets goodness: this kind of charismatic chain-reaction lies at the root of virtuosity. But the good manners and good sense of noble people do not only influence the thoughts and actions of other people: they deal with the physical environment in the same thoughtful way. "Thus Heaven and Earth

---

221. *Laozi* ch. 49. See chs. 15 and 20 for descriptions of the doubtful mind metaphorically described as "muddied" (濁) or "dim" (昏).
222. The bifurcation is primarily one of convenience, as the two figures probably overlap much more than they differ.
223. *Liji* ch. 1 (曲禮上); cf. Legge, *Li Chi*, 1:86.
224. *Zhuangzi* ch. 33 (天下); cf. Watson, *Zhuangzi*, 287.
225. *Liji* ch. 10 (禮器); cf. Legge, *Li Chi*, 1:394.

produce noble people, and noble people [in turn] organize Heaven and Earth; noble people form a triad with Heaven and Earth, lead the myriad things, and act as parents to the people." (故天地生君子，君子理天地；君子者，天地之參也，萬物之摠也，民之父母也。)[226] They are as parents to the people, but they also "organize" the world and "lead" the things within it. They did this by mapping the movements of the objects in the sky, by maintaining the calendar, by deciding on the best times for planting and harvesting, by creating sustainable guidelines for hunting . . . in general, by observing the natural environment and organizing ways for humans to competently and responsibly live within it. Thus, noble people affect not only social and political interactions among people, but also the physical interactions between people and the world.

Virtuous people are sometimes characterized as naive in popular culture, but our sources maintain that this is not actually the case. The following is a brief exchange between Kongzi and his student Zai Wo. "Zai Wo asked: 'If a good person were told that there was a good person who had fallen into a well, would he go in after them?' The scholar said: 'Why would he do that? A noble person would go [to the well], but he wouldn't fall in; he might be deceived, but he won't be fooled.'" (宰我問曰：「仁者，雖告之曰『井有仁焉』其從之也？子曰：「何為其然也？君子可逝也，不可陷也；可欺也，不可罔也。」)[227] The point of the question seems to be: would a good person be dumb enough to jump into a well to save someone without an exit plan? That is: would his goodness blind him to practical exigencies? The answer, for Kongzi, is: definitely not.

But just because noble people are virtuous and clever, this does not make them infallible. For smaller issues, Kongzi's student Zixia admits as much: "Great virtuosity does not exceed the boundaries, but lesser virtuosity is more flexible." (大德不踰閑；小德出入可也。)[228] Mengzi analyzes the situation from a different point of view, saying "Noble people of old did make mistakes, but then they rectified them." (古之君子，過則改之。)[229] Here the issue is not "being right on the big things," but rather, being fallible yet willing to learn from one's mistakes.

---

226. *Xunzi* ch. 9 (王制); cf. Hutton, *Xunzi*, 75.

227. *Lunyu* 6.26; cf. Slingerland, *Analects*, 62.

228. *Lunyu* 19.11; cf. Slingerland, *Analects*, 224.

229. *Mengzi* 2B9 (公孫丑下); cf. Van Norden, *Mengzi*, 57. Partially quoted in chap. 3, n. 112.

A third way of assessing differences among noble people is to look at their circumstances, which will likely cause them to act in different ways.

> Noble people, when ambitious, respect Heaven and [follow] the [human] way; when modest, they revere propriety and are orderly; when learned, they understand thoroughly and [think] categorically; when unlearned, they begin with sincerity and [think] lawfully; when followed, they are courteous and restrained; when ignored, they are respectful and even-handed; when delighted, they are harmonious and principled; when concerned, they are tranquil and principled; when successful, they are civil and percipient; when unsuccessful, they are frugal and prudent.
>
> (君子大心則敬天而道，小心則畏義而節；知則明通而類，愚則端愨而法；見由則恭而止，見閉則敬而齊；喜則和而理，憂則靜而理；通則文而明，窮則約而詳。)[230]

Noble people come in a variety of conditions: ambitious or not, smart or not, recognized or not, happy or not, financially successful or not. And these conditions have an effect upon their virtuosity. Ambitious noble people think big, whereas those with more limited worldviews may be more concerned about keeping their own houses in order. Learned noble people can infer things based upon limited observation, whereas those who are less educated may be more inclined to follow established customs. *Vive la différence.*

A final note. A second potential characterization of noble people is that they would not argue or debate, either because they are confident in themselves, or because they think argument does not solve problems. But our authors were scholars, academics, so of course they were fond of precisely such exchanges of ideas. Xunzi claimed, rather bluntly: "Noble people certainly argue." (君子必辯。)[231] Noble people are not aloof, but are, rather, keenly engaged. To engage with other people necessitates honest and objective debate. As counterintuitive as it may sound, social harmony is grounded in argument, insofar as argument allows people to speak their minds, and encourages them to speak reasonably, since reasonableness is (at least sometimes) persuasive. Of course, there is a time and place for everything, as our next chapter will attempt to argue.

---

230. *Xunzi* ch. 3 (不苟); cf. Hutton, *Xunzi*, 18.
231. *Xunzi* ch. 5 (非相); cf. Hutton, *Xunzi*, 37.

Chapter 5

Timeliness (時)

"Now if a person does not encounter the right time, then even if they are worthy, how could they get anywhere?"

—*Xunzi* ch. 28

今有其人，不遇其時，雖賢，其能行乎？《荀子。宥坐》

Timeliness, like several other early Chinese self-cultivation factors, is amenable to a Yin-Yang analysis. It is a response first to our temporal and geographical environment, though it also comes into play with our social surroundings. Timeliness and wisdom might both be cultivated while alone on a desert island, but timeliness is primarily described as a response to the physical environment while wisdom is primarily described as a response to the social environment. This is why timeliness does not appear among the various social virtuosities examined in the previous chapter. But it is nevertheless an important factor in early Chinese self-cultivation. Laozi said: "In movement, competence is found in timeliness" (動善時).[1] And Kongzi was described by perhaps his most ardent follower as precisely a (perhaps even *the*) "sage of timeliness" (聖之時者也).[2] While each of these claims may be explained in

---

1. *Laozi* 老子 ch. 8.
2. *Mengzi* 孟子 ch. 5B1.5 (萬章下): "[When one] should go, he went; [when one] should stay, he stayed; [when one] should remain, he remained; [when one] should serve, he served: [this] was Kongzi. . . . Kongzi was a sage of timeliness." (可以速而速，可以久而久，可以處而處，可以仕而仕：孔子也. . . . 孔子，聖之時者也。) cf. Bryan Van Norden, *Mengzi: With Selections from Traditional Commentaries* (Indianapolis: Hackett, 2008), 132. There is a similar narrative at *Mengzi* 2A2 (公孫丑上); cf. Van Norden, *Mengzi*, 42.

particular ways specific to their context,³ it is also possible to discern the general parameters of "timeliness" by considering the larger context of early Chinese Scholars' texts. As with the other virtuosities, timeliness is flexible, and very much apt to being employed slightly differently depending on the situation. But the value of timeliness should not be underestimated, whether one is on a desert island or amidst the web of social relations that constitutes an important background for most human lives.

In this chapter, I argue that the virtue of timeliness is predicated on variables of time and location, that it may be defined as a set of six practices, and that it results in three related outcomes. For the variables, *temporal* variables include circumstances that are either inevitable or that require effort to bring about. Growing and changing present us with different living circumstances both within our own skins and among the people we live with, and each of these scenarios will likely require its own means for optimal behavior. Additionally, one may choose to embark upon one or more specific courses of self-cultivation, each one possibly having its own agenda and process. And where we stand—literally, *geographically* stand—while undergoing these voluntary and involuntary changes will of course matter a great deal. Different places, after all, will present different opportunities and limitations. These factors, taken together, demonstrate that timeliness is anything but a static endeavor, particularly when situated within the paradigm of an ever-changing world. A timely person must be on their toes amid all of this change:

> As a general rule, [all] humans and things are [produced by] the developments of Yin and Yang. Yin and Yang are created and completed by Heaven. With Heaven there is definitely decline, insufficiency, ruination, and debilitation, as well as flourishing, surplus, accumulation, and reinvigoration. With humans, similarly, there are difficulties, privations, frustrations, and deficiencies, as well as fullnesses, fruitions, successes, and breakthroughs. All of these are encompassed by Heaven, are in the [natural] principles of things, and are calibrations of inevitability. Therefore, ancient sages did not allow their feelings of [narrow] self-interest to harm their spirits but instead simply and acceptingly awaited [what was to be].

---

3. That is, for Laozi, always be responsive and humble, like water; for Kongzi, be responsive to the reception one is given by the ruler.

(凡人物者,陰陽之化也。陰陽者,造乎天而成者也。天固有衰嗛廢伏,有盛盈坌息。人亦有困窮屈匱,有充實達遂。此皆天之容、物理也,而不得不然之數也。古聖人不以感私傷神,俞然而以待耳。)[4]

Both the situation of the individual and the particular environmental situation (i.e., "what was to be") are always simultaneously changing. Before we consider the evolving position of individual persons, let us consider the changing world in which we stand.

Contexts

The practice of timeliness occurs within the cosmological paradigm of the Heaven-Earth dyad discussed in chapter 1. It is a universal order to which humans belong as naturally as any of our other co-inhabitants, from hydrogen atoms to dinosaurs. While humans may only be a subset of the larger schema of the "myriad things," a modified, aspirational version of this paradigm includes humanity within the dyad, creating a triad. While this participation potentially extends to every individual, it is not something that can be inherited but must be attained. As we saw in chapter 2, it was people of "full honesty," who could "complete" both their own human natures as well as the natures of others, and who "assisted" Heaven and Earth, such that these people could join with the latter two to create this triad.[5] Xunzi, less keen to rely on the individual self-sufficiency of human honesty, stressed "practice and habit" (習俗) as the means to change one's nature, concluding "Focusing on one thing [i.e., changing your inner nature for the better] and not two may result in a connection with spiritous percipience, and the creation of a triad with Heaven and Earth."[6] While these authors differed on whether one's inner nature should be "completed" (盡) or "developed" (化), they agreed that its cultivation was key, and that success might ultimately lead to realizing a kind of unity with Heaven and Earth. These paradigms—the Heaven-Earth dyad and the Heaven-Earth-human triad—set the stage

---

4. *Lüshi chunqiu* 呂氏春秋 ch. 20.3 (知分); cf. John Knoblock and Jeffrey Riegel, *The Annals of Lü Buwei* (Stanford: Stanford University Press, 2000), 519. The first two sentences were quoted in chap. 1, n. 21.

5. *Liji* 禮記 ch. 31 (中庸). See chap. 2, n. 27.

6. *Xunzi* 荀子 ch. 8 (儒效). Quoted with fuller context in chap. 1, n. 2.

for the analysis of timeliness that follows. We should remember that even if one has no desire to form any sort of trio with Heaven and Earth, it is still the case that every human must function within the boundaries set by the person-specific vicissitudes of space and time.

Given, then, that each of us must take at least some of our cues from the cosmos, one might do well to ask *how* and *what* we can learn from the Heaven-Earth dyad when, unlike other "ultimate" entities revered in other parts of the world, it dispatches no prophets and inspires no infallible scriptures. The "how" is certainly to be accomplished by observation and investigation. The cosmos holds secrets for us that are there for the taking. Thus, the "investigation of things" (格物), mentioned briefly in chapter 3 and to be discussed fully in chapter 6, is the first step in self-cultivation, and indeed the first step toward world peace.[7] Certainly, Heaven is inspiring, if not verbally forthcoming: just ask Neil deGrasse Tyson, or any other physicist, astro- or otherwise.

But *what* could one possibly hope to learn from Heaven and Earth? One thing is to discern the order(s) underlying the never-ending change. The seasons are always changing, and we, accordingly, should "respond to circumstances in an infinite variety of ways" (應形於無窮).[8] But they are always changing with a definite pattern, a certain logic. Similarly, "Sages change with the seasons but remain untransformed [by them], follow along with things but remain unmoved [by them]." (聖人與時變而不化，從物而不移。)[9] Agile responsiveness from an inner firmness—an inner logic—is key to timeliness. The Earth, meanwhile, has other lessons for us, as Laozi avers, when he observes that, at least ideally, "people comply with the Earth" (人法地).[10] Being low, it has stability, "a low center of gravity," one might say. Its "lowliness" seems a natural metaphor for humility. "Solid as a rock" denotes strength and tranquility. It is, or at least some parts of it are, very productive, hence our expression "*Mother* Earth." After millennia of human

---

7. *Liji* ch. 42 (大學); cf. James Legge, *Li Chi: Book of Rites* (1885; rpt. New York: University Books, 1967), 2:412.

8. *Sunzi* 孫子 ch. 6 (虛實); cf. Ralph Sawyer, *The Seven Military Classics of Ancient China* (Boulder: Westview Press, 1993), 168. The circumstances Sunzi is referring to are, of course, military circumstances, but the advice holds in general.

9. *Guanzi* 管子 ch. 49 (內業); cf. W. Allyn Rickett, *Guanzi: Political, Economic, and Philosophical Essays from Early China* (Princeton: Princeton University Press, 1985, 1998), 2:43.

10. *Laozi* ch. 25. A fuller quote is in chap. 4, n. 214.

depredation, we should say it is forgiving and adaptable. It can be very peaceful, as a walk in the woods will show. As far as role models go, it is blissfully reticent.[11] Water, that model of flexibility and persistence, follows *it*.

As Heaven and Earth change, so do we. We saw in chapter 3 that Kongzi articulated his own stages of life, which have since become something of an aspirational template for others. "At fifteen I set my mind upon learning; at thirty I took my place [in society]; at forty I became free from doubts; at fifty I understood Heaven's mandate; at sixty my ear was accordant [to it]; and at seventy, I could follow my heart's desires without overstepping the bounds."[12] Clearly, different things are to be expected of people at different points in their lives. While the learning that he set his mind upon as a teenager was a life-long effort underlying all the other stages, it resulted in different actions at different times. Gaining a degree of confidence at age thirty, he became quite sure that the path he was on was the correct one only a decade later. "Knowing Heaven's mandate" is an interesting phrase that we will consider in chapter 9. Suffice it to say here that he became sure of how he, personally, ought to spend his time. Precisely what his ear became accordant to at age sixty is left to the reader to decide. Perhaps it was the details of the "Heavenly mandate" (as the bracketed "to it" avers), or to the teachings that he had been studying for the past forty-five years; perhaps it was to the needs of his students, or to the "mind within the mind"—Socrates's *daimon*, a "still, small voice."[13] Only at age seventy did he finally feel confident in his actions being correct. These stages disclose an evolving relationship between the individual and the world around us and call for us to consider how different responses to challenges and circumstances will probably depend on just where we are in life.

A different place or time in one's life may also provide a number of opportunities for various methods of self-cultivation. These methods, meanwhile, often entail a certain number of "steps," from as few as Christianity's two-step "milk to meat" to the well-known twelve-step programs employed

---

11. One of Kongzi's students said that he "only spoke when the time was right, and so people never grew tired of listening to him" (時然後言，人不厭其言), whereas Kongzi himself said he would prefer to go without speaking ("予欲無言"), noting that, after all: "What does Heaven ever say?" (天何言哉？) See *Lunyu* 14.13 and 17.19.

12. *Lunyu* 2.4, see chap. 3, n. 52.

13. *Guanzi* chs. 37 (心術下) and 49 (內業), quoted in chap 3, n. 96. The other two references are from Plato's *Apology* 31d and "1 Kings" 19.12.

by various substance-abuse organizations.¹⁴ Shizi's observation that "learning is the sharpening of the self" (夫學，身之礪砥也) certainly implies a gradual process.¹⁵ The "sharpening" here literally refers to two kinds of whetstones, coarse and fine, which are perhaps echoed in Xunzi's distinction between lesser and greater Ruists (Confucians): "One who is impartial, cultivated, and capable may be called a lesser Ru. [Whereas] one whose intentions are at ease in impartiality, whose conduct is at ease in cultivation, and whose understanding thoroughly unifies the categories [of things]: one like this may be called a greater Ru." (公修而才，可謂小儒矣。志安公，行安修，知通統類：如是則可謂大儒矣。)¹⁶ Given Xunzi's emphasis on the process of education, I would argue that here he is simply referring to the amount of time and effort one has put into the Ruist program, and not to any underlying, genetic capacity that might separate the "lesser" from the "greater."¹⁷ But passages such as these clearly indicate specific degrees of attainment.

The most clearly articulated self-cultivation curriculum in early Chinese literature is probably the seven-step program promulgated by the otherwise-unknown "Woman Crookback."¹⁸ She refers to her plan as "the way of the sage" (聖人之道), but specifies the "ultimate" goal of this plan not (specifically) as harmony with the Way, but as "calmness within turmoil" (攖寧), which we might call "remaining calm within the storm." It is likely, however, that this is simply another name for such harmony. Step one is to "forget the world" (外天下), literally to "put the world out [of your mind]." In Woman Crookback's description, her student Buliang Yi took three days to master this initial step, though it does bear repeating that he already "had the talent of a sage" (有聖人之才); thus, your results may vary. After seven more days of practice under her guidance, he was able to "put [all] things out [of his mind]" (外物). Just what is the difference between "the world" and "all things," and why would the latter take twice as long to forget? I suggest the former refers to everything outside the home: politics, social

---

14. For the former, see "1 Corinthians" 3:2.

15. *Shizi* 尸子 ch. 10 (廣); cf. Paul Fischer, *Shizi: China's First Syncretist* (New York: Columbia University Press, 2012), 58.

16. *Xunzi* ch. 8 (儒效); cf. Hutton, *Xunzi*, 67.

17. Such human capacity, or native substance (質), was briefly discussed in the first part of chapter 2, and is commented upon by Kongzi in *Lunyu* 6.18 and 12.8.

18. *Zhuangzi* ch. 6 (大宗師); cf. Watson, *Zhuangzi*, 46–47. Another famous program is outlined in chapter 6 below.

issues, your employment, friends, etc. While "all things" is a considerably more radical and inclusive rubric: your family—parents, siblings, spouse, children—as well as the physical objects that currently surround you. With these two steps, she exhorts us to disregard the "background noise" in our lives in order to better concentrate. Nine days later, he achieved step three: "putting [his own] life outside out [of his mind]" (外生). If the world and everything in it has now been put safely out of mind, then "forgetting" one's own life may recall the interior stages of meditation that the Buddha is said to have gone through during his enlightenment experience, wherein he freed himself from his own distracting thoughts, then his own desires, then finally even his own emotions.[19] In any case, a mental space of quiet equilibrium has by now been achieved. It is perhaps significant that for the next four steps, no time frame is given. I suspect that this is due to the "timeless" nature of Buliang Yi's state of consciousness. If everything outside of one has been forgotten, and the inner landscape has likewise been subdued, then calculating the passing of time would probably only be a distraction or intrusion. Alternatively, perhaps Zhuangzi did not want to set up expectations for his readers, given that different people will likely achieve the steps in time frames that vary considerably.

Armed now with a sharpened mind, a pointed focus, the fourth step arrives, when "the morning sun breaks through" (朝徹)—similar to our own idiom of a creative idea "*dawning* upon" us. While this too may recall the Buddha's enlightenment, Woman Crookback's way neither induces one to recall previous incarnations nor to perceive the universal "dependent arising" (*pratitya-samutpada*) of all phenomena. What it is that "breaks through" to her student is not specified, and this is no doubt intentional, as it is probably a description of the subjective experience itself. Step five is to "perceive with detachment" (見獨), which signals awareness that is not unduly influenced by emotion and desire. The final two steps will dispatch with the remaining two fetters of time and space. To "be without past or present" (無古今) is the penultimate step; freeing one from the measured flow of time, however one might conceive it, linear or cyclical. The seventh and last step is to "enter the undying/unborn" (入於不死不生), to become detached from ontological conceptions of self and other as discrete living processes. Which is not to say that you cease to *be* a living process—only

---

19. Donald Mitchell, *Buddhism: Introducing the Buddhist Experience* (2002; 2nd ed. New York: Oxford University Press, 2008), 18–19.

that you stop identifying with your memories of, or unfounded beliefs about living. The ever-changing worlds both outside and inside of oneself create the flux, the turmoil, in which the sage maintains tranquility. Hence the culmination of "calmness within turmoil" (攖寧).

These learning stages are specific to the "way" of Woman Crookback, and may even have been specific to fledgling sages like Buliang Yi, and thus unfit for general consumption. In no way does Woman Crookback insinuate that this seven-step plan is the only plan, or that all plans must have seven steps. A one-size-fits-all panacea would be an inflexible chimera. We would not, of course, expect early Chinese scholars to be supporters of a kind of global thinking that would posit one way for all of us. First, they did not know about "the globe" as we know it, and second, they, like most writers of antiquity, were rather ethnocentric. Nevertheless, we can glean a certain open-mindedness from them. Xunzi said, without any apparent condescension toward these named cultural groups, that "the children of Han, Yue, Yi, and Mo are born making the same sounds, but they grow up having different customs because their teachings have caused them to be thus." (干、越、夷、貉之子，生而同聲，長而異俗，教使之然也。)[20] These cultural differences may very well necessitate different ways of self-cultivation.

It is true that Mengzi, quite possibly the most doctrinaire of early Chinese scholars, did say that "the way is one and only one" (夫道一而已矣),[21] but this claim may be ameliorated in several ways. On the face of it, we might consider whether or not he meant that he only knew of one way, or thought that there was only one right way for himself, or for his followers, or for his culture. Fortunately, however, we need not engage in such speculation because the context of this statement is Mengzi telling a doubtful ruler that the one and only goal is to become a noble person. Thus, the singular "way" here is the "way of the noble person," which is the standard human ideal for humans. But this does not thereby imply that there is only one way to *become* a noble person. Buttressing this claim, Mengzi later in the text returns to the issue. After describing the different courses of actions taken by three sages, Bo Yi, Yi Yin, and Liuxia Hui, he specifically says "these three scholars had different ways, but their aim was

---

20. *Xunzi* ch. 1 (勸學); cf. Hutton, *Xunzi*, 1.

21. *Mengzi* ch. 3A1 (滕文公上); cf. Van Norden, *Mengzi*, 63; *Mengzi* 4A6 contradicts this when it claims: "Kongzi said, 'There are only two [human] ways: being good and not being good.'" But it is not difficult to see the prior "one way" as meaning "one [proper] way." Quoted in chap 4, n. 125.

one" (三子者不同道,其趨一也。)²² So when he said above that "the way is one and only one," what he *should* have said (to avoid contradiction), was "the *goal* is one and only one."

If even Mengzi is not averse to contemplating a variety of self-cultivation programs due to the vagaries of circumstance and, we might add, time and geography, then we may conclude this section on the contexts of timeliness. We live in a Heaven-Earth cosmos that is always moving and transforming, yet nevertheless provides us with a number of useful, aspirational metaphors for our own behavioral standards. We grow and mature inexorably through a variety of life stages, each of which seems to promise an increase in our understanding of both ourselves and the world around us. We may choose to adopt one or more learning programs, each with its own enumerated gradations and goal(s). And we each are limited and defined to a certain significant degree by the time and place that we inhabit. This is the context in which and to which we are advised to respond with timeliness. There may be some constants within this flux. Mengzi suggested that his audience should strive to become noble people in society. That is a worthy goal. Zhuangzi, meanwhile, alludes to an *inner* constant, reflected in his description of his own aspirational objective. In chapter 3, we saw him say that "fulfilled people use their mind like a mirror—going after nothing, welcoming nothing, responding but not storing."²³ The "constant" here may well be an emptiness, a contentless attitude, an open-mindedness, but it is in clear contradistinction to a soul carried along by tides and disturbances both exterior and interior. And yet timeliness does have to do with "going along with" things. Is there a contradiction here? What, after all, is the difference between being "carried away by" things and "going along with" things? Or does the problem lie with our metaphors? This issue will resolve itself in the following discussion of the six practices of timeliness.

Practices

Within the changing natural world and amidst a changing inner landscape the timely person carries a small arsenal of best practices. At the most

---

22. *Mengzi* ch. 6B6 (告子下); cf. Van Norden, *Mengzi*, 164. Kongzi also implies this in *Lunyu* 11.22, where he specifies that different students need different kinds of instruction.
23. *Zhuangzi* ch. 7 (應帝王); see chap. 3, n. 7.

fundamental level, this means paying attention to the seasons. Awareness of, and responding to, the seasons is, as mentioned above, the original meaning of timeliness (時). Certainly, for one to flourish, we would do well to plant and build and weave along with the cycles afforded us by our cosmic parents. Working in coordination with certain given situations, like seasonal weather patterns, naturally gives rise to one kind of human skillfulness. It may well be that most modern humans are completely disconnected from any seasonal consciousness insofar as it relates to our food, but this, of course, in no way diminishes its elementary relevance. Metaphorically too, as Mengzi's "sprouts" and even the English word "self-*cultivation*" attest, the agricultural dependence on seasonality is an appropriate device for self-cultivation.

At one remove from the farming life is another kind of seasonality that was of great significance to many early Chinese scholars. This was the fluctuating opportunities for employment at the state courts, where most scholars—in the time before the invention of academia—sought to ply their wares. Kongzi said of these noble scholars, seeking some kind of tenure from the politicians of the day, "If it is not the proper time, then they did not show themselves" (非時不見).[24] These scholars did want jobs, but certainly not at the cost of their professional dignity: if they were not welcome, they could either go to another court or retire with their books into the countryside. Or they could, as Kongzi did, teach. It is ironic that Mengzi described Kongzi as a "timely sage," given that the times were surely against him. Having never been taken seriously by any of the rulers that he solicited, one observer exclaimed that "The world has been without the [human] way for a long time now, and Heaven is going to use this scholar as its warning bell." (天下之無道也久矣，天將以夫子為木鐸。)[25] This description, not unlike that of Socrates as a "gadfly" to uncomprehending Athenian politicians,[26] serendipitously led to the establishment of the enduring Ruist (Confucian) tradition. But responsiveness to the vagaries of those in power is an enduring motif in Chinese history, from the plangent verses of the *Chuci* to the prodding tweets of modern China. Timeliness, it seems, plays a role in the job market as surely as it does in the farmers' market.

---

24. *Kongzi jiayu* 孔子家語 ch. 5 (儒行解); cf. Robert Kramers, *K'ung Tzu Chia Yu: The School Sayings of Confucius* (Leiden: E.J. Brill, 1949), 216.

25. *Lunyu* 3.24; cf. Slingerland, *Analects*, 27.

26. Plato, *Apology* 30e, translated by Hugh Tredennick in Edith Hamilton and Huntington Cairns, eds., *Plato: The Collected Dialogues* (Princeton, Princeton University Press, 1961), 17.

As a general rule extrapolated from these two examples of annual and political seasonality, "paying attention" may be said to be a key component of timeliness, and a core tenet of self-cultivation. In one of his "skill stories," Zhuangzi relates the tale of a cicada-catcher who succeeds at catching cicadas because of his "undivided attention and concentrated spirit" (用志不分，乃凝於神).²⁷ Paying attention to an exterior object—one's crops, one's boss, one's prey—involves one kind of attentiveness, but watching yourself involves quite another. Recall the story of Zhuangzi and the "peculiar magpie" (異鵲).²⁸ The moral of the story was that, while you do want to pay attention to the world around you, you should not thereby forget your own position in it, the reality of your own relationality. "Paying attention" involves a degree of self-awareness.

The *Laozi* has an enigmatic passage about nurturing life. "Those competent at assisting life, when walking on land do not encounter rhinoceroses or tigers, and when entering battle do not encounter armed warriors. [Therefore] rhinoceroses have no place to stick their horns, tigers have no place to sink their claws, and soldiers have no place to put their blades. Why is this? Because they have no 'place for death.'" (善攝生者，陸行不遇兕虎，入軍不被甲兵。兕無所投其角，虎無所措其爪，兵無所容其刃。夫何故？以其無「死地」。)²⁹ Some readers take the claim that these people can have no "place for death" to mean the *Laozi* promises immortality, but I prefer Zhuangzi's oblique interpretation: "For people of fulfilled virtuosity, fire cannot burn them and water cannot drown them; neither heat nor cold can harm them; neither birds nor beasts can hurt them. This is not to say that they treat these things lightly, but rather that they discern where there is safety and danger, remain calm in both good and bad fortune, are cautious about what to flee and what to approach: thus, nothing can harm them." (至德者，火弗能熱，水弗能溺，寒暑弗能害，禽獸弗能賊。非謂其薄之也，言察乎安危，寧於禍福，謹於去就：莫之能害也。)³⁰ In this interpretation, a rhino would "have no place to stick its horn" because you would have

---

27. *Zhuangzi* ch. 19 (達生); cf. Watson, *Zhuangzi*, 147. It is perhaps interesting that, when asked, this cicada-catcher confessed that he indeed "had a way" of catching cicadas ("我有道也"), whereas a skillful swimmer described later in the same chapter, when asked, admitted that he "had no way" for his skill ("吾無道").
28. *Zhuangzi* ch. 20 (山木); see chap. 3, n. 75.
29. *Laozi* ch. 50.
30. *Zhuangzi* ch. 17 (秋水); cf. Watson, *Zhuangzi*, 132.

been paying attention, spotted the rhino in advance, and made sure to not get close enough for it to gore you. This may be a comparatively prosaic reading of Laozi, but Zhuangzi's emphasis on "discerning" (察) danger and being "cautious" (謹) about one's surroundings neatly illustrates a kind of timeliness—most pointedly, of *not* being in the wrong place at the wrong time—that never loses relevance.

The advice to "pay attention" is certainly broad and a potential list of things one ought to pay attention to could go on indefinitely, but early Chinese authors are specific about several of them. Both Zhuangzi and Xunzi warn us of the shifting semantic range of words, a topic that will be discussed in the following chapter.[31] One might also make a case for Xunzi warning us of what we now call "confirmation bias": "In general, people's problems are from their own biases harming them. [They] see what they want, but then do not consider what may be undesirable [about it]; they see what may be beneficial [to themselves], but then do not consider what may be harmful [about it]." (凡人之患，偏傷之也。見其可欲也，則不慮其可惡也者；見其可利也，則不慮其可害也者。)[32] Knowing what you prefer is one thing to keep in mind when confronting new data; knowing your own limitations is yet another. Realizing that your own specificity entails significant perspectival blind areas is a major theme of the *Zhuangzi*. His "frog in the well" image is especially popular: "One cannot discuss the ocean with well-frogs [because they] are constrained in space, one cannot discuss ice with summer insects [because they] are limited in time, and one cannot discuss the Way with partisan scholars [because they] are bound by what they have been taught." (井䵷不可以語於海者，拘於虛也；夏蟲不可以語於冰者，篤於時也；曲士不可以語於道者，束於教也。)[33] No one can escape personal perspectivism, one can only hope to become sufficiently cognizant of its effects.

One way to potentially and partially escape the bounds of our own immediate subjectivity is to think ahead. Kongzi opined that "A person who does not consider what is distant will certainly come to have anxiety about what is nearby." (人無遠慮，必有近憂。)[34] What is "distant" could refer to

---

31. In the meantime, see *Zhuangzi* ch. 2 (齊物論): "words have never had any constant sustainability" (言未始有常), or *Xunzi* ch. 22 (正名): "names have no invariable appropriateness" (名無固宜).

32. *Xunzi* ch. 3 (不苟); cf. Hutton, *Xunzi*, 22.

33. *Zhuangzi* ch. 17 (秋水); cf. Watson, *Zhuangzi*, 126.

34. *Lunyu* 15.12; cf. Slingerland, *Analects*, 179.

things or events removed in either space or time or both: the context does not make this clear. The *Zuozhuan* is more specific. In 545 BCE, the army of the state of Song marched to attack the state of Chu, but the king of Chu died en route. While deciding whether or not to continue the difficult winter march, a Song counselor advised his duke that "A noble person has thought for the future, [while] the inferior person follows [only] what is immediate." (君子有遠慮，小人從邇。)[35] What was "immediate" in this situation was the desire to conquer Chu *now*, despite the hunger and cold of the troops, while the struggle with Chu, in the opinion of the counselor, should properly be seen as a long-term consideration. In the end, Song made a tactical retreat.

Han Ying explicitly ties thinking ahead to our topic: "Self-cultivation is [something about which you] must be careful. . . . [If you] do not ponder deeply and think ahead, of what use will regret be?" (修身不可不慎也. . . . 不深念遠慮，後悔何益？)[36] Regret, imagined or experienced, may well act either as something to be avoided or as a corrective to future action. Either way, it is thinking ahead (遠慮), along with pondering deeply (深念)—which is not unlike the mental focus (摶心) mentioned in the previous chapter—that are relevant to the process(es) of self-cultivation. Developing foresight is no doubt one of the primary goals of using divination texts like the *Yijing*. The book can be used as something of a crystal ball in its role as an oracle, but in its role as a wisdom text it can also serve as a reminder to think about the future with some care. Using this text as a source of wisdom will prompt us to think ahead, regardless of what we think of the text's underlying assumptions. As Shang Yang said, repeating a saying of his time, "Stupid people are befuddled by matters [even] after they have been completed, while wise people are perceptive about [matters] before they have [even] sprouted." (愚者闇於成事，知者見於未萌。)[37] This kind of far-sightedness, which perceives incipience in affairs as an attentive botanist might spy a tiny sprout, leads us directly to a fourth practice of timeliness.

---

35. *Zuozhuan* 左傳 (襄公 28); cf. Stephen Durrant, Wai-yee Li, David Schaberg, *Zuozhuan: Commentary on the 'Spring and Autumn Annals'* (Seattle: University of Washington Press, 2016), 2:1229.

36. *Hanshi waizhuan* 韓詩外傳 ch. 9.19; cf. James Hightower, *Han Shih Wai Chuan: Han Ying's Illustrations of the Didactic Application of the Classic of Songs* (Cambridge: Harvard University Press, 1952), 308.

37. *Shangjunshu* 商君書 ch. 1 (更法); cf. Yuri Pines, *The Book of Lord Shang: Apologetics of State Power in Early China* (New York: Columbia University Press, 2016), 120.

One of the more poetic bits of advice to be gleaned from these texts is that of doing things early. This observation is a natural extension from the admonition to pay attention, insofar as if you are keeping an eye on a given situation, you will be much more likely to note when events warrant your intervention. Laozi notes: "That which is steady is easy to secure. That which is incipient is easy to plan for. That which is brittle is easy to break apart. That which is fragile is easy to scatter. [Therefore,] act on things before they become [fully] formed, and order things before they become [too] disordered. A tree whose circumference fills one's embrace grew from a downy sprout. A terrace nine stories tall arose from a pile of dirt. A journey of a thousand miles began from a single step." (其安易持，其未兆易謀。其脆易泮，其微易散。為之於未有，治之於未亂。合抱之木，生於毫末；九層之臺，起於累土；千里之行，始於足下。)[38] Shizi warns us that thinking fast and acting early will sometimes have the counterintuitive result of precluding the notice of other people. He gives the examples of people who take the trouble to caulk their chimney cracks and parents who take the trouble to raise their children with manners. The courageous efforts of firemen battling a house on fire, and the frantic battle of parents attempting to persuade a judge to release their child from jail may each be newsworthy, but the actions of those who acted early, before these problems arose, will go unnoticed.[39] As much as this may suit the temperament of the circumspect heroes among us, it may prove a stumbling block to those who seek the spotlight. But the logic of getting a handle on things before they get out of hand seems unequivocal.

Chimney-caulking and child-raising are quite different scenarios, inviting quite different responses, and in recognition of this, our texts recommend that we always take into consideration the "dynamism" (勢) of a particular situation, the "lay of the land" so to speak, and that we "rely upon" (因) or "accord with" that situation, rather than imposing upon it our own preconceptions. There are, after all, many kinds of chimneys and many kinds of children. In his *Bingfa*, or *The Art of War*, Sunzi explores the semantic range of the term *shi* 勢 (the dynamism, or lack thereof, in any given location or situation). Illustrating the importance of momentum and timing—both of which are greatly influenced by geography and the situation in general—he writes: "The speed of torrential water that has reached the point of overturning rocks is *dynamism*; the strike of a bird of prey that has reached the point of breaking

---

38. *Laozi* ch. 64.

39. *Shizi* ch. 2 (貴言); cf. Fischer, *Shizi*, 67–68.

[the bones of its prey] is *timing*." (激水之疾，至于漂石者，勢也。鷙鳥之擊，至于毀折者，節也。)[40] The impact of a flash-flood, a diving hawk, or a surprise military attack depends precisely on timeliness, and these instances of timeliness depend on the specifics of the terrain and the moment.

After noting that discerning the circumstances is important for deciding how to correctly respond to them, it is good to remind oneself that some circumstances cannot be changed and that we will have to adjust our actions accordingly. An open mind, once again, proves to be useful in this situation. The *Guanzi* makes the related claims that, for noble people: "Their responses [to things] are without assumptions and their interactions [with things] are without preferences." (其應也，非所設也，其動也，非所取也。)[41] It goes on to explain this advice by saying "This is called 'accordance.' Those who are accordant take things, rather than themselves, as the rule. To sense [a particular thing] and *then* to respond is to be 'without assumptions.' To act following [natural] principles is to be 'without preferences.'" (此言「因」也。因也者，舍己而以物為法者也。感而後應，「非所設」也。緣理而動，「非所取」也。)[42] What sets the stage for human action should be the things with which humans inevitably interact, rather than humans always imposing their own ideas on everything. To misquote Protagoras, maybe "man is *not* the measure of all things."[43]

Finally, extrapolating from those "things," the wider context for human timeliness is of course the natural context. This natural context is not merely the world "out there," but also includes what comes to us naturally from within. "Delight and anger, sadness and happiness, planning and disappointment, transformation and inertia, capricious abandonment and brash posturing: [like] music coming out of [tree] hollows or steamy mist creating mushrooms. Day and night alternating before [our very eyes], with no one knowing from whence they sprout." (喜怒哀樂，慮嘆變慹，姚佚啟態；樂出虛，蒸成菌。日夜相代乎前，而莫知其所萌。)[44] Several self-cultivation regimes will articulate just how we are to deal with our emotions, as we saw in chapter 2, but it is noteworthy that early Chinese

---

40. *Sunzi* ch. 5 (兵勢); cf. Sawyer, *Seven Military Classics*, 165.
41. *Guanzi* ch. 36 (心術上); cf. Rickett, *Guanzi*, 2:74.
42. *Guanzi* ch. 36 (心術上); cf. Rickett, *Guanzi*, 2:80. Quoted at greater length in ch. 3 n. 37.
43. Plato, *Theaetetus* 152a, translated by F.M. Cornford in Hamilton and Cairns, eds., *Plato: The Collected Dialogues*, 856.
44. *Zhuangzi* ch. 2 (齊物論); cf. Watson, *Zhuangzi*, 8.

authors recognized their natural inevitability and never sought to ignore them or shut them down. The natural context is both constantly changing and not amenable to our ultimate control, which suggests that we can really only "follow" its way by not following any final, conclusive code that we might be able to formulate. This is why Zhuangzi paradoxically points out that only "when you do not follow anything and have no [human] way [as your guide] will you begin to attain the Way." (無從無道始得道。)[45] This "way of having no way" may cause perplexity, but if we assume an ultimate goal of harmony, however defined—as we certainly may with early Chinese texts—then we will have the logical foreground necessary for this "non-way" to work.

The six practices of timeliness, then, begin with an awareness of seasonality—both the seasonality that was created by the Heaven-Earth dyad as well as human-created seasonalities, like economic cycles or the rhythms of the academic or political calendars. Paying attention to the specifics within these seasons is second: the cycles of cicadas, for example, or specified hunting seasons, as well as interior "threats" like confirmation bias. Third is considering the future and planning for eventualities and uncertainties. Some people find divination to be a helpful aid in this endeavor. Acting early and avoiding procrastination is fourth. We considered situations associated with homeownership and child-raising above. The fifth practice was the consideration of the (shifting) dynamics of a given situation and how these should help us determine how to calibrate our response to them. Finally, repeating advice from chapter 3, we saw that real timeliness implies an unbiased responsiveness to things as they actually are, and not as we would like them to be. This applies both to the world around us as well as the emotional landscape within.

Outcomes

The practice of timeliness has several outcomes. One is decisiveness. Recall the cicada-catcher described above, catching cicadas with only a glue-stick and his wits; or the image of the attacking hawk: resolve and timeliness go hand in hand. It should come as no surprise that Xunzi also makes this claim, given his emphasis on the role of human effort to realize the

---

45. *Zhuangzi* ch. 22 (知北遊); cf. Watson, *Zhuangzi*, 176.

Heaven-Earth-human triad. "When Heaven and Earth unite, then the myriad things are produced. When Yin and Yang interact, then transformations and developments arise [among them]. When [human] nature and *contrivance* [i.e., deliberate effort] unite, then the world becomes ordered." (天地合而萬物生，陰陽接而變化起，性偽合而天下治。)[46] The Heaven-Earth and Yin-Yang interactions are natural events, with no consciousness providing motivation. Human nature too is a natural phenomenon. Only the contrivance (偽) of humans is within the purview of self-cultivation, though it is through precisely this that all the others are affected, for good or ill. Xunzi would not make the claim that without human intervention the cosmos would be *dis*ordered, exactly, but he does think that we bring, or can bring, a certain kind of order otherwise unknown in the natural world. Domesticated plants and animals, neat rows of irrigated crops, considered land management . . . in addition to domesticating our unruly desires, taming our potentially aggressive interactions with others, passing on the fruits of civilization to our descendants: these are the kinds of order that deliberate human effort—human contrivance (which for other authors, but not Xunzi, has a negative connotation)—can achieve.

Combining the elusiveness of a stable situation in an ever-changing world with the oft-times waffling decision-making process of humans faced with an array of options could lead to paralysis. Decisiveness can thus be seen as a good in itself, even apart from any larger self-cultivation scheme. The following passage lauds human ingenuity in dealing with circumstantial infelicities, along the lines of "When life gives you lemons, make lemonade," but with a broader scope. "When wise people begin a project, they always rely on timeliness, [but since] timeliness may not always manifest, their human activities are not thereby neglected." (智者之舉事必因時，時不可必成，其人事則不廣。)[47] That is, if the "right time" does not come along within the timeframe that we have in mind, do not simply give up: improvise. Timeliness surely requires our attention to the inner and outer landscapes, but it also requires the perspicacity to know when the time is right, the intelligence to choose the response that best fits the situation, and the courage to act decisively when the time comes. Sometimes a decisive response will be to a unique situation; other times it will be required just to keep a proper rhythm. In the latter case, practice may be necessary.

---

46. *Xunzi* ch. 19 (禮論); cf. Hutton, *Xunzi*, 210.
47. *Lüshi chunqiu* ch. 15.6 (不廣); cf. Knoblock and Riegel, *The Annals of Lü Buwei*, 360. Note: 廣 = 曠

Skillfulness is another consequence of timeliness. Zhuangzi is famous for telling skill stories, including those of a butcher, a swimmer, and a carpenter, where "practice makes perfect." Insofar as almost all of us have a skill, this analogy is easily relatable. And the focus on practice in these stories makes a great antidote for facetious readings among neophytes of Daoist "spontaneity." But the mystery of skillfulness is also very much worth considering. As an old wheelwright, commenting on his boss's penchant for reading the classics, opined of his own skillfulness: "It cannot be put into words, yet there's a knack to it somewhere. I cannot explain it to my son, and he cannot get it from me. This is why I've done it for seventy years and am still chiseling wheels. The people of antiquity [whom you are now reading] died along with those things that cannot be handed down. So what you are reading is nothing but the chaff and dregs of the people of antiquity." (口不能言，有數存焉於其間。臣不能以喻臣之子，臣之子亦不能受之於臣，是以行年七十而老斵輪。古之人與其不可傳也死矣。然則君之所讀者，古人之糟魄已夫。)[48] The "knowing that" versus "knowing how" distinction is very useful in this situation.[49] It certainly helps to know that early Chinese texts have a lot of potentially useful advice for one interested in self-cultivation. To understand their worldview, it also helps to know that the cosmic paradigm consists of a Heaven-Earth dyad in constant flux, a flux not controlled by any deity. And to know the importance of timeliness as one potential facet of self-cultivation may be surprising to those with more passive belief systems. But no amount of "knowing that" will help you attain the skillfulness that only comes with focused practice.

The final outcome of the cultivation of timeliness is a certain grace. Skillfulness usually exhibits gracefulness, but it comes in several forms. One is in appropriate silence, bred of the confidence that skill imparts, which several of our texts call for. Kongzi pointed out that Heaven, though a role model, is silent.[50] Perhaps aware of the irony of a professional speaker advocating quiet time, Xunzi notes: "To speak when it is fitting is wisdom; to be silent when it is fitting is also wisdom. Thus, knowing when to be silent is just as good as knowing when to speak." (言而當，知也；默而當，亦知也。故知默猶知言也。)[51] Another outcome is a graceful attitude.

---

48. *Zhuangzi* ch. 13 (天道); cf. Watson, *Zhuangzi*, 107.
49. From Gilbert Ryle, *The Concept of Mind* (Chicago: University of Chicago Press, 1949).
50. *Lunyu* 17.19; see note 11 above.
51. *Xunzi* ch. 6 (非十二子); cf. Hutton, *Xunzi*, 43.

Sometimes an optimal state of mind can be maintained with a light touch, an attitude that brings to mind the maxim to "get out of your own way." It is a relaxed but alert mental posture that can accompany us when feeling particularly fluid or free.

> Genuine people of antiquity did not think to be joyful about life or hate death; emerging without elation, submerging again without resistance; just freely coming in, and freely going out again; not forgetting where they came from and not asking where they would end up; receiving it [i.e., life], and delighting in it; forgetting about it, and giving it back. This is what it means not to use the mind to abandon the Way, not to use the human to [try to] "help" the Heavenly. Such is what is called being a genuine person.
>
> (古之真人，不知說生，不知惡死；其出不訢，其入不距；翛然而往，翛然而來而已矣；不忘其所始，不求其所終；受而喜之，忘而復之。是之謂不以心捐道，不以人助天。是之謂真人。)[52]

"The Heavenly" is a delightfully vague phrase here. It is something more diffuse and inchoate than "the Way." It is the generative force within the cosmos, the blind will to live, as it were. (The Way, meanwhile, is something more articulate. While the Heavenly is like life reproducing itself, by any means necessary, the Way is more like the principle of natural selection.) To "not use the human to [try to] 'help' the Heavenly" is in fact very much like "getting out of your own way," even if the latter saying does not specify for what it is we are getting out of the way. But "Heaven" is a sufficiently vague yet powerful concept to take on that role. One might also insert their deity of choice here, or simply "the universe." In any case, the will to step aside, "trying not to try,"[53] is easier said than done, especially when actively pursuing a course of self-cultivation.

We began this chapter with Mengzi's description of Kongzi as a "timely" sage. One way that he was timely was in his tailoring of advice to different students. Such a context-specific, adaptive technique makes it more difficult for those who wish to derive timeless advice from his sayings, but

---

52. *Zhuangzi* ch. 6 (大宗師); cf. Watson, *Zhuangzi*, 43.
53. See Edward Slingerland, *Trying Not to Try* (New York: Crown Publishing, 2014).

this practice is clearly in line with doing things according to the situation (勢), as considered above. Gracefulness is a difficult attribute to discern in the *Lunyu* because the form of that text is aphorisms and short exchanges with students, though there undeniably is a kind of grace in the very brevity of this kind of writing. There is also one interesting passage at the end of a chapter that deals primarily with his attention to protocol. No one seems to know for sure what it is doing there. "[Changing] countenance, [a bird] thus rose up, circled in the air and then alighted [on a branch]. [Kongzi] said: 'The pheasant on the mountain ridge: how timely!' Zilu bowed to it, then it spread its wings three times and flew off." (色斯舉矣，翔而後集。曰：「山梁雌雉，時哉時哉！」子路共之，三嗅而作。)[54] Presumably Kongzi was commending the bird's response to their arrival: at first reflexively ascending to survey the newly changed situation on the ground, then calmly returning to perch in a nearby tree. Without explicitly saying as much, presenting this simple visual image is sufficient to bring to mind nearly all of the aspects of timeliness discussed in this chapter: a natural, outdoor context; the bird paying attention to its surroundings; decisively acting early to avoid possible capture; responding to the situation and even changing course after perceiving there to be no threat; the obvious skill of taking off and landing on treetops; and the gracefulness of feathered flight. What could be more fitting?

---

54. *Lunyu* 10.27; cf. Slingerland, *Analects*, 109–10.

PART III

OBJECTS (物)

Chapter 6

Learning (學)

"To learn without tiring is that by which one brings the self into order."

—*Shizi* ch. 1

學不倦所以治己也。《尸子 · 勸學》

Learning as Self-Cultivation

We have so far discussed self-cultivation as it applies to our persons, both as individuals and as selves enmeshed within our social and physical environments. In this chapter and the next, we look at two material self-cultivation aids: books and music. This chapter is specifically on learning, and while learning is certainly not confined to books, books are useful tools for self-cultivation and have a long and venerable history in Chinese (and global) intellectual history.

It may be difficult, these days, to find someone who is seriously against education. If we contextualize early Chinese scholars, and particularly Kongzi and Laozi, the traditional founders of Ruism (Confucianism) and Daoism, within the global field of philosophy, then their advice to learn is unremarkable. But if we view them within the field of religion, then this focus is more unusual. Education, broadly speaking, is not crucial to the Buddhist enterprise of extinguishing suffering, the Muslim goal of creating a community submissive to the will of Allah, or the Christian aim of saving one's immortal soul. In our sources, however, learning is quite important for self-cultivation. In keeping with the agricultural metaphor of self-*cultivation*, it is said: "To learn is to grow; to not learn is to wither." (夫學，殖也；不學將落。)[1] Similarly, it is also said: "Learning is the means to develop oneself and to take care of oneself." (夫學者所以自化，所以自撫。)[2]

There is probably no more definitive synopsis for early Chinese thought in general, and of the role of learning in particular, than the opening lines of a text called "The Great Learning" (大學):

> The way of great learning lies in illuminating luminous virtuosity, in being close to the people, and in coming to rest in full competence. After knowing where to rest, one can then become settled; after being settled, one can then become tranquil; being tranquil, one can then be calm; being calm, one can then deliberate; with deliberation one can then attain [this way].
>
> Things have their roots and their branches; affairs have their ends and their beginnings. Knowing what comes first and what comes last, one approaches the way [of great learning].
>
> Those in antiquity who wished to illuminate luminous virtuosity within the world first ordered their states; wishing to order their states, they would first bring equilibrium to their families; wishing to bring equilibrium to their families, they would first cultivate their persons; wishing to cultivate their persons, they would first rectify their minds; wishing to rectify their minds, they would first make their thoughts true; wishing to make their thoughts true, they would first extend their knowledge. The extension of knowledge lies in the investigation of things.
>
> (大學之道，在明明德，在親民，在止於至善。知止而後在定，定而後能靜，靜而後能安，安而後能慮，慮而後能得。
> 物有本末，事有終始。知所先後，則近道矣。
> 古之欲明明德於天下者，先治其國。欲治其國者，先齊其家，欲齊其家者，先修其身。欲修其身者，先正其心。欲正其心者，先誠其意。欲誠其意者，先致其知。致知在格物。)[3]

---

1. *Zuozhuan* 左傳 (昭公 18); cf. Stephen Durrant, Wai-yee Li, David Schaberg, *Zuozhuan: Commentary on the "Spring and Autumn Annals"* (Seattle: University of Washington Press, 2016), 3:1557.

2. *Guanzi* 管子 ch. 66 (版法解); cf. W. Allyn Rickett, *Guanzi: Political, Economic, and Philosophical Essays from Early China* (Princeton: Princeton University Press, 1985, 1998), 1:147.

3. *Liji* 禮記 ch. 42 (大學); cf. James Legge, *Li Chi: Book of Rites* (1885; rpt. New York: University Books, 1967), 2:411–12.

This human way begins with three articulated aims. The first is the cultivation of our individual (presumably natural and inborn) "luminous virtuosity," which was the subject of chapter 4. The second situates us within our community, in "being close to the people," which we may construe as social harmony, which is the general goal of all early Chinese scholars. The verb phrase "being close to" (親) can also mean, in noun form, one's "parents," so community as family is the objective here, articulated in a later passage as "peace on earth." The third connects our individualized potential with the greater good within the practice of competence in our actions. The "full" is aspirational, not a *sine qua non*. The six-step program here is somewhat different from the seven-step program mentioned in the previous chapter. Though both describe inward journeys, there the goal was mental equanimity, while here it is ordered states (and in the following passage, world peace). After realizing the importance of competence in one's actions, we are advised to pursue that competence by becoming "settled" in body, "tranquil" in emotion, "calm" in mind, and "deliberate" in attention. After these steps, the resulting mental acuity will allow us to attain this "way of great learning."

The second short paragraph returns to the subject of deliberation, to our attention, which is rather key. The "roots and branches" are metaphors for degrees of importance: roots are more important than branches for the life of a tree. The "first and last" refer to the order in which things should be done. For example, in the six-step program here, being settled in body precedes mental equanimity because trying to reach and maintain mental equanimity is decidedly more difficult when there is bodily discomfort or there are sensory distractions. Likewise, the seven steps of the program in the last paragraph are also described as contingent.

The third paragraph may be written for the benefit of a ruler, but it is easily extrapolated to the rest of us. That is, should we wish to cultivate our virtuosity—"within the world," as distinct from only in the privacy of our own homes—then we should want an ordered community, just as we would want a settled body prior before turning our attention to attaining a tranquil mind. The ruler is in the best position to "order" the state, but citizens can also contribute to bringing about order in their communities in a number of ways, not least by simply setting an example of what it means to be a good citizen. Bringing "equilibrium" to one's family shrinks the scope from one's community to one's family. Just as filiality was construed as foundational for other virtuosities, so being committed to a harmonious home is here posited as foundational for commitment to a harmonious society. Sharpening the focus even more, we arrive at the subject of the present monograph: self-cultivation. In this passage, self-cultivation is pursued via rectifying the mind (正心) and, more specifically, through honesty (誠), both of which were discussed in chapter 6. As there is no verb form of the English word "honesty," I here translated it as "to make true." Finally, crucially, the ultimate and—since this list is temporally backward—primary means to all these contingent ends is the iconic "investigation of things."

The "investigation of things" is probably a sufficiently clear piece of advice that no explanation is needed, but I will risk belaboring the point to add two implied activities popular in our sources: asking questions and thinking. Elsewhere in the same text as the quote above, it says "Noble people honor [their] virtuosic natures and follow the way of asking and learning, reaching to the expansive yet scrutinizing the tiniest, [finally] arriving at lofty percipience yet following the way of centered engagement: cherishing the old yet knowing the new." (君子尊德性而道問學，致廣大而盡精微，極高明而道中庸：溫故而知新。)[4] The "way of asking," then, implies inquiring broadly. But inquiry alone is not enough; to truly acquire knowledge is to make it your own, which requires some amount of rumination. Kongzi said, "To learn without thinking [about what you have learned] is futile; to think without learning [new things] is dangerous." (學而不思則罔，思而不學則殆。)[5] The former claim seems intuitively true, as information must be processed to be memorable and useful. The latter claim points to the "danger" of personal bias and one-sidedness.

Xunzi picks up on the latter claim and says: "In general, people's suffering [comes from] being circumscribed by one-sided partiality, while remaining ignorant of the great [natural] principles." (凡人之患，蔽於一曲，而暗於大理。)[6] He goes on to say that we can be circumscribed—blinded—by a number of things: our own desires or aversions, the beginnings or endings of problems, things distant or near, broad or narrow, past or present.[7] But partiality is not just due to limited exposure to external data; we are also constrained by several cognitive biases, one of which is the relatively well-known "Dunning-Kruger effect."[8] This effect describes the

---

4. *Liji* ch. 31 (中庸); cf. Legge, *Li Chi*, 2:323.

5. *Lunyu* 論語 2.15; cf. Edward Slingerland, *Confucius: Analects with Selections from Traditional Commentaries* (Indianapolis: Hackett, 2003), 13.

6. *Xunzi* 荀子 ch. 21 (解蔽); cf. Eric Hutton, *Xunzi: The Complete Text* (Princeton: Princeton University Press, 2014), 224.

7. *Ibid*.

8. Justin Kruger and David Dunning, "Unskilled and Unaware of It: How Difficulties in Recognizing One's Own Incompetence Lead to Inflated Self-Assessment," *Journal of Personality and Social Psychology* 77.6 (1999): 1121–34.

tendency to underestimate what we do not know, to disregard the possibility and extent of "unknown unknowns." Zhuangzi seems to have anticipated this bias when he said: "Those who know what Heaven does and know what people do, will be fulfilled. Those who know what Heaven does, are Heavenly and alive [i.e., live naturally]. [But] those who [also] know what people do, *take the knowledge of what they know to nourish what they know they don't know*, living out their Heaven-mandated years without dying along the way: this is the fullness of knowledge." (知天之所為，知人之所為者，至矣。知天之所為者，天而生也。知人之所為者，以其知之所知以養其知之所不知，終其天年而不中道夭者：是知之盛也。)[9] To "know what we don't know" is to say that we can keep in mind that there is much that we do not know and to act accordingly.

Considering context and other analytical angles, as well as having humility about the current state of our own knowledge, then, are hedges against one-sided learning. Persistence can help all of these potential deficiencies, as it often takes time to realize the broader context, to think of or learn about other analytical angles, and to become aware of the Dunning-Kruger effect. Xunzi says, pithily, that "By taking half-steps without stopping, [even] a lame turtle [can traverse] a thousand leagues." (故蹞步而不休，跛鱉千里。)[10] He elaborates in a later chapter that this is the case for everyone, not just sages or noble people: "Now if the people on the street were to submit to the arts and practice learning, to focus the mind and unify the will, to think about [how to] investigate [things] and fully examine [them], then add to this day upon day, extending quite some time, and accumulate competence without ceasing, then [this may] result in a connection with spiritous percipience, and the creation of a triad with Heaven and Earth." (今使涂之人伏術為學，專心一志，思索孰察，加日縣久，積善而不息，則通於神明，參於天地矣。)[11] Persistence is what connects the resolve to study with the ultimate goal of living in harmony with the cosmos. The "arts" here refers to what are now called "fields" of study, the "teachings" of various early Chinese scholars, as well as broader "methods" for doing a variety of particular things. The term applies to pursuits as disparate as bodily self-cultivation, rhetoric, getting a job, astrology, military affairs, and

---

9. *Zhuangzi* 莊子 ch. 6 (大宗師); cf. Burton Watson, *The Complete Works of Zhuangzi* (New York: Columbia University Press, 1968; 2013), 42.
10. *Xunzi* ch. 2 (修身); cf. Hutton, *Xunzi*, 13.
11. *Xunzi* ch. 23 (性惡);` cf. Hutton, *Xunzi*, 254.

funeral rites. One "art" that may provide a starting point and context for the others is history.

What to Learn (I): History

We saw above that we should "cherish the old yet know the new." Kongzi said it was this attitude that could make one a teacher.[12] Learning history is not for an abstract production of knowledge, but rather to help us understand the present: "A bright mirror is for reflecting images, [just as] returning to the past is for knowing the present." (夫明鏡者所以照形也，往古者所以知今也。)[13] The "past," for many of our authors, was transmitted via a number of different cultural pursuits: ancient songs and poems, famous political speeches, a variety of traditional protocols articulated for a wide array of life events, music for a range of state and public ceremonies, cosmological and divinatory texts, and records of local events specific to a number of locales.[14] Add to these foundational arts the philosophies of the various scholars, military strategy, and medical techniques, and this will give you an idea of the "curriculum" of early Chinese students of cultural history. We are asked to engage with such cultural heritage texts quite comprehensively; the "them" below specifically refers to the Chinese classics, though I suspect Xunzi would be fine if modern readers made use of other classics:

> [Use] them once and [you will find that they] can be used again and again; acquire them and [you will find that they] can have lasting [value]; broaden them and [you will find that they] can be communicative; ponder them and [you will find that they] can bring stability; repeatedly follow up in examining them and [you will find that they] can be even more enjoyable. Use [them] to order [your] inclinations and [you] will find benefit; use [them] to make a name [for yourself] and [you] will find glory; use [them] to create community and [you] will find harmony; use

---

12. *Lunyu* 2.11; cf. Slingerland, *Analects*, 11.

13. *Hanshi waizhuan* 韓詩外傳 ch. 4.18; cf. James Hightower, *Han Shih Wai Chuan: Han Ying's Illustrations of the Didactic Application of the Classic of Songs* (Cambridge: Harvard University Press, 1952), 178.

14. These six came together as the Six Classics (詩, 書, 禮, 樂, 易, 春秋).

[them] in solitude and [you] will find sufficiency: aren't these such happy thoughts?

(一之而可再也，有之而可久也，廣之而可通也，慮之而可安也，反鈆察之而俞可好也。以治情則利，以為名則榮，以群則和，以獨則足：樂意者其是邪！）[15]

The word to "broaden" (廣) can also mean to "extend," so the third phrase may mean that we should take the lessons learned from studying history and extend them into our daily life, using them as cultural touchstones that our audience will understand. But I have taken it to mean that we can and should "broaden" our historical learning with our own experience, much as Kongzi said, with a synonymous word, "It is people that can broaden the way . . ." (人能弘道) in the introduction.[16] Thus informed with our own experience, we can use the combination of historical precedent and individual observation to create speech that is both socially recognizable and personally agreeable: that is, "communicative." Similarly, tapping into cultural precedent can confer a degree of "stability" insofar as interlocutors will share similar reading experiences and vocabulary upon which they can draw. The practical uses of learning the "canon" are here summed up in four applications, and the first, "to order [your] inclinations," is explicitly related to our topic of self-cultivation. That such pursuits can be "happy" is a topic we shall turn to shortly.

History is not static. As any teacher of history knows, history is more like an assortment of descriptions and snapshots of a multitude of crime scenes, and history books are attempts to identify and articulate (overlapping and competing) narratives about those scenes. This insight is reflected in the suggestion, noted above, that we are to "broaden" the history we read. But this should remind us that the writers of history books—even the venerable classics—had particular points of view and had specific audiences in mind when they were writing. Our learning of history, therefore, should be broad and take in a spectrum of viewpoints. A Ruist (Confucian) once had the broadmindedness to write: "[Good] books do not only come from the followers of Zhongni [i.e., Kongzi], [just as good] medicine does not only come from [the famous physician] Bian Que: those [books] that accord with

---

15. *Xunzi* ch. 4 (榮辱); cf. Hutton, *Xunzi*, 30.
16. *Lunyu* 15.29, quoted in the introduction, n. 63 and chap. 4, n. 200.

competence may be used as models, adapted to the times, and judiciously acted upon." (書不必起仲尼之門，藥不必出扁鵲之方：合之者善，可以為法，因世而權行。)[17] One might object that to "accord with competence" is a subjective judgment, but "competence" suggests that, as with science, we should go with what works and what fits the available evidence, rather than with what fits our personal theories.

What to Learn (II): Rhetoric

Early Chinese intellectuals were cognizant of the problems in communication caused by the shifting semantic range of words. Their solution is summarized in the well-known phrase the "rectification of names" (正名). The starting point for learning about this problem and how to deal with it lies in the observation that "names [for things] have no invariable appropriateness" (名無固宜).[18] A second basic observation is that this is problematic. "In general, disorder derives from things and their names not matching." (凡亂者，形名不當也。)[19] The "disorder" here refers of course to confusion in communication. The importance of this problem is illustrated in a dialogue between Kongzi and one of his students. The student asked the scholar what his first order of business would be should he be employed in governing a state, and Kongzi surprised him by responding that it would "certainly be the rectification of names" (必也正名乎)![20] Otherwise, he explained, "things just wouldn't get done" (事不成).

Thoughts on how to use words correctly and clearly usually were expressed as desires to have words correspond with reality.[21] It is hard to imagine any honest person disagreeing with that assessment, even though it sometimes seems, in more cynical moments, that many people make their livelihood on deception and the dishonest manipulation of words. But what

---

17. *Xinyu* 新語 ch. 2 (術事); cf. Ku Mei-kao, *A Chinese Mirror for Magistrates* (Canberra: Australian National University, 1988), 77.
18. *Xunzi* ch. 22 (正名); cf. Hutton, *Xunzi*, 239. Quoted in chap. 5, n. 31.
19. *Lüshi chunqiu* 呂氏春秋 ch. 16.8 (正名); cf. John Knoblock and Jeffrey Riegel, *The Annals of Lü Buwei* (Stanford: Stanford University Press, 2000), 401.
20. *Lunyu* 13.3; cf. Slingerland, *Analects*, 139.
21. *Zhuangzi* ch. 18 (至樂): In the days when sages ruled, "Names [for things] remained with reality, and propriety was established on what was moderate." (名止於實，義設於適。) cf. Watson, *Zhuangzi*, 143.

exactly does it mean to make words correspond with reality? In effect, it means to speak as clearly as possible, taking care when choosing words to express yourself. Metaphor, hyperbole, ambiguity, generalizations, and the like do have their place in human communication, certainly, but when important agreement is at stake, clarity is key. In such situations, honest people will "work toward clarifying their aims and intentions" (務白其志義).²² "Aims and intentions" sounds rather bloodless, but miscommunication often arises with value judgments and their attendant emotions. Xunzi examines a few that were on his mind. One is the saying "To kill a robber is not to kill a person." (殺盜非殺人也。)²³ Xunzi does not elaborate on this saying, which he objected to, but it seems to juxtapose the emotional and legal term "robber" with the broader and emotionally-neutral term "person," producing the effect of rationalizing state executions. This is roughly akin to the modern phrase "abortion is murder," which uses the same juxtaposition, with "murder" as the emotional and legal term: though abortion is not, legally speaking, murder, the desired effect is to make the listener conjure the emotions as if it were.

Two sayings that Xunzi does elaborate on, and disagrees with, in his pursuit to "rectify names," are: "To be insulted is not [the same as] being disgraced" (見侮不辱) and "[Human] inclinations have but few desires" (情欲寡).²⁴ These hinge on the hazy semantic parameters of "disgrace" and "few." For the first saying, Xunzi spends a few pages arguing against it, but in the course of his analysis, it becomes clear that his hypothetical interlocutor would probably actually agree with him. He says the term "disgrace" has two types, one external and situational (a 勢 type) and the other internal and ethical (an 義 type), and he claims that one can be disgraced in both ways. That is, someone can disgrace you by punching you and you can disgrace yourself by being greedy. But the original saying, "To be insulted is not [the same as] being disgraced," was almost certainly only referring to the latter, internal definition of "disgrace," counseling us to *not* feel ashamed about things that are out of our control, like getting punched. To my mind, Xunzi's argument is no argument at all, but a rhetorical problem, a miscommunication predicated on not agreeing on a definition for "disgrace." A

---

22. *Xunzi* ch. 22 (正名); cf. Hutton, *Xunzi*, 242.
23. *Xunzi* ch. 22 (正名); cf. Hutton, *Xunzi*, 239.
24. *Xunzi* ch. 22 (正名), with further discussion in ch. 18 (正論); cf. Hutton, *Xunzi*, 239–40, and 197–200.

modern example might be the definition of "modesty." The socially acceptable clothing-to-exposed-skin ratio of any given outfit varies widely, not only by the situation (the beach versus, say, a wedding), but also by the culture in which one was raised and in which one currently lives.

Xunzi's disagreement with the second saying, "[Human] inclinations have but few desires," centers on the ambiguity in the word "few," and the miscommunication is evident once the reader notices that, in Chinese, "few" can modify both quantity and quality.[25] For example, let us consider someone who is hungry and desires food. With quantity in mind, we might wonder if he desires one steak or ten; with quality, we may wonder if he desires a bowl of gruel or a steak. Xunzi argues that he will certainly take steak over gruel which, to him, demonstrates that (human) inclinations are excessive, but it seems quite possible that a hypothetical interlocutor—one who is not present to explain or defend his claim that "[human] inclinations have but few desires"—meant that the average person would not take ten steaks when one would suffice. If that is the case, then, as above, there really may be no quarrel (assuming that Xunzi would agree with this assessment), just a miscommunication due to elastic semantic parameters.

One might also wonder what, exactly, is meant by "desire." To extrapolate from our sources to another tradition, the second of the Buddha's "Four Noble Truths" is "dissatisfaction derives from desire" or, perhaps more accurately, "dissatisfaction derives from the craving that leads to rebirth."[26] Thus, we may ask: which desires or cravings (Pali: *tanha*; Sanskrit: *trishna*), exactly, cause our dissatisfaction and lead to rebirth? Does it include "everyday" desires like those for food and sleep? Since the Buddha himself ate and slept, presumably not, but that still leaves us unclear about the semantic parameters of this word, so crucial to the Buddhist narrative.

Rhetoric in early China was not logocentric. That is, although the "rectification of names" was a relatively widespread and important consideration, scholars acknowledged that "names [for things] have no invariable appropriateness." One ramification of this "language skepticism" is a kind of centered ambivalence that manifests in rhetorical caution. Such prudence is evident in this description of Kongzi: "The scholar rejected four [things]: conjecture, absolutism, obstinance, and self-centeredness." (子絕四：毋意，

---

25. This makes more sense for the Chinese word *gua* 寡 than the English "few." Perhaps "scant" would be a better translation, except that "[Human] inclinations have but scant desires" sounds awkward.

26. Donald Mitchell, *Buddhism: Introducing the Buddhist Experience* (2002; 2nd ed. New York: Oxford University Press, 2008), 47–51.

毋必,毋固,毋我。)[27] The first three of these are easily related to the idea that rhetoric is inherently problematic, and even the fourth, rather than moral opprobrium, may be a nod to the problem of confirmation bias, which is, in part, an undue preference for one's own narrative. Our sources contain a good cautionary tale about confirmation bias:

> There was a person who lost an ax and suspected his neighbor's son. He "observed" the stealing of the ax in his gait, his demeanor, and his speech: every action and attitude [of the neighbor's son affirmed his] stealing of the ax. [Later, while] clearing his ditch he found his ax. When he again observed his neighbor's son on another day, his actions and attitude were *not* those of an ax stealer. There had been no change in the neighbor's son, [rather] he himself had changed. This change was in nothing other than [the man's] prejudice.
>
> (人有亡鈇者,意其鄰之子。視其行步竊鈇也,顏色竊鈇也,言語竊鈇也:動作態度無為而不竊鈇也。相其谷而得其鈇。他日復見其鄰之子,動作態度無似竊鈇者。其鄰之子非變也,己則變矣。變也者無他,有所尤也。)[28]

This is not to claim that guilty people never act in nervous ways that might tip off a keen observer, but rather that if you already suspect somebody of something, your assessment of their speech (and actions) will likely not be very objective. This is the sense of "self-centeredness" that I think Kongzi rejected above.

Analogous with the problem of confirmation bias is the problem of the argument from authority. Where the former privileges one's own viewpoint, the latter privileges that of an authority. Authorities that are competent will adduce evidence for their claims, and it is that evidence that non-authorities should focus on, rather than on the name or fame of the authority. Our sources often do defer to the authority of "prior sage-kings," but this move is as much a rhetorical device as it is a logical fallacy; when it came to their actual contemporaries, early Chinese scholars typically gave no ground based on name alone. Kongzi said: "Noble people going about in the world

---

27. *Lunyu* 9.4; cf. Slingerland, *Analects*, 87.
28. *Lüshi chunqiu* ch. 13.3 (去尤); cf. Knoblock and Riegel, *The Annals of Lü Buwei*, 286–87. Note: 相 = 扫.

neither affirm nor deny [anyone uncritically]; they [simply] associate with those who are proper." (君子之於天下也，無適也，無莫也，義之於比。)²⁹ One could counter that noble people in fact "deny" improper people, but the point of the saying is that various people in a variety of settings can be proper, and that the judgment of propriety always lies with us, not with the authority, or the social or political affiliation, of others. Arguments from authority prevent our learning of rhetoric by circumventing our responsibility to weigh arguments based on the words and logic of a given argument.

We might fight confirmation bias and deny automatic credence to authority figures in favor of scrutinizing the words and sentences of a given argument, but that does not mean we should not consider the perspective of the author of said argument. Zhuangzi, among our sources, was most keenly aware of the vagaries of perspective. He noted not only that any given individual perspective is only one among many, but also that the human perspective itself is only one among many. He reminds us that, in a dispute, while it is possible that one person is right and the other wrong, it might also be that both are right or both are wrong.³⁰ Consider the example above about modesty: since dress codes vary from person to person, place to place, and time to time, two people could well disagree on whether a given outfit is or is not modest, and depending upon which definition we appeal to, one could be right and one wrong, or both right, or both wrong. He goes on to remark that the perspective of our species is just as limited: "[We] calculate the number of things as myriad, and humans are but one among them. . . . Comparing us with the myriad things, are we [humans] not as a tiny tip of hair on a horse's body?" (號物之數謂之萬，人處一焉 . . . 此其比萬物也，不似豪末之在於馬體乎？)³¹ For readers of Dr. Seuss, this is *Horton Hears a Who* (1954) in early China. Contextual assumptions, word choice, implications, and the like are all greatly influenced by an author's particular perspective.

The most famous anecdote about language skepticism comes from the same author: "Fish traps are for fish: [once you] get the fish, the trap can be forgotten. [Likewise,] rabbit snares are for rabbits: [once you] get

---

29. *Lunyu* 4.10; cf. Slingerland, *Analects*, 32.
30. *Zhuangzi* ch. 2 (齊物論): "If one is right, must the other be wrong? Couldn't both be right or both be wrong?" (其或是也，其或非也邪？其俱是也，其俱非也邪？) cf. Watson, *Zhuangzi*, 17.
31. *Zhuangzi* ch. 17 (秋水); cf. Watson, *Zhuangzi*, 127.

the rabbit, the snare can be forgotten. [Similarly,] words are for meaning: [once you] get the meaning, the words can be forgotten. How might I get a person who has forgotten words so that I may have a word with them?" (荃者所以在魚，得魚而忘荃；蹄者所以在兔，得兔而忘蹄；言者所以在意，得意而忘言。吾安得夫忘言之人而與之言哉？)[32] Words are flexible and their semantic parameters evolve over time, sometimes in quite arbitrary ways. It is important to both recognize this fact yet still work to reduce miscommunication by clarifying what we mean by the rhetoric we use. All things considered, whether we are learning history or rhetoric—which, construed broadly, includes everything that has ever happened and every way that humans use to talk about it—if we are cognizant of the problems inherent in human authorship and human learning, there are few better words of advice than "Examine what you know *and* examine what you do not know." (察所知察所不知。)[33] This simple maxim entails a whole variety of virtuosities: humility (謙), courage (勇), caution (慎), flexibility (柔), and honesty (誠) among them.

Hence: Reality-Based (實)

Being "reality-based," for humans, involves three things: the reality out there, our ability to perceive it, and our ability to speak about what we have perceived. These three—reality, veracity, and truth—are all denoted in the word "reality-based" (實). In the following passage, it has the first meaning:

> Improve names by scrutinizing reality, [then] fix names in accordance with reality. Names and reality [should] mutually produce each other and, conversely, mutually create truth. If names and reality match, then there is order; if they do not match, then there is disorder. Names [should] be produced from reality; reality is produced from the virtuosities [of things]; the virtuosities [of things] are produced from [natural] principles; [natural] principles are produced from harmony, and harmony is produced from what is appropriate.

---

32. *Zhuangzi* ch. 26 (外物); cf. Watson, *Zhuangzi*, 233. The pun is intended.
33. *Yucong, yi* 語叢一; cf. Scott Cook, *The Bamboo Texts of Guodian* (Cornell: Cornell University East Asia Program, 2012), 2:830.

(修名而督實,按實而定名。名實相生,反相為情。名實當則治,不當則亂。名生於實。實生於德,德生於理,理生於智,智生於當。)³⁴

Ultimate causes, like "what is appropriate," in our sources, are typically vague. This may well indicate a refreshing humility about the ultimate causes of all reality. And, of course, it is not always feasible to have such a concise, reality-based, vocabulary. Another author noted that "[Those who] are cold shiver, [but] those who are afraid also shiver: this is the same word but [it denotes] different realities." (寒顫,懼者亦顫:此同名而異實。)³⁵

"Reality" in the context of a modern reader may bring to mind questions about the supernatural. Early China certainly had its share of supernatural beliefs—chief among them the influence of astrology, nature spirits, and the souls of dead people—but our sources are notable for not being very interested in these subjects. We saw in chapter 1 that Kongzi said "Attending to the propriety of the people, and respecting the ghosts and spirits *while yet keeping them at a distance*, can be called wisdom."³⁶ This is probably a fair overall description of the attitude toward the supernatural in our sources (which, recall, are primarily the Scholars' texts, not *all* early Chinese texts), but other authors had a less sanguine attitude toward such matters. Han Fei claimed: "Now, when priestly incantors intone for someone saying: 'May you live for a thousand, [or even] ten thousand years!' the sound of the 'thousand, [or even] ten thousand years' simply grates upon the ear, since not even a single day's longevity has ever been evidenced to people [as a result of such incantations]: this is why people disdain priestly incantors." (今巫祝之祝人曰:「使若千秋萬歲。」千秋萬歲之聲聒耳,而一日之壽無徵於人:此人所以簡巫祝也。)³⁷ Repudiating priests is not the same as repudiating the supernatural entities with which they claim to commune—probably not many humans on c. 300 BCE earth would be willing to do that—but the emphasis on "evidence" (徵) is remarkable. It implies our ability to perceive

---

34. *Guanzi* ch. 55 (九守); cf. Rickett, *Guanzi*, 2:236–37. Note: 智 = 和. The text does not specify what is being harmonized, but one plausible guess is Yin and Yang.

35. *Huainanzi* 淮南子 ch. 16 (說山); cf. John Major, Sarah Queen, Andrew Meyer, and Harold Roth, *The Huainanzi: A Guide to the Theory and Practice of Government in Early Han China* (New York: Columbia University Press, 2010), 654.

36. *Lunyu* 6.22. Quoted in chap. 1, n. 89.

37. *Hanfeizi* 韓非子 ch. 50 (顯學); cf. Burton Watson, *The Basic Writings of Han Fei Tzu* (New York: Columbia University Press, 1964), 127.

reality accurately. Thus, when people make suspicious claims, the listener should "certainly verify their [actual] abilities" (必實其能).[38]

To predicate claims on evidence is no longer particularly controversial, if it ever was. But much of what we might wish to claim may not be amenable to direct or immediate observation. Reason allows us to also derive general principles from discrete, observable phenomena. These "(natural) principles" were discussed in chapter 3. We also noted in chapter 3 that "Statements that are thought to be wrong often are right, and those that seem right are often wrong."[39] Thus, the sage is said to "investigate and [seek] evidence for things" (察而徵之),[40] the "evidence" being either indications (表) that we are able to observe or principles (理) that we are able to consider (and work into our theories).

The third aspect of "reality-based" learning is talking about what has been perceived; "In general, discourse is [only] valuable insofar as distinctions are fitting and insofar as it accords with verification." (凡論者貴其有辨合，有符驗。)[41] To have "distinctions" that are "fitting" is, as we may say, to "call a spade a spade": it is to speak clearly and precisely and, should there be a dispute about definition, to clarify your own definition before proceeding. To "accord with verification," meanwhile, is simply to keep one's claims from exceeding the evidence. To return to our priest-distrusting author, "One who insists on something for which there is no adduced verification is stupid." (無參驗而必之者，愚也。)[42] In this way, one may say that claims are actually "reality-based"—that is, are actually true—to the extent that there is evidence to support them.[43] "'Truthfulness and honesty, generosity and charity, thoughtfulness and considerateness are called the arts of the mind." (實也誠也、厚也施也、度也恕也，謂之心術。)[44] The difference between "truthfulness" and "honesty" is that the former refers to

---

38. *Hanfeizi* ch. 8 (八姦); cf. Watson, *Han Fei Tzu*, 47.
39. *Lüshi chunqiu* ch. 22.6 (察傳). See chap. 3, n. 117.
40. *Guanzi* ch. 38 (白心); cf. Rickett, *Guanzi*, 2:91.
41. *Xunzi* ch. 23 (性惡); cf. Hutton, *Xunzi*, 252.
42. *Hanfeizi* ch. 50 (顯學); cf. Watson, *Han Fei Tzu*, 119.
43. A claim may also be true without evidence, insofar as guesses sometimes turn out to be true. These two senses of the word "true," one predicated of a claim that has no evidence to support it (yet), and one predicated of a claim that does, are thus distinguished as "potentially true" and "actually true."
44. *Guanzi* ch. 6 (七法); cf. Rickett, *Guanzi*, 1:129.

an external artifact—a particular sentence, a claim—and the latter describes one's intent, insofar as even honest people may unwittingly utter untruths. Honesty is an impetus to study so that one may be truthful.

Why Learn? Ethics (道德) and Joy (說/悅)

Truthfulness is not the only reason to learn. The *Xingzi mingchu*, regarding the subset of learning that is facilitated by a teacher, explicitly says: "Teaching is that by which virtuosities are produced within [you]." (教所以生德于中者也。)[45] Other texts only imply a connection between learning and ethics. For example, an *Yijing* commentary implies connection via juxtaposition: "Noble people learn in order to gather things, ask [questions] in order to differentiate things, are generous in order to abide with things, and are good in order to act along with things." (君子學以聚之，問以辯之，寬以居之，仁以行之。)[46] Here, the implicit connection is between learning and the virtuosities of generosity and goodness. Other authors, however, make more explicit connections. We saw above that Kongzi said of noble people—who certainly prized learning—that propriety was fundamental.[47] But he elsewhere broadens the scope of his claim considerably, explicitly tying six virtues to six problematic "obfuscations" (蔽) of those virtues. He specified that goodness, wisdom, trustworthiness, straightforwardness, courage, and certainty (仁知信直勇剛) could, without the benefit of learning, turn into foolishness, indecisiveness, betrayal, convolution, disorderliness, and a disregard for others (愚蕩賊絞亂狂).[48]

A third reason for learning, in addition to helping one's claims be more truthful and one's actions be more ethical, is for the sheer joy of it. It is perhaps no accident that the opening sentence of the most famous and influential of all our sources reads: "To learn and then to have the opportunity to practice it: *is this not a joy?*" (學而時習之，不亦說乎？)[49]

---

45. *Xingzi mingchu* 性自命出; cf. Scott Cook, *The Bamboo Texts of Guodian* (Cornell: Cornell University East Asia Program, 2012), 2:712.

46. *Yijing* 易經 #1 (乾), "Wen yan" (文言) commentary; cf. Richard Lynn, *The Classic of Changes: A New Translation of the* I Ching *as Interpreted by Wang Bi* (New York: Columbia University Press, 1994), 133.

47. *Lunyu* 4.10. See note 29 above.

48. *Lunyu* 17.8; cf. Slingerland, *Analects*, 203.

49. *Lunyu* 1.1; cf. Slingerland, *Analects*, 1.

Kongzi elsewhere further opines that "wise people are happy" (知者樂).⁵⁰ When he asked his favorite student why he didn't pursue government office, particularly since his family was relatively poor, Yan Hui replied: "[I] don't want to be an official. I have eight acres of farmland outside the city walls, sufficient to provide [me] with porridge and gruel . . . with silk and hemp; playing the zither is sufficient for my entertainment; and that which I have learned of the scholar's way is sufficient for my happiness." (不願仕。回有郭外之田五十畝，足以給饘粥 . . . 為絲麻；鼓琴足以自娛；所學夫子之道者足以自樂也。)⁵¹ Even in antiquity, with all its attendant hardships that are probably quite difficult for modern people to comprehend, learning was connected to joy.

Teachers (師)

Our sources generally hold teachers in high regard. This, in turn, has had notably far-reaching influences on all subsequent East Asian cultures. One source places teachers among the highest of cosmic and earthly figures. Though patriarchal (and biologically deficient), it says: "Heaven produces the seasons and Earth produces resources; humans are produced by their fathers and are instructed by teachers." (天生時而地生財，人其父生而師教之。)⁵² This list of four things that a wise ruler makes use of (i.e., Heaven, Earth, fathers, and teachers) ends there. Teachers are, moreover, integral to the subject of self-cultivation. We saw in chapter 1 that for cultivating the body and mind, nothing is more important than getting a (good) teacher.⁵³ These claims speak to the importance and relevance of teachers in our sources.

Teachers, however, do not have to be human, as one might take Heaven or the cosmic Way as one's teacher.⁵⁴ You can even take nature, or natural principles, as your teacher. The sage-hero Yu successfully stopped the deadly flooding of the Yellow River by channeling its waters, rather than by trying to dam it, as his predecessor had unsuccessfully done. His cooperation with

---

50. *Lunyu* 6.23; cf. Slingerland, *Analects*, 60. Kongzi at *Lunyu* 7.19 describes himself as happy.
51. *Zhuangzi* ch. 28 (讓王); cf. Watson, *Zhuangzi*, 246.
52. *Liji* ch. 9 (禮運); cf. Legge, *Li Chi*, 1:378.
53. *Xunzi* ch. 2 (修身); see chap. 1, n. 103.
54. *Zhuangzi* chs. 25 (則陽) and 6 (大宗師), respectively; cf. Watson, *Zhuangzi*, 216, 52.

the natural tendencies of river water was depicted as both clever and humble, with himself in the role of student. Thus: "Yu's dredging of the river was due to his taking the waters as his teacher." (禹之決瀆也，因水以為師。)[55] But here I am primarily concerned with human teachers. Who is qualified to be a teacher? Really, anyone can, in theory, be a teacher. On the most basic level, we might follow the aspirational saying that "competent people are the teachers of incompetent people" (善人者，不善人之師).[56] But this does not reflect the broader complications of *finding* a competent teacher.

Kongzi is now revered as China's "first teacher," and even in his own day he had acquired a significant following of students, but this does not mean that he was universally regarded as beyond reproach.[57] Teachers, then, are not always simply those who present themselves as teachers. In one sense, finding a teacher is contingent on having the willingness to learn from others. Kongzi said: "When walking with two other people, there is certain to be a teacher for me among them: [I] identify their competencies to emulate them, and [identify] their incompetencies to reform them [in myself]." (三人行，必有我師焉：擇其善者而從之，其不善者而改之。)[58] In another sense, ethical inclinations were generally thought to be common to human beings. We saw in chapter 2 that Mengzi and Xunzi disagreed about whether or not human nature was good, but as interesting as that argument is and was, the idea that we are, at least potentially, good was more mainstream. Someone once asked one of Kongzi's students who Kongzi had studied under, and that student replied: "The way of [kings] Wen and Wu has not yet fallen to the ground, but resides in the people. Worthy people recognize its great aspects and unworthy people recognize its minor aspects, but no one is without the way of [kings] Wen and Wu within them. With whom did the scholar *not* study and, indeed, how could he have had [only a single] constant teacher?" (文武之道，未墜於地，在人。賢者識其大者，不賢者識其小者，莫不有文武之道焉。夫子焉不學，而亦何常師之有？)[59] Despite this eminently humanist claim, not everyone is actually up to the

---

55. *Huainanzi* ch. 1 (原道); cf. Major, Queen, Meyer, and Roth, *Huainanzi*, 55.
56. *Laozi* ch. 27.
57. Mozi and Zhuangzi are well-known critics, but even ostensibly Ruist texts sometimes paint unflattering pictures of Kongzi; see *Yanzi chunqiu* 晏子春秋 ch. 8.1; cf. Olivia Milburn, *The Spring and Autumn Annals of Master Yan* (Leiden: Brill, 2016), 400–402.
58. *Lunyu* 7.22; cf. Slingerland, *Analects*, 71. Similarly, see also *Lunyu* 4.17.
59. *Lunyu* 19.22; cf. Slingerland, *Analects*, 228.

task of being a teacher. One author noted, unfortunately without context but with apparent wryness, that "The trouble with people is that they love acting as other people's teachers." (人之患,在好為人師。)[60] The lesson is that, while anyone *might* be a teacher to us, we should be wary of anyone who positively *wants* to be our teacher.

Teachers are neither magicians nor even, primarily, purveyors of content; they are more like sports coaches who proffer considered advice: the real work is up to the athlete and student. In this vein, it was noted that "A carpenter or wheelwright can give another person their compass or T-square, but they cannot make another person skillful." (梓匠輪輿,能與人規矩,不能使人巧。)[61] The "compass" and "T-square" of teachers are reason and ethics, and the business of teachers is to engage students on the implementation of both tools. Thus: "The task of those who would be teachers lies in the championing of [natural] principles and in the doing of what is proper." (為師之務,在於勝理,在於行義。)[62] Both of these endeavors have indispensable roots in history. We noted above that "cherishing the old yet knowing the new" was something that noble people pursued. Kongzi used the same maxim to define teachers: "To cherish the old yet know the new—[one who] is able to do this [may] become a teacher." (溫故而知新,可以為師矣。)[63]

Richard Dawkins's claim that "memes" transmit ideas about natural principles and ethics (among other things) from the past to the present is itself a new way of expressing an old idea.[64] It contrasts the importance of the cumulative "wisdom" of human culture with the genetic information with which we are born. Xunzi makes much the same point when he says: "If people have no teachers or models, then they will venerate [human] nature [as their teacher and model]; if they have teachers and models, then they will venerate the accumulation [of human knowledge as their teacher and model]." (人無師法,則隆性矣;有師法,則隆積矣。)[65] All animals make

---

60. *Mengzi* 孟子 ch. 4A23 (離婁上); Bryan Van Norden, *Mengzi: With Selections from Traditional Commentaries* (Indianapolis: Hackett, 2008), 100.
61. *Mengzi* ch. 7B5 (盡心下); cf. Van Norden, *Mengzi*, 186.
62. *Lüshi chunqiu* ch. 4.2 (勸學); cf. Knoblock and Riegel, *The Annals of Lü Buwei*, 120.
63. *Lunyu* 2.11; cf. Slingerland, *Analects*, 11. We saw the first part of this sentence in another text, quoted in chap. 3, n. 22 and from the *Lunyu*, above, n. 12.
64. Richard Dawkins coined the term "meme" to be a cultural analog of genetic "genes" in *The Selfish Gene* (New York: Oxford University Press, 1976).
65. *Xunzi* ch. 8 (儒效); cf. Hutton, *Xunzi*, 65.

use of the genes they were born with, but the accumulation of memes, of transmitted ideas that evolve over time and which make up culture, is what distinguishes humans from the rest. One problem in the transmission of cultural knowledge is bias, from which teachers are not exempt. We saw above that the goal was to be "reality-based," which is to say, objective, but this is a difficult goal. Zhuangzi rhetorically asks: "[If one] follows one's completed mind and makes it one's teacher, who would then be without a teacher?" (夫隨其成心而師之，誰獨且無師乎？)[66] "Completed" here means "biased" or "closed." A "completed mind" is never a good thing, because new information about natural principles and ethics is, practically speaking, limitless.

Teachers present, critically assess, and creatively improvise uses for cultural ideas, to and with students, by means of explanation. The task of explanation was described thus: "The arts of discussion and exposition [are these]: establish it with even-handed seriousness, situate it with utmost honesty, grasp it with steady strength, illustrate it with clear explanations, clarify it with distinctive differentiation, and transmit it with a pleasant fragrance." (夫談說之術：齊莊以立之，端誠以處之，堅強以持之，辟稱以喻之，分別以明之，歡忻芬芳以送之。)[67] The "it" is simply the idea under discussion, and while the advice to "transmit it with a pleasant fragrance" goes unexplained, I take it to mean "with a cheerful attitude," so that students are not subjected to tedious instruction by a bored teacher. But the advice to establish (i.e., articulate), situate (i.e., give context), grasp (i.e., focus on), illustrate (i.e., give examples, use metaphors), and clarify (i.e., distinguish it from other, similar ideas) is quite sound.

Another goal of teachers is to encourage students to get to the point where they are capable and willing of being their *own* teachers; to inculcate a love of learning. Kongzi conveyed this when he said "If [one's learning] is [only] as big as an ant-hill yet [they try] to advance [it], I will join them. If [it] is [even] as big as a hill, yet [they] stop, I will be finished [with them]." (如垤而進，吾與之；如丘而止，吾已矣。)[68] Motivation is key, and, though self-motivation is the Platonic ideal, how to get unmotivated students to be motivated is a perennial problem. Back in c. 500 BCE, it was more of a *sine qua non*. Kongzi, accordingly, summarized his view on this issue by saying:

---

66. *Zhuangzi* ch. 2 (齊物論); cf. Watson, *Zhuangzi*, 9.
67. *Hanshi waizhuan* ch. 5.22; cf. Hightower, *Han Shih Wai Chuan*, 180.
68. *Xunzi* ch. 28 (宥坐); cf. Hutton, *Xunzi*, 322.

"[I] will not open [the door] for the unmotivated, nor will [I] encourage [those who] do not try to articulate themselves. [If I] hold up one corner [of a problem, and the student] does not [even try to] come back to me with the other three, then [I] will not [attempt to instruct them] again." (不憤不啟，不悱不發。舉一隅不以三隅反，則不復也。)[69] This, however, may well have been more of a practical expedient than a philosophical stand.[70]

---

69. *Lunyu* 7.8; cf. Slingerland, *Analects*, 66.

70. This stated desire for motivated students should be weighed against the statement directly preceding this one, where Kongzi says he has never refused a student who had come to him with even the smallest token for tuition.

Chapter 7

Music (樂)

"In general, music is a harmonization of Heaven and Earth, a blending of Yin and Yang."

—*Lü shi chunqiu* ch. 5.2

凡樂,天地之和,陰陽之調也。《呂氏春秋。大樂》

Music in Self-Cultivation

The role of music in self-cultivation makes eminent sense in the naturalistic context of early China, if one accepts the wind in the trees or a chorus of cicadas as "music." Given the perception that humans are but an extension of the natural environment—albeit intelligent ones powerful enough to form "a triad with Heaven and Earth"—it makes sense to claim that at least some "human extrapolations" from nature would be construed as deriving from a plane more fundamental than the human one. One classic text claims: "Heaven is above and Earth is below, with the myriad things dispersed and differentiated [between them], and with protocol constituting their activities. [These primordial conditions] flowed without ceasing, harmoniously coming together and developing, and music arose among them. Spring arousal and summer maturation are [their] goodness; autumn gathering and winter storing are [their] propriety. [This] goodness is akin to [our] music and [this] propriety is akin to [our] protocol." (天高地下,萬物散殊,而禮制行矣。流而不息,合同而化,而樂興焉。春作夏長,仁也;秋斂冬藏,義

也。仁近於樂，義近於禮。)[1] A few more details on "these primordial conditions" consisting of Heaven, Earth, and everything between them come a few paragraphs later, hinting at just how music might have arisen in this context. "Earthly *qi*-substance ascends evenly while Heavenly *qi*-substance descends compliantly, Yin and Yang come into contact with each other, Heaven and Earth wash over each other, drumming the other with thunder claps, arousing the other with wind and rain, moving the other with the four seasons, warming the other with sun and moon, and the multitudinous developments arose among them. Given these, then, music is the harmony of Heaven and Earth." (地氣上齊，天氣下降，陰陽相摩，天地相蕩，鼓之以雷霆，奮之以風雨，動之以四時，暖之以日月，而百化興焉。如此，則樂者天地之和也。)[2] Here we have the sounds of thunder, wind, and rain amid the harmonious contact, the visceral embrace, of Heaven and Earth.

But these are not the only natural sounds that might be construed as music. Thunder and rain are not merely the effects of "contact," but are also signifiers of cosmic coitus between Heaven and Earth, which results in the production of the myriad things, the most immediately visible of which are plants. "Sprouts sprout initiated by thunder, and coalesce into their forms. [These] forms have hollows, all of which make sounds [in the wind]. [These] sounds come forth harmoniously, and [this] harmony comes forth in moderation. [With this] harmony and moderation, prior kings established music: it was from this [that human-made music] was produced." (萌芽始震，凝寒以形。形體有處，莫不有聲。聲出於和，和出於適。和適先王定樂，由此而生。)[3] Elsewhere, the sounds that come forth from wind in the hollows of bushes and trees is called "the piping of Earth" (地籟), after the bamboo pan-pipes used by the early Chinese, and is characterized as something of a natural symphony.[4] This extrapolation from nature, then, is the precedent for human music.

Music of the human variety, despite the correspondence to "harmony" made above, can be used for good or ill. "The origination of music is

---

1. *Liji* 禮記 ch. 19 (樂記); cf. James Legge, *Li Chi: Book of Rites* (1885; rpt. New York: University Books, 1967), 2:102–103.

2. *Liji* ch. 19 (樂記); cf. Legge, *Li Chi*, 2:104.

3. *Lüshi chunqiu* 呂氏春秋 ch. 5.2 (大樂); cf. John Knoblock and Jeffrey Riegel, *The Annals of Lü Buwei* (Stanford: Stanford University Press, 2000), 137.

4. *Zhuangzi* 莊子 ch. 2 (齊物論); cf. Burton Watson, *The Complete Works of Zhuangzi* (New York: Columbia University Press, 1968; 2013), 7–8.

venerable, and certainly cannot be discarded. [Music] has [those whom] it regulates and [those whom] it makes profligate; it has [those whom] it corrects and [those whom] it corrupts. Worthy people use it to flourish, while unworthy people use it to fail." (樂所由來者尚也，必不可廢。有節有侈，有正有淫矣。賢者以昌，不肖者以亡。)[5] It is not clear which kinds of music were thought to make people profligate and corrupt, but one source says, rather offhandedly, that "Music taken to the extreme leads to anxiety." (樂極則憂).[6] Reading between the lines, we can safely say that music that is not harmonious is not good, but what, exactly, constitutes extreme or unharmonious music is left to the reader to decide.[7] Which is probably as it should be, given the variety of people's preferences for music.

Here we are specifically interested in music for self-cultivation, which ostensibly has a long pedigree. "In general, when the kings of the [first] three dynasties taught their princes, they certainly [did so] with protocol and music. Music is that by which [one's] *interior* is cultivated; protocol is that by which [one's] *exterior* is cultivated." (凡三王教世子必以禮樂。樂，所以修內也；禮，所以修外也。)[8] But music for self-cultivation is not, of course, reserved solely for princes of yore; everyone can reap the benefits of musical harmony. One of these benefits is a kind of elegance. "Music is that which moves [us] internally. . . . music brings about fullness, yet [also] introspection, and [we can] use [this] introspection to become cultured." (樂也者，動於內者也. . . . 樂盈而反，以反為文。)[9] Being cultured is a goal that is realized both inwardly and outwardly, and music is thought to help achieve inward harmony.

Music influences us inwardly by affecting our minds, just as protocol influences us outwardly by guiding our behavior. This interior influence can be calming and aid focus: "Music is an abiding harmony, and protocol is an abiding [natural] principle. . . . The combination of protocol and music brings order to people's minds." (樂也者，和之不可變者也；禮也者，理之

---

5. *Lüshi chunqiu* ch. 5.5 (古樂); cf. Knoblock and Riegel, *The Annals of Lü Buwei*, 146.

6. *Liji* ch. 19 (樂記); cf. Legge, *Li Chi*, 2:102.

7. Erica Brindley suggests that a Yin-Yang balance in music was desirable: "tonal imbalance in one's immediate environment affects the seasons of the body just as cosmic imbalance affects the seasons of Earth"; see Erica Brindley, *Music, Cosmology, and the Politics of Harmony in Early China* (Albany: State University of New York Press, 2012), 134.

8. *Liji* ch. 8 (文王世子); cf. Legge, *Li Chi*, 1:349.

9. *Liji* ch. 19 (樂記); cf. Legge, *Li Chi*, 2:126.

不可易者也. . . . 禮樂之統，管乎人心矣。)¹⁰ And music does more than help to bring order to the mind, it also helps to foster its ultimate goal of mental acuity: "Sagacity and wisdom are that which are produced from protocol and music." (聖知，禮樂之所由生也。)¹¹ The harmony with which music is associated also aids the pursuit of virtuosity, which is in constant dialogue with desire. "Music is that by which [one] guides happiness, and [the musical instruments of] metal, stone, silk, and bamboo are those by which one guides virtuosity." (樂者，所以道樂也，金石絲竹，所以道德也。)¹² How might music achieve this?

Two specific ways by which music helps us further our virtuosity are by inhibiting anger and by inhibiting excessive desire. We already saw in chapter 2 that "For regulating [the potential excesses of] anger, nothing is better than music."¹³ Excessive desire, a *bête noire* in China since ancient times, is also targeted. "Prior kings instituted protocol and music, not to satiate the desires of the mouth, belly, ears, and eyes, but rather to instruct the people to make equanimous their likes and dislikes and to return to the correct human way." (先王之制禮樂也，非以極口腹耳目之欲也，將以教民平好惡而反人道之正也。)¹⁴ Desires, as well as likes and dislikes, are to be made equanimous and corrected, that is, channeled in a positive direction that benefits both the individual and the community; music can help.

Another source posits two steps for creating music, one that functions to regulate desire and a second that builds upon the state of already having had one's desires regulated: "Creating music has a capability, [insofar as it] certainly regulates strong attractions and desires. When strong attractions and desires are not aberrant, then music may be concentrated on. Concentrating on music has an art [to it], [insofar as it] certainly derives from equanimity, and equanimity derives from impartiality." (成樂有具，必節嗜慾。嗜慾不辟，樂乃可務。務樂有術，必由平出，平出於公。)¹⁵ The author does not

---

10. *Xunzi* 荀子 ch. 20 (樂論); cf. Eric Hutton, *Xunzi: The Complete Text* (Princeton: Princeton University Press, 2014), 221. The word for "bring order to" (管) also refers to an ancient bamboo flute.

11. *Wuxing* 五行; cf. Scott Cook, *The Bamboo Texts of Guodian* (Cornell: Cornell University East Asia Program, 2012), 1:506.

12. *Xunzi* ch. 20 (樂論); cf. Hutton, *Xunzi*, 221. Note: 道 = 導.

13. *Guanzi* 管子 ch. 37 (心術下). See chap. 2, n. 45.

14. *Liji* ch. 19 (樂記); cf. Legge, *Li Chi*, 2:96.

15. *Lüshi chunqiu* ch. 5.2 (大樂); cf. Knoblock and Riegel, *The Annals of Lü Buwei*, 137.

explain just how "creating music" regulates desires: perhaps it too draws upon a state of impartiality, one of the virtuosities considered in chapter 4. If so, then "creating music" and "concentrating on music" would be functionally identical. If not, then the former would be a kind of step one, while the latter would be step two. Either way, "concentrating on music," at least, draws upon impartiality to bring equanimity to (that is, to harmonize) our excessive desires. If we construe impartiality as a *mental* state and excessive desire as an *emotional* state, then this will be a case of the mind exerting some degree of calming influence over the heart. Music alone, however, may be insufficient, as we have seen in the foregoing quotes that it was often paired with protocol. Kongzi, therefore, places music toward the end of the process of self-cultivation: "Inspire [yourself] with poetry, establish [yourself] with protocol, complete [yourself] with music." (興於詩，立於禮，成於樂。)[16]

Music Results in: Personal Happiness (樂)

We saw above that music can help with mental orderliness, which is a goal of self-cultivation, but it has an added benefit of making us happy, which is another, perhaps underestimated, goal of self-cultivation. "Mastering music in order to bring order to the mind results in an easy-going yet correct, caring, and forgiving mind being spontaneously produced. A mind that is easy-going, correct, caring, and forgiving will be happy, and if happy, then secure, and if secure, then long-lived. . . ." (致樂以治心，則易、直、子、諒之心油然生矣。易直子諒之心生則樂，樂則安，安則久. . . .)[17] Happiness is a part of our human nature, and music is an extension of it. This is reflected in the fact that the same Chinese graph (i.e., 樂) denotes both happiness and music. Their relation is perhaps best summarized thus:

> Music is happiness, and is unavoidable given human inclinations. The reason why humans cannot do without music is that when they feel happy they often express it in music and song, embody it in movement and stillness. Thereby, the human way, [including] music and song, movement and stillness, and the mutable arts

---

16. *Lunyu* 論語 8.8; cf. Edward Slingerland, *Confucius: Analects with Selections from Traditional Commentaries* (Indianapolis: Hackett, 2003), 80.

17. *Liji* ch. 19 (樂記); cf. Legge, *Li Chi*, 2:125. Note: 子 = 慈.

of [human] nature are fulfilled in it [i.e., music]. Thus people cannot be without happiness, and happiness then cannot be without embodiment, but if the embodiment does not [help] create the [human] way, then it will not fail to create chaos.

(夫樂者，樂也，人情之所必不免也。故人不能無樂，樂則必發於聲音，形於動靜；而人之道，聲音、動靜，性術之變盡是矣。故人不能不樂，樂則不能無形，形而不為道，則不能無亂。)[18]

Music and song can be "embodied" in "stillness" when, for example, singing in a choir where not everyone sings at once. Unfortunately, neither the phrase "the mutable arts of [human] nature" nor "arts of [human] nature" appears elsewhere in the text, but they no doubt refer to a variety of ways that human nature manifests itself, in addition to the present topic of happiness. In any case, the initial connection between happiness and music, as well as the subsequent connection between good music and the proper human way, may be seen as a reciprocal one.

Music may naturally spring from happiness, but its utility extends beyond just being an emotional outlet. Another text claims that music can be used as a deterrent. "For stopping anger, nothing is better than poetry, for being rid of worry, nothing is better than music." (止怒莫若詩，去憂莫若樂。)[19] Thus, music can be used to properly channel happiness and effectively unburden oneself from worry. Emotions can disturb the mind; music can help with this. Thus: "Noble people listen to it [i.e., music] in order to make equanimous their minds, and when the mind is equanimous, virtuosity is harmonious." (君子聽之以平其心，心平，德和。)[20]

Music Results in: Social Harmony (合)

Music is beneficial for the cultivation of personal happiness, but it is also useful for the common weal. This begins at the cosmic level. We saw above

---

18. *Xunzi* ch. 20 (樂論); cf. Hutton, *Xunzi*, 218. This passage is also found at *Liji* ch. 19 (樂記), with minor, but interesting, differences.

19. *Guanzi* ch. 49 (內業); cf. W. Allyn Rickett, *Guanzi: Political, Economic, and Philosophical Essays from Early China* (Princeton: Princeton University Press, 1985, 1998), 2:52.

20. *Zuozhuan* 左傳 (昭公 20); cf. Stephen Durrant, Wai-yee Li, David Schaberg, *Zuozhuan: Commentary on the "Spring and Autumn Annals"* (Seattle: University of Washington Press, 2016), 3:1587–89.

that "music is the harmony of Heaven and Earth." But, if forced to choose, it has a closer affinity to the former. "Music emphasizes harmony, leads the spirit, and follows Heaven; protocol distinguishes proprieties, settles ghosts, and follows Earth. Thus sagely people create music in order to respond to Heaven, and institute protocol in order to accompany Earth." (樂者敦和，率神而從天；禮者別宜，居鬼而從地。故聖人作樂以應天，制禮以配地。)[21] This assessment could refer to the creative aspect of music, whereas protocol is often learned passively, as part of our cultural upbringing. In any case, pairing music with protocol implies harmony should be conceived as social as well as personal. Music might also be connected to natural principles. We saw above that "prior kings instituted protocol and music" in order to pacify the "likes and dislikes" of the people. Another source has that same sentence, but rather than ending with "to return to the correct human way," it ends by claiming that prior kings instituted music and protocol to cause the people "to act with [natural] principles and propriety" (行理義也).[22] We also saw in chapter 1 that natural principles derive from the interaction of Heaven *and* Earth, so while music may "follow Heaven," it is nevertheless implicated in both aspects of the cosmic dyad.

Music, with its roots in the cosmic, affects the entire natural environment and all its inhabitants.

> When great people extol protocol and music, then Heaven and Earth will be reflected in them [i.e., in the protocol and music]. [Similarly,] when Heaven and Earth happily unite, Yin and Yang mutually obtain, warmly covering and nurturing the myriad things. Afterwards, grasses and trees flourish, small sprouts rise up, feathers and wings ruffle, horns and antlers grow, hibernating insects revive, feathered animals warm their eggs, furred animals nurture their young, those that have live young have none that are stillborn, and those that lay eggs have none that do not hatch: the way of music comes together in these.
>
> (大人舉禮樂，則天地將為昭焉。天地訢合，陰陽相得，煦嫗覆育萬物。然後草木茂，區萌達，羽翼奮，角骼生，蟄蟲昭蘇，羽者嫗伏，毛者孕鬻，胎生者不殰，而卵生者不殈：則樂之道歸焉耳。)[23]

---

21. *Liji* ch. 19 (樂記); cf. Legge, *Li Chi*, 2:103.
22. *Lüshi chunqiu* ch. 5.4 (適音); cf. Knoblock and Riegel, *The Annals of Lü Buwei*, 145.
23. *Liji* ch. 19 (樂記); cf. Legge, *Li Chi*, 2:115.

This picture of flourishing nature may not always conjure an aural image—after all, what do growing antlers sound like?—but taken together, it represents a symphony of outdoor sounds: the wind in the trees, wings flapping, cicadas serenading, and the cooing and murmurs that mothers and their young often make to one another. It is a romantic picture, but an old and appealing one.

Music also has an effect on individuals at the physical level. I suspect most people who have been to a live concert can confirm this. In the following quote, "*qi*-substance" is a vague, but physiological, term that probably means something like "enthusiasm" or "energy" in this context. One might imagine punk and classical music as modern instances of these two kinds of music: "In general, when vulgar sounds move people, a perverse *qi*-substance [within them] responds to it, and when this perverse *qi*-substance takes shape, then disorderliness is produced within them. [Alternatively,] when correct sounds move people, an accordant *qi*-substance [within them] responds to it, and when this accordant *qi*-substance takes shape, then orderliness is produced within them." (凡奸聲感人而逆氣應之，逆氣成象而亂生焉。正聲感人而順氣應之，順氣成象而治生焉。)[24] "Perverse" and "accordant" could also be translated as "anti-social" and "social" (in the sense of enjoying the company of others). Thus, though music affects us on an individual level, the result is one that influences our sociability, and, thereby, our society.

Music has another social aspect insofar as musical performances are sometimes social events. "Thus, when music is performed, human relationships are clarified, ears and eyes are made perceptive, blood and *qi*-substance are harmonized, customs and culture are modified, and the world is calmed." (故樂行而倫清，耳目聰明，血氣和平，移風易俗，天下皆寧。)[25] Human relationships are analogs to various players in a band or orchestra: different people play different roles, in both the family and the community. Hence music can "clarify" who does what, both on and off stage. In this way, musical performance both creates in us individually a harmonious spirit and presents us with an idealized example of what social harmony might look like: an orchestra. Accordingly, though music and protocol have often been presented in tandem in several of the passages above, one author could claim, of the traditional music of his time, that "if this music is lost, then protocol will follow it" (夫樂亡而禮從之).[26] Music helps keep the social

---

24. *Xunzi* ch. 20 (樂論); cf. Hutton, *Xunzi*, 220.
25. *Liji* ch. 19 (樂記); cf. Legge, *Li Chi*, 2:111.
26. *Yanzi chunqiu* 晏子春秋 ch. 1.6; cf. Olivia Milburn, The *Spring and Autumn Annals of Master Yan* (Leiden: Brill, 2016), 172.

contract effective by creating social harmony in the individual and modeling social harmony as a symphony.

Three specific instantiations in our sources of music creating social harmony are musical performances at the royal ancestral temple, at clan meetings in the village square, and at home. These performances bring together people of different status and facilitate them in fulfilling their various roles. At the royal court, this results in "harmonious respect" (和敬); among clans at the village level, "harmonious accordance" (和順); and within the family, "harmonious familiality" (和親).[27] Music, then, has a role to play at all levels, and for all members, of society.

These foregoing claims about the harmonizing power of music may be a little surprising in the context of Western philosophy, but I do not find them too counterintuitive. Sometimes, however, our sources do press the issue a bit far. Referring to a particular song written by a sage-king of old, it was said of the five-tone scale employed in that song:

> [When one] heard the *gong* tone, it caused the people to be conscientious and generous; [when one] heard the *shang* tone, it caused the people to be modest and proper; [when one] heard the *jiao* tone, it caused the people to be compassionate and good; [when one] heard the *zhi* tone, it caused the people to be nourishing and giving; and [when one] heard the *yu* tone, it caused the people to be respectful and to love protocol."
>
> (聞其宮聲，使人溫良而寬大；聞其商聲，使人方廉而好義；聞其角聲，使人惻隱而愛仁；聞其徵聲，使人樂養而好施；聞其羽聲，使人恭敬而好禮。)[28]

While different musical tones certainly do elicit generalizable responses from an audience, the specificity of these five, at least in this description, seems too unequivocal to modern ears.

Mozi is the most famous skeptic of the social utility of music in our sources. Recounting the music created during successive reigns of the past, he correlated those songs with what was generally agreed to be the declining effectiveness of the successive rulers. (Early Chinese scholars were mostly

---

27. *Liji* ch. 19 (樂記); cf. Legge, *Li Chi*, 2:127–28.
28. *Hanshi waizhuan* 韓詩外傳 ch. 8.31; cf. James Hightower, *Han Shih Wai Chuan: Han Ying's Illustrations of the Didactic Application of the Classic of Songs* (Cambridge: Harvard University Press, 1952), 285.

a romantic lot, assuming a golden age in remote antiquity that gradually declined until the then-present, decadent age. Your grandfather may have a similar view of the world.) Given this correlation, Mozi did not doubt that traditional music could instill harmony in its listeners, but he did think that the increasing complexity of the newer music became less and less effective at this task: "Thus, when their music became increasingly elaborate, their orderliness increasingly diminished. Seen this way, music is *not* the means by which to order the world." (故其樂逾繁者，其治逾寡。自此觀之，樂非所以治天下也。)²⁹ By his own admission, then, music per se is not insufficient for this task, but rather "elaborate" music is. We can only wonder if increasingly elaborate music did not entail increasing elaborate predictions, as in the previous quote, of their effects.

It is also possible that by "elaborate" music, Mozi was not in fact referring to the music itself, but rather to elaborate royal *performances* of music. Elsewhere in his text he says: "Nowadays, kings, dukes, and grand officers cannot do without creating music, excessively diminishing and confiscating the resources that the people use for clothing and food, in order to have music performed in this manner. This is why Scholar Mozi said: Making music is wrong." (今王公大人唯毋為樂，虧奪民衣食之財，以拊樂如此多也。是故子墨子曰：「為樂非也。」)³⁰ Here, too, it is not music itself that is under attack, only music that is so costly to perform that the taxes needed to pay for it adversely affect the livelihoods of the people. Music, at the level of the state, was thus not a priority for this author, but this is not a criticism of the use of music for self-cultivation. Therefore, we may remain confident of the claim made in chapter 4, that "noble people take goodness as their benevolence, propriety as their principle, protocol as their behavior, and music as their harmony."³¹ Because our sources describe music as an inevitable outcome of our emotions, having an effect both upon our persons and our community, it must be considered a significant avenue of self-cultivation.

---

29. *Mozi* 墨子 ch. 7 (三辯); cf. John Knoblock and Jeffrey Riegel, *Mozi: A Study and Translation of the Ethical and Political Writings* (Berkeley: University of California, Berkeley, 2013), 77.

30. *Mozi* ch. 32 (非樂上); cf. Knoblock and Riegel, *Mozi*, 278.

31. *Zhuangzi* ch. 33 (天下); see chap. 4, n. 224.

PART IV
COSMOS (天)

Chapter 8

Fate (命)

"Thoroughly pursue [natural] principles and fully follow [human] nature in order to apprehend fate."

—*Yijing*, "Explaining the Hexagrams"

窮理盡性以至於命。《易經。說卦》

Introduction

Fate consists of those things that inform us and affect us which we cannot avoid. It refers to things like when and where we were born, who our parents and siblings are, the color of our hair and eyes and, indeed, our entire genetic makeup.[1] Our cultural inheritance is also fated, insofar as we did not choose the culture(s) in which we grew up, though once we come of age, we can begin to interact with our culture in novel ways and begin to challenge its received wisdom. Fate, then, exists on a spectrum. On one end there are things that it would really be better to simply accept: we cannot change our ethnicity or the era in which we were born. On the other end, there are situations into which we were born that we *can* change: we can

---

1. Karl Marx famously remarked: "Men make their own history, but they do not make it as they please; they do not make it under self-selected circumstances, but under circumstances existing already, given and transmitted from the past." Karl Marx, "The Eighteenth Brumaire of Louis Bonaparte," *Die Revolution* (1852), translated by Saul Padover. https://www.marxists.org/archive/marx/works/download/pdf/18th-Brumaire.pdf

dye our hair, wear contacts, move away from our hometown, and embrace different cultural norms. In the middle are those things that we cannot eradicate, but we may be able to ameliorate: we might have inherited a gene that predisposes us to certain physical or psychological conditions that we can keep at bay. Or we may have imbibed certain cultural or cognitive biases that are best dealt with using persistent vigilance. The semantic range of the idea of fate is, thereby, broad to the point of sometimes being unwieldy.[2] For this reason, I will distinguish between "fate" and "destiny," the latter of which will be discussed in the following chapter. "Fate" will refer to that which is inescapable, while "destiny" will refer to that which can (and often should) be changed.

Fate in early Chinese thought is said to derive from Heaven. The Chinese graph for "fate" (命) is the same graph for "command" or "mandate," so that which Heaven "commands" is referred to as the "Heavenly mandate" (天命), which at the level of the individual is "fate." This is a central tenet of early Chinese thought and we have already encountered it several times. We saw in the introduction, for example, that Heaven mandates our shared human nature.[3] In chapter 1, we saw that we are all fated to die.[4] In these basic senses, our fates are unremarkable, and we can agree, taking "Heaven" to be "nature," that "the fate of humans lies with Heaven" (人之命在天).[5] But the implications are nevertheless broad and definitely worth considering for their impact upon self-cultivation.

Heaven, as the active, Yang half of the Heaven-Earth dyad, would stand in for "nature" in the so-called "nature versus nurture" dichotomy.[6] But the circumstances in which we find ourselves—"nature" as context—may appear to favor some people more than others. Whereas other cultures might attribute the disparity to a "universal law" of karma or the machinations of a theistic judge, Heaven in early China was often conceived as something that "sends rain on the just and the unjust alike."[7] Zhuangzi tells the story

---

2. For an edited volume that addresses this unwieldiness, see Christopher Lupke, ed., *The Magnitude of Ming: Command, Allotment, and Fate in Chinese Culture* (Honolulu: University of Hawaii Press, 2005).

3. *Liji* 禮記 ch. 31 (中庸). See introduction, n. 65.

4. *Liji* ch. 4 (檀弓下). See chap. 1, n. 72.

5. *Xunzi* 荀子 ch. 16 (彊國); cf. Eric Hutton, *Xunzi: The Complete Text* (Princeton: Princeton University Press, 2014), 163.

6. As we saw in the introduction, "Heaven" in earlier texts is more anthropomorphic and less so in later texts, ending up, for some writers, as simply another word for "nature."

7. "Matthew" 5:45.

of a poor and unfortunate person who nevertheless does not blame Heaven for his woe: "Heaven impartially covers [all], and Earth impartially carries [all], so why would Heaven and Earth specifically impoverish *me*? [I] have looked within them for a doer but without success. Thus, my extreme condition must be fate!" (天無私覆，地無私載，天地豈私貧我哉？求其為之者而不得也。然而至此極者，命也夫！)[8] Fate, then, is not amenable to appeal, but that does not mean that it is not open to inquiry.

Insofar as the time and place of one's demise will likely be out of our hands, it is a matter of circumstance, or fate. Similarly, whether or not we enjoy a long or short lifespan may also be a matter of fate.[9] This should not be taken to imply fatalism. We still have at least a modicum of control over when and how we die, not least through care of the body, as discussed in chapter 1. There is also the matter of timeliness, the topic of chapter 5. Timeliness and fate are explicitly brought together by Zhuangzi in a discussion of the perennial decision of whether to engage in politics to better one's community or to stay clear of the sausage factory and be a (political) recluse. "With appropriate timing and fate, [worthy recluses would have undertaken] great actions in the world, so [they could then] return to oneness without leaving a trace. Without appropriate timing and fate, [such recluses would have only] great destitution in the world, so [they would] deepen [their] roots, perfectly calm, and wait. This is the way self-preservation." (當時命而大行乎天下，則反一無迹。不當時命而大窮乎天下，則深根寧極而待。此存身之道也。)[10] Thus, fate can be construed as either appropriate or not appropriate to one's goals and of particular consequence for which actions should and should not be pursued.

Perceiving fate in circumstances goes well beyond construing circumstance as merely favorable or unfavorable. We can in fact equate "fate" with whatever it is that we come across in life: "circumstances [we] encounter are called fate" (節遇謂之命).[11] This is particularly true when the circumstances are unexpected or inexplicable: "Fate is that which happens even though

---

8. *Zhuangzi* 莊子 ch. 6 (大宗師); cf. Burton Watson, *The Complete Works of Zhuangzi* (New York: Columbia University Press, 1968; 2013), 54.

9. *Hanfeizi* 韓非子 ch. 50 (顯學): "Long life is [a matter of] fate" (壽命也); cf. Burton Watson, *The Basic Writings of Han Fei Tzu* (New York: Columbia University Press, 1964), 126.

10. *Zhuangzi* ch. 16 (繕性); cf. Watson, *Zhuangzi*, 124.

11. *Xunzi* ch. 22 (正名); cf. Hutton, *Xunzi*, 236. *Jie* 節 as "circumstances" is somewhat unusual but can also be found in *Xunzi* ch. 17.

we do not know why it happens thus." (命也者，不知所以然而然者也。)[12] It is in this sense that "knowing fate" might be understood as "expect the unexpected." In this way, fate is that which sets the scene in which we may pursue physical or ethical self-cultivation.

Though we are all fated to find ourselves in situations beyond our control, it is not the case that we each face circumstances of equal advantage: some fates are simply better than others. "Of those that receive their fate from Earth, pines and cypresses especially can persist through winter and summer and stay green. Of those that receive their fate from Heaven, Shun especially was correct, and was fortunate to be able to correct his life, in order to correct a multitude of lives." (受命於地，唯松柏獨也在冬夏青青。受命於天，唯舜獨也正，幸能正生，以正眾生。)[13] In this example, Shun was "fortunate" to be fated as he was, but his "correctness" was not a foregone conclusion—it was not "preordained"—because he was born only with the "ability" (能) to correct himself. As the next chapter will make clear, the opportunities afforded by fate must often still be met with the hard work of fulfilling one's destiny.

Fate as circumstance pairs naturally with how we act in a given circumstance. That is, fate may be thought of as an "outer" context that interacts with an "inner" element. There are at least three examples of such inner elements: human nature, virtuosity in general, and the motivational virtuosity of propriety in particular. One pairing of "[human] nature and fate" (性命) correlates human nature with Heaven and fate with Earth.[14] Mengzi, meanwhile, contrasts what is "within ourselves" yet can still be lost—i.e., virtuosity—with external things like wealth, the obtaining of which involves fate.[15] Finally, Zhuangzi more specifically juxtaposes fate with propriety: "The world has two great strictures: the first is fate, the second is propriety. A child's love for their parents is fate, as it cannot be

---

12. *Lüshi chunqiu* 呂氏春秋 ch. 20.3 (知分); cf. John Knoblock and Jeffrey Riegel, *The Annals of Lü Buwei* (Stanford: Stanford University Press, 2000), 521.

13. *Zhuangzi* ch. 5 (德充符); cf. Watson, *Zhuangzi*, 35. Shun was the fifth of the mytho-historical "five thearchs" (五帝). Chen Guying amends these sentences significantly, but the gist of a fortunate fate remains. See Chen Guying 陳鼓應, *Zhuangzi jinzhu jinyi* 莊子今註今譯, 2 vols. (臺北: 臺灣商務印書館, 1974; revised ed. 1999), 1:157, note 18.

14. *Liji* 禮記 ch. 19 (樂記); cf. James Legge, *Li Chi: Book of Rites* (1885; rpt. New York: University Books, 1967), 2:104.

15. *Mengzi* 孟子 ch. 7A3 (盡心上); cf. Bryan Van Norden, *Mengzi: With Selections from Traditional Commentaries* (Indianapolis: Hackett, 2008), 172.

unbound from their heart. A minister's service to their ruler is propriety, as no matter where you go there will be rulers." (天下有大戒二：其一，命也；其一，義也。子之愛親，命也，不可解於心。臣之事君，義也，無適而非君也。)[16] Children, at least generally speaking and at least up to a certain age, naturally love their parents. Ministers, on the other hand, and particularly during the Warring States era in China, have a choice about which ruler to serve. The motivation to serve derives from an inner sense of propriety, and the decision to serve hinges on whether the minister's sense of propriety perceives the ruler to be good or bad.

Thus fate is not trivial. Kongzi said: "[Those who] do not understand fate lack [one of] the means to become a noble person." (不知命，無以為君子也。)[17] *Why* this is the case is the subject of this chapter.

Ameliorable Fate

Death is ultimately a matter of fate because most of us have no choice in the time and place of our own demise. But this does not mean that we can thereby act carelessly or as if we could not hasten our end. Kongzi spelled it out for us:

> People have three ways to die that are not fated but rather that they choose for themselves. Those who live in places that are not principled [i.e., orderly], those who eat and drink without moderation, and those who are either inactive or active in excessive measure: *sickness* will kill them all. Those who occupy an inferior position yet like to oppose their superiors, those who are insatiably addicted to desires, and those who seek and demand endlessly: [state] *punishment* will kill them all. Those with few [allies] who make enemies of the many, those who are weak yet insult the strong, and those who cannot control their

---

16. *Zhuangzi* ch. 4 (人間世); cf. Watson, *Zhuangzi*, 27.
17. *Lunyu* 論語 20.3. The passage continues: "[Those who] do not understand protocol lack [one of] the means to establish [themselves]. [Those who] do not understand words lack [one of] the means to understand other people." (不知禮，無以立也。不知言，無以知人也。) cf. Edward Slingerland, *Confucius: Analects with Selections from Traditional Commentaries* (Indianapolis: Hackett, 2003), 234.

anger: *weapons* will kill them all. Thus are there three ways to die that are not fated but rather that they choose for themselves.

(人有三死而非命也者,自取之也。居處不理,飲食不節,佚勞過度者,病共人殺之。居下而好干上,嗜欲無厭,求索不止者,刑共殺之。少以敵眾,弱以侮強,忿不量力者,兵共殺之。故有三死而非命者,自取之也。)[18]

Sickness at home, punishment as a citizen of a body politic, and death by weaponry in domestic and international society: these can often be ameliorated by, roughly speaking, (health) science, ethical orderliness, and prudence.

Kongzi here adduces one's living situation, dietary habits, and exercise regimen as potential causes of death that one cannot blame on fate. Home can thus be a dangerous place if one is not careful. One potentially life-threatening "home" situation that *was* thought to be a matter of fate was pregnancy.[19] Given the increase of scientific knowledge about biological reproduction since that opinion was expressed, one might venture a guess that getting pregnant would no longer be considered a matter of fate. Or not, given the still somewhat haphazard nature of getting pregnant. Similarly, another author thought that "getting injured is fate" (有疾,命矣).[20] The injury in question was an axe that was knocked from where it hung, falling and cutting off a man's foot. Here the cause of injury was not mysterious at all, but the unexpectedness of the event seems to have qualified it for consideration as fated. In fact, later in this same text, another person is incredulous at the habit of ascribing to fate what really belongs in the explainable realm of what we now might call "science." He asked, rhetorically, "The natural occurrence of fortune and misfortune are taken by the masses to be matters of fate, but how could they not know where they come from?" (禍福之所自來,眾人以為命,焉不知其所由?)[21] This was

---

18. *Hanshi waizhuan* 韓詩外傳 ch. 1.4; cf. James Hightower, *Han Shih Wai Chuan: Han Ying's Illustrations of the Didactic Application of the Classic of Songs* (Cambridge: Harvard University Press, 1952), 15.

19. *Shijing* 詩經 #51 (螽蜥); cf. Arthur Waley, *The Book of Songs: The Ancient Chinese Classic of Poetry* (1937; edited with additional translations by Joseph Allen; New York: Grove Press, 1996), 43. Pregnancy in premodern times was potentially "life-threatening" due to the higher risk of maternal mortality.

20. *Lüshi chunqiu* ch. 6.3 (音初); cf. Knoblock and Riegel, *The Annals of Lü Buwei*, 161.

21. *Lüshi chunqiu* ch. 20.4 (召類); cf. Knoblock and Riegel, *The Annals of Lü Buwei*, 522.

in the context of things that the author thought were logically explainable: how different notes on stringed instruments resonate with other notes, for example, or how a poorly managed state tends to attract those who would take advantage of the disorder to enrich themselves. In all these examples, "fate" may or may not be fate, depending on the degree to which one understands the circumstances.[22]

While facts about the world are one thing, human ethics are quite another. As we saw in chapter 2, our sources are not in agreement about whether or not human nature tends toward the good, the bad, neither, or both, but Mengzi is a champion of the first option. He makes an interesting distinction between perception and virtuosity, noting that both are influenced by both human nature and fate, but says the one that takes more effort lies—or should be conceptualized as lying, possibly for ethical rather than ontological reasons—more in our nature, with the reverse being true of fate.

> The way the mouth is to flavors, the eyes to colors, the ear to sounds, the nose to smells, and the four limbs to comfort: these *are* in [human] *nature*, but there is fate in them [too], so the noble person does *not* call them "[human] *nature*" [because they do not need to be cultivated]. The goodness between fathers and sons, the propriety between rulers and ministers, the protocol between guests and hosts, the wisdom among the worthy, and the sage in relation to the way of Heaven: these *are fated*, but there is [human] nature in them [too], so the noble person does *not* call them "*fated*" [because they need to be cultivated].
>
> (口之於味也，目之於色也，耳之於聲也，鼻之於臭也，四肢之於安佚也：性也，有命焉，君子不謂性也。仁之於父子也，義之於君臣也，禮之於賓主也，智之於賢者也，聖人之於天道也：命也，有性焉，君子不謂命也。)[23]

We see here an interesting awareness of the elasticity of semantic parameters. Human mouths generally like sweet things and human fathers are generally good to their children. Given this near-inevitability, these inclinations

---

22. For this reason, Sarah Allan, in *The Way of Water and Sprouts of Virtue* (Albany: State University of New York, 1997), sometimes translates "fate" (命) as "the natural order." See pp. 98ff.

23. *Mengzi* ch. 7B24 (盡心下); cf. Van Norden, *Mengzi*, 189.

might be attributed to either human nature or to fate, to either an "inner" genetic proclivity or to an "outer" circumstantial probability. Nevertheless, a distinction is made, and while the deciding factor remains unstated in this passage, the implication is that the latter are more amenable to cultivation than the former.

The ambiguity about what precisely counts as "fate" is highlighted in the fact that Zhuangzi above classified filiality as "fated" (as opposed to being a matter of propriety) while Mengzi instead classifies parent-child goodness (which may be taken to include filiality) as "[human] nature" rather than as a matter of fate (even though he said that it partook of both). Despite this apparent discrepancy, I do not think these authors are at odds over this matter. Both seem to have been comparing more or less "natural" proclivities, and both drew a line between verbal and non-verbal inclinations. If we take Zhuangzi's example of children's love for their parents, we may well assume a pre-verbal or non-verbal bond. Mengzi, on the other hand, specifically contrasted interior, bodily proclivities with exterior relationships, beginning with the father-son bond, and if we construe this as a kind of teacher-student relationship, then the problem resolves itself. Relationships that are dependent on communication are potentially more fraught with the problem of miscommunication, and therefore take more cultivation. Zhuangzi, in fact, goes on to elaborate precisely this problem. "For two people to communicate [things like] delight and anger with words is one of the most difficult things in the world. Their delight often gets exaggerated into words of flattery, while their anger often gets exaggerated into words of hatred. Such exaggeration is reckless, and this recklessness leads to the breakdown of trust." (夫傳兩喜兩怒之言，天下之難者也。夫兩喜必多溢美之言，兩怒必多溢惡之言。凡溢之類妄，妄則其信之也莫。)[24] Given this analysis, both authors agree that we can do little about the innate feelings that humans are fated to experience, but there is much work to do on inevitable relationships that depend on interpersonal communication. Rhetoric is inherently problematic, but death from miscommunication is an ameliorable fate.

The third of Kongzi's three types of avoidable death is that wrought by weaponry. This kind may be ameliorated by prudence, by paying attention. Zhuangzi notes that if you wander around between an archer and his target, you ought to expect to get shot: in such a situation, getting shot is not a matter of fate, rather, *not* getting shot would be exceptional, and thus a matter of fate, or what we might call "luck."[25] Wandering the field

---

24. *Zhuangzi* ch. 4 (人間世); cf. Watson, *Zhuangzi*, 27.
25. *Zhuangzi* ch. 5 (德充符); cf. Watson, *Zhuangzi*, 36.

of an archery course may be analogous to working in politics: you have to keep an eye on the people who can do you harm. The ruler, certainly, may be said to hold the fate of the people in his hands.[26] This means that one should be careful and consider the possible outcomes of your actions. This is called "foresight" (先見). "To first consider how they [i.e., your actions] will change [the situation] and only then act is to understand the inclinations of [human] nature and fate." (先見其化而已動,達乎性命之情也。)[27] The "inclinations" of fate are tricky and seemingly unexpected, but this situation can, to an extent, be mitigated by forethought or prudence.

One way to analyze prudence is to posit two foci. The first is a particular person whose reactions we should try to anticipate, and the other is the general situation itself: the archer *and* the archery field. As another example, one may be fated to have a particular president and one may also be fated to have been born into a representative democracy, as opposed to, say, a monarchy. Xunzi, in contrast, analyzed prudence as inner and outer.

> Minnows are fish that float in the sunlight, but when they are [already] on their sides on the sand yet thinking about being in the water, it is too late. To be [already] hung up in misfortune and yet thinking of being cautious is [similarly] of no use. Those who know themselves do not blame others, and those who know fate do not blame Heaven. Those who blame others are [simply] desperate, while those who blame Heaven [simply] lack willpower. Their own faults perversely assigned to others: is this not far [from the truth]?
>
> (鯈䱖者,浮陽之魚也,胠於沙而思水,則無逮矣。挂於患而思謹,則無益矣。自知者不怨人,知命者不怨天;怨人者窮,怨天者無志。失之己,反之人,豈不迂乎哉?)[28]

---

26. *Lüshi chunqiu* ch. 20.6 (行論): "The ruler . . . holds the people's fate [in his hands]." (人主 . . . 執民之命.) cf. Knoblock and Riegel, *The Annals of Lü Buwei*, 531.
27. *Lüshi chunqiu* ch. 16.2 (觀世); cf. Knoblock and Riegel, *The Annals of Lü Buwei*, 381. Note: 遺 = 達.
28. *Xunzi* ch. 4 (榮辱); cf. Hutton, *Xunzi*, 25. Many commentators argue that *zhi* 志 (willpower) should be *shi* 識 (knowledge [of fate]) because this is the locution in *Xunzi* ch. 30: 怨人者窮,怨天者無識 (Those who blame others are [simply] desperate, while those who blame Heaven [simply] lack knowledge [of fate]). Either reading supports the point being made here.

Like the stranded fish or the imprudent person wandering on an archery field, one has only oneself to blame for any injury. Risk assessment is a crucial part of knowing oneself. Thus, if you know your own risk tolerance, you may have to blame yourself, rather than the archer who shoots you, or the other individuals in your school of fish that nudged you too close to the shore. Similarly, if you find yourself "hung up" in a bad situation, it may well be your own lack of caution, your own lack of resolve to be prudent, that is to blame, not the situation and not Heaven (in either its earlier, anthropomorphic guise or in its later, "natural order" form).

Fate as Fatalism

In English, the word "fate" often occurs in sentences with potentially misleading syntax and it also has unfortunately wide semantic parameters. By "misleading syntax," I mean that it is often paired with the verb "to believe," such that it is common to hear something like "Those people believe in fate." But if one takes "fate" to be "those things that inform us and affect us which we cannot avoid," then the tentative nature of "believe" is entirely unwarranted, as no one would deny that there are, in fact, things that inform us and affect us which we cannot avoid. Fate, in this sense, is what actually, factually happens to us: no "belief" is required. Its semantic parameters, moreover, regrettably include definitions that include intentionality. Thus, to say "I was fated to have green eyes" can mean both "I had no say in the matter, because it is a matter of genetics" and "some anthropomorphic supernatural entity consciously *caused* me to have green eyes." Indeed, in Greek mythology, there are the three female Fates (*Moirai*): Clotho, Lachesis, and Atropos. The first "spun" the thread of human fate, the second "allotted" its length, and the third did the actual cutting. In Hesiod's *Theogony* (c. 700 BCE), the three sisters "give mortal humans both good and bad [fortune] to have."[29] China, for its part, as we have seen, has a more ambiguous entity in Heaven, which some people took to be anthropomorphic and others did not.

Mozi believed in an anthropomorphic Heaven (as well as other supernatural entities that could influence our fates), but it was one that reliably rewarded human goodness and punished human badness. He had opponents in a group of people that we might call "fatalists" (執有命者) who believed, as did Hesiod, that human fate was not influenced by our

---

29. Hesiod, *Theogony*, lines 904–905; cf. *Hesiod and Theognis*, translated by Dorothea Wender in Betty Radice, ed. (New York: Penguin Books, 1973), 52.

actions. Mozi said that this group thought the wealth or poverty, large or small population, and orderliness or disorderliness of a state, as well as long or short lives for the people, are entirely fated, and "Though one struggle mightily with fate, what good will it do?" (命雖強勁，何益哉？)[30] Mozi's primary argument against this idea was to adduce examples of good people that had good fates and ascribe the latter to the action of Heaven. Today this argument would be considered flawed, as the evidence is cherry-picked, and the correlation is not necessarily evidence of causation.

Mozi, then, denied the existence of "fate" in the deterministic, fatalistic sense of the term, but since he identified fatalism as the primary referent of this word (i.e., *ming* 命), and did not want his idea of supernatural anthropomorphic entities rewarding and punishing good and bad human behavior with good and bad consequences mixed up with such fatalism, he rejected the word entirely. His was a minority position, however, at least among our sources, which continued to use the term with the ambiguities of its semantic parameters. Knowing that some people in early China referred to fate in a fatalistic way, it then becomes somewhat difficult to know when it is and is not being used in this way. For example, when a powerful minister of the state of Lu told Kongzi that he, the minister, could kill someone who had slandered Kongzi's student, Kongzi replied: "Whether or not the [human] way will be carried out is fated. Whether or not the [human] way is discarded is [also] fated." (道之將行也與：命也。道之將廢也與：命也。)[31] Because of the elliptical nature of this text, it is hard to discern if Kongzi is saying that there is nothing that humans can do to affect the fate of his student (because, perhaps, it is decided by Heaven); or if he is saying that he trusts that his student has done no wrong and that "the truth will out," so that the minister won't feel the need to kill the slanderer; or if he is alarmed at the minister's suggestion to kill the slanderer and wants only to nip that murder plot in the bud by shifting the responsibility from the minister to simply "let the chips fall where they may."

Earlier in the same text, a presumably common saying is repeated: "Life and death are fated, wealth and honor [are decided] by Heaven." (死生有命，富貴在天。)[32] Here the context makes clear that Kongzi is not promoting fatalism: we are to do the best we can and, given the circumstances,

---

30. *Mozi* 墨子 ch. 35 (非命上); cf. John Knoblock and Jeffrey Riegel. *Mozi: A Study and Translation of the Ethical and Political Writings* (Berkeley: University of California, Berkeley, 2013), 289.

31. *Lunyu* 14.36; cf. Slingerland, *Analects*, 168.

32. *Lunyu* 12.5; cf. Slingerland, *Analects*, 127.

if that is not enough to succeed, so be it. Try your best but accept defeat gracefully. Mengzi says as much when he described his teacher: "Kongzi arrived with protocol and departed with propriety: [but] whether or not he [actually] got what he came for, he said was a matter of fate." (孔子進以禮，退以義；得之不得曰「有命」。)³³ In fact, Mengzi upped the rhetorical ante when he elsewhere claimed that "everything" is a matter of fate: "Everything is fated; [still, one should only] accord with and accept what is correct in it [i.e., in everything]. For this reason, one who understands fate does not stand beneath a precipitously leaning wall [i.e., one about to collapse]. Dying after fully pursuing the way is one's correct fate. Dying in fetters [i.e., as a criminal] is not one's correct fate." (莫非命也，順受其正。是故，知命者，不立乎巖牆之下。盡其道而死者，正命也。桎梏死者，非正命也。)³⁴ This clarifies matters. We cannot control the environment, but we can be perceptive and act intelligently, and one subset of acting intelligently is to act ethically, insofar as it is intelligent to act for social harmony if you want to stay alive and out of prison.

Returning to the topic of fatalism, we saw above that some people believed that human fortunes were decided by supernatural anthropomorphic entities who assigned fates to humans regardless of human action. We call these people fatalists; they are referred to but not represented in our texts. Others, like Mozi, believed that human fortunes were decided by supernatural anthropomorphic entities who assigned fates to humans based on their actions. We might call these people "religious." Most of our sources are either ambivalent or agnostic on this—simply put, on whether or not Heaven is anthropomorphic—with some, like Xunzi, being positively atheistic. This ambivalence generally took the form that Kongzi and Mengzi outlined above: be intelligent and ethical and let the chips fall where they may. Whether or not "prayer" should be included in "intelligent" activity would, in this analysis, be a personal decision.

If one *were* to pray, a representative example might be found in the following anecdote about Yu, the founder of the Xia dynasty. Recall that "mandate" and "fate" are the same word:

> Yu was inspecting the south [of his kingdom], and just when he was crossing the Jiang river, a yellow dragon lifted the boat on its

---

33. *Mengzi* ch. 5A8 (萬章上); cf. Van Norden, *Mengzi*, 128.
34. *Mengzi* ch. 7A2 (盡心上); cf. Van Norden, *Mengzi*, 171.

back. The people on the boat turned five different colors [with fright]. Yu lifted his head, faced Heaven, and sighed: "I received the mandate from Heaven, and have expended all my energy in sustaining the people. Life is a matter of [human] nature and death is a matter of fate. [So] why should I be worried about this dragon here?" The dragon then lowered its head, dropped its tail, and departed. Thus did Yu understand the allocation of life and death and the mainstays of benefit and harm.

(禹南省,方濟乎江,黃龍負舟。舟中之人,五色無主。禹仰視天而歎曰:「吾受命於天,竭力以養人。生,性也;死,命也。余何憂於龍焉?」龍俛耳低尾而逝。則禹達乎死生之分,利害之經也。)[35]

Was that a prayer, and did Heaven cause the dragon to leave? No. There is nothing in the text to imply that Heaven caused the dragon to go, and while facing Heaven and talking to it certainly looks like what might be called a prayer, the last sentence implies otherwise. The final sentence makes no mention of the piety of calling out to Heaven; indeed, it does not mention Heaven at all. It summarizes the story by noting that Yu understood that it might indeed be time for his death, but that his apparent equanimity stemmed from his ethics, from knowing that his was a life well-lived, insofar as he had known "the standards of benefit and harm" for himself and his people and had pursued the former and avoided the latter as much as possible.

Yu was no doubt more cautious than Xunzi, but then, assuming the historicity of Yu, two thousand years would have passed between them. Xunzi, for his part, had a decidedly clear conception of the separate roles that Heaven and humans had and thought that each had their own responsibilities.

> To exalt Heaven and *think about* it: how can this compare to domesticating [living] things and *managing* them? To follow Heaven and *praise* it: how can this compare to managing Heaven's mandate and *using* it? To observe the seasons and *wait upon* them: how can this compare to responding to the seasons and *making use* of them? To rely on things and *increase* them [as they are]: how can this compare to expediting their potential and *developing* them? To think about things and *consider* them [as such]: how can this

---

35. *Lüshi chunqiu* ch. 20.3 (知分); cf. Knoblock and Riegel, *The Annals of Lü Buwei*, 519.

compare to understanding things and *not losing* them? To covet the means to *start* things: how can this compare to having the means to *complete* them? Thus, to turn your back on that which humans do while pining for that which Heaven does is to lose hold of the inclinations of the myriad things.

(大天而思之，孰與物畜而制之？從天而頌之，孰與制天命而用之？望時而待之，孰與應時而使之？因物而多之，孰與騁能而化之？思物而物之，孰與理物而勿失之也？願於物之所以生，孰與有物之所以成？故錯人而思天，則失萬物之情。)[36]

For Xunzi, then, Heaven's mandate—our fate—is something that is not only "manageable" in the more passive sense of the word, but also something that we humans can and should actively work to improve upon: domesticate crops and farm animals, anticipate and exploit the regularity of the seasons, utilize natural resources to create new things never before seen (from basic farm tools to supercomputers), seek to understand the patterns and logic that underlie natural phenomena rather than passively letting things go to waste or go extinct . . . we humans appear to uniquely possess the explanatory knowledge to accomplish these goals. To relinquish our responsibility in these practical areas in favor of spending time on metaphysics—"pining for that which Heaven does"—is, for Xunzi, something of a category error.

Divination (占卜 / 策龜)

There were several types of divination used in early China.[37] But while divination was both ancient and widespread, the Scholars' texts make relatively few references to these practices. It seems to have been an activity primarily pursued by rulers, though there are a number of notable exceptions.[38] Xunzi curated a list of court officers and their duties, and between

---

36. *Xunzi* ch. 17 (天論); cf. Hutton, *Xunzi*, 180.

37. See, for example, Stephen Field, *Ancient Chinese Divination* (Honolulu: University of Hawaii Press, 2008).

38. For some of these, see Donald Harper, "Warring States Natural Philosophy and Occult Thought" in *The Cambridge History of Ancient China*, eds. Michael Loewe and Edward Shaughnessy (New York: Cambridge University Press, 1999), 813–84. For examples specific to the *Yijing*, see Kidder Smith, "*Zhouyi* Interpretation From Accounts in the *Zuozhuan*," *Harvard Journal of Asiatic Studies* 49.2 (Dec. 1989): 421–63.

the "Master of Craftsmen" (工師) and the "Overseer of Public Places" (治市) he noted the following: "The duties of the hunchback priestesses and lame priests are to examine Yin and Yang, prognosticate portents and omens, bore turtle shells and arrange hexagrams, preside at [ceremonies for] repelling and attracting the five [types of] divination cracks, and to know their propitious, unpropitious, inauspicious, and auspicious [implications]." (相陰陽，占祲兆，鑽龜陳卦，主攘擇五卜，知其吉凶妖祥，傴巫跛擊之事也。)³⁹ Just as blind people were thought to be particularly well-suited to being musicians in early China, so the hunchbacked and the lame were thought to be especially well-suited to being diviners, though this certainly does not mean that the practice of divination was limited to them. Still, these diviners do not appear to have been paradigmatic figures for the kind of self-cultivation that is our focus here.⁴⁰

Indeed, there is evidence that divination in general was considered to be somewhat suspect by the authors under consideration here. Some sorts of questions seemed not to be amenable to divination. Qu Yuan was the archetypical honest minister who lost his job due to slander at court. After he was exiled, he approached a diviner and asked if it is better to be honest and bereft or to lower one's standards and "go along to get along." After hearing the problem, the diviner declined to even consult his instruments and said that some things are not amenable to divination.⁴¹ Further, though according to Xunzi it was typical for rulers to have diviners, other sources opined that the practice of divination was perhaps not a good idea, or at least that an over-reliance on it was not a good idea. "If rulers rely on turtle and yarrow [divination], and indulge their priestesses and doctors, then ghosts and spirits will hasten their misfortune." (上恃龜筮，好用巫醫，則鬼神驟祟。)⁴² Context does not indicate whether the author thought

---

39. *Xunzi* ch. 9 (王制); cf. Hutton, *Xunzi*, 78. Note: 擊 = 覡. To "bore" a tortoise shell is to drill an indentation into a turtle plastron, after which a hot poker was put into the indentation, which resulted in a 卜-shaped crack on the other side that was then interpreted by a diviner.

40. In fact, in a later chapter, Xunzi clearly implies that such diviners do not have true knowledge. See *Xunzi* ch. 18 (正論); cf. Hutton, *Xunzi*, 187.

41. *Chuci* 楚辭 ch. 6 (卜居). Specifically, the diviner said: "Given your attitude and your intentions, turtle and yarrow [divination] is honestly unable to know this matter." (用君之心，行君之意，龜策誠不能知事。) cf. David Hawkes, *Ch'u Tz'u: The Songs of the South* (1959; rpt. Boston: Beacon Press, 1962), 88–90.

42. *Guanzi* 管子 ch. 3 (權修); cf. W. Allyn Rickett, *Guanzi: Political, Economic, and Philosophical Essays from Early China* (Princeton: Princeton University Press, 1985, 1998), 1:96.

divination was completely to be avoided, or if they thought a ruler should not rely upon it to the exclusion of other considerations.

Divination within the context of mental self-cultivation was also sometimes thought to be superfluous. "[Are you] able to concentrate, [are you] able to focus? [Are you] able to *not* divine with tortoise or milfoil and yet know the propitious and unpropitious? [Are you] able to stop [when you ought]? [Are you] able to finish [where you ought]? [Are you] able to *not* inquire of other people but rather obtain it within yourself?" (能專乎？能一乎？能毋卜筮而知凶吉乎？能止乎？能已乎？能毋問於人，而自得之於己乎？)[43] Here, attention, timeliness, and introspection are presented as superior alternatives to divination. Another chapter in the same text puts it more bluntly still, saying that sages simply "do not divine with turtles or yarrow, yet prudently know the propitious from the unpropitious" (不卜不筮，而謹知吉凶).[44] As we saw in chapter 3, sages do pay attention to "evidence and indications" (徵表) but these, presumably, are of the natural kind.[45] Other types of divination were also looked at askance in our sources, including physiognomy and astrology.[46] Recourse to the *Yijing*, in particular, would in later centuries come to be held in high regard, and the divergent views on whether the text should primarily be used to foretell the future or as a suggestive guide for introspection have persisted to this day.

Outcome: Contentment (知足)

There is sometimes only a razor's edge between being content with one's unavoidable lot in life and working to better oneself and one's community, both social and natural. Most of us probably toggle back and forth between the two, perhaps spurred by nothing more than small changes in mood. The difference between complacence and contentment may thus be in the eye of the beholder. But contentment with what is truly unavoidable is what it means to accept your fate, and this attitude is well represented in our sources. We saw Laozi opine, in chapter 3, that "no misfortune is greater than not knowing contentment."[47] Contentment, moreover, manifests itself

---

43. *Guanzi* ch. 37 (心術下) and ch. 49 (內業); cf. Rickett, *Guanzi*, 2:60 and 50–51.
44. *Guanzi* ch. 38 (白心); cf. Rickett, *Guanzi*, 2:89.
45. From *Lüshi chunqiu* ch. 20.5 (觀表); see chap. 3, n. 115.
46. For a negative assessment of physiognomy, see *Xunzi* ch. 5 (非相); for astrology, see *Hanfeizi* ch. 19 (飾邪).
47. *Laozi* ch. 46. See chap. 3, n. 64.

in a variety of ways. At a basic level, there is a lack of resentment. "Noble people . . . rectify themselves and are not demanding of others, thus they are without resentment. Above, [they] do not resent Heaven, and below [they] do not blame others. This is why noble people abide in change while awaiting fate; petty people [on the other hand], act recklessly while chasing a lucky break." (君子 . . . 正己而不求於人，則無怨。上不怨天，下不尤人。故君子居易以俟命。小人行險以徼幸。)[48] One could read this, superficially, as rather intolerably passive, insofar as we are asked to "await fate." But such a reading would be mistaken: we are not being asked *only* to await fate, but rather to take responsibility ourselves, through self-rectification, that is, self-cultivation. We must do our part, but without sanctimony or anger, without blaming anyone else when things do not go as we would wish, while embracing inevitable change, that is, fate.

Contentment goes deeper than just avoiding resentment, however. One author claims that, fundamentally, "those who understand fate are free from anxiety" (知命者不憂).[49] A commentary to the *Yijing* elaborates on this idea:

> [If one] is like Heaven and Earth, then there will be no contrariness. [If one] knows the myriad things everywhere, and [one's] way helps the world, then there will be no excessiveness. [If one] acts with the incidentals but is not carried away [by them], and delights in Heaven and in knowing its mandate, then there will be no anxiety. [If one] is secure in one's surroundings and generous in goodness, then there will be the ability for love.
>
> (與天地相似，故不違。知周乎萬物，而道濟天下，故不過。旁行而不流，樂天知命，故不憂。安土敦乎仁，故能愛。)[50]

In this passage we see that an acceptance of fate (that is, Heaven's "mandate") entails not only a lack of specific resentment, and not only a lack of more generalized anxiety, but also a positive "delight in Heaven," even

---

48. *Liji* 禮記 ch. 31 (中庸); cf. James Legge, *Li Chi: Book of Rites* (1885; rpt. New York: University Books, 1967), 2:306–07.

49. *Huainanzi* 淮南子 ch. 14 (詮言); cf. John Major, Sarah Queen, Andrew Meyer, and Harold Roth, *The Huainanzi: A Guide to the Theory and Practice of Government in Early Han China* (New York: Columbia University Press, 2010), 572.

50. *Yijing* 易經, "Xici zhuan I" 繫辭上傳; cf. Richard Lynn, *The Classic of Changes: A New Translation of the* I Ching *as Interpreted by Wang Bi* (New York: Columbia University Press, 1994), 52.

with the constant changes that it inevitably occasions. Further, a delight in Heaven is connected to a feeling of security and an increase of goodness, which together result in what is, for the cultural West, the holy grail of affirmative love.[51]

A lack of anxiety is not the same thing as a sense of security, though the former is requisite for the latter. Zhuangzi implies that the difference between the two may be a matter of virtuosity: "To know what you cannot do anything about and to be secure in it as with fate: only one with virtuosity can do this." (知不可奈何而安之若命,唯有德者能之。)[52] Laozi, meanwhile, implicates the even more positive state of "tranquility" in place of being "secure," and implies that becoming comfortable with one's fate is only a matter of time, at least for some of us (i.e., sages): "Returning to one's root is called 'being tranquil'; it is called 'returning to fate.' 'Returning to fate' is called 'abiding.' 'Knowing how to abide' is called 'percipience.' Not knowing how to abide, one is foolishly aroused to violence [in trying to escape fate]. Knowing how to abide brings tolerance; tolerance brings impartiality; impartiality brings completion." (歸根曰「靜」:是謂「復命」。「復命」曰「常」。「知常」曰「明」。不知常,妄作凶。知常容;容乃公;公乃全。)[53] Here a "return to fate" is equated with "abiding," which in this text refers to a positive mental attitude comfortable with fate and its permutations. It is elsewhere in the text equated with a feeling of harmony.[54]

Zhuangzi's Kongzi (i.e., the character of Kongzi in Zhuangzi's text) elaborates on the connection between accepting fate and abiding in harmony; though he does not use the term "contentment," its presence is certainly implied:

> Life and death, preservation and loss, success and failure, wealth and poverty, worthiness and unworthiness, fame and obscurity, hunger and thirst, cold and heat: the alterations of these matters can be the workings of fate. Day and night they supplant each other before [our eyes], yet our understanding is unable [even] to glimpse their beginnings. Thus [they should] be insufficient to disorder our harmony, and should not be allowed into the

---

51. Love is certainly an important ingredient in early Chinese thought generally (the term appears in the *Lunyu*, for example, nine times), and self-cultivation specifically, but it is not as central a concept as in the Christian-dominant West.
52. *Zhuangzi* ch. 5 (德充符); cf. Watson, *Zhuangzi*, 36.
53. *Laozi* ch. 16.
54. *Laozi* ch. 55: "To know harmony is called 'abiding.'" (知和曰常。)

"numinous storehouse" [i.e., the mind]. [Rather] cause it [i.e., the mind] to be harmonious and easygoing, perceptive but without a loss of joy; cause it day and night without respite to get along with things as in springtime: this is to apprehend things in the mind as at the time of their birth. This [attitude] is what is called having "replete capacity."

(死生存亡，窮達貧富，賢與不肖毀譽，飢渴寒暑，是事之變，命之行也；日夜相代乎前，而知不能規乎其始者也。故不足以滑和，不可入於「靈府」。使之和豫，通而不失於兌；使日夜無郤而與物為春，是接而生時於心者也。是之謂「才全」。)[55]

Things change—are always changing—and they do not appear to change in accordance with any appreciable sense of justice. Some cultures address this disparity with ideas of redress in another life or an afterlife, but in early China we are asked to make the best of it and not let it get to us. Indeed, we should aspire to be easygoing and even happy, while not averting our gaze. The method outlined here is "to get along with things as in springtime," which is to say, with an optimistic eye to the potential of things.

Outcome: Acceptance of Death

Life and death—that is, when and where one is born and when and where one dies—are the classic examples of fate. "Whether you are worthy or unworthy is a matter of your capacity; what you do or do not do is a matter of your person; what you encounter or do not encounter is a matter of timeliness; [but when and where] you are born and die is a matter of fate." (夫賢不肖者，材也；為不為者，人也；遇不遇者，時也；死生者，命也。)[56] Given this situation, Xunzi goes on to exhort us to "study broadly, plan carefully, and cultivate ourselves . . . in order to await our time" (博學、深謀、修身 . . . 以俟其時). We can thus be at least somewhat prepared for what is to happen to us, for what we may or may not encounter. Mengzi goes a step further in advising us to not "feel divided" by the thought of death: "Not feeling divided by early death or by living on, but cultivating oneself in order to await it, is how to stand firm in your fate." (殀壽不貳，修身以

---

55. *Zhuangzi* ch. 5 (德充符); cf. Watson, *Zhuangzi*, 39.
56. *Xunzi* ch. 28 (宥坐); cf. Hutton, *Xunzi*, 323–324.

俟之,所以立命也。)⁵⁷ Qu Yuan, due to his forced exile, often thought of death, but he said that he faced it without fear. "The lives of the myriad people each have their placement. [Therefore, with] a settled mind and a broad attitude, where is there room for aversion or fear? . . . [I] know that death cannot be deferred, [therefore I] would rather not love [life]." (萬民之生,各有所錯兮。定心廣志,余何畏懼兮? . . . 知死不可讓,願勿愛兮。)⁵⁸

It is Zhuangzi, however, that has, among our sources, the most audacious attitude toward death. We saw in chapter 1 that he described his wife's death as a "transformation" as natural as a change in seasons.⁵⁹ In that story, his good friend asked him why he was not weeping for this dear person with whom he had grown old. Zhuangzi, implying that he had, in fact, initially wept, replied: "When someone lies down to sleep in the 'big room,' were I to follow after, wailing and crying for them, I would think that I did not understand fate, so I stopped." (人且偃然寢於巨室,而我噭噭然隨而哭之,自以為不通乎命,故止也。)⁶⁰ Understanding fate, then, implies an equanimous acceptance of death, even the death of a loved one.

In the same text, when Zhuangzi himself was facing death, he was again able to wax poetic.

> Zhuangzi was on the verge of dying, and his followers wanted to give him a lavish funeral. Zhuangzi said: "I have Heaven and Earth as my coffins, the sun and moon as my linked jades, the stars and constellations as my rounded and squared gemstones, and the myriad things as my gifts and presents! My funeral thus fully prepared, what could be lacking? What could possibly be added to these?"
>
> (莊子將死,弟子欲厚葬之。莊子曰:「吾以天地為棺槨,以日月為連璧,星辰為珠璣,萬物為齎送!吾葬具豈不備邪?何以加此?」)⁶¹

---

57. *Mengzi* ch. 7A1 (盡心上); cf. Van Norden, *Mengzi*, 171.
58. *Chuci* ch. 4 (九章); cf. Hawkes, *Ch'u Tz'u*, 72.
59. From *Zhuangzi* ch. 18 (至樂); see chap. 1, n. 68.
60. *Zhuangzi* ch. 18 (至樂); cf. Watson, *Zhuangzi*, 141. The "big room" is the space between Heaven and Earth.
61. *Zhuangzi* ch. 32 (列禦寇); cf. Watson, *Zhuangzi*, 286. I don't know if Zhuangzi was really wealthy enough to be able to afford to be buried with jades and gemstones or if he was just being aspirational (or poetic) here.

This kind of naturalism, of completely being at home in this world, is an important background for the acceptance of death that results from fully accepting fate. But Zhuangzi was not only contextualizing his death among the moon and stars; he goes on to relate that he was quite content to remain unburied after he died, even while knowing what that would entail. With what we might now call "gallows humor," he responded to his followers' concern that an unburied body would attract the attention of scavengers: "From above crows and kites will feed, and from below crickets and ants will feed; to take from the one to give to the other: why such favoritism?" (在上為烏鳶食，在下為螻蟻食；奪彼與此：何其偏也？)[62] Why indeed.

Genuine People (真人)

The aspirational figure of the "genuine person" is no stranger to death, insofar as he is said to "wander in the wilds of destruction and loss" (游于滅亡之野).[63] But acceptance of death is not the genuine person's primary feature. Neither is the health of the body, the subject of chapter 1, though the genuine person *is* described as unusually healthy.[64] We have already met the genuine person in chapter 5, where they are described as, more or less, "going with the flow."[65] This figure appears primarily in two texts, the *Zhuangzi* and *Huainanzi*, and the *Zhuangzi* ranks the genuine person above common people, scholars, worthies, and even sages.[66] It is possible that Zhuangzi coined the term in order to describe an aspirational figure outside the Ruist (Confucian) scholastic norm. He was critical of what we might call "traditional education," thinking, among other things, that actions speak louder than words. Regarding the classics, the "curriculum" of Kongzi and his followers, Zhuangzi said: "The 'six classics' are [but] the worn footprints of prior kings: how could they be that which *caused* the footprints? Now that which you [i.e., Kongzi] are talking about is similar to such footprints. Footprints are caused by walking, but how could footprints walk?" (夫六經，先王之陳迹也：豈其所以迹哉？今子之所言，猶迹也。夫

---

62. *Ibid.*
63. *Huainanzi* ch. 2 (俶真); cf. Major, Queen, Meyer, and Roth, *Huainanzi*, 97.
64. *Lüshi chunqiu* ch. 3.3 (先己); cf. Knoblock and Riegel, *The Annals of Lü Buwei*, 102.
65. From *Zhuangzi* ch. 6 (大宗師); see chap. 5, n. 52.
66. *Zhuangzi* ch. 15 (刻意); cf. Watson, *Zhuangzi*, 121.

迹，履之所出，而迹豈履哉？）⁶⁷ It is precisely this kind of iconoclasm that may explain why "genuine people" are not more widely depicted in our sources. Further, it is this kind of rejection of authority that leads us to the crux of what it means to be a genuine person.

Laozi does not use the term "genuine people," but he does connect genuineness to self-cultivation, saying "Cultivate it [i.e., the Way] in your person, and your virtuosity will then be genuine." (修之於身，其德乃真。)⁶⁸ Another source defines them in a wider context: "Genuine people of old took their stand on the root of Heaven and Earth, and centered themselves on fully leisurely wandering." (古之真人，立於天地之本，中至優游。)⁶⁹ Unfortunately, the text does not elaborate on just what "the root of Heaven and Earth" is, and the phrase does not appear elsewhere in it (nor does it appear in the *Zhuangzi*, but a similar phrase is in *Laozi* ch. 6, where it appears to be a metaphor for the Way). Ultimately, however, genuine people have a certain attitude toward reality that sets them apart.

When reading texts that are poetic, one perennial problem for the reader is deciding when to take their claims literally and when to take them metaphorically. The *Zhuangzi* is certainly a poetic text. Let us end this examination of genuine people with an iconic and enigmatic description from it:

> The "genuine people" of old did not reject the inadequate, were not over-confident with success, and did not scheme for things. As such, when in error they were without anguish, and when correct they were without self-satisfaction. As such, [they could] climb heights without fear, enter water without [feeling] wet, and enter fire without [feeling] hot. [Only] those whose knowledge ascends to, and relies upon, the Way are like this.
>
> The "genuine people" of old: they slept without dreaming, and awakened without worries; they ate simply and breathed deeply. "Genuine people" breathe from their heels, while the masses breathe from their throats. Humble and accommodating, they [reluctantly] choke out words like vomiting. Those in whom preferences and desires are deep are those in whom the "Heavenly function" is shallow.

---

67. *Zhuangzi* ch. 14 (天運); cf. Watson, *Zhuangzi*, 118.
68. *Laozi* ch. 54.
69. *Huainanzi* ch. 2 (俶真); cf. Major, Queen, Meyer, and Roth, *Huainanzi*, 88.

(古之真人,不逆寡,不雄成,不謨士。若然者,過而弗悔,當而不自得也。若然者,登高不慄,入水不濡,入火不熱。是知之能登假於道者也若此。

古之真人:其寢不夢,其覺無憂,其食不甘,其息深深。真人之息以踵,眾人之息以喉。屈服者,其嗌言若哇。其耆欲深者,其「天機」淺。)[70]

Let us unpack this passage. To "not reject the inadequate" refers to being comfortable with one's own inadequacies as well as the shortcomings of others. It is to be okay with partial understanding, with not always having perfectly persuasive evidence: it is a recognition that our comprehension of "Heaven and Earth" is not always as complete as we might like. When, on the other hand, we *do* have persuasive evidence, when our understanding *is* (relatively) complete and successful, genuine people are not arrogant about it, because things—evidence—can always change. This is why they were said to "go with the flow" above: we may know what we know, but there is much that we do not know, and this deficit may well affect what we are currently confident about. Not "scheming" for things refers to not indulging in confirmation bias. It means being impartial: genuine people follow the evidence and do not selectively emphasize only that which supports their case. They are flexible but are not thereby spineless. Being right or wrong without self-satisfaction or regret is simply an extension of this.

The next line presents us with the choice to read either literally or metaphorically. To "climb heights without fear" points to the general fearlessness of genuine people; to not fear being right or wrong has already been established. But the rest of the sentence has scholars split: is the author claiming that genuine people can "enter water without (*getting*) wet" or is that locution a metaphor for the claim that they can "enter water without (*feeling*) wet"? The literal reading implies genuine people who can do magic. The metaphorical reading, on the other hand, implies that genuine people are open-minded, that they are capable of reducing their theory-laden perception to the point where they can enter water or fire without feeling wet or hot (at least, at first) simply because they were without the preconceptions that would have made them expect to feel wet or hot.[71] It is, to be

---

70. *Zhuangzi* ch. 6 (大宗師); cf. Watson, *Zhuangzi*, 42. Note: 士 = 事, 假 = 至.

71. This would be the opposite of the "fire walking" that one hears about, wherein people "psych themselves up" to walk on hot coals by telling themselves that it is just a case of "mind over matter."

sure, a hyperbolic—that is, poetic—claim, but it fits with Zhuangzi's habit of using magical realism to make a philosophical point. (Recall the person who "sometimes thinks he is a horse and sometimes thinks he is an ox" from chapter 3.) The following sentence makes it clear that this degree of open-mindedness is something of an aspirational attitude.

To "sleep without dreaming and awake without worry" is likewise a metaphor for being comfortable with oneself. The genuine person's eating and breathing habits reflect unfussiness and calm. "Breathing from the heels" for some scholars indicates esoteric yogic practices; alternatively, it could just be a metaphor for equanimity. "Humble and accommodating" describes the tentative nature of those who know they do not have all the answers, while "they [reluctantly] choke out words like vomiting" is droll hyperbole: it is behavior opposite to what we might now ascribe to a slick politician or an unctuous used-car salesman. Zhuangzi's relativism encourages humility and precludes over-confidence, resulting in a hesitation to claim certainty. Genuine people's words, then, are tentative, and their forced articulation is here parodied as "choking" and "vomiting."

The final sentence disparages "preferences and desires," which, in the context of this text, refers to socially inculcated ideas that obscure more than they illuminate. These are the "preferences and desires" that obfuscate open-mindedness. The passage ends with a technical term, "Heavenly function," which is something that operates most pristinely in genuine people. In the context of this sentence, it refers to the attitude that is the opposite of having (excessive or contrived) "preferences and desires," which is to say, open-mindedness. Open-mindedness is a key theme in the *Zhuangzi* and is a key feature in genuine people, but for open-mindedness to be kept from floating away into untethered idealism and flights of fancy, it must be balanced with a dose of reality, with that which is unavoidable, with that which is fated.

Chapter 9

Destiny (天)

"Being skilled in the Heavenly and competent at the human: only 'complete people' can do this."

—*Zhuangzi* ch. 23

夫工乎天而俍乎人者,唯全人能之。《莊子。庚桑楚》

Introduction

As discussed at the beginning of the previous chapter, I make a distinction between the inevitabilities of fate and the potentialities of destiny. Through the lens of self-cultivation, the goal vis-à-vis *fate* is contentment with, and making the best of, what cannot be changed, while the goal vis-à-vis *destiny* is to fulfill our individual potential. The differences between the two words and ideas are often elided, however, in both Chinese and English, but they are nevertheless implicit in our sources and can be articulated with sufficient attention to context. The ambivalence toward the degree to which the vicissitudes of life are amenable to human influence or control is discernible even in the earliest texts.

The "Heavenly mandate" (天命) that was used to justify dynastic change in early China was never inevitable: it was always connected to the virtuosity of the incoming dynastic house, which is to say, it was always something of an achievement. In this earliest sense, the "mandate" is more destiny than fate. I used the word "fate" for "mandate" in the previous chapter because at a fundamental individual level, Heaven is described as mandating human birth and death, which are matters of fate and not ethical achievements. But at the political and dynastic level, the mandate *was* a matter of ethical achievement and thus a matter of destiny. The fungibility of dynastic destiny is evident in the *Shijing*, which notes that even for the illustrious first king of the illustrious Zhou dynasty, "Heaven's mandate is not constant" (天命靡常).[1] Indeed, his successors were exhorted to try to "match," that is, "live up to," the mandate (i.e., 配命).[2] Some readers may be inclined to extend this advice to all people, as Mengzi seems to have done.[3] We saw in chapters 2 and 8 that Mengzi explicitly tied destiny to self-cultivation, whereby the latter is the means to realize the former.[4]

There are passages in our sources that lack the context for us to confidently read them as referring to fate or destiny. (Dealing with such ambiguity is the fate of a text critic.) For example, one source says: "There are those who are cautious with themselves and yet still harm themselves [because they] do not understand the inclinations of [their own] natures and fates/destinies. [If they] do not understand the inclinations of their fates/destinies: of what use is caution?" (有慎之而反害之者，不達乎性命之情也。不達乎性命之情，慎之何益？)[5] It seems possible that one could harm oneself by not understanding either one's fate *or* destiny. By way of explanation, the author goes on to add, "This is [like] a deaf person who, when raising their infant, steps out of the house just when it is thundering." (是聾者之養嬰兒也，方雷而窺之于堂。) Deaf people may know that infants fear thunder, but they are hampered in being cautious about it. But is the moral of the

---

1. *Shijing* 詩經 #235 (文王); cf. Arthur Waley, *The Book of Songs: The Ancient Chinese Classic of Poetry* (1937; edited with additional translations by Joseph Allen; New York: Grove Press, 1996), 228. Similarly, someone who presumably worked for the Zhou dynastic house later noted, upon observing an ominous solar eclipse which for him may have indicated the collapse of the dynasty, that "Heaven's mandate is unclear" (天命不徹). See *Shijing* #193 (十月之交); cf. Waley, *The Book of Songs*, 172.
2. *Shijing* #235 (文王); cf. Waley, *The Book of Songs*, 227–28.
3. *Mengzi* 孟子 ch. 4A4 (離婁上); Bryan Van Norden, *Mengzi: With Selections from Traditional Commentaries* (Indianapolis: Hackett, 2008), 91.
4. *Mengzi* chs. 7A1 (盡心上) and 7B24 (盡心下) at chap. 2, n. 21 and chap. 8, n. 23.
5. *Lüshi chunqiu* 呂氏春秋 ch. 1.3 (重己); cf. John Knoblock and Jeffrey Riegel, *The Annals of Lü Buwei* (Stanford: Stanford University Press, 2000), 67–68. In context, the pronoun *zhi* 之 ("themselves") refers to the topic of the section from which this quote is taken, *ji* 己 ("oneself ").

story that we should understand, and come to terms with, the inclinations of fated conditions like congenital deafness? Or is it that we should seek to understand, and make the best of, the inclinations of our destinies, which may include idiosyncratic conditions like non-congenital deafness? In any case, most passages that deal with these topics can, thankfully, be parsed as referring to *either* fate *or* destiny.

The Heavenly and the Human

Realizing our individual destinies requires our effort. Thus, one author says: "Sagely people *nourish* their singular natures, *manage* their six *qi*-substances, *control* their singular destinies, and *regulate* their taste for the delicious." (聖人養一性而御六氣，持一命而節滋味。)[6] Since fate, by definition, is not amenable to our "control," this must refer to destiny, and "control" (持)—literally "to take by the hand"—itself necessitates our active involvement. Similarly, another author says "For sagely people of ancient times, their harmonious joy and calm tranquility were [matters of their] natures, while their conscious achievements and implementation of the Way were [matters of] destiny. This is why it is only when [human] nature meets destiny that it [i.e., nature] can *proceed*, and it is only when destiny meets with [human] nature that it [i.e., destiny] can be *perceived*." (古之聖人，其和愉寧靜，性也；其志得道行，命也。是故性遭命而後能行，命得性而後能明。)[7] An emotionally calm attitude or nature needs the direction of destiny to proceed; likewise, we can only properly understand our destiny when we come to terms with our inherited human nature (whether general or specific). More to our point, destiny here is explicitly a matter of "conscious achievement" and an "implementation of the Way." It is a matter entirely within the realm of our control and requires our attention and cultivation.

Destiny, like fate, derives from Heaven. This matters because it contextualizes individual human destiny within the larger picture of the cosmos

---

6. *Hanshi waizhuan* 韓詩外傳 ch. 5.31; cf. James Hightower, *Han Shih Wai Chuan: Han Ying's Illustrations of the Didactic Application of the Classic of Songs* (Cambridge: Harvard University Press, 1952), 189. Some scholars say the *liu* 六 (six) should be *fu* 夫 (their) or *da* 大 (great), but this is not especially relevant here.

7. *Huainanzi* 淮南子 ch. 2 (俶真); cf. John Major, Sarah Queen, Andrew Meyer, and Harold Roth, *The Huainanzi: A Guide to the Theory and Practice of Government in Early Han China* (New York: Columbia University Press, 2010), 107.

of which we are a part. This cosmos, unlike a chaos, is conceived as an ordered—and therefore rational—place:

> Examine Heavenly destiny, put in order the mind's procedures, make reasonable [your] likes and dislikes, moderate [your] inclinations and nature, and [your] ordering of the [human] way will be complete. If [you] examine Heavenly destiny, then [you] will not be confused about fortune and misfortune; and if [you] are not confused about fortune and misfortune, then in [both] action and stillness [you] will accord with reason.
>
> (原天命，治心術，理好惡，適情性，而治道畢矣。原天命則不惑禍福，不惑禍福則動靜循理矣。)[8]

Here, too, the verbs—examine, order, make reasonable, make appropriate—all point to facets of self-cultivation. If I know my destiny, then I will know that I am not, for example, cut out to be an astronaut, and would thereby encounter misfortune should I try. It would be an unreasonable quest. The same could be said of fate too, but the context makes clear that this is a narrative about an interior endeavor: "These four things [i.e., the four activities described in the first four clauses of the quote above] are not to be sought in externalities, nor do they rely upon others; [rather,] turn to them within oneself and sustain [them]." (四者不求於外，不假於人，反諸己而存矣。)[9] Like the procedures of my mind, my likes and dislikes, and my inclinations and nature, my destiny too is a proper object of self-inquiry and examination. Fate, on the other hand, is only something to be aware of and become reconciled to.

That Heaven is the ultimate source of our destinies does not seem to imply that Heaven should thus become the object of our investigation here. This is likely due to the author conceiving of Heaven as "nature" rather than as an anthropomorphic entity. As we saw in the introduction, Xunzi is one scholar who thought that "Heaven" was just another name for "nature."[10] With regard to self-cultivation, he can therefore say: "If [you] nourish [yourself] sufficiently and act in a timely manner, then Heaven cannot make you ill, and if [you] cultivate the [human] way and are not

---

8. *Hanshi waizhuan* ch. 2.34; cf. Hightower, *Han Shih Wai Chuan*, 73.
9. *Hanshi waizhuan* ch. 2.34; cf. Hightower, *Han Shih Wai Chuan*, 74.
10. *Xunzi* 荀子 ch. 17 (天論). See introduction, n. 38.

distracted, then Heaven cannot bring you misfortune." (養備而動時，則天不能病；修道而不貳，則天不能禍。)[11]

Other authors described Heaven as a reified symbol of the Heavenly mandate, as it applies to ordinary humans; which is to say, fate, the topic of the previous chapter. For example, one text describes the transfer of power from one mytho-historical sage-king to another: "That Shun [happened to] meet Yao was a *Heavenly* [matter], but that Shun plowed on Mt. Li, made pottery on the banks of the Yellow River, fished in Thunder Marsh, that the world delighted in him, and that excellent officials followed him, were *human* [matters]." (夫舜遇堯，天也；舜耕於歷山，陶於河濱，釣於雷澤，天下說之，秀士從之，人也。)[12] Here, "Heavenly [matters]" refer to fate, the things beyond our control, while "human [matters]" refer to destiny, the things that we can and should do to realize our potential. Shun, the fifth of the pre-dynastic Five Thearchs (五帝), was not a member of the royal house of Yao, who was the fourth of the Five Thearchs. He was a natural leader who inspired confidence and loyalty wherever he went—that is, "the world delighted in him." For this reason, through a chance encounter with Yao, Yao subsequently decided to abdicate to Shun rather than to his own son, even though primogeniture was already the norm. Here, then, Shun realized his destiny to be the ruler of early China not through waiting for fate to bestow the honor upon him, but by exerting himself in the world, from Mt. Li to Thunder Marsh. His ultimate success was due to a combination of fate *and* destiny. The moral of the story is that we should always pursue our destiny, whether or not fate "decides" to smile upon us.

It is reasonable to assume that pursuing our destiny will result in increased effectiveness, given that our destinies are what we are already inclined—physically or mentally, or both—to do. Zhuangzi, who among our authors was the most interested in individual destiny, tells a story of an old swimmer connecting destiny and effectiveness. When asked why he was so good at swimming, even in dangerous waters, the swimmer replied: "I began with the given, developed my [human] nature, and completed [my skill] in accord with my destiny." (吾始乎故，長乎性，成乎命。)[13] When asked to

---

11. *Xunzi* ch. 17 (天論); cf. Eric Hutton, *Xunzi: The Complete Text* (Princeton: Princeton University Press, 2014), 175.

12. *Lüshi chunqiu* 呂氏春秋 ch. 14.6 (慎人); cf. John Knoblock and Jeffrey Riegel, *The Annals of Lü Buwei* (Stanford: Stanford University Press, 2000), 323.

13. *Zhuangzi* 莊子 ch. 19 (達生); cf. Burton Watson, *The Complete Works of Zhuangzi* (New York: Columbia University Press, 1968; 2013), 152.

elaborate, he helpfully replied: "I was born on land and feel comfortable on land: this is 'the given.' [I] grew up with water and became comfortable with water: this [adaptability] is [part of human] 'nature.' Not knowing why I am the way I am: this is my 'destiny.'" (吾生於陵而安於陵，故也；長於水而安於水，性也；不知吾所以然而然，命也。)[14]

We saw in chapter 3 that uncontrived action is efficacious.[15] Zhuangzi, extending the idea that individual destiny is "from" Heaven—or rather, *is* Heavenly—brazenly equates the two: "Uncontrived action is called 'Heavenly.'" (無為為之之謂天。)[16] The uncontrived swimming of the old swimmer in the previous paragraph has his "Heavenly destiny" to thank for his skill. He describes his destiny as "not knowing why I am the way I am" because destiny is always something of a mystery. As individuals, we all have certain proclivities and abilities, but discovering what those are, and then articulating them into a "way," is not usually an obvious pursuit.

The Heavenly of the Human

Zhuangzi also pursues the idea of "the Heavenly" within humans more than any other early Chinese author. Regarding self-cultivation, he asks us explicitly, in different anecdotes, to "complete" (成) and "develop" (開) the Heavenly within us, as well as to "match" (合) the Heavenly within us to the Heavenly outside of us. Let us briefly look at these three passages. In the first, he is describing sagely people, whom we considered in chapter 3. He says: "[They] have the physical form of other people, but are without other people's inclinations. Having the physical form of other people, [they] thus socialize with other people, but being without other people's inclinations, [they] thus do not internalize the 'right and wrongs' [of other people]. How insignificant and small are the ways in which they are categorized with other people! How outstanding and great is the solitary completion of their Heavenly [aspect]." (有人之形，無人之情。有人之形，故羣於人，無人之情，故是非不得於身。眇乎小哉，所以屬於人也！警乎大哉，獨成其天！)[17] We discussed aspirational ethics in chapter 4, so we need not

---

14. *Ibid.*
15. See chapter 3 ". . . Leads to Noncontrivance (無為)."
16. *Zhuangzi* ch. 12 (天地); cf. Watson, *Zhuangzi*, 85.
17. *Zhuangzi* ch. 5 (德充符); cf. Watson, *Zhuangzi*, 40. "Solitary" (獨) might also be read as "detached."

reiterate here why sages do not "internalize the 'right and wrongs' [of other people]." Rather, our concern is with the locution of the final phrase, "the solitary completion of their Heavenly [aspect]." Here, "Heaven" is neither "up there" as the traditional and literal wording would have it, nor is it "nature" "out there" as Xunzi would have it, nor even is it abstracted as uncontrived action as in the previous paragraph. Rather, it is an internal aspect of individuals, a part of each of us, and an object of self-cultivation.

In another chapter, Zhuangzi revisits and expands on this idea, advising us: "Do not [only] develop the 'Heavenly' of the human, but [also] develop the Heavenly of Heaven. Those who 'develop Heaven' will produce virtuosity, while those who [only] 'develop the human' will produce harm. Neither disdain the Heavenly nor neglect the human, and people will draw near to their genuineness!" (不開人之天，而開天之天。開天者德生，開人者賊生。不厭其天，不忽於人，民幾乎以其真！)[18] The anecdotes directly before and after this passage unfortunately do not provide any obvious help in understanding these three sentences. If we use Zhuangzi's equation of "the Heavenly" with "uncontrived action," as we saw above, and if we take the non-sagely human "inclinations" regarding "right and wrong" that we also saw above as "the human," we could conclude that "uncontrived action" is good while absolute social norms about ethics are bad. Alternatively, if we analyze "the Heavenly" as destiny and "the human" as fate (think of our genetic limitations), then focusing on the latter could "produce harm" insofar as it could turn people into fatalists, thinking that everything is fated and that individuals cannot by their actions change anything. I prefer the latter interpretation for two reasons. First, it sounds incongruous to say that we should "develop" the social norms that are, when divorced from uncontrived action, deleterious. And second, taking this passage along with the preceding quote, it also sounds odd to say we should "complete" uncontrived action. On the other hand, it sounds reasonable to both "develop"—here, literally, "open the door to" (開)—one's fate and "complete" one's destiny. Finally, the "genuineness" that we might draw near to is the same adjective used to describe the "genuine people," reconciled to their fates, in the previous chapter.

In the third example that we will touch upon in this section, Zhuangzi uses a third verb to connect the Heavenly within to Heaven "up/out there." This is one of the "skill stories" for which this author is duly famous, and we have already encountered it in chapter 1. Woodworker Qing went to the

---

18. *Zhuangzi* ch. 19 (達生); cf. Watson, *Zhuangzi*, 147.

forest to choose a tree to make into an exquisite bell-stand. After fasting and focusing his mind, he says "I go into a mountain forest, and observe the Heavenly nature [of the trees, to see which has] the perfect shape. After this I see the completed bell-stand [in my mind's eye], and after this, I put my hand to it; otherwise, I leave it alone. In this way the Heavenly is matched with the Heavenly. Utensils that are suspected of being the result of spirits are due to this!"[19] Trees do not have destinies in the way I am using the word here for humans, because they lack the conscious capacity to assess their fate, assess their capabilities and inclinations, and conceive of a "way" of living that best suits them. But for Woodworker Qing, who seems to know his destiny is to be a great woodworker, to "match" or "harmonize" his "Heavenly" destiny with the specific "Heavenly" nature of a particular tree, is to undertake a profound act of self-cultivation that situates him, or even *subsumes* him, within the natural environment. It ties together self-cultivation, destiny, and the making of art so good that it amazed his contemporaries.

Fulfilled People (至人)

The aspirational figure of the "fulfilled person" is described as one who "does not depart from the genuine" (不離於真).[20] What is "genuine" to the individual, within the individual, is their unique destiny. Those fortunate enough to have discovered their destiny, and courageous enough to follow that path, should find it particularly suitable (if not necessarily easy) to follow. It may or may not match up with social norms (or parental wishes), which make or may not make them social outsiders, but they should feel comfortable within their own skins and within the cosmos as a whole. Another text describes this situation: "Fulfilled people eat according to the capacity of their stomachs, dress according to the measurements of their bodies, wander wherever relaxes their persons, move wherever accords with their inclinations. . . . [They] abide in the great hall of the cosmos . . . and play with Heaven and Earth in the palms of their hands." (至人，量腹而食，度形而衣，容身而游，適情而行. . . . 處大廓之宇 . . . 玩天地於掌握之中。)[21] This sounds like someone who has found their niche in life and has succeeded in at least starting out on that path.

---

19. *Zhuangzi* ch. 19 (達生); see chap. 1, n. 114.
20. *Zhuangzi* ch. 33 (天下); cf. Watson, *Zhuangzi*, 287.
21. *Huainanzi* ch. 7 (精神); cf. Major, Queen, Meyer, and Roth, *Huainanzi*, 259.

Once one embarks upon this path, the going should become easier with time. The goal is to achieve an unselfconscious and uncontrived state of mind that does not meander off course due to exterior pressure that does not really warrant a change of direction. The spontaneity that derives from this state of mind is another trait of the fulfilled. "The orderliness of the fulfilled person: their mind dwells with spirit and their body is coordinated with [inner] nature; when tranquil they embody virtuosity and when active they comprehend [natural] principles; they accord with the spontaneity of [their inner] nature and follow along with inevitable developments; they are profoundly uncontrived and naturally harmonize with the world." (至人之治也：心與神處，形與性調；靜而體德，動而理通；隨自然之性而緣不得已之化；洞然無為而天下自和。)[22] This is to say, fulfilled people are creative and feel at home in their own skins, they act effectively and intelligently (because they are not hamstrung by being of two minds about choices), and they feel at home in the ever-changing world.

Returning to the poetic use of "the Heavenly" as part of the human organism that we saw in the previous section, our sources also describe fulfilled people as "guarding" this Heavenly aspect. Fulfilled people, Zhuangzi says, "unify their [inner] nature, nourish their *qi*-substance(s) [i.e., their bodies], and harmonize their virtuosity, in order to fully understand how things are created. Those who are like this: their 'Heavenly [aspect]' is guarded and complete, and their spirit is without discord, so how could things get into them [i.e., 'get under their skin']?" (壹其性，養其氣，合其德，以通乎物之所造。夫若是者：其天守全，其神無郤，物奚自入焉？)[23] We saw above that we should complete, develop, and harmonize with the Heavenly within us; here we are additionally asked to guard it carefully, lest we lose it. This possibility lends self-cultivation an edge of urgency. Destiny too is often thought of as something precarious, something that we must keep in balance, lest we get thrown off course by the vicissitudes of fate and the vagaries of ever-changing social expectations.

Xunzi singles out "subtlety" as the defining feature of fulfilled people. In an anecdote preceding the passage quoted below, he notes how some people can be excessive in the pursuit of goodness. For example, by burning your hand to keep yourself awake to study, or by divorcing your spouse for a slight impropriety. Neglecting your studies and social improprieties is not ideal, but Xunzi's point is that "the punishment should fit the crime." Fulfilled people, on the other hand, are models of due proportion. Being thus balanced,

---

22. *Huainanzi* ch. 8 (本經); cf. Major, Queen, Meyer, and Roth, *Huainanzi*, 274.
23. *Zhuangzi* ch. 19 (達生); cf. Watson, *Zhuangzi*, 146.

they can operate with smaller gestures. They thus have no need of traits like having the forbearance to deal with a burned hand or the forcefulness to divorce your spouse for a minor incident. "The subtle person is the fulfilled person. Fulfilled people: why [would they need to exhibit such] forbearance? Or forcefulness? Or precariousness? Thus, the muddled perceive the external situation while the astute perceive the internal situation." (夫微者，至人也。至人也：何忍？何強？何危？故濁明外景，清明內景。)[24] This equanimity and emphasis on interiority lends itself to the kind of mental acuity that can recognize subtlety: the "light touch" that is also the right touch.

Fulfilled people are described as having extraordinary mental focus. This too may be construed as a result of the tranquility that is a consequence of following one's destiny. Confident in their own course of living, they do not need to fight with others. "Fulfilled people, along with everyone else, acquire food from Earth and happiness from Heaven; but they do not fight with people or things for the sake of profit or loss; they do *not*, along with everyone else, do strange things or devise schemes or contrive matters: they innocently arrive and freely go." (夫至人者，相與交食乎地而交樂乎天；不以人物利害相攖；不相與為怪，不相與為謀，不相與為事；儵然而往，侗然而來。)[25] Fulfilled people go along with others when it accords with their destiny, but otherwise are quite content to go it alone.

The focus of fulfilled people extends beyond just the social context. While unusually attuned to the natural world, they are not thereby distracted by it. "Fulfilled people. . . . [can] forget Heaven and Earth and [can] disregard the myriad things, yet their spirit will not experience any difficulty as a result." (至人....外天地，遺萬物，而神未嘗有所困也。)[26] But though they can forget the world, they are still profoundly at home within it. When it is the time for focus, their mind's eye is turned inward, but when it is time to wander freely, then they remain at ease even while engaged with everything around them. "Fulfilled people can look up into azure Heaven, dive down to the Yellow Springs, and saunter and explore in [all] the eight directions, without a change in their spirit or *qi*-substance [i.e., body]." (夫至人者，上闚青天，下潛黃泉，揮斥八極，神氣不變。)[27] This is the very picture of equanimity.

---

24. *Xunzi* ch. 21 (解蔽); cf. Hutton, *Xunzi*, 232.
25. *Zhuangzi* ch. 23 (庚桑楚); cf. Watson, *Zhuangzi*, 193.
26. *Zhuangzi* ch. 13 (天道); cf. Watson, *Zhuangzi*, 106.
27. *Zhuangzi* ch. 21 (田子方); cf. Watson, *Zhuangzi*, 174. The "Yellow Springs" probably refers simply to what is underground. See Poo Mu-chou 蒲慕州, *In Search of Personal*

A fulfilled person, firmly on the path of their destiny, travels through the social and natural worlds with confidence. But confidence and humility have always had a counterintuitive relationship. On the one hand, they can be construed as opposites, insofar as one who is confident about a particular claim is often thought to thereby have no doubts about said claim. Zhuangzi's fallibilism turns this perspective on its head and brings confidence together with "the torch of slippery doubt."[28] Combining confidence and doubt, or humility, fulfilled people can thereby achieve (or approach) objectivity. As we saw in chapter 3, "Fulfilled people use their minds like a mirror, neither seeing [things] off, nor welcoming them: responding but not storing."[29] It is this calm objectivity, this kind of informed humility, that connects fulfilled people with a kind of selflessness. Though confident, they are not arrogant—quite the opposite—and they have reconciled themselves with both their fate and their destiny. In this way, Zhuangzi can say that "fulfilled people are selfless" (至人無己).[30]

Destiny may appear chimerical, especially to younger people who have only just begun to consider their place in the world. But realizing one's destiny is an important step in the early Chinese program of self-cultivation. Apprehending your destiny is a little like realizing that you are in love: both often begin with a tentative intuition that may or may not pan out into the real thing. But once you have it, you may well come to feel quite comfortable and confident with it, and it can indeed become a central part of your life. "Fulfilled people lean on an immovable pillar, walk on an unobstructed road, receive from an inexhaustible storehouse, learn from a deathless teacher. Wherever [they] go, [they] arrive; wherever [they] reach, [they] comprehend. Life is insufficient to ensnare [their] intentions, and death is insufficient to darken [their] spirits." (夫至人倚不拔之柱，行不關之塗，稟不竭之府，學不死之師。無往而不遂，無至而不通。生不足以挂志，死不足以幽神。)[31]

Welfare: A View of Ancient Chinese Religion (Albany: State University of New York Press, 1998), 65.

28. *Zhuangzi* ch. 2 (齊物論). Quoted in chap. 4, n. 169.
29. *Zhuangzi* ch. 7 (應帝王). See chap. 3, n. 7.
30. *Zhuangzi* ch. 1 (逍遙遊); cf. Watson, *Zhuangzi*, 3.
31. *Huainanzi* ch. 7 (精神); cf. Major, Queen, Meyer, and Roth, *Huainanzi*, 252–53.

Chapter 10

Spiritousness (神)

"When Yin and Yang cannot be fathomed, it is called 'spiritous.'"

—*Yijing*, Xici zhuan

陰陽不測之謂神。《易經‧繫辭上傳》

Spirit and Spiritous (神)

The single graph translated as "spirit" or "spiritous" conveys the same kind of ambiguity as "Heaven," an ambiguity that often lies at the heart of religious poetry. In each case, it is up to the reader to decide if the author is referring to a supernatural entity or to a noteworthy but natural phenomenon. We saw in the introduction that "Heaven" for some authors denotes an anthropomorphic entity, while others use the same word for the natural world or "nature." Sometimes we may be justified as reading the former as a metaphor for the latter. But the ambiguity inherent in precisely *when* we are so justified is what keeps the literal-minded and metaphorical-minded members of the community together. Similarly, "spirit" can refer to a supernatural entity, to a mysterious aspect of nature, or to mysterious-seeming animal (including human) abilities, like creativity or foresight.

Take, for example, the story of a white ape that was considered to be either a spirit or spiritous, insofar as it was consistently able to elude the arrows of the king's best archers.[1] It was finally shot and killed by the hero

---

1. *Lüshi chunqiu* 呂氏春秋 ch. 24.5 (博志); cf. John Knoblock and Jeffrey Riegel, *The Annals of Lü Buwei* (Stanford: Stanford University Press, 2000), 619. It is described as a "spiritous white ape" (神白猿). Its unusual color may also have had something to do with the locution, but its color is treated as superfluous in the story.

of the story, a superlative archer who succeeded where others had failed because he was able to envision hitting the ape before actually doing so. Be that as it may, how is the reader to decide whether the author thought the white ape was some kind of supernatural being, or was merely extraordinarily clever (i.e., "spiritous"), or lucky? Since the ape was, in the end, killed, we *might* suspect one of the latter. However, this assessment assumes that spirits in early China were considered immortal but, while no doubt long-lived, I do not know of any evidence that suggests that spirits could or would never "die." Thus, there is no way to know exactly what the author was conveying with his description of this ape. If I had to choose, I would still assume that the framing of the anecdote was a contest between a clever archer and his clever prey, and that the "spiritous white ape" indicates an "unusually clever white ape." As noted in previous chapters, while early China had its fair share of superstition and religion, the authors of the Scholars' texts under consideration here were relatively agnostic on such issues.

Certainly not all our authors were in complete agreement on the existence or nonexistence of spirits, but given his authority and influence, let us consider what Kongzi said about them. The term appears in six anecdotes of the *Lunyu*.² The strongest evidence that Kongzi *did* believe in spirits is in two of these passages: once where he defines "wisdom" as, in part, "respecting the ghosts and spirits [even] while keeping them at a distance" (敬鬼神而遠之), and once where he praises the culture hero Yu for "bringing utmost filiality to [his treatment of] ghosts and spirits" (致孝乎鬼神).³ These pronouncements, however, should be weighed against two more that are somewhat more ambivalent. In perhaps this text's best-known observation on the matter, it says that one should "sacrifice to spirits as if they were present" (祭神如神在).⁴ It is the "as if" that arouses the reader's doubt.⁵ Similarly, when Kongzi got sick, a follower asks if he should perhaps

---

2. *Lunyu* 論語 3.12, 6.22, 7.21, 7.35, 8.21, and 11.12.

3. *Lunyu* 6.22 and 8.21; cf. Edward Slingerland, *Confucius: Analects with Selections from Traditional Commentaries* (Indianapolis: Hackett, 2003), 60, 85. The first was quoted in chap. 1, n. 89 and chap. 6, n. 36.

4. *Lunyu* 3.12; cf. Slingerland, *Analects*, 21.

5. This "as if" may be construed in two quite different ways: as indicative of Kongzi's doubt in the *existence* of spirits, or of his doubt about whether the spirits are *currently present*. If Kongzi did *not* believe in (literal) spirits, then the reader may wonder why he made the previous two comments (i.e., in *Lunyu* 6.22 and 8.21); and if Kongzi *did* believe in spirits, we may wonder why they didn't play a more prominent role in his philosophy.

say a prayer. After asking if there even *were* such things, and then hearing an example of such a prayer, to "upper and lower spirits and earth-spirits" (上下神祇), Kongzi cryptically says that he has in fact already been praying for a long time.[6] Scholars have long taken Kongzi's improbable ignorance in this matter and his final reply to indicate that he thought his ethical life itself constituted his lifelong "prayer." This assessment does not imply that Kongzi did not believe in spirits but, rather like Socrates' opaque relationship to the Greek gods, it does indicate a certain ambivalence. In addition to the two sayings that seem unequivocal and the two that are uncertain, there are two more that indicate Kongzi did not really speak much about the matter. One baldly claims that he did not speak about spirits—but, given the preceding, this is clearly hyperbolic—while another reports that, upon being asked about how to "serve" (事) ghosts and spirits, Kongzi evasively retorted "[You] are not yet able to serve *people*, so how [will you] be able to serve *ghosts*?" (未能事人，焉能事鬼？)[7]

What are we to make of this? There is an equal amount of evidence for both the standard cultural belief in spirits and the intellectual-elite doubt toward such entities, coupled with evidence that Kongzi, like the Buddha, did not really like to speak of such matters. Given this, perhaps ambivalence and caution are the best attitudes to take while reviewing the source material for the present chapter. In any case, the *Lunyu* provides no unambiguous examples of "spirit" used in the sense of "spiritous," as I construed the white ape mentioned above. And it is precisely these uses that make "spiritousness" relevant to the topic of self-cultivation. But the rhetorical problem of semantic parameters remains.

Spirits in early China were considered part of the natural landscape, and it may be that spiritousness was too. In the following passage on cosmology, one could parse the phrase *shen qi* 神氣 either as "spirits and *qi*-substance" or "spiritous *qi*-substance." I chose the latter.

> Heaven has four seasons—spring, autumn, winter, summer—[with their] wind, rain, frost, and dew: each has their lessons [for us]. Earth conveys spiritous *qi*-substance—the spiritous *qi*-substance in

---

6. *Lunyu* 7.35; cf. Slingerland, *Analects*, 76. Scholars are unanimous in taking Kongzi's query "*Are* there such things?" (有諸？) to refer to prayers, but given his reputation for knowledge about protocol, and especially end-of-life protocol, I wonder if he was not actually questioning the existence of the *recipients* of such prayers, i.e., spirits.

7. *Lunyu* 7.21 and 11.12; cf. Slingerland, *Analects*, 71, 115. The latter was quoted, with fuller context, in chap. 1, n. 88.

wind and thunder—the wind and thunder that carry along the bodies by which so many things come forth and are born: each has their lessons [for us]. When pure percipience is in oneself, the *qi*-substance of your intentions are like a spirit. [Then, when] aspirations and desires are about to arrive, they will certainly unfold with prior [intuitions about how to successfully realize them, just as] when rain is going to fall, the land [first] sends forth rainclouds.

(天有四時,春秋冬夏,風雨霜露:無非教也。地載神氣,神氣風霆,風霆流形,庶物露生;無非教也。清明在躬,氣志如神。嗜欲將至,有開必先;開降時雨,山川出雲。)[8]

I chose the latter because I think "spirituous *qi*-substance" makes more sense. The rainclouds that are blown into place preceding rainfall are notable here for their reliable ability, so to speak, to be in the right place at the right time. It could be that they are timely in this way because the world's wind and thunder are possessed by spirits, but the crux of this passage focuses on the useful human intuition that ostensibly comes as a result of cultivating "pure percipience," not on the existence of supernatural entities. If clever spirits were available for consultation, then to realize our "aspirations and desires," why not just consult them, rather than rely on our own "pure percipience"?[9] Therefore, while recognizing that many early Chinese people did believe in the existence of literal spirits, many others also used the term as an adjective denoting astuteness, just as modern English speakers may describe an action as "devilishly clever" or "fiendishly difficult" without thereby necessarily believing in the literal existence of devils or fiends.

In any case, literal spirits were a part of the imaginative, cultural landscape.[10] One text recounts an imperial order to the people to "offer sacrifice

---

8. *Liji* 禮記 ch. 29 (孔子閒居); cf. James Legge, *Li Chi: Book of Rites* (1885; rpt. New York: University Books, 1967), 2:281–82. The "bodies by which so many things come forth and are born" refers to seeds and pollen.

9. The preference for relying on one's own (cultivated) perception, or "percipience," over appeal to unseen intelligences may be exemplified in the slow, centuries-long shift from divination with ancestors and spirits to the (cultivated) perception of the lines of the *Yijing* and the visible realities that those lines were thought to mysteriously represent.

10. For a thoughtful historical survey and analysis of the relationship between humans and literal spirits, see Michael Puett, *To Become a God: Cosmology, Sacrifice, and Self-divinization in Early China* (Cambridge: Harvard University Press, 2002).

to august Heaven and the thearch(s) above, as well as to the spirits of the eminent mountains, great rivers, and four directions" (供皇天上帝，名山大川、四方之神).[11] Elsewhere in the same text, five spirits are mentioned by name, each of whom appears subordinate to a named, but little-understood, "thearch" (帝).[12] They were capable of both helping and harming humans.[13] It appears that spirits wanted respect and that at least some of them wanted the occasional sacrifice. They also seemed to respond well to human virtuosity (德), propriety (義), prudence (詳), and social orderliness (倫).[14]

For their part, spirits were invisible, were active in the "embodiment of things" (體物), were themselves virtuous, and could, on occasion, send omens, and even speak to people in dreams.[15] More to the point here, spirits also had a reputation for being focused and skillful. One text refers to "a ferryman that handled his boat like a spirit" (津人操舟若神), as well as to a woodworker who carved skillfully, "like a spirit" (猶神).[16] A third "skill story" in the same chapter edges us, grammatically speaking, from

---

11. *Lüshi chunqiu* ch. 6.1 (季夏); cf. Knoblock and Riegel, *The Annals of Lü Buwei*, 154. The "thearch(s)" mentioned here are not the "Five Thearchs" mentioned in the introduction, but refer either to a single, totemic, primarily Shang-dynasty-era "First Ancestor" (see chap. 1, n. 44 for more on this); to the five thearchs mentioned by name elsewhere in the *Lüshi chunqiu* (see next note); or more generally to a class of supernatural entities called "thearchs" about which little is known.

12. The names of these spirits are Goumang 句芒, Zhurong 祝融, Houtu 后土, Rushou 蓐收, and Xuanming 玄冥. See *Lüshi chunqiu* chs. 1.1 (孟春), 4.1 (孟夏), 6.1 (季夏), 7.1 (孟秋), 10.1 (孟冬) and elsewhere; cf. Knoblock and Riegel, *The Annals of Lü Buwei*, 60, 115, 156, 172, 223. Shennong 神農 ("Spiritous Farmer") was the third of the "Three Sovereigns" (三皇), and was also known as Yan Di 炎帝 ("Ardent Thearch"); presumably he would be classed as a human thearch, and while "spiritous," clearly he was not a "spirit."

13. *Lüshi chunqiu* ch. 22.5 (求人); cf. Knoblock and Riegel, *The Annals of Lü Buwei*, 581.

14. *Zuozhuan* 左傳 (宣公 15, 成公 16); *Hanshi waizhuan* 韓詩外傳 ch. 3.12; cf. Stephen Durrant, Wai-yee Li, David Schaberg, *Zuozhuan: Commentary on the 'Spring and Autumn Annals'* (Seattle: University of Washington Press, 2016), 1:681, 2:829; James Hightower, *Han Shih Wai Chuan: Han Ying's Illustrations of the Didactic Application of the Classic of Songs* (Cambridge: Harvard University Press, 1952), 88.

15. *Liji* ch. 31 (中庸); *Guanzi* 管子 ch. 12 (樞言); *Lü shi chunqiu* ch. 14.2 (本味); cf. Legge, *Li Chi*, 2:307; W. Allyn Rickett, *Guanzi: Political, Economic, and Philosophical Essays from Early China* (Princeton: Princeton University Press, 1985, 1998), 1:221; Knoblock and Riegel, *The Annals of Lü Buwei*, 307.

16. *Zhuangzi* 莊子 ch. 19 (達生); cf. Burton Watson, *The Complete Works of Zhuangzi* (New York: Columbia University Press, 1968; 2013), 148, 152.

the concept of "spirit" to the idea of "spiritousness." In it, a cicada-catcher practiced his art until he could hold his arm out as motionless as "a branch on a dead tree." Given the degree of carefulness requisite for catching cicadas, he was finally described as "using undivided attention for the concentration of spirit/ousness" (用志不分，乃凝於神).[17] Here, a noun is called for, but both "spirit" and "spiritousness" would work. Either way, we are now clearly talking about a human, psychological faculty rather than a nonhuman, supernatural entity. In a cosmological sense, this is a significant category shift, but in a grammatical or literary sense, the needle has barely moved.

Spirit/ous(ness) (神)

I argued in chapter 1 that "essence" (精) and "spirit" (神) were like two sides of the same coin of cosmological creativeness, with the former being an active ingredient in all things and the latter being used primarily in relation to sentient things. Living humans have a spirit, which may or may not, for non-ordinary people, persist temporarily after death. But humans and other animals are not the only sentient beings with spirit/ousness. The aforementioned "thearch(s) above" are described by a different author as spiritous, here meaning intelligent and effective. "If the thearch above *is* spiritous, then it cannot be deceived, and if the thearch above is *not* spiritous, then prayers [to it] are useless." (上帝神，則不可欺；上帝不神，祝亦無益。)[18] Ghosts, too, are characterized as spiritous, and in this case, given that Zhuangzi is a Daoist, the spiritousness derives from the Way. "The Way. . . . made ghosts and thearchs spiritous, and produced Heaven and Earth." (夫道. . . . 神鬼神帝，生天生地。)[19]

Furthermore, human spiritousness can harmonize itself with supernatural entities. Sages are said to be able to "harmonize their spirit/ousness with the Great One . . . and their essences [can] commune with ghosts and spirits" (神合乎太一 . . . 精通乎鬼神).[20] The Great One, like Heaven, sometimes refers to an anthropomorphic figure and other times refers, like "the thearch above," to the North Star—though these two characterizations should not

---

17. *Zhuangzi* ch. 19 (達生); cf. Watson, *Zhuangzi*, 147. Quoted in chap. 5, n. 5.
18. *Yanzi chunqiu* 晏子春秋 ch. 1.12; cf. Olivia Milburn, *The Spring and Autumn Annals of Master Yan* (Leiden: Brill, 2016), 182.
19. *Zhuangzi* ch. 6 (大宗師); cf. Watson, *Zhuangzi*, 45. A more literal translation would use "spirit/ous" as a verb, whereby it "*spiritized* ghosts and *spiritized* thearchs."
20. *Lüshi chunqiu* ch. 17.4 (勿躬); cf. Knoblock and Riegel, *The Annals of Lü Buwei*, 420.

be taken as necessarily mutually exclusive, and both may be reified symbols of the cosmic Way. Like so many other imaginative accounts, it is difficult to know whether to take such a "harmonization" literally or figuratively, though given the pervasive undercurrent of doubt in most of our sources, I lean towards the latter. In this case, the one whose spirit and essence are so "harmonizing" and "communing" is the aspirational sage-king who rules with perfect attention to both the orderly workings of the cosmos and the potentially orderly relationships among the citizenry.

Spirit/ousness is often described as something that moves about, both inside and outside the body. It is, in this regard, something like "attention," which we also describe as something that moves and wanders, that can be dissipated or focused. Sometimes spirit/ousness can wander out in sagely musings;[21] other times it can depart as an unwanted result of distraction or despair.[22] Conversely, spirit/ousness can also enter into one and take up residence, as it were. One passage says that if one is balanced in their living arrangements, diet, speaking, thinking, and intentionality, then "spirit/ousness will reside in them" (神居之).[23] Another text says that "[If you] become empty of desire, spirit/ousness will then enter and dwell [in you]." (虛其欲，神將入舍。)[24] In case this is too gnomic, the author explains that getting rid of (excessive) desire leads to tranquility (靜), which leads to detachment (獨立), which leads to percipience (明), which leads to spiritousness; thus, we are informed that if we "do not clean [our minds], then spirit/ousness will not abide" (不潔則神不處).[25]

The metaphor of "spirit" for "spiritousness" can sometimes lend itself to hyperbole. We saw in chapter 1 that Mengzi described his ethically cultivated *qi*-substance hyperbolically as "fill[ing] the space between Heaven and Earth."[26] Similar rhetorical flourishes may be found describing the activities of our spirit/ousness. Later in chapter 1 we saw that "spirit/ousness can cover the cosmos" (神覆乎宇宙).[27] The same text also says our

---

21. *Lüshi chunqiu* ch. 17.2 (君守); cf. Knoblock and Riegel, *The Annals of Lü Buwei*, 413.
22. *Chuci* 楚辭 ch. 5 (遠遊); cf. David Hawkes, *Ch'u Tz'u: The Songs of the South* (1959; rpt. Boston: Beacon Press, 1962), 82.
23. *Hanshi waizhuan* ch. 8.29; cf. Hightower, *Han Shih Wai Chuan*, 283.
24. *Guanzi* ch. 36 (心術上); Rickett, *Guanzi*, 2:72.
25. *Guanzi* ch. 36 (心術上); Rickett, *Guanzi*, 2:76.
26. *Mengzi* 孟子 ch. 2A2 (公孫丑上). See chap. 1, n. 28.
27. *Lüshi chunqiu* ch. 1.2 (本生). See chap. 1, n. 58.

"spirit/ousness [can] fathom the six directions" (神通乎六合).[28] Given that the human imagination does seem rather unconstrained (for some people anyway), it is perhaps fitting that our creative spirit/ousness is described in our sources as unbounded in these ways.

The "movement" of spirit/ousness also lends itself to literary creativity. On the one hand, it is said to move outside and inside of our bodies; on the other, it can also move other people, in the sense of, for example, "moving someone to tears." Viewed in this manner, spirit/ousness is connected to honesty:

> Those who are genuine are the utmost of essence and honesty. Without essence or honesty, [you] will not be able to move other people. Thus, those who force tears, though they [may] grieve, will not [move others to] sadness, [just as] those who force anger, though they [may] be stern, will not [move others to] awe, and those who force affection, though they [may] laugh, will not [move others to] harmony. [Conversely,] genuine grieving, even when soundless, will [move others to] sadness; [just as] genuine anger, even before it is expressed, will [move others to] awe; and genuine affection, even before sharing a laugh, will [move others to] harmony. Those who are genuine within, their spirit/ousness will move the outside [world].
>
> (真者，精誠之至也。不精不誠，不能動人。故強哭者雖悲不哀，強怒者雖嚴不威，強親者雖笑不和。真悲無聲而哀，真怒未發而威，真親未笑而和。真在內者，神動於外。)[29]

The ability to move others may be related to the ability to persuade others, though our texts stipulate that both of these abilities are predicated on being honest. One author says "[If] speakers and rulers are not honest, their [ability to] move the minds of other people will not be spiritous." (說與治不誠，其動人心不神。)[30] This is true not only in social and political spheres, but also in education: "For those who are honest, their spiritousness [creates] responsiveness in other people: how could words [alone] be sufficient for instructing them?" (誠有之則神應乎人矣：言豈足以諭之哉？)[31]

---

28. *Lüshi chunqiu* ch. 17.1 (審分); cf. Knoblock and Riegel, *The Annals of Lü Buwei*, 408.
29. *Zhuangzi* ch. 31 (漁父); cf. Watson, *Zhuangzi*, 275–76. "Laugh" (笑) could also be translated as "smile."
30. *Lüshi chunqiu* ch. 18.8 (具備); cf. Knoblock and Riegel, *The Annals of Lü Buwei*, 472.
31. *Lüshi chunqiu* ch. 26.1 (士容); cf. Knoblock and Riegel, *The Annals of Lü Buwei*, 645.

Spiritousness, unsurprisingly, is spirited. (That is, creativity is often expressed with enthusiasm.)

One author says spiritousness can be expressed in loyalty,[32] but honesty seems to be of particular importance. Xunzi expands on this connection. "If [you] preserve goodness with an honest mind, then [you] will be able to embody [it], and if [you] embody it, then [you] will be spiritous, and you will be able to develop [things]." (誠心守仁則形，形則神，垂能化矣。)[33] This spiritous ability to develop things can continue even after one has died. Another text said of the virtuous sage-kings of yore: "Even after they died, later generations were developed [by them] as if by spirits." (身已終矣，而後世化之如神。)[34] So spirit/ousness can itself move; can move, persuade, instruct, and develop other people; and it has an important ethical dimension.

Due to these factors, and because our spirit/ousness is the pointy end of our creative consciousness, it naturally may assume the position of leader, though only if we allow it to. One text says that "spiritous *qi*-substance" (神氣) can "lead" (將) us.[35] Another is more specific: "Development has five [key] *qi*-substances: [those of the mind, mentioned earlier,] will, thought, spirit/ousness, and virtuosity; [but] spirit/ousness is its unifying leader." (化有五氣者，志也、思也、神也、德也；神其一長也。)[36] We saw above that spiritousness depends upon tranquility, and we will return to this theme below, but here we might note that leadership implies competence, and competence begins with good planning. Thus, "When the mind is secure and tranquil then spiritous plans are produced [in it]; when deliberation is deep and far-reaching, then calculative strategies [can] be completed. When spiritous plans are produced, then the will will not be disorderly, and when calculative strategies are completed, then achievement will not be blocked." (心安靜則神策生，慮深遠則計謀成；神策生則志不可亂，計謀成則功不可間。)[37] As has already been noted above, that this antique recipe for success still resonates may give one pause, even if we do just chalk it up to "common sense."

---

32. *Lüshi chunqiu* ch. 9.5 (精通); cf. Knoblock and Riegel, *The Annals of Lü Buwei*, 221.
33. *Xunzi* 荀子 ch. 3 (不苟); cf. Eric Hutton, *Xunzi: The Complete Text* (Princeton: Princeton University Press, 2014), 19.
34. *Lüshi chunqiu* ch. 19.5 (適威); cf. Knoblock and Riegel, *The Annals of Lü Buwei*, 494.
35. *Lüshi chunqiu* ch. 3.2 (盡數); cf. Knoblock and Riegel, *The Annals of Lü Buwei*, 101.
36. *Guiguzi* 鬼谷子 ch. 15 (本經陰符七術); cf. Thomas Cleary, *Thunder in the Sky* (Boston: Shambhala, 1994), 57–58. This was noted in passing in chap. 1, n. 113.
37. *Guiguzi* ch. 15 (本經陰符七術); cf. Cleary, *Thunder in the Sky*, 37.

Successful planning entails foresight, and foresight is another idea that, with just the slightest dash of hyperbole, can implicate ideas of supernatural "foreknowledge." Recall the quote in chapter 3 wherein "the masses" erroneously took accurate foresight "to be the work of spirits or [just] good luck."[38] It should perhaps not be surprising that the classic divination text of the *Yijing* claims that "With spiritousness the future is known, and in wisdom the past is stored." (神以知來, 知以藏往。)[39] But most of our sources have a more prosaic attitude toward prudence and foresight, even while making use of the flexible parameters of the somewhat mysterious term "spirit/ousness." Conversely, we should not be surprised to learn that Xunzi—who takes "Heaven" to be prosaic "nature"—defines spirit/ousness in equally non-fantastical terms: "What is it to be focused? [I] say: 'to grasp spiritousness firmly.' What is it to be spiritous? [I] say: 'to be fully competent and to firmly grasp orderliness' is called spiritousness." (曷謂一? 曰: 執神而固。曷謂神? 曰: 盡善挾治之謂神。)[40] "Spiritousness" is thus as flexible a concept as we will have come to expect by now, but it nevertheless has specific touchstones of timely, and competent, perceptivity.

In fact, "spiritousness" can be used to describe not just the creative attentiveness of sentient beings, but also the incipience of events. Shizi noted that "Misfortunes, at the beginning, are easily dispelled. As for those that cannot be dispelled, avoid them. Because when they are fully manifested, [though you might] desire to dispel them [you will] be unable, and [though you might] desire to avoid them [you will] be unable. Those who deal with [problems] while [still] spiritous: their activities are few but their achievements are many." (禍之始也易除。其除之不可者避之。及其成也, 欲除之不可, 欲避之不可。治於神者, 其事少而功多。)[41] He goes on to adduce several examples of such behavior: cutting down (unwanted) trees before they get too big, putting out (unwanted) fires before they spread, daubing cracks in the chimney before sparks fly out, and instilling ethics in children before they land themselves in prison.[42] He then concludes: "Sagely people

---

38. *Lüshi chunqiu* ch. 20.5 (觀表). See chap. 3, n. 115.

39. *Yijing* 易經, "Xici zhuan I" 繫辭上傳; cf. Richard Lynn, *The Classic of Changes: A New Translation of the* I Ching *as Interpreted by Wang Bi* (New York: Columbia University Press, 1994), 64.

40. *Xunzi* ch. 8 (儒效); cf. Hutton, *Xunzi*, 60.

41. *Shizi* 尸子 ch. 2 (貴言); cf. Paul Fischer, *Shizi: China's First Syncretist* (New York: Columbia University Press, 2012), 67.

42. Some of these were noted in chap. 5, n. 39.

deal with [things] when [they] are yet spiritous; stupid people contend with [things] after [they] have become obvious. . . . Therefore [sages] are called 'spiritous people.'" (聖人治於神，愚人爭於明也. . . . 故曰神人。)[43] These passages widen the scope of the term "spirit/ous" such that it may also be used to describe the physical conditions that create opportunities for timely success for those paying attention to such things. Here, the first "spiritous" refers to liminal events, to beginnings that are as yet inchoate, events that "spiritous people" with foresight are competent at capitalizing on. We will discuss the aspirational figure of the "spiritous person" at the end of this chapter, but first there are two important phrases that incorporate the idea of spiritousness that should be examined: "essential spiritousness" and "spiritous percipience."

Essential Spiritousness (精神)

Recall from chapter 1 that "essence" refers to the creative edge of the *qi*-substances that constitute what we call "matter," while "spirit" is roughly the same thing but is employed when describing sentience. The two terms can be used as two separate nouns, "essence and spirit," but can also be put together as an adjective-noun term: "essential spirit/ousness." It is not always obvious which reading is more likely to be correct. We saw both uses in chapter 1, with the more descriptive analysis concluding that excessive physical conditions had a detrimental effect on one's essence, while excessive emotions had a detrimental effect on the spirit.[44] But another quote made clear, in context, that they belonged together, insofar as "the essential spirit belongs to Heaven, while the skeletal system belongs to Earth."[45] Since "skeletal system" is a clear adjective-noun phrase, and since classical Chinese favors grammatical parallelism, it is a good bet that "essential spirit" here should be preferred to "essence and spirit."

Essential spiritousness is not restricted to humans, nor even to sentient beings. We saw in the previous paragraph that "essential spirit/ousness belongs to Heaven," and Zhuangzi was described as one who "came and went alone with the essential spiritousness of Heaven and Earth" (獨與天

---

43. *Shizi* ch. 2 (貴言); cf. Fischer, *Shizi*, 68–69.
44. *Lüshi chunqiu* ch. 3.2 (盡數). See chap. 1, n. 107.
45. *Huainanzi* 淮南子 ch. 7 (精神). See chap. 1, n. 23.

地精神往來).⁴⁶ The essential spiritousness of jade is located specifically in the Earth.⁴⁷ Xunzi described clouds as displaying essential spiritousness.⁴⁸ Zhuangzi, again, is the one to wax poetic: "Essential spiritousness flows throughout the four directions: no place is out of reach. Converging with Heaven above, extending over Earth below: it develops and nurtures the myriad things. [Because] nothing compares [to it], it may be called 'the equal of thearchs.'" (精神四達並流：無所不極。上際於天，下蟠於地：化育萬物。不可為象，其名為同帝。)⁴⁹ In a later chapter he avers, unsurprisingly, that "essential spiritousness is produced by the Way" (精神生於道).⁵⁰ High praise, indeed. From all this we may conclude that essential spiritousness is essential to the order of things, extensive throughout the cosmos, and exalted beyond ordinary creative activities.

Despite the pervasiveness of essential spiritousness, its persistence within humans can be jeopardized. It can be "drained by outer spectacles" (竭於外貌) or "disordered" (亂) by "external things" (外物).⁵¹ More specifically, it can be "agitated and unsettled" (搖蕩) by an excess of external stimulation or by "strange things" (奇物).⁵² One author cautions us to not "wear out essential spiritousness in what is inferior and shallow" (敝精神乎蹇淺).⁵³ Another says it is possible for "essential spiritousness to be overworked until it dissipates" (精神勞則越).⁵⁴ An army facing defeat is described as "fearfully quavering, [with their] essential spiritousness exhausted" (單蕩精神盡).⁵⁵ Perhaps most salient for us is the observation that arrogant people

---

46. *Zhuangzi* ch. 33 (天下); cf. Watson, *Zhuangzi*, 296. The "alone" (獨) might instead be read as "detachedly."

47. *Liji* ch. 48 (聘義); cf. Legge, *Li Chi*, 2:464.

48. *Xunzi* ch. 26 (賦); cf. Hutton, *Xunzi*, 281. Or they could be read as having "essence and spirit/ousness."

49. *Zhuangzi* ch. 15 (刻意); cf. Watson, *Zhuangzi*, 121.

50. *Zhuangzi* ch. 22 (知北遊); cf. Watson, *Zhuangzi*, 180.

51. *Hanfeizi* 韓非子 chs. 20, 21 (解老, 喻老); cf. Liao Wengui, *The Complete Works of Han Fei Tzu* (London: Arthur Probsthain, 1939, 1959), 1:205, 221.

52. *Huainanzi* 淮南子 ch. 8 (本經); cf. John Major, Sarah Queen, Andrew Meyer, and Harold Roth, *The Huainanzi: A Guide to the Theory and Practice of Government in Early Han China* (New York: Columbia University Press, 2010), 283.

53. *Zhuangzi* ch. 32 (列禦寇); cf. Watson, *Zhuangzi*, 281.

54. *Huainanzi* ch. 9 (主術); cf. Major, Queen, Meyer, and Roth, *Huainanzi*, 325.

55. *Lüshi chunqiu* ch. 8.2 (論威); cf. Knoblock and Riegel, *The Annals of Lü Buwei*, 195.

will "squander" (耗) their essential spiritousness in trying to outdo others.[56] From all the examples in this paragraph, we may conclude that "essential spiritousness is slippery soft and delicately subtle" (精神滑淖纖微).[57] What, then, should we do with our spirit/ousness?

Essential spiritousness should be "protected" (保), "preserved" (守), and "treasured" (寶).[58] In more proactive terms, it should also be "cleaned" (澡), "rested" (休), "loved" (愛), and "nourished" (養).[59] If we provide it with a "tranquil" (靜) abode, it will respond by becoming more "full" (充) and "strong" (壯).[60] Our sources sometimes also address this issue with more poetic advice. Sages are described as those whose "essential spiritousness preserves its root, and life and death create no vacillation in their persons: thus [they] are called fully spiritous" (精神守其根，死生無變於己：故曰至神).[61] Elsewhere we learn that "Fulfilled people return their essential spiritousness to 'the beginningless' and to the sweet depths of 'the land of without-any-form.'" (至人者，歸精神乎「無始」而甘冥乎「無何有之鄉」。)[62] "The root," "the beginningless," and "the land of without-any-form" are not identified here, but they presumably refer to either the cosmic Way or to an introspective state of mind.

The functionality of essential spiritousness is sometimes described in terms of normal mental functions like willpower or determination (志),[63] or the wordless communication that can sometimes occur between close family members,[64] but it seems more often to be used in poetic descriptions of

---

56. *Huainanzi* ch. 1 (原道); cf. Major, Queen, Meyer, and Roth, *Huainanzi*, 76.

57. *Huainanzi* ch. 19 (修務); cf. Major, Queen, Meyer, and Roth, *Huainanzi*, 779.

58. *Huainanzi* chs. 1 (原道), 7 (精神); cf. Major, Queen, Meyer, and Roth, *Huainanzi*, 59, 244, 247.

59. *Zhuangzi* ch. 22 (知北遊); *Huainanzi* chs. 7 (精神), 21 (要略); cf. Watson, *Zhuangzi*, 180; Major, Queen, Meyer, and Roth, *Huainanzi*, 256, 852.

60. *Huainanzi* ch. 1 (原道); cf. Major, Queen, Meyer, and Roth, *Huainanzi*, 76.

61. *Huainanzi* ch. 7 (精神); cf. Major, Queen, Meyer, and Roth, *Huainanzi*, 247.

62. *Zhuangzi* ch. 32 (列禦寇); cf. Watson, *Zhuangzi*, 282.

63. *Hanshi waizhuan* ch. 5.31: "Sagely people . . . preserve their essential spiritousness in order to augment their centeredness: this is called determination." (聖人 . . . 存其精神，以補其中：謂之志。) cf. Hightower, *Han Shih Wai Chuan*, 189.

64. *Lüshi chunqiu* ch. 9.5 (精通): "Spiritousness comes out in [familial] loyalty and finds response in [the other's] mind, and the two essences connect with each other: what need is there for words?" (神出於忠，而應乎心，兩精相得：豈待言哉？) cf. Knoblock and Riegel, *The Annals of Lü Buwei*, 221.

creative consciousness. When depicted as operating *outside* the body, it is said to be able to "penetrate the myriad things" (通於萬物) and even "ascend the distance to the [cosmic] Way" (登假於道).[65] When described as operating *inside* the body, it is said to be able to "return to full genuineness" (反於至真) and even, in a clear precursor of centuries-later Zen stories of "sudden enlightenment," to abruptly "understand clearly" (曉泠).[66] One passage situates essential spiritousness between stubbornness and reasonableness, implying control of the one and awareness of the other.

> If [your] volatile will operates without bias, then essential spiritousness can be made replete and *qi*-substance can be undissipated. If [your] essential spiritousness is replete and *qi*-substance is not dissipated, then there can be reasonableness. If there is reasonableness, then there can be balance; if there is balance, then there can be understanding; if there is understanding, then there can be spiritousness; and if there is spiritousness, then there may be nothing that is unseen, nothing that is unheard, and nothing that is unachievable.
>
> (教志勝而行之不僻，則精神盛而氣不散矣。精神盛而氣不散則理，理則均，均則通，通則神，神則以視無不見，以聽無不聞也，以為無不成也。)[67]

In this passage, essential spiritousness seems to refer to a mental *attitude* while spiritousness refers to a mental *ability*. Such an attitude comports well with the image of a still pool of water that accurately mirrors the reality of the world. This is why Zhuangzi is able to exclaim: "Tranquil water is clear, but how much more so is essential spiritousness!" (水靜猶明，而況精神！)[68] The word translated here as "clear," when describing human cognition, may be translated as "percipient" or "perceptive." (If the Buddhists had not already laid claim to the word "enlightened," that might be a preferable translation, but that ship has sailed.)

---

65. *Huainanzi* chs. 8 (本經), 7 (精神); cf. Major, Queen, Meyer, and Roth, *Huainanzi*, 278, 249.
66. *Huainanzi* chs. 8 (本經), 19 (修務); cf. Major, Queen, Meyer, and Roth, *Huainanzi*, 280, 781.
67. *Huainanzi* ch. 7 (精神); cf. Major, Queen, Meyer, Roth, *Huainanzi*, 243.
68. *Zhuangzi* ch. 13 (天道); cf. Watson, *Zhuangzi*, 98.

Spiritous Percipients / Percipience (神明)

If spiritousness is creative mental *action*, and essential spiritousness is the tranquil mental *attitude* underlying it, then spiritous percipience is the intelligent *acuity* of our creative minds. But the term "spiritous percipience" can, like "essential spiritousness," be read either as two nouns—spirits and percipients or spiritousness and percipience—or as an adjective-noun phrase. In the following sentence, it appears that two separate things are being referred to: "Yin and Yang [mingle in] the four seasons, but not [specifically] to produce the myriad things; rain and dew seasonally fall, but not [specifically] to nourish the grasses and trees: [rather,] spirits and percipients join, Yin and Yang harmonize, and the myriad things are produced." (陰陽四時，非生萬物也；雨露時降，非養草木也；神明接，陰陽和，而萬物生矣。)[69] It is not impossible that "spirits and percipients" should be instead taken as a number of "spiritous percipients" that join with one another, but the precedent of "Yin and Yang" as well as "rain and dew" is, again assuming a penchant for grammatical parallelism, evidence for the former. Another text adds the Heaven-Earth dyad, furthering the implication that there are two separate things at work in each dualism: "Heaven and Earth responded by assisting each other: this was to create spirits and percipients. Spirits and percipients responded by assisting each other: this was to create Yin and Yang." (天地復相輔也：是以成神明。神明復相輔也：是以成陰陽。)[70] No one knows just what entities are being referred to in passages like these; perhaps this is a generic appellation for celestial objects or supernatural sentience (or both).

Spiritousness and percipience are also found separately in human anthropology. One text uses the terms separately *and* together in the same passage: "To see what other people do not see is called 'percipience,' and to know what other people do not know is called 'spiritousness.' The spiritously percipient are the first to triumph." (見人所不見，謂之明；知人所不知，謂之神。神明者，先勝者也。)[71] Another uses the terms to describe not knowledge and vision, but rather the contexts in which decisions are made. "Sagely people strategize in private, and thus are called spiritous; they carry out [their plans] in public, and thus are called percipient." (聖人謀

---

69. *Huainanzi* ch. 20 (泰族); cf. Major, Queen, Meyer, and Roth, *Huainanzi*, 800.
70. *Taiyi shengshui* 太一生水; cf. Scott Cook, *The Bamboo Texts of Guodian* (Cornell: Cornell University East Asia Program, 2012), 1:345.
71. *Huainanzi* ch. 15 (兵略); cf. Major, Queen, Meyer, and Roth, *Huainanzi*, 612.

之於陰，故曰神；成之於陽，故曰明。)[72] Examples such as these reveal the flexibility inherent in these words.

The *Liji* uses "spiritous percipience" in relation to grave goods that were presumably for use by the recently deceased, which strongly implies that the ghost(s) or spirit of the dead remained in something like a conscious state (i.e., of "spiritous percipience") for a time after death.[73] It also uses the term in relation to royal sacrifices, and says that participants can in some sense "interact with" (交) the recipients of the sacrifice.[74] Unfortunately, it is usually not entirely clear if these recipients are dead ancestors or cultural heroes like the Five Thearchs or nature spirits, or all of the above (and possibly more).

Three paragraphs above, we saw that in some cosmogonies "spirits" and "percipients" played active roles. In others, a singular "spiritous percipience" is at work.

> Heaven displays the sun and moon, arranges the stars and planets, allocates Yin and Yang, and spreads the four seasons; by day exposing them and at night resting them, with wind drying them and with rain and dew moistening them. In its production of things, none see that by which it nourishes, yet things grow; in its killing of things, none see that by which it mortifies, yet things perish: these [processes] are called its 'spiritous percipience.'

> (天設日月，列星辰，調陰陽，張四時；日以暴之，夜以息之，風以乾之，雨露以濡之。其生物也，莫見其所養而物長；其殺物也，莫見其所喪而物亡：此之謂神明。)[75]

It seems more likely that the final sentence of this passage is *not* referring to supernatural entities called "spiritous percipients" but is rather describing

---

72. *Guiguzi* ch. 8 (摩篇); cf. Cleary, *Thunder in the Sky*, 35.
73. *Liji* chs. 3, 4 (檀弓上, 下); cf. Legge, *Li Chi*, 1:148, 172. For an account of Kongzi being reticent on this issue, see chap. 1, n. 67.
74. See, for example, *Liji* ch. 11 (效特牲); cf. Legge, *Li Chi*, 1:434.
75. *Huainanzi* ch. 20 (泰族); cf. Major, Queen, Meyer, and Roth, *Huainanzi*, 795. It may or may not be notable that the cosmological quote from *Zhuangzi* ch. 15 on "essential spiritousness" (above, note 49) was re-told with nearly identical wording in the *Huainanzi* ch. 12, but with "spiritous percipience" rather than "essential spiritousness" in the creative role. See *Huainanzi* ch. 12 (道應); cf. Major, Queen, Meyer, and Roth, *Huainanzi*, 473.

the mysterious creative and destructive powers of nature. Should the author have intended us to think that Heaven had minions called "spiritous percipients" that did its creative work for it, there would be evidence for such a reading within the passage. The "percipience" does suggest the author is attributing something like anthropomorphic consciousness to Heaven, but I would suggest that this is merely poetic metaphor.

A similar passage from the same text describes the spiritous percipience not of Heaven but of the Way. Whereas Heaven was used to describe cosmic creativity, the way of the Way is about flexibility.

> That which is called the Way embodies the circular but [also] models the square; it shoulders the Yin but [also] embraces the Yang; it on the one hand is flexible but on the other is firm; it treads in darkness but [also] carries the bright; it transforms and develops without constancy, and attains the well-spring of oneness, in order to be responsive everywhere: this is called its spiritous percipience.
>
> (所謂道者，體圓而法方；背陰而抱陽；左柔而右剛；履幽而戴明；變化無常，得一之原，以應無方：是謂神明。)[76]

Here, the five introductory, "both A *and* B" phrases culminate in a spiritous percipience that cannot but be interpreted as eminently responsive to the circumstances.

Besides being cosmically creative and flexible, spiritous percipience also exhibits a virtuosity that we humans are advised to connect with. The *Yijing* says it is a text that can be used "to connect with the virtuosity of spiritous percipience, and to conform to the inclinations of the myriad things" (以通神明之德，以類萬物之情).[77] This passage does not elaborate on what such virtuosity might include, but other texts connect spiritous percipience specifically with social precedence (e.g., the "affiliations between fathers and sons, rulers and ministers" 父子君臣之節) and more generally with "competence" (善).[78]

---

76. *Huainanzi* ch. 15 (兵略); cf. Major, Queen, Meyer, and Roth, *Huainanzi*, 582.
77. *Yijing*, "Xici zhuan"; cf. Lynn, *The Classic of Changes*, 77.
78. *Liji* ch. 19 (樂記); *Guanzi* ch. 30 (君臣上); cf. Legge, *Li Chi*, 2:115; Rickett, *Guanzi*, 1:410.

Careful reading indicates that there may be "spirits and percipients," "spiritous percipients," and the "spiritous percipience" of non-human entities like Heaven and the Way, as well as nearly-human entities like the recently dead. Who else might possess this ability? One author claims that "Ancient sage-kings all took ghosts and spirits as spiritously percipient." (古聖王皆以鬼神為神明。)[79] Another attributes spiritous percipience to Huang Di, first of the Five Thearchs.[80] A third says of the six humans who invented writing, the calendar, clothing, agriculture, ale, and carts, respectively: "These six people: all had the way of spiritous percipience and [left] footprints of sagely wisdom." (此六人者：皆有神明之道，聖智之跡。)[81] So we can add ghosts, spirits, cultural heroes, and inventors to our list.

It is not clear if all humans were thought to possess spiritous percipience or not. Xunzi may have implied we do when he said: "The mind is the ruler of the body and the master of spiritous percipience."[82] But the two other quotes using "spiritous percipience" cited in chapter 1 both suggest that it is contingent on mental focus or invigorated essence.[83] And a third text avers that only some people are able to achieve it, implying elsewhere that even among noble people, only some are able to make use of it.[84] The same text also implies contingency when it says "When spiritous percipience is settled in the world, then minds will revert to their original [state]; when minds revert to their original [state], then the people's natures will be competent." (神明定於天下而心反其初，心反其初而民性善。)[85] This leads me to believe that humans are not born with it, but it is rather an ability that we can achieve, though self-cultivation, as well as lose, through neglect.

The spiritous percipients "out there" in the invisible realm are entities that we should "respect" (敬) and "hold in awe" (畏).[86] Some authors

---

79. *Mozi* 墨子 ch. 48 (公孟); cf. John Knoblock and Jeffrey Riegel, *Mozi: A Study and Translation of the Ethical and Political Writings* (Berkeley: University of California, Berkeley, 2013), 357.

80. *Guanzi* ch. 41 (五行); Rickett, *Guanzi*, 2:123.

81. *Huainanzi* ch. 19 (修務); cf. Major, Queen, Meyer, and Roth, *Huainanzi*, 778.

82. *Xunzi* ch. 21 (解蔽). Quoted in chap. 1, n. 57.

83. *Xunzi* ch. 8 (儒效) and *Zuozhuan* (昭公 7). See chap. 1, n. 2 and 75.

84. *Huainanzi* chs. 2 (俶真), 19 (修務); cf. Major, Queen, Meyer, and Roth, *Huainanzi*, 101, 779.

85. *Huainanzi* ch. 8 (本經); cf. Major, Queen, Meyer, and Roth, *Huainanzi*, 272.

86. *Zuozhuan* (襄公 14); *Xunzi* ch. 16 (修國); cf. Durrant, Li, Schaberg, *Zuozhuan*, 2:1025; Hutton, *Xunzi*, 163.

construed them as entities that we should also "serve" (事) or, what amounts to the same thing, "follow due protocol toward" (禮), via sacrifice.[87] Others saw them as entities that one should somehow harmonize with. Zhuangzi says we should "move with" (往與), "match" (配), and even "abide with" (居) them, which indicates a decidedly different kind of relationship than one of "service."[88] I suspect that the discrepancy is resolved precisely along literal versus metaphorical lines: the former text conceives them as literal entities that could cause us harm, while the latter author construes them as metaphorical entities that represent the more mysterious aspects of the functioning of our cosmos.

Another kind of extrapolation may be made from the spiritous percipients "out there" to the spiritous percipience within humans. This is an ability that can be "labored" (勞) and even "lost" (失), and should therefore be "protected" (保).[89] It should come as no surprise by now that "tranquility and stillness are the abode of spiritous percipience" (夫靜漠者，神明之宅也).[90] Still, the poetic imagery of spiritous percipience as being "out there" persists, even when it should literally be thought of as an ability "in here," in the human mind. Consider the claim that sage-kings of yore "looked equally upon life and death, assimilated [the world's] transformations and developments, and embraced the minds of great sages in order to mirror the inclinations of the myriad things. [They] befriended spiritous percipience above and made companions of creative developments below." (齊死生，同變化，抱大聖之心，以鏡萬物之情。上與神明為友，下與造化為人。)[91] At first it may appear that it would make more sense to talk about "befriending" external entities "above" as spiritous *percipients*, rather than spiritous *percipience*. But the second half of that sentence also talks about "making companions" of "creative developments" in the natural world. Thus, we should conclude that it is the "befriending" and "making companions" that are being used metaphorically here, and that the objects of these actions are abstractions of cosmic (and anthropological) creativity and development.

---

87. *Liji* ch. 25 (祭統); *Guanzi* ch. 31 (君臣下); cf. Legge, *Li Chi*, 2:239; Rickett, *Guanzi*, 1:419.
88. *Zhuangzi* ch. 33 (天下); cf. Watson, *Zhuangzi*, 295–96, 288, 294.
89. *Zhuangzi* ch. 2 (齊物論); *Huainanzi* ch. 2 (俶真); *Chuci* ch. 5 (遠遊); cf. Watson, *Zhuangzi*, 11; Major, Queen, Meyer, and Roth, *Huainanzi*, 98; Hawkes, *Ch'u Tz'u*, 83.
90. *Huainanzi* ch. 7 (精神); cf. Major, Queen, Meyer, and Roth, *Huainanzi*, 241.
91. *Huainanzi* ch. 11 (齊俗); cf. Major, Queen, Meyer, and Roth, *Huainanzi*, 414.

Spiritous percipience in humans is an embodied mental ability. It operates through normal sensory channels: "The openings and apertures [of the body] are the doors and windows of spiritous percipience." (空竅者，神明之戶牖也。)[92] Further, it knows things in a particular way that sets it apart from regular knowing. "The utmost of spiritous percipience radiantly knows the myriad things." (神明之極，照乎知萬物。)[93] Precisely what it means to "radiantly" know something is not explained anywhere in the text, but we might infer that it means to know something clearly and without bias. Sometimes spiritous percipience is used to refer to cleverness; for example, it describes a king who knows he cannot always trust his ministers to get things done.[94] Cleverness implies a degree of mental flexibility, able to apprehend and keep track of a number of options. Zhuangzi says "spiritous percipience is fully essential [i.e., creative, which allows it] to go along with these myriad developments" (神明至精，與彼百化)[95] But its essential creativity is necessarily grounded in tranquility, which allows Xunzi to further say: "Spiritous percipience is broad and great yet fully moderate." (神明博大以至約。)[96] Mental moderation is itself a form of objectivity, of combatting bias.

Finally, spiritous percipience, while primarily a particularly creative strain of mental acuity, also has an ethical component. Xunzi claims that if one "accumulates competence and achieves virtuosity, then spiritous percipience will naturally obtain" (積善成德，而神明自得).[97] Another author goes further, saying that spiritous percipience is in fact superior to conventional ethics: "After [you] know spiritous percipience, [you] will know the inadequacy of the [ordinary human] way and virtuosity." (知神明然後知道德之不足為也。)[98] But this ethical factor should not be surprising, as ethical concerns usually are part and parcel of the early Chinese worldview even for its more secular thinkers.

---

92. *Hanfeizi* ch. 21 (喻老); cf. Liao, *Han Fei Tzu*, 1:221.

93. *Guanzi* ch. 49 (內業); cf. Rickett, *Guanzi*, 2:45.

94. *Hanfeizi* ch. 30 (內儲說上：七術) has two such stories; cf. Liao, *Han Fei Tzu*, 1:306, 308.

95. *Zhuangzi* ch. 22 (知北遊); cf. Watson, *Zhuangzi*, 178.

96. *Xunzi* ch. 9 (王制); cf. Hutton, *Xunzi*, 77.

97. *Xunzi* ch. 1 (勸學); cf. Hutton, *Xunzi*, 3. A similar quote, from *Xunzi* ch. 23, was adduced in chap. 6, n. 11.

98. *Huainanzi* ch. 8 (本經); cf. Major, Queen, Meyer, and Roth, *Huainanzi*, 273.

The Numinous (靈)

Numinosity is a general term describing things that are mysterious. It too carries supernatural implications, though nothing quite as discrete as "spirits" or "percipients." It fits with our theme of self-cultivation because it too is employed imaginatively to describe the finer aspects of certain cognitive functions. The general editor of the *Huainanzi*, a primary source for this entire chapter, says of this text: "[It] traces to the source the mental arts, and [it] rationalizes [human] nature and inclinations in order to [properly] house the numinosity of pure equanimity, and to clearly perceive the essence of spiritous percipience, in order to be wrapped up snugly with Heavenly harmony." (原心術，理性情，以館清平之靈，澄徹神明之精，以與天和相嬰薄。)[99] While this text purports to accomplish this for its readers, it is also an injunction for us to consciously try to do the same. Here, "numinosity" is used to describe the mysterious importance of having an underlying attitude of equanimity so that spiritous percipience may function well (i.e., "essentially," which is to say, "creatively").

Lots of things in early China were thought to be numinous. Spirits were, of course.[100] As was the First Ancestor, the "thearch above."[101] Both ancestral temples (宗廟) and the altars of earth and soil (社稷), as sacrificial venues, were considered numinous.[102] The priests who were employed for such events were described as numinous.[103] The tortoises whose shells were used in divination were certainly thought to possess magical properties.[104] In fact, there were four animals that were thought to be numinous: dragons, phoenixes, tortoises, and a chimerical antlered-horse creature called a *lin*

---

99. *Huainanzi* ch. 21 (要略); cf. Major, Queen, Meyer, and Roth, *Huainanzi*, 857.

100. *Laozi* 老子 ch. 39.

101. *Shijing* 詩經 #245 (生民); cf. Arthur Waley, *The Book of Songs: The Ancient Chinese Classic of Poetry* (1937; edited with additional translations by Joseph Allen; New York: Grove Press, 1996), 245. Or perhaps it was Hou Ji 后稷, the first ancestor of the Zhou dynasty; the poem can be read either way.

102. *Liji* ch. 6 (月令) or *Lü shi chunqiu* ch. 6.1 (季夏); cf. Legge, *Li Chi*, 1:276; Knoblock and Riegel, *The Annals of Lü Buwei*, 154.

103. *Mozi* ch. 68 (迎敵祠); cf. Ian Johnston, *The Mozi: A Complete Translation* (New York: Columbia University Press, 2010), 837.

104. *Yijing* #27 (頤); *Mozi* ch. 1 (親士); *Huainanzi* ch. 4 (墬形); cf. Lynn, *The Classic of Changes*, 306; Knoblock and Riegel, *Mozi*, 44; Major, Queen, Meyer, and Roth, *Huainanzi*, 169.

麟, more popularly known as a *qilin* 麒麟.¹⁰⁵ Perhaps less obvious recipients of this honor are the Shang dynasty capital city itself, as well as a timely rainfall.¹⁰⁶ Returning to the numinosity of spirits, this attribute of theirs was thought to be something that we humans could somehow tap into, by "harmonizing" with it. As such, it is of a piece with the contextualization of self-cultivation within the environment as a whole: "Great people harmonize with the virtuosity of Heaven and Earth, with the brightness/percipience of the sun and moon, with the numinosity of ghosts and spirits, and with the trustworthiness of the four seasons." (大人者，與天地合德，日月合明，鬼神合靈，與四時合信。)¹⁰⁷

Chinese rulers often received a posthumous name that was supposed to summarize their rule. Kongzi was born during the reign of Ji Xiexin 姬泄心 (r. 571–545), who was posthumously, and now popularly, known as Zhou King Ling (周靈王), or "the 'numinous' king of the Zhou dynasty." An early court chronicle describes him thus: "King Ling was born with a mustache. He was quite spiritously sagacious, and garnered no ill-will from the various marklords." (靈王生而有髭。王甚神聖，無惡於諸侯。)¹⁰⁸ I suppose being born with something of a mustache was seen as mysteriously significant, and the fact that he succeeded in keeping the various local rulers happy over the course of his twenty-six-year reign during this tumultuous period of political history was no doubt, in retrospect, seen as nothing short of miraculous. Hence his posthumous name, and his "spiritous" wisdom.

Even the cosmic Way is described as numinous. "The Way is the beginning of Heaven and Earth, and oneness is its precept. Whatever is created by things, whatever is produced by Heaven, contains [within it both] a great formlessness and developing *qi*-substance that were made prior [even] to Heaven and Earth. None can see its form, none know its name: [thus we] call it 'spiritously numinous.'" (道者，天地之始，一其紀也。物之所造，天之所生，包宏無形，化氣先天地而成。莫見其形，莫知其名，謂之神靈。)¹⁰⁹ The mystery here is how the Way operates through a cyclical life-death or form-formless process that characterizes the ceaseless change of the universe. The inclusive balance between the two is called "oneness,"

---

105. *Liji* ch. 9 (禮運); cf. Legge, *Li Chi*, 1:384.
106. *Shijing* #305 (殷武), #50 (定之方中); cf. Waley, *The Book of Songs*, 323, 42.
107. *Huainanzi* ch. 20 (泰族); cf. Major, Queen, Meyer, and Roth, *Huainanzi*, 798.
108. *Zuozhuan* (昭公 26); cf. Durrant, Li, Schaberg, *Zuozhuan*, 3:1667.
109. *Guiguzi* ch. 15 (本經陰符七術); cf. Cleary, *Thunder in the Sky*, 56.

and the creativeness and mystery of the process are portrayed as "spiritous" and "numinous."

Sometimes the term is used as a noun. We saw above that tomb goods were buried with the dead for the sake of the "spiritous percipience" that persisted for a while after their death. Some of those tomb goods were called "straw numens" (芻靈) because they were made of straw or hay.¹¹⁰ An entirely different definition is used in another text, which says: "Heavenly spirits are called numens, Earthly spirits are called sprites, and human spirits are called ghosts." (天神曰靈，地神曰祇，人神曰鬼。)¹¹¹ The most common use, however, is as an adjective, as in the preceding paragraphs.

Like essential spiritousness and spiritous percipience, not all humans have numinosity, and those that have it can lose it. Zhuangzi said that "The biggest fools will go their whole lives without numinosity." (大愚者，終身不靈。)¹¹² But one of his characters did feel that they depended on "returning to numinosity for life" (復靈以生),¹¹³ though this probably indicates a certain *quality* of life rather than the biological fact of life itself. One reason given for a lack of numinosity is impatience, which is to say, a lack of tranquility. "The numinous *qi*-substance in the mind comes and goes: [though] its subtlety [is such that] there is nothing too small [for it to reach], and its magnitude [is such that] there is nothing outside [its reach]; the reason we lose it is that it takes impatience as harmful [to it]." (靈氣在心，一來一逝：其細無內，其大無外；所以失之，以躁為害。)¹¹⁴

The first Zhou dynasty king was King Wen (r. 1056–1050), and he was said to have built a "numinous rostrum" (靈臺) as a monument to his success with his people.¹¹⁵ Zhuangzi used this literal raised platform, from which one may obtain a less parochial view of things, as a metaphor for the mind, or rather, for a mysteriously objective and responsive *potential aspect* of the mind. Both of his text's two uses of this metaphor are brief. The first articulates an unhesitating responsiveness: "Artisan Chui's freehand

---

110. *Liji* ch. 4 (檀弓下); cf. Legge, *Li Chi*, 1:173. These objects are probably a larger category subsuming the "straw dogs" (芻狗) mentioned in *Laozi* ch. 5.
111. *Shizi*, fragment #106; Fischer, *Shizi*, 153.
112. *Zhuangzi* ch. 12 (天地); cf. Watson, *Zhuangzi*, 95.
113. *Zhuangzi* ch. 27 (寓言); cf. Watson, *Zhuangzi*, 235.
114. *Guanzi* ch. 49 (內業); cf. Rickett, *Guanzi*, 2:55.
115. It is briefly described at *Shijing* #242 (靈臺); cf. Waley, *The Book of Songs*, 239–40.

drawing could match [the lines of] a compass or square [because] his fingers responded along with the things [he was drawing] and he did not hesitate with his mind: thus his 'numinous rostrum' was unified and unfettered." (工倕旋而蓋規矩，指與物化而不以心稽：故其靈臺一而不桎。)[116] His mind was unified with the ceaseless change of the environment as well as unfettered by preconceived notions and personal or social biases.

The second use is only slightly longer, and is in a story about the importance of contextualization:

> All things [should] be taken to guide [one's] person: take them in without expectations in order to vitalize the mind; respectfully be centered [on them] in order to [truly] apprehend them; if [one is] like this and a myriad troubles [still] arrive, [then they] are all of Heaven [i.e., fate] and not of the human [i.e., destiny], and [therefore should] not be sufficient to derail [one's] completion, and [should] not be allowed into [one's] 'numinous rostrum.' The 'numinous rostrum' has that which guides it [i.e., the Way], but though it does not [fully] comprehend that which guides it, it cannot be the guider [of itself].
>
> (備物以將形：藏不虞以生心，敬中以達彼；若是而萬惡至者，皆天也，而非人也，不足以滑成，不可內於靈臺。靈臺者有持，而不知其所持，而不可持者也。)[117]

This passage contextualizes humans within the larger environment of "all things," a favorite Daoist perspective. Human action should always take into account context, both for making decisions and for assessing consequences. In this way our minds are "rooted" in the world around us, and in this way our minds may be said to be "vitalized" by realizing its context. This advice is not, the author is at pains to say, going to make life problem-free; it is, however, going to shift the focus from the individual to the entire interrelated ecosystem. Our "completion" refers to our self-cultivation: problems in life should not derail the program; they should not "get into our head" and impel us to abandon the task of self-inquiry. Just as Artisan Chui was guided by the objective reality of the things he drew, allowing him to respond to them objectively, so this passage closes by saying that the mental ability

---

116. *Zhuangzi* ch. 19 (達生); cf. Watson, *Zhuangzi*, 153.
117. *Zhuangzi* ch. 23 (庚桑楚); Watson, *Zhuangzi*, 194.

to respond to things objectively depends upon the realization that in order to apprehend things clearly, and then respond to them appropriately, we must first understand that we are so "embedded" in the cosmos, and that we are not separate, individual loci of consciousness that can proceed *in* the world as if we were not also *of* the world.[118] Numinous responsiveness rests upon this prior understanding.

Zhuangzi also inverted the image of a "numinous rostrum," which brings to mind an elevated terrace from which to survey one's surroundings, with his metaphorical "numinous storehouse," evoking the image of a private, interior repository. This image appears only once in the *Zhuangzi*, which we saw in chapter 8.[119] There, I parenthetically equated the "numinous storehouse" with the mind in general but, while I did not want to digress in that chapter, I do not think its meaning is quite that broad. Both the "numinous rostrum" and the "numinous storehouse" refer to different, specific aspects of the mind. The "numinous rostrum" relates to the ability to be responsive to objective reality. The "numinous storehouse," on the other hand, describes an underlying attitude of being "harmonious and easygoing, perceptive but without a loss of happiness."[120] In Zhuangzi's memorable phrase, having a fully-stocked "numinous storehouse" results in "get[ting] along with things as in springtime" (與物為春).[121] These two phrases, "numinous rostrum" and "numinous storehouse," thus may be paired to form a Heaven-Earth or Yin-Yang dyad, one active, the other receptive, their border another "razor's edge" to be tread on the way of self-cultivation.

Spirit/ousness in Self-Cultivation

Spiritousness, like other elements of our anthropology, can be "wasted" (費) by, for example, not delegating authority and micromanaging.[122] It can also

---

118. Thus, from Zhuangzi's point of view, Protagoras was both right and wrong when he said that "Man is the measure of all things." He is correct to point out that it is humans, and not meddling deities, that truly guide human action, but he was wrong to focus on the human to the exclusion of the rest of the natural world. See chap. 5, n. 43.
119. *Zhuangzi* ch. 5 (德充符). See chap. 8, n. 55.
120. *Ibid.*
121. *Ibid.*
122. *Lüshi chunqiu* ch. 2.4 (當染); cf. Knoblock and Riegel, *The Annals of Lü Buwei*, 89.

"be harmed by feelings of self-interest" (以感私傷神),[123] or by excessive expression of emotions.[124] We saw above that it was imagined as "taking up residence" within one's person, something like an honored guest:

> There is a spirit/ousness that [may] spontaneously reside in the body, [but] no one can [fully] apprehend its coming and going: lose it and [you] will certainly be disordered; obtain it and [you] will certainly be ordered. Respectfully clean its lodging place, and [this] essence will spontaneously arrive. With essential [i.e., creative] thinking apprehend it; with calm reflection order it. With a serious demeanor and circumspect respect, [this] essence will arrive and become settled: [if you] attain it and do not abandon it, [your] eyes and ears will not be profligate, and [your] mind will have no extrinsic contrivances. With a rectified mind within [you], the myriad things [that you encounter will all] attain their due measure [of attention].
>
> (有神自在身，一往一來，莫之能思：失之必亂，得之必治。敬除其舍，精將自來。精想思之，寧念治之。嚴容畏敬，精將至定：得之而勿捨，耳目不淫，心無他圖。正心在中，萬物得度。)[125]

The "lodging place" of spiritousness is, of course, your own person, and your "cleaning" of this lodging place neatly stands in for the process of self-cultivation as a whole. "Cultivation" is an agricultural metaphor, and its animal-husbandry equivalent, including caring for humans such as one's parents, is the verb "to nourish" (養). Thus, sage-kings of yore were said to have "nourished their spiritousness and cultivated their virtuosity" (養其神，修其德).[126]

---

123. *Lüshi chunqiu* ch. 20.3 (知分); cf. Knoblock and Riegel, *The Annals of Lü Buwei*, 520. "Feelings of self-interest" (感私), however, are ostensibly not the same as (a degree of) "self-indulgence," in so far as the same text says—at least for the individual to whom it was told—that "If you cannot control yourself, then indulge yourself: your spirit/ousness will not be hurt." (不能自勝則縱之，神無惡乎。) *Lü shi chunqiu* ch. 21.4 (審為); cf. Knoblock and Riegel, *The Annals of Lü Buwei*, 559. This kind of self-indulgence is only possibly with an anthropology that assumes a good human nature.

124. *Zhuangzi* ch. 11 (在宥); see chap. 1, n. 54 and 65.

125. *Guanzi* ch. 49 (內業); cf. Rickett, *Guanzi*, 2:45–46. Partially quoted in chap. 1, n. 52.

126. *Lüshi chunqiu* ch. 17.4 (勿躬); cf. Knoblock and Riegel, *The Annals of Lü Buwei*, 420.

What spiritousness prefers, as we have seen above, is tranquility. Zhuangzi says if we "enfold spiritousness in tranquility, then the body will correct itself" (抱神以靜，形將自正).[127] Besides this, he also said, as we saw above, that we should "concentrate" (凝) spiritousness, a theme that he elaborates on in another chapter: "Being pure and unmixed; tranquil, unified and unchanging; calm and uncontrived; acting but with Heavenly movement: this is the way of nourishing spiritousness." (純粹而不雜，靜一而不變，惔而無為，動而以天行：此養神之道也。)[128] Another author tells us to "Unify [your] *qi*-substances and enlarge [your] spiritousness, preserving [them even] in the middle of the night; attain them with open-mindedness, [even] before [acting] uncontrivedly." (壹氣孔神兮，於中夜存；虛以待之兮，無為之先。)[129] Though the metaphors of "concentrating" and "unifying" may not mesh perfectly with that of "enlarging" the spirit, they do not thereby necessarily clash, insofar as it is possible to enlarge something by concentrating *on* it: if we concentrate on self-cultivation, the process will become enlarged within our field of attention.

So the cultivation of spiritousness involves tranquility and focus. One synonym for "focus" is "one(ness)" or "unity" (一 or 壹, both of which can be translated either way) which, as chance would have it, like other terms reviewed in this chapter, has a cosmological component that matches the anthropological. In the following quote, the term the "One" is a metaphor for the cosmic Way.[130] This "One" is explicitly tied to the pursuit of self-cultivation. (The "it" in the following is "the way of ruling," but the advice can certainly be extrapolated to the rest of us.)

> What does it mean to inquire after it in oneself? [It is] to moderate the senses and regulate the desires, be free of "wise" [i.e., wily] strategies and be rid of scheming rationalizations, in order to let awareness roam in the temporary lodging of the limitless and engage the mind on the path of spontaneity. If [one] is like this then there will be nothing to harm one's Heavenly

---

127. *Zhuangzi* ch. 11 (在宥); cf. Watson, *Zhuangzi*, 78.
128. *Zhuangzi* ch. 15 (刻意); cf. Watson, *Zhuangzi*, 121.
129. *Chuci* ch. 5 (遠遊); cf. Hawkes, *Ch'u Tz'u*, 83.
130. See *Laozi* chs. 10, 22, and 39. It is also important in the *Guanzi*, *Zhuangzi*, *Guiguzi*, *Lüshi chunqiu*, and *Huainanzi*. This concept is anthropomorphized in the person of Taiyi 太一 ("Great One"), a drawing of whom was found in an excavated tomb in Mawangdui in 1973.

[destiny]. If there is nothing to harm one's Heavenly [destiny], then one will know essence, and if [one] knows essence, then [one] will know spiritousness, and to know spiritousness means to attain the "One."

(何謂反諸己也？適耳目，節嗜欲，釋智謀，去巧故，而游意乎無窮之次，事心乎自然之塗。若此則無以害其天矣。無以害其天則知精，知精則知神，知神之謂得一。)[131]

Attaining this "One," which requires tranquility in the face of all the demands upon our attention, as well as the pursuit of our individual destiny, involves "essence," which is to say, creativity, which is dependent upon open-mindedness, on "getting along with things as in springtime." Out of that general creativity, spiritousness develops, the cognitive acuity that is the only thing sufficient to apprehend "the One."

But while the "One" denotes a peerless singularity, the same (Chinese) word, "unity," implies a bringing together of disparate parts, for example, Yin and Yang. This "unity" signifies the ceaseless, cyclical interplay of form and formlessness that constitutes the functioning of the universe. From this initial concept, "unity" can be extrapolated to a number of other concerns, including the cosmic, the anthropological, and the ethical. A secondary cosmic extrapolation denotes the multiplicity-within-unity that characterized the various *qi*-substances before they evolved into the cosmos that we know today. Anthropologically, it describes the necessity of the physical active-sleep cycle, and the mental creativity-out-of-tranquility equilibrium (symbolized by the numinous rostrum and storeroom discussed above), as well as the mental interface-with-exterior-reality exemplified by Artisan Chui above. Ethically, it underlies the virtues of humility and flexibility and compromise, with what Zhuangzi calls the ability to "walk two roads" (兩行), which we now might call "splitting the difference."[132]

The cultivation of spiritousness, like self-cultivation in general, includes both inner and outer practices that must be unified. Inner practice includes introspection:

> Close the four gates [of perception], and stop the five delusions, then [you can] be immersed in the Way. In this way spiritous

---

131. *Lüshi chunqiu* ch. 3.4 (論人); cf. Knoblock and Riegel, *The Annals of Lü Buwei*, 106.
132. *Zhuangzi* ch. 2 (齊物論); cf. Watson, *Zhuangzi*, 11.

percipience will be ensconced within in the formless, and essential spiritousness can return to full genuineness: thus [your] eyes will be clear but not used for looking, [your] ears will be sharp but not used for listening, and [your] mind will be orderly and penetrating but not used for apprehending or deliberating. [You] will be cooperative but not contriving, harmonious but not arrogant.

(閉四關，止五遁，則與道淪。是故神明藏於無形，精神反於至真：則目明而不以視，耳聰而不以聽，心條達而不以思慮。委而弗為，和而弗矜。)[133]

The "four gates [of perception]" are the eyes, ears, mouth, and mind. "Closing" these certainly suggests something like inward-looking meditation. The "five delusions" need not concern us here, but refer to the things on which a ruler could potentially overspend tax-dollars.[134] More to our point, in such an introspective mode, spiritous percipience returns to its resting state, in order to "recharge its batteries," so to speak, while essential spiritousness returns to "full genuineness," meaning that it "gets back on track," which is to say, returns you to your destiny.

Outer practice, which depends upon inner practice just as our waking actions depend upon our sleeping, includes things like learning. As we saw in chapter 6: "Now if the people on the street were to submit to the arts and practice learning, to focus the mind and unify the will, to think about [how to] investigate [things] and fully examine [them], then add to this day upon day extending quite some time, and accumulate competence without ceasing, then [this may] result in a connection with spiritous percipience, and the creation of a triad with Heaven and Earth."[135]

Outcome: Making Use of (Incipient Heavenly) Principles (理)

One final note about the cultivation of spiritousness is its resulting apprehension of the principles inherent in nature. We have already discussed

---

133. *Huainanzi* ch. 8 (本經); cf. Major, Queen, Meyer, and Roth, *Huainanzi*, 280.

134. These potential areas of extravagance are divided via the Five Phases: buildings (wood), moats and ponds (water), walls and roads (earth), bells and sacrificial vessels (metal), and cooking and burning forests (fire).

135. *Xunzi* ch. 23 (性惡). See chap. 6, n. 11.

natural principles in chapter 3, but the connection to spiritousness warrants a brief revisit. We saw above that spiritousness is described as something that may come to "reside" in us, dependent on factors such as tranquility and a lack of excessive or contrived desires. One text that records such advice further declares: "Clean the 'mansion' [of your mind], open the 'gates' [of your perception], be rid of selfishness and do not speak [excessively]: [then] spiritous percipience will abide in [you]." (潔其宮，開其門，去私毋言，神明若存。)[136] Given what we have already considered, this is not surprising. But the text later helpfully goes on to explain itself, including the following two notes. First, "'Clean it' means to rid [oneself] of [excessive] likes and dislikes." (潔之者，去好過也。)[137] And second, "[While having *some*] dislikes, do not lose the [natural] principles, and [while having *some*] desires, do not be excessive in [following your] inclinations." (惡不失其理，欲不過其情)[138] We should not be excessive in following our inclinations because "those who [excessively] express their inclinations will harm their spiritousness" (信其情者傷其神)[139] As for not losing natural principles, we saw in chapter 3 that "To act following [natural] principles is to be 'without preferences'" (緣理而動，非所取也).[140]

These "[natural] principles" play an important role in spiritousness. In the following quote, they are implicated in everything that follows:

> The lives of sages are a Heavenly process, their deaths a transformation of things. In tranquility their virtuosity is unified with Yin; in activity, their flow is unified with Yang. [They] act neither to initiate gain, nor to start misfortune. [They] respond when moved, act when pressed, and initiate when it is unavoidable. [They] get rid of [contrived] knowledge and rationalizations, and follow along with the [natural] principles of Heaven. Thus [they] are without Heavenly disasters, without entanglement with things, without opprobrium from other people, and without censure from ghosts. Their life is like floating [on a river], their death like taking a rest. [They] neither envision nor deliberate,

---

136. *Guanzi* ch. 36 (心術上); cf. Rickett, *Guanzi*, 2:73.
137. *Guanzi* ch. 36 (心術上); cf. Rickett, *Guanzi*, 2:79. Note: 過 = 惡.
138. *Guanzi* ch. 36 (心術上); cf. Rickett, *Guanzi*, 2:80.
139. *Guanzi* ch. 35 (侈靡); cf. Rickett, *Guanzi*, 2:312.
140. *Guanzi* ch. 36 (心術上). See chap. 3, n. 37 or chap. 5, n. 41.

SPIRITOUSNESS (神) 313

neither anticipate nor plan; [they] are bright but not ostentatious, trustworthy but not expecting [others to be the same]. They sleep without dreaming and wake without worries. Their spirit/ousness is pure and their [ethereal] *hun*-soul is not fatigued. Open and indefinite, serene and quiet, [they] thereby are harmonized with Heavenly virtuosity.

(聖人之生也天行，其死也物化。靜而與陰同德，動而與陽同波。不為福先，不為禍始。感而後應，迫而後動，不得已而後起。去知與故，循天之理。故無天災，無物累，無人非，無鬼責。其生若浮，其死若休。不思慮，不豫謀。光矣而不燿，信矣而不期。其寢不夢，其覺無憂。其神純粹，其魂不罷。虛無恬惔，乃合天德。)[141]

The first two sentences situate anthropology within cosmology: human tranquility and activity correspond to the first principles of Yin and Yang. The next two speak to sagely equanimity. In sentence five, we meet the "[natural] principles of Heaven," which are to take precedence over our own individual and cultural inclinations and biases. The remaining six sentences, beginning with "Thus," all flow from following these principles. The first of these six indulges us in a bit of hyperbole, since no one seriously thinks that sages never encounter problems of any kind: it is just that they avoid causing themselves unnecessary trouble. The same is true of the claim that they "neither envision nor deliberate," which indicates that since sages are objective, open-minded, and flexible, they do not spend time scheming about how to impose their views or will upon the world. That their spirit/ousness is "pure," which we saw above, is a poetic foreshadowing of the explicit open-mindedness in the final sentence, while the unfatigued ethereal soul reflects back on the requisite tranquility at the beginning of the paragraph.

Heavenly principles refer to how objective reality functions and can be perceived both in the world outside us as well as the one within us. The *Yijing*, as a divination text that claims to represent these natural principles, primarily refers to exterior principles.[142] The *Liji*, the classic of protocol, perhaps unsurprisingly avers that the principles of both Heaven and Earth can

---

141. *Zhuangzi* ch. 15 (刻意); cf. Watson, *Zhuangzi*, 120. The first two sentences of this quote appeared in chap. 3, n. 99.
142. See, for example, *Yijing* #2 (坤), "Wen yan" (文言) commentary on line five; "Xici zhuan;" and "Shuo gua 說卦"; cf. Lynn, *The Classic of Changes*, 149, 49, 120.

be "destroyed" (滅, 絕).¹⁴³ We saw in chapter 2 that the principles of Heaven within us can actually be "destroyed" by over-indulging our biases.¹⁴⁴ And we saw in chapter 3 that to follow natural principles, we should "investigate, examine, and study them, and when you finish, then start again."¹⁴⁵ That sentence, in the original text, is followed by: "Be open-minded by means of tranquility and humility; do not depend on yourself." (虛以靜後，未嘗用己。)¹⁴⁶ The same author in a later chapter summarizes his view concisely: "Rely on [natural] principles and discard [selfish] desires" (任理去欲).¹⁴⁷

Elsewhere, the same author makes an interesting comment on the idea of frugality in the *Laozi*, bringing together our present topics of spiritousness and natural principles: "Most people use their spiritousness impatiently: with impatience comes much wastefulness, and much wastefulness is called extravagance. Sagely people use their spiritousness tranquilly: with tranquility comes minimal wastefulness, and minimal wastefulness is called frugality. To be frugal is an art, and is produced by the Way and [natural] principles." (眾人之用神也躁，躁則多費，多費之謂侈。聖人之用神也靜，靜則少費，少費之謂嗇。嗇之謂術也生於道理。)¹⁴⁸ Frugality was not among the fifteen virtuosities that we surveyed in chapter 4, but were there space to add a sixteenth, frugality would likely be it.

Zhuangzi relates the most famous story among our sources that connects spiritousness with natural principles. In his "Butcher Ding" story, a ruler asks about Butcher Ding's "competence" (善) in carving up an ox. Mr. Ding answers:

> That which I like is the Way, which goes farther than skillfulness. When I began carving oxen, I could never *not* see the entire ox. After three years [of carving], I [finally] experienced *not* seeing the entire ox. These days, I use my spirit/ousness in apprehending [the ox] rather than using my eyes to see it: my sensory perception pauses while spirit/ousness proceeds. Relying

---

143. *Liji* chs. 19 (樂記), 6 (月令); cf. Legge, *Li Chi*, 2:96, 1:257.
144. *Liji* ch. 19 (樂記). See chap. 2, n. 36.
145. *Hanfeizi* ch. 8 (揚權). See introduction, n. 49 or chap. 3, n. 38.
146. *Hanfeizi* ch. 8 (揚權); cf. Burton Watson, *The Basic Writings of Han Fei Tzu* (New York: Columbia University Press, 1964), 36.
147. *Hanfeizi* ch. 18 (南面); cf. Watson, *Han Fei Tzu*, 93.
148. *Hanfeizi* ch. 20 (解老); cf. Liao, *Han Fei Tzu*, 1:181.

upon the Heavenly principles, I strike the clefts and guide [the knife through] the larger hollows, relying upon them confidently. I don't even experience [striking] the branching networks of tendons, much less the larger bones. Good cooks change their knives yearly, [because] they cut, while average cooks change their knives monthly, [because] they hack. Now I've had my knife for nineteen years, and have used it to butcher several thousand oxen, yet the knife blade is as [sharp as] having just come from the whetstone. Those [oxen] joints have clefts, while my knife edge [is so sharp that one might say it] has no thickness: [thus,] in using what has no thickness to enter the clefts, readily and certainly does such a moving blade [find] the extra space [it needs] . . . . Even so, every time I come to a tangle, I look at how difficult it will be, and apprehensively proceed with caution: my vision pauses, my movements slow down, and I move the knife with great subtlety. [Eventually, the problem] disentangles and resolves, like a dirt-clod crumbling to the earth. [Then] I lift my knife, stand up straight, and carry on while glancing around; I carry on, satisfied and content, then I take care of my knife and put it away.

(臣之所好者道也，進乎技矣。始臣之解牛之時，所見無非全牛者。三年之後，未嘗見全牛也。方今之時，臣以神遇而不以目視：官知止而神欲行。依乎天理，批大郤，導大窾，因其固然。技經肯綮之未嘗，而況大軱乎！良庖歲更刀，割也；族庖月更刀，折也。今臣之刀十九年矣，所解數千牛矣，而刀刃若新發於硎。彼節者有閒，而刀刃者無厚：以無厚入有閒，恢恢乎其於遊刃必有餘地矣。. . . 雖然，每至於族，吾見其難為，怵然為戒：視為止，行為遲，動刀甚微。謋然已解，如土委地。提刀而立，為之四顧，為之躊躇滿志，善刀而藏之。)[149]

In using his creative spiritousness rather than everyday, discursive consciousness, Butcher Ding pointedly "relies upon the Heavenly principles" in the subject at hand; in this case, an ox carcass. But cutting up an animal's body is a metaphor for analyzing any complex thing, including abstract things like situations and ideas. Whatever the object of consideration, the first thing to do is to figure out the natural, objective principles operating in that thing

---

149. *Zhuangzi* ch. 3 (養生主); cf. Watson, *Zhuangzi*, 19–20. Note: 技 = 枝; 善 = 繕.

or situation. In physical objects, like ox carcasses, such principles reveal themselves in how different parts—like bone, muscle, and tendons—are connected to one other. Knowing these principles allows one to deal with them more skillfully and easily.

There are three further points to be gleaned from this passage. The first is that such skill takes time and practice. It took Butcher Ding three years just to be able to focus on a specific problem, rather than only being able to see the ox as a whole (scary problem), as novice butchers might. Only after practicing somewhere between three and nineteen years was he able to acquire the skill that brought him to the attention of his ruler. The second point is that while describing his knife blade as "having no thickness" can be taken literally to mean it had no dull (i.e., "thick") points along the edge, it can also be taken metaphorically as referring to spiritousness itself, which is literally invisible, and hence without "thickness." Third, and perhaps most importantly, even skilled butchers (and analysts) meet with problems that force them to slow down and be careful. The final sentence conveys an air almost of bewilderment, as if he himself were surprised by what he had just accomplished.

"Spiritousness" relying on "Heavenly" principles makes double use of metaphor, given the semantic parameters of the literal and metaphorical uses of "spirit/ousness" and "Heaven/nature." One might wonder how a story like that of Butcher Ding might translate to more literal language. Recall the opening lines of the "Great Learning," which I suggested might be the definitive synopsis for early Chinese thought in general.[150] It had a six-part chain of advice, with the middle four parts mapping neatly onto an ostensible guide to self-cultivation: (1) know where to rest (知止); (2) be settled (定); (3) be tranquil (靜); (4) be calm (安); (5) deliberate (慮); (6) attain (your goal) (得). The first and the last refer us either to the human way of "great learning" or, if one inclines toward Daoism, to the cosmic Way. The other four, however, work quite well as an analysis of the Butcher Ding story, even though the technical language does not overlap. First, Mr. Ding first "settled" himself when, as an apprentice butcher, he chose his mark but could only see the entire ox. Second, he became "tranquil" when he was, after years of practice, able to focus on a specific part of the problem. Third, "these days," he was decidedly "calm" when he was able to make use of his spiritousness. Fourth, when he "came to a tangle," he was "deliberative" in being cautious and moving slowly.

---

150. *Liji* ch. 42 (大學). See chap. 6, n. 3.

SPIRITOUSNESS (神)

Another way of thinking about these four steps is to pair them with our anthropology: a *settled* body, a *tranquil* sensing of the exterior world, a *calm* mind in analyzing the sensory data along the lines of natural principles, and a *deliberative* spiritousness that makes use of caution and results in creativity. It may be the ordinary mind that apprehends the natural principles in the world around us, but it is only a special aspect of our minds—spiritousness—that is able to, at least sometimes, be unbiased and objective enough to rely on those principles rather than our personal inclinations and cultural prejudices.

Spiritous People (神人)

Spiritous people appear in three lists of aspirational figures. One is a list of four, comprised of spiritous people (神人), sagely people (聖人), worthy people (賢人), noble people (君子), and the non-aspirational petty people (小人).[151] These are analyzed each as being more "relaxed" (佚) than the next one on the list, who is characterized as being more "strained" (勞). The goals for everyone are more tranquility (靜) and calm (寧), which by now should surprise no one.

A second list of five omits worthy people and adds two other types that we have already met:

> *Heavenly* people do not depart from the ancestor; *spiritous* people do not depart from essence; *fulfilled* people do not depart from the genuine; *sagely* people take Heaven as ancestor, take virtuosity as the root, take the Way as the gate, and can foretell transformations and developments; *noble* people take goodness as their benevolence, propriety as their principle, protocol as their procedure, and music as their harmony: they are imbued with caring goodness.

> (不離於宗，謂之天人。不離於精，謂之神人。不離於真，謂之至人。以天為宗，以德為本，以道為門，兆於變化，謂之聖人。以仁為恩，以義為理，以禮為行，以樂為和，薰然慈仁，謂之君子。)[152]

---

151. *Zhuangzi* ch. 26 (外物); cf. Watson, *Zhuangzi*, 233.
152. *Zhuangzi* ch. 33 (天下); cf. Watson, *Zhuangzi*, 287. Partially quoted at chap. 4, n. 224 or chap. 7, n. 31.

In the first list, spiritous people comprised the highest group, while in the second they are in second place, after "Heavenly people." Little else can be said of these "Heavenly people," other than they "forget the human" (忘人)¹⁵³ and do not depart from the Way. Spiritous people, meanwhile, are identified here with "essence," or more colloquially, creativity.

A third list has only three types in it, and it reverses the second and third places of the previous list: "Fulfilled people are selfless, spiritous people are without [ostensible] merit, and sagely people are not famous." (至人無己，神人無功，聖人無名。)¹⁵⁴ This claim comes in the middle of a narrative that provides us with examples of all three of these aspirational figures. In reverse order, Song Rongzi, elsewhere known as Song Xing, was a sage who did not care what the world thought of him, whether it praised him or insulted him. Liezi, who has a whole chapter in the *Zhuangzi* named after him, as well as an entire eponymous book attributed to him, is said to be a spiritous person "without [ostensible] merit" because he was not calculating about wealth. But, it should be added, he could not only "ride the wind" (御風), but was "coolly competent" (泠然善) in doing so. We looked at "fulfilled people" in the previous chapter, though we did not consider there the sentence that is quoted here. This aspirational figure appears a couple of paragraphs later where, confusingly, he appears as an anonymous "spiritous person" living on a mountain. I take this spiritous person to also be a fulfilled person, even though he is not identified as such, because he fits the description of being "selfless." He, like Liezi, could fly (on dragons, no less), and could "concentrate" (凝) his spiritousness, but unlike Liezi, "This person, with his virtuosity, will lean on the extensive myriad things in order to become unified with them." (之人也，之德也，將旁礴萬物以為一。)¹⁵⁵ Thus, the sagely Song Xing still clung to a desire for success, and the spiritous Liezi still clung to his idea of himself, but the mysterious spiritous person living alone on the mountain was able to unify himself with everything, thereby losing his particular, individual self.

Other sundry details about spiritous people include their appearing to be useless within a society that only values financial success, and their dislike of crowds.¹⁵⁶ More useful to our purposes is the description of

---

153. *Zhuangzi* ch. 23 (庚桑楚); cf. Watson, *Zhuangzi*, 198,

154. *Zhuangzi* ch. 1 (逍遙遊); cf. Watson, *Zhuangzi*, 3. The first of these three was quoted at chap. 9, n. 30.

155. *Zhuangzi* ch. 1 (逍遙遊); cf. Watson, *Zhuangzi*, 4. Note: 旁 = 傍.

156. *Zhuangzi* chs. 4 (人間世), 24 (徐无鬼); cf. Watson, *Zhuangzi*, 31–32, 212.

spiritous people as having foresight. We saw above that sagely people who dealt with things when they were still "spiritous" were also called spiritous people (further muddling the lines between aspirational figures).[157] They are the unsung heroes who fix things before they need fixing: "They promote good fortune: none see it and yet good fortune is promoted. They avert disaster: none know it and yet disaster is averted. Therefore they are called spiritous people." (其興福也：人莫之見而福興矣。其除禍也：人莫之知而禍除矣。故曰神人。)[158] Invisible spirits are perhaps reified versions of the "invisible" work that spiritous people perform.

The final description of spiritous people that we shall consider describes two aspects of their being, echoing, once again, a Yin-Yang analysis: "Superior spiritous [people] ride upon sunbeams, [where they] disintegrate and perish along with [their] forms [i.e., bodies]: this is called 'shining spaciously.' [When they] fulfill [their] destinies and realize [their] inclinations, [share in] the joy of Heaven and Earth, dissolve and perish [among] the myriad matters, and [along with] the myriad things return to [their original] inclinations: this is called 'darkly deep.'" (上神乘光，與形滅亡：此謂照曠。致命盡情，天地樂而萬事銷亡，萬物復情：此之謂混冥。)[159] The states of being "shiningly spacious" and "darkly deep" are neologisms coined by Zhuangzi, and appear nowhere else, but they do reflect the cyclical dynamic that characterizes early Chinese thought. In this case, the self-cultivation of spiritous people consists of becoming selfless by "disintegrating" in two different ways: once in the Heavenly rays of the sun, and once again among all the other creatures of the Earth.

---

157. *Shizi* ch. 2 (貴言). See note 41 above.
158. *Shizi* ch. 2 (貴言); cf. Fischer, *Shizi*, 68–69.
159. *Zhuangzi* ch. 12 (天地); cf. Watson, *Zhuangzi*, 94.

Works Cited

Primary Sources & Select Translations

Note: Though it would be easier, and in a sense more accurate, to list the primary sources for this book alphabetically, I nevertheless think a rough chronological order may be helpful for some students. Dating texts, along with analyzing which sections of them may be earlier or later, and deciding and how the texts took their final form, is a complex enterprise far beyond the scope of this bibliography.[1] Thus, the dates below should only be taken as rough estimates for when perhaps most of the text was authored (and by "authored" I do not mean "written down," and certainly not when the written text took its final form, which, for most, if not all of them, would be centuries later, during the Han dynasty). In early China there were six classics, but the *Music Classic* was subsequently lost, thus there are only five listed here.

CLASSICS

1. *Yi jing* 易經 (Changes Classic; c. 1000–800 BCE), aka *Zhou Yi* 周易 (Zhou Changes); but the commentaries, known as the *Shi yi* 十翼 (Ten Wings; c. 250 BCE), are much later. (Many scholars, including myself, refer to the text alone as the *Zhou Yi* and the text plus commentaries as the *Yi jing*.)

    Lynn, Richard. *The Classic of Changes: A New Translation of the I Ching as Interpreted by Wang Bi*. New York: Columbia University Press, 1994.

---

1. For example, I have "dated" the *Shu jing* to 1000–700 BCE, but for an interesting and relatively brief analysis theorizing three "layers" of the New Text chapters of this text, see Mark Lewis, *Writing and Authority in Early China* (Albany: State University of New York, 1999), 101–05.

2. *Shu jing* 書經 (Documents Classic; c. 1000–700 BCE), aka *Shang shu* 尚書 (Venerated Documents); there are 28 or 29 older "New Text" (今本) chapters and 58 later "Old Text" (古本) chapters written c. 325 CE, but this assessment is contested; I cite only New Text chapters in this book.

   Legge, James. *The Shoo King*. 2nd ed. 1894; rpt. Hong Kong: Hong Kong University Press, 1960.

3. *Shi jing* 詩經 (Odes Classic; c. 1000–600 BCE)

   Waley, Arthur. *The Book of Songs: The Ancient Chinese Classic of Poetry*. 1937; edited with additional translations by Joseph Allen; New York: Grove Press, 1996.

4. *Chun qiu* 春秋 (Spring and Autumn [Annals]; 722–463 BCE); with three commentaries, *Zuo zhuan* 左傳 ([Mr.] Zuo's Account; c. 450 BCE), *Gongyang zhuan* 公羊傳 ([Mr.] Gongyang's Account; c. 150 BCE), and *Guliang zhuan* 穀梁傳 ([Mr.] Guliang's Account; c. 150 BCE): I use only the *Zuo zhuan* in this book.

   Durrant, Stephen, Wai-yee Li, David Schaberg. *Zuozhuan: Commentary on the "Spring and Autumn Annals."* Seattle: University of Washington Press, 2016.

5. *San Li* 三禮 (Three Protocol [texts]): *Li ji* 禮紀 (Protocol Records; c. 150 BCE), *Yi Li* 儀禮 (Ritual and Protocol; c. 150 BCE), and *Zhou Li* 周禮 (Zhou Protocol); c. 150 BCE): I mostly use only the *Li ji* in this book.

   Legge, James. *Li Chi: Book of Rites*. 1885; rpt. New York: University Books, 1967.

Scholars' Texts

Note: This is not a complete list of Scholars' Texts; these are only those cited in this book. As with the Classics above, authorship is far more complex than the traditional attributions given below.

6. *Lun yu* 論語 (Collected Sayings, aka Analects; c. 450 BCE) by Kong Qiu 孔丘 (551–479) and his students

   Slingerland, Edward. *Confucius: Analects with Selections from Traditional Commentaries*. Indianapolis: Hackett, 2003.

7. *Sun Zi bingfa* 孫子兵法 (Scholar Sun's Military Methods; c. 450 BCE) by Sun Wu 孫武 (c. 500 BCE) and his students

   Sawyer, Ralph. *The Seven Military Classics of Ancient China*. Boulder: Westview Press, 1993.

WORKS CITED 323

8. *Yan Zi chunqiu* 晏子春秋 (Scholar Yan's Annals; c. 450) by students of Yan Ying 晏嬰 (c. 500 BCE)

   Milburn, Olivia. *The Spring and Autumn Annals of Master Yan*. Leiden: Brill, 2016.

9. *Guo yu* 國語 (State Sayings; c. 420 BCE) attributed to Zuo Qiuming 左丘明 (c. 420 BCE)

   Untranslated

10. *Lao Zi* 老子 (Scholar Lao; c. 400 BCE) aka *Daode jing* 道德經 (The Way and Virtuosity Classic); by Li Er 李耳 (c. 400 BCE)

    Many translations

11. *Mo Zi* 墨子 (Scholar Mo; c. 400 BCE) by students of Mo Di 墨翟 (480–390)

    Partial translation by Knoblock, John and Jeffrey Riegel. *Mozi: A Study and Translation of the Ethical and Political Writings*. Berkeley: University of California, Berkeley, 2013. Full translation by Johnston, Ian. *The Mozi: A Complete Translation*. New York: Columbia University Press, 2010.

12. *Mu Tianzi zhuan* 穆天子傳 (Biography of Heavenly Scion Mu; c. 350 BCE); author unknown

    Cheng Te-k'un. "The Travels of Emperor Mu." *Journal of the North China Branch of the Royal Asiatic Society* 64 (1933): 124–149 [chs. 1–3] and 65 (1934): 128–149 [chs. 4–6].

13. *Xiao jing* 孝經 (Filiality Classic; c. 350 BCE) by students of Kong Zi;

    Rosemont, Jr., Henry and Roger Ames. *The Chinese Classic of Family Reverence: A Philosophical Translation of the* Xiaojing. Honolulu: University of Hawaii Press, 2009.

14. *Gongsun Ni Zi* 公孫尼子 (Scholar Gongsun Ni; c. 350 BCE) by Gongsun Ni 公孫尼 (c. 350 BCE). Fragmented text in Ma Guohan 馬國翰 (1794–1857). *Yuhan shanfang ji yi shu* 玉函山房輯佚書 (Reconstructed lost texts from the Jade-armor mountain retreat). c.1855; rpt. in 4 vols. 上海: 上海古籍出版社, 1990; rpt. in 5 vols. 揚州: 廣陵書社, 2004.

    Untranslated.

15. *Shang jun shu* 商君書 (The Shang Lord's Writings; c. 340 BCE) by Gongsun Yang 公孫鞅 (aka Shang Yang 商鞅 or Wei Yang 衛鞅; c. 390–338)

    Pines, Yuri. *The Book of Lord Shang: Apologetics of State Power in Early China*. New York: Columbia University Press, 2016.

16. *Shi Zi* 尸子 (Scholar Shi; c. 330 BCE) by Shi Jiao 尸佼 (c. 390–330)

    Fischer, Paul. *Shizi: China's First Syncretist*. New York: Columbia University Press, 2012.

17. *Chu ci* 楚辭 (Chu elegies; c. 325 BCE) by Qu Yuan 屈原 (c. 325), et al.

    Hawkes, David. *Ch'u Tz'u: The Songs of the South*. 1959; rpt. Boston: Beacon Press, 1962.

18. *Meng Zi* 孟子 (Scholar Meng; c. 310 BCE) by Meng Ke 孟軻 (c. 390–305) and students

    Van Norden, Bryan. *Mengzi: With Selections from Traditional Commentaries*. Indianapolis: Hackett, 2008.

19. *Zhuang Zi* 莊子 (Scholar Zhuang; c. 300 BCE) by Zhuang Zhou 莊周 (c. 369–286) and followers

    Watson, Burton. *The Complete Works of Zhuangzi*. New York: Columbia University Press, 1968; 2013.

20. *Guan Zi* 管子 (Scholar Guan; c. 300 BCE) by Jixia 稷下 academics at Linzi 臨淄 in Qi 齊, fl. c. 319–301

    Rickett, W. Allyn. *Guanzi: Political, Economic, and Philosophical Essays from Early China*. 2 vols. Princeton: Princeton University Press, 1985, 1998.

21. *Kong Zi jia yu* 孔子家語 (Scholar Kong's School Sayings; c. 300 BCE) by followers of Kong Zi

    Kramers, Robert. *K'ung Tzu Chia Yü: The School Sayings of Confucius*. Leiden: E.J. Brill, 1949.

22. *Guigu Zi* 鬼谷子 (The Guigu Scholar; c. 300 BCE); author unknown

    Cleary, Thomas. *Thunder in the Sky*. Boston: Shambhala, 1994.

23. *Tai Yi sheng shui* 太一生水 (Great One Creates Water; c. 300 BCE), anonymous, excavated at Guodian

    Cook, Scott. *The Bamboo Texts of Guodian*. Cornell: Cornell University East Asia Program, 2012.

24. *Liu de* 六德 (Six Virtuosities; c. 300 BCE), anonymous, excavated at Guodian

    Cook, Scott. *The Bamboo Texts of Guodian*. Cornell: Cornell University East Asia Program, 2012.

25. *Wu xing* 五行 (Five Conducts; c. 300 BCE), anonymous, excavated at Guodian

   Cook, Scott. *The Bamboo Texts of Guodian*. Cornell: Cornell University East Asia Program, 2012.

26. *Xing zi ming chu* 性自命出 ([Human] Nature Comes from the Mandate; c. 300 BCE), anonymous, excavated at Guodian

   Cook, Scott. *The Bamboo Texts of Guodian*. Cornell: Cornell University East Asia Program, 2012.

27. *Zhong xin zhi dao* 忠信之道 (The Way of Loyalty and Faithfulness; c. 300 BCE), anonymous, excavated at Guodian

   Cook, Scott. *The Bamboo Texts of Guodian*. Cornell: Cornell University East Asia Program, 2012.

28. *Yu cong* 語叢 (Sayings Thicket; c. 300 BCE), in four parts; anonymous, excavated at Guodian

   Cook, Scott. *The Bamboo Texts of Guodian*. Cornell: Cornell University East Asia Program, 2012.

29. *Heng xian* 恆先 (Abiding Antecedent; c. 300 BCE), anonymous, excavated, now in the Shanghai Museum

   Brindley, Erica, Paul Goldin, Esther Klein. "A Philosophical Translation of the *Heng Xian*." *Dao: A Journal of Comparative Philosophy* 12 (2013) 12:145–151.

30. *Xun Zi* 荀子 (Scholar Xun; c. 240 BCE) by Xun Kuang 荀況 (c. 310–215)

   Hutton, Eric. *Xunzi: The Complete Text*. Princeton: Princeton University Press, 2014.

31. *Heguan Zi* 鶡冠子 (Pheasant Cap Scholar; c. 240 BCE) by Heguan Zi 鶡冠子 (c. 240 BCE?)

   Untranslated, but many passages translated in Defoort, Carine. *The Pheasant Cap Master: A Rhetorical Reading*. Albany: State University of New York Press, 1997.

32. *Lü shi chunqiu* 呂氏春秋 (Mr. Lü's Annals; 239 BCE), edited by Lü Buwei 呂不韋 (c. 285–235)

   Knoblock, John and Jeffrey Riegel. *The Annals of Lü Buwei*. Stanford: Stanford University Press, 2000.

33. *Han Fei Zi* 韓非子 (Scholar Han Fei; c. 233) by Han Fei 韓非 (c. 280–233) and his students

> Partial translation by Watson, Burton. *The Basic Writings of Han Fei Tzu*. New York: Columbia University Press, 1964. Full translation by Liao Wengui. *The Complete Works of Han Fei Tzu*. 2 vols. London: Arthur Probsthain, 1939, 1959.

34. *Xin yu* 新語 (New Sayings; c. 200 BCE) by Lu Jia 陸賈 (215–150?)

> Ku Mei-kao. *A Chinese Mirror for Magistrates*. Canberra: Australian National University, 1988.

35. *Han shi wai zhuan* 韓詩外傳 (Han's Unofficial Account of the *Odes*; c. 150 BCE) by Han Ying 韓嬰 (c. 200–120)

> Hightower, James. *Han Shih Wai Chuan: Han Ying's Illustrations of the Didactic Application of the Classic of Songs*. Cambridge: Harvard University Press, 1952.

36. *Huainan Zi* 淮南子 (The Huainan Scholar; 139 BCE), edited by Liu An 劉安 (179–122)

> Major, John, Sarah Queen, Andrew Meyer, and Harold Roth. *The Huainanzi: A Guide to the Theory and Practice of Government in Early Han China*. New York: Columbia University Press, 2010.

Secondary Sources: English

Note: This is a list of "works cited" in this book and not a list of the many more works that influenced this book.

Allan, Sarah. *The Way of Water and Sprouts of Virtue*. Albany: State University of New York, 1997.
Allan, Sarah. "On the Identity of Shang Di 上帝 and the Origin of the Concept of a Celestial Mandate (*Tian Ming* 天命)." *Early China* 31 (2007): 1–46.
Allan, Sarah. *Buried Ideas: Legends of Abdication and Ideal Government in Early Chinese Bamboo-Slip Manuscripts*. Albany: State University of New York Press, 2015.
Ames, Roger. *Confucian Role Ethics: A Vocabulary*. Honolulu: University of Hawaii Press, 2011.
Angle, Stephen. *Sagehood: The Contemporary Significance of Neo-Confucian Philosophy*. New York: Oxford University Press, 2009.
Aristotle, *Metaphysics*. Translated by W.D. Ross in *The Basic Works of Aristotle*, edited by Richard McKeon. New York: Random House, 1941.

Brashier, Kenneth. *Ancestral Memory in Early China*, Cambridge: Harvard University Asia Center, 2011.
Brindley, Erica. *Individualism in Early China: Human Agency and the Self in Thought and Politics*. Honolulu: University of Hawaii Press, 2010.
Brindley, Erica. *Music, Cosmology, and the Politics of Harmony in Early China*. Albany: State University of New York Press, 2012.
Cai Zong-qi. "The *Yi-Xiang-Yan* Paradigm and Early Chinese Theories of Literary Creation." In *The Rhetoric of Hiddenness in Traditional Chinese Culture*, edited by Paula Varsano, 333–57. Albany: State University of New York Press, 2016.
Cook, Constance. *Ancestors, Kings, and the Dao*. Cambridge: Harvard University Asia Center, 2017.
Dawkins, Richard. *The Selfish Gene*. New York: Oxford University Press, 1976.
de Bary, Wm. Theodore and Irene Bloom, eds. *Sources of Chinese Tradition: From Earliest Times to 1600*. New York: Columbia University Press, 1999.
Deutsch, David. *The Beginning of Infinity*. New York: Penguin Books, 2011.
Field, Stephen. *Ancient Chinese Divination*. Honolulu: University of Hawaii Press, 2008.
Fischer, Paul. "Authentication Studies (辨偽學) Methodology and the Polymorphous Text Paradigm." *Early China* 32 (2008–2009): 1–43.
Fischer, Paul. "The Creation of Daoism." *Journal of Daoist Studies* 8 (2015): 1–23.
Geisel, Theodore Seuss. *Horton Hears a Who*. New York: Random House, 1954.
Harper, Donald. *Early Chinese Medical Literature: The Mawangdui Medical Manuscripts*. New York: Kegan Paul International, 1998.
Harper, Donald. "Warring States Natural Philosophy and Occult Thought." In *The Cambridge History of Ancient China*, edited by Michael Loewe and Edward Shaughnessy, 813–84. New York: Cambridge University Press, 1999.
Harris, Sam. *Free Will*. New York: Free Press, 2012.
Hesiod. *Theogony*. Translated by Dorothea Wender in *Hesiod and Theognis*, edited by Betty Radice. New York: Penguin Books, 1973.
Ing, Michael. *The Vulnerability of Integrity in Early Confucian Thought*. New York: Oxford University Press, 2017.
Kruger, Justin and David Dunning. "Unskilled and Unaware of It: How Difficulties in Recognizing One's Own Incompetence Lead to Inflated Self-Assessment." *Journal of Personality and Social Psychology* 77.6 (1999): 1121–34.
Lai Guolong. *Excavating the Afterlife: The Archaeology of Early Chinese Religion*. Seattle: University of Washington Press, 2015.
Lakoff, George and Mark Johnson. *Metaphors We Live By*. Chicago: University of Chicago Press, 1980.
Lewis, Mark. *Writing and Authority in Early China*. Albany: State University of New York Press, 1999.
Lewis, Mark. *The Construction of Space in Early China*. Albany: State University of New York Press, 2006.
Lloyd, G.E.R. *Demystifying Mentalities*. Cambridge: Cambridge University Press, 1990.

Loewe, Michael, ed. *Early Chinese Texts: A Bibliographical Guide*. Berkeley: The Society for the Study of Early China, 1993.

Lupke, Christopher, ed. *The Magnitude of Ming: Command, Allotment, and Fate in Chinese Culture*. Honolulu: University of Hawai'i Press, 2005.

Martin, Dale. *The Corinthian Body*. New Haven: Yale University Press, 1995.

Mitchell, Donald. *Buddhism: Introducing the Buddhist Experience*. 2002; 2nd ed. New York: Oxford University Press, 2008.

Moeller, Hans-Georg. *The Moral Fool: A Case for Amorality*. New York: Columbia University Press, 2009.

Munro, David. *The Concept of Man in Contemporary China*. Ann Arbor: The University of Michigan Press, 1977.

Ortega y Gasset, Jose. *Toward a Philosophy of History*. Translated by Helene Weyl, Eleanor Clark, and William Atkinson. New York: W.W. Norton, 1941.

Pankenier, David. *Astrology and Cosmology in Early China: Conforming Earth to Heaven*. Cambridge: Cambridge University Press, 2013.

Perkins, Franklin. *Heaven and Earth are Not Humane: The Problem of Evil in Classical Chinese Philosophy*. Bloomington: Indiana University Press, 2014.

Pines, Yuri. *Envisioning Eternal Empire: Chinese Political Thought of the Warring States Era*. Honolulu: University of Hawaii Press, 2009.

Pirsig, Robert. *Zen and the Art of Motorcycle Maintenance*. New York: William Morrow, 1974.

Plato. *Apology*. Translated by Hugh Tredennick in *Plato: The Collected Dialogues*, edited by Edith Hamilton and Huntington Cairns. Princeton: Princeton University Press, 1961.

Plato. *Theaetetus*. Translated by F.M. Cornford in *Plato: The Collected Dialogues*, edited by Edith Hamilton and Huntington Cairns. Princeton: Princeton University Press, 1961.

Poo Mu-chou 蒲慕州. *In Search of Personal Welfare: A View of Ancient Chinese Religion*. Albany: State University of New York Press, 1998.

Poo Mu-chou 蒲慕州. "The Concept of Ghost in Ancient Chinese Religion." In *Religion and Chinese Society, Volume I: Ancient and Medieval China*, edited by John Lagerwey, 173–91. Hong Kong: The Chinese University of Hong Kong Press, 2004.

Puett, Michael. *To Become a God: Cosmology, Sacrifice, and Self-divinization in Early China*. Cambridge: Harvard University Press, 2002.

Ryle, Gilbert. *The Concept of Mind*. Chicago: University of Chicago Press, 1949.

Slingerland, Edward. "Metaphor and Meaning in Early China." *Dao: A Journal of Comparative Philosophy* 10.1 (2011): 1–30.

Slingerland, Edward. *Trying Not to Try*. New York: Crown Publishing, 2014.

Slingerland, Edward. *Mind and Body in Early China: Beyond Orientalism and the Myth of Holism*. New York: Oxford University Press, 2019.

Smith, Kidder. "*Zhouyi* Interpretation From Accounts in the *Zuozhuan*." *Harvard Journal of Asiatic Studies* 49.2 (Dec. 1989): 421–63.

Wang, Robin. *Yinyang: The Way of Heaven and Earth in Chinese Thought and Culture.* New York: Cambridge University Press, 2012.

Yu, Anthony. "Reading the *Daodejing*: Ethics and Politics of Rhetoric." *Chinese Literature: Essays Articles Reviews* 25 (Dec. 2003): 165–187.

Ziporyn, Brook. *Ironies of Oneness and Difference: Coherence in Early Chinese Thought; Prologomena to the Study of* Li 理. Albany: State University of New York, 2012.

Ziporyn, Brook. *Beyond Oneness and Difference*: Li 理 *in Chinese Buddhist Thought and Its Antecedents.* Albany: State University of New York Press, 2013.

Secondary Sources: Chinese

Note: I translate the titles here but do not translate them in the book. As with the English sources above, this list is only of works cited, not of all those that influenced the writing of this book.

Chen Guying 陳鼓應 (1935–). Zhuangzi *jinzhu jinyi* 莊子今註今譯 (Modern notes and translation to *Scholar Zhuang*). 2 vols. 臺北: 臺灣商務印書館, 1974; revised ed. 1999.

Chen Qiyou 陳奇猷 (1917–2006). Lü shi chunqiu *jiaoshi* 呂氏春秋校釋 (Collated Explanations of *Mr. Lü's Annals*). 2 vols. 1984; rpt. 臺北: 華正書局, 1988.

Fang Po 方破. "儒家憂與靜矛盾的分析" (An Analysis of the 'Contradiction' of Confucian Anxiety and Tranquility), 《簡帛》第十輯 (*Bamboo and Silk* 10 [2015]): 37–49.

Fang Po 方破. "《老子》中本體論的'無'為心理上的'思想開明'" (Ontological Emptiness as Metaphorical Open-mindedness in the *Laozi*). In 治氣養心之術—中國早期的修身方法 (The Arts of Ordering the Body and Cultivating the Mind—Methods of Early Chinese Self-Cultivation), edited by 方破 and 林志鵬, 215–22. 上海: 復旦大學出版社, 2017.

Lü Zuqian 呂祖謙 (1137–1181). *Lü Donglai wenji* 呂東來文集 (Collected Writings of Lü Donglai). 台北: 臺灣商務, 1968.

Ma Chengyuan 馬承源 (1927–2004), ed. *Shanghai bowuguan cang zhanguo Chu zhushu* 上海博物館藏戰國楚竹書 (Bamboo Texts from the Warring States [State of] Chu in the Shanghai Museum). Vol. 3. 上海: 上海古籍出版社, 2003.

Wei Litong 魏荔彤 (1670–?). *Da Yi tongjie* 大易通解 ch. 13. Chinese Text Project (ctext.org). Accessed 2021 June 07, http://ctext.org/wiki.pl?if=en&chapter=483549

Xu Shen 許慎 (55–149?). *Shuowen jiezi* 說文解字 (Explanation of Simple Graphs and Explication of Compound Graphs; 121 CE). 台北: 天工書局, 1991.

Zhu Xi 朱熹 (1130–1200). *Zhongyong zhangju* 中庸章句 (Glosses on *Centered Engagement*). In 《四部備要。四書集注》, 1927–35; rpt. 台北: 中華書局, 1984.

Index

Note: Index items followed by the Chinese, except for proper nouns, are followed by the page numbers on which the Chinese graphs appear.

accord with, accordant, accordance (順), 47, 49, 87, 120, 155, 164, 165, 179, 242, 243, 258; *also* translated as "obedient," 56; *also* translated as "go along with," 87
achieve, achievements (功), 1, 46, 291, 292; *also* translated as "merit," 175, 318
allocate, allocative, allocation, allotments, distinctive, separated, separately (分), 38, 46, 49, 87, 114, 156, 159, 164, 165, 201 (不分, "undivided"), 232, 259, 288 (不分, "undivided")
anger (怒), 40, 68, 72, 73, 91, 92, 98, 99, 205, 240, 254, 290
animosity, blame, enmity, resentful, resentment (怨), 29, 120, 165, 187, 255, 263
anthropology, 35, 46, 50, 66, 297, 307, 308, 313, 317
anxiety, anxious, concern, worry, worried, worries (憂), 71, 72, 96, 97, 108, 145, 146, 167, 189, 202, 237, 240, 259, 263, 269, 313

appropriate, correct, fitting, match, matching (當), 10, 24, 54, 115, 116, 208, 220, 226, 249, 269
appropriate (宜), 71, 94, 118, 155, 159, 202, 220; *also* translated as "proprieties," 241
"argument from authority," 12, 223
art, arts, procedures, technique (術), 68, 70, 76, 177, 217, 227, 232, 238, 240, 274, 303, 314
Artisan Chui (工倕), 305, 306, 310

benevolence (恩), 164, 165, 187, 317
Bian Que 扁鵲, 219
blame: see *animosity, blame, enmity, resentful, resentment*
blame, prejudice (尤), 28, 263
blessings, fortune, fortunate, gain, good fortune (福), 17, 65, 171, 201, 252, 274, 313, 319
Bo Yi 伯夷, 198
Boyou 伯有, 59
Buddha, Buddhists, Buddhism, 29, 55, 63, 81, 109, 128, 130, 184, 197, 213, 222, 285, 296
Buliang Yi 卜梁倚, 196, 197, 198

331

Butcher Ding (庖丁), 185, 314, 315, 316

calm, calmed, calmness (寧), 51, 178, 196, 198, 201, 242, 249, 273, 308, 317

calm, comfort, comfortable, composed, at ease, relaxing, secure, securely, security, settled, stable, stability (安), 16, 28, 33, 34, 67, 71, 73, 74, 118, 135, 145, 158, 174, 196, 201, 214, 219, 239, 253, 263, 264, 276, 291, 316

careful, carefully, caution, cautious, prudence (慎), 99, 113, 145, 157, 165, 170, 171, 174, 203, 225, 272

caring (慈), 164, 165, 176, 187, 239, 317

centered, centeredness, central, at its core (中), 72, 98, 99, 112, 123, 156, 216, 268, 295, 306

ceremony, norm, rites, ritual (儀), 40, 43, 49, 65, 145, 155, 158

Christian, Christianity, 29, 30, 34, 35, 55, 63, 65, 144, 184, 195, 213, 264

Chuci 楚辭, 121, 138, 200, 261, 266, 289, 301, 309

Chunqiu 春秋, 3

Chunqiu fanlu 春秋繁露, 175

circumstances, situation, position, the "dynamism" of a particular situation or location (勢), 27, 90, 92, 106, 204, 205, 210, 221

civil, civility, civilized display, cultural refinement, culture, cultured (文), 79, 87, 89, 145, 155, 158, 164, 165, 189, 237; *also* translated as "patterns," 159

classics (經), 1, 3, 17, 28, 145, 161, 208, 218, 219, 235, 267, 292, 313

competence (善), 19, 28, 44, 75, 87, 92, 111, 112, 114, 130, 145, 151, 157, 183, 184, 187, 191, 201, 214, 217, 220, 230, 292, 299, 300, 302, 314, 318

complete person (成人, 全人), 120, 167, 271

concern: see *anxiety, anxious, concern, worry, worried, worries* (憂)

confirmation bias, 106, 116, 125, 129, 202, 206, 223, 224, 269

Confucius: see *Kongzi*

conscientiousness, good, good-naturedness (良), 85, 108, 164, 165, 243, 315

conscious, consciously, consciousness, 11, 33, 47, 56, 57, 58, 61, 64, 93, 105, 108, 109, 115, 129, 180, 187, 197, 200, 207, 256, 273, 278, 291, 296, 298, 299, 303, 307, 315

considerate, considerateness (恕), 130, 175, 176, 177, 227

contrivance (偽), 89, 107, 115, 117, 159, 177, 207, 308; *also* another graph translated as "contrivance" (圖), 308

content, contentment (知足), 124, 125, 262

correct, correctness, properly, rectify, rectification (正), 16, 52, 53, 72, 88, 98, 104, 151, 155, 172, 214, 216, 237, 238, 242, 250, 258, 263, 308, 309

cosmos, cosmological, cosmology, 2, 14, 33–37, 44–48, 50, 53, 54, 66, 94, 113, 114, 116, 124, 126, 128, 129, 131–135, 143, 176, 177, 185, 193, 194, 199, 207, 209, 217, 218, 245, 273, 274, 278, 285, 288, 289, 294, 298, 301, 307, 309, 310, 313

INDEX

courage, courageous (勇), 146, 152, 153, 154, 156, 157, 173, 225, 228; *also* translated as "brave," 132

courteous (恭), 145, 156, 157, 189; *also* untranslated as part of the binome "respectful" (恭敬), 174, 243

create, creative, creativity (造), 41, 57, 111, 193, 279, 301, 304

cultivate, cultivation (修), 1, 25, 28, 49, 75, 89, 99, 101, 134, 137, 145, 155, 157, 166, 170, 176, 178, 196, 203, 214, 237, 265, 268, 275, 308; *also* translated as "improve" and "improving," 67, 226

Daoist, Daoism, 22, 129, 208, 213, 288, 306, 316

Dawkins, Richard, 231

delight (喜), 40, 68, 72, 91, 92, 98, 99, 189, 205, 209, 254

desire, want, wish to (欲), 7, 19, 57, 80, 86, 87, 91, 95, 116, 118–122, 124, 133, 137, 156, 159, 165, 166, 174, 176, 181, 195, 202, 214, 221, 238, 252, 266, 269, 286, 289, 292, 310, 312, 314, 315

destiny, 2, 28, 89, 93, 104, 123, 133, 248, 250, 271–281, 306, 310, 311

detached, detachment, 26, 74, 118, 121–124, 197, 276, 289, 294

Deutsch, David, 174

develop, developed, development (化), 20, 34, 41, 45, 46, 51, 57, 59, 87, 89, 91, 110, 130, 131, 144, 168, 176, 193, 207, 214, 235, 236, 260, 279, 291, 294, 299, 301, 302, 304, 317; *also* translated as "change/s," 71, 122, 255; *also* translated as "transformation," 134, 313; *and* as part of "untransformed," 194; *also* translated as "responded," 306

divination, divinatory, diviner, 3, 203, 206, 218, 260, 261, 262, 286, 292, 303, 313

Dunning-Kruger effect, 125, 216, 217

Earth (地), 4, 14–17, 19, 20, 22, 24, 26, 33, 34, 36–39, 42, 44, 46, 49, 51, 54, 58, 61, 80, 91, 94, 95, 99, 108, 114, 132, 134–136, 155, 172, 176, 185, 188, 194, 207, 217, 229, 235, 236, 241, 249, 250, 263, 266, 268, 278, 280, 286, 288, 294, 297, 304, 305, 319

equanimity, equanimous (平), 16, 68, 85, 98, 108, 135, 148, 238, 240, 242, 303

emotion, emotions, emotional, 8, 17, 23, 24, 26, 27, 36, 40, 53, 55, 70–72, 77, 78, 80, 91–96, 98–100, 107, 108, 112, 118, 119, 122–124, 129, 138, 178, 197, 205, 206, 215, 221, 239, 240, 244, 273, 293, 308

enmity: see *animosity, blame, enmity, resentful, resentment*

essence, essential (精), 35, 40, 42, 43, 48, 51–55, 59, 60, 63, 67, 71, 72, 103, 121, 133, 134, 288, 290, 293–296, 302, 303, 308, 310, 311, 317; *also* as "integrity," 146; *and* untranslated as part of the binome "tiniest" (精微), 216

eudaimonia (well-being), 1

evidence (徵), 132, 137, 138, 226, 227, 262

excess, profligate (淫), 19, 40, 80, 87, 126, 237, 308; *also* translated as "malevolent," 59

fallibilism, 174, 281

Fan Chi 樊遲, 64, 164

fatalism, fatalists, 249, 256, 257, 258, 277

fate, 2, 28, 49, 56, 58, 65, 82, 89, 93, 123, 167, 247–260, 262–267, 270–275, 277–279, 281, 306
fear, fearful (恐), 56, 57, 72, 99; *also* translated as "afraid," 20
fear, fearful (懼), 72, 91, 132, 266; *also* translated as "afraid," 74, 146, 226; *also* translated as "apprehensive," 99
filial, filiality (孝), 56, 57, 65, 146, 161, 163, 284
Five Phases (五行), 79, 80, 311
Five Thearchs (五帝), 5, 250, 275, 287, 298, 300
flexible, flexibility (柔), 108, 145, 171–174, 225, 299; *also* translated as "yielding," 42
focus, focusing (摶心, 并一, 一, 壹), 34, 70, 73, 74, 75, 105, 106, 108, 125, 126, 203, 217, 262, 292, 309
foresight, 137, 138, 203, 255, 283, 292, 293, 319
form (有, 形), formlessness (無, 無形), 15, 36–38, 40, 42, 46, 49, 51, 57, 61, 109, 111, 131, 132, 135, 144, 204, 236, 276, 295, 304, 311, 319
fulfilled people (至人), 103, 123, 124, 134, 278–281, 295, 317, 318
Fuxi 伏羲 (2nd of the Three Sovereigns), 42

genuine (真), genuine people (真人), 71, 82, 134, 139, 176, 209, 267–269, 277, 278, 290, 296, 311, 317
ghost (鬼), 59, 60, 62–64, 76, 241, 261, 284, 285, 288, 300, 304, 305, 313
Gongsun Nizi 公孫尼子, 69, 72
good, goodness (仁), 6, 26, 74, 83–86, 97, 113, 130, 143, 146, 148, 150, 164–167, 175, 176, 183, 184, 186–188, 228, 235, 236, 243, 253, 263, 291, 317
Great One (太一), 40, 288, 309
Greek, Greeks, 1, 2, 34, 36, 55, 111, 169, 256, 285
grief, grieving (悲), 92, 290
Guan Zhong 管仲, Guanzi, *Guanzi* 管子, 15, 16, 18, 22, 24, 28, 39, 48, 51–53, 63, 65, 66, 68, 74, 82, 92, 95, 98, 102, 104, 108, 110, 114, 117, 119, 121, 125–127, 132, 134, 135, 138, 144, 146, 152, 159, 164–168, 170, 175–177, 194, 195, 205, 214, 226, 227, 238, 240, 261, 262, 287, 289, 299–302, 305, 308, 309, 312
Guiguzi 鬼谷子, 47, 118, 127, 134, 291, 298, 304, 309
Guo Pu 郭璞, 146
Guoyu 國語, 148, 150, 164

Han Ying 韓嬰, *Hanshi waizhuan* 韓詩外傳, 18, 50, 68, 114, 157, 203, 218, 232, 243, 252, 273, 274, 287, 289, 295
Han Fei 韓非, *Hanfeizi* 韓非子, 21, 63, 82, 104, 117, 124, 149, 155, 157–159, 163–165, 226, 227, 249, 262, 294, 302, 314
happy, happiness (樂), 27, 40, 68, 74, 92, 94, 97–99, 123, 130, 160, 179, 205, 219, 229, 238–240, 280; *also* translated as "delights in," 263; *also* untranslated as part of the binome "nourishing" (樂養; literally, "happily nourishing"), 243; *also* translated as "joy of," 319
harmony, harmonize (和), 39, 51, 54, 67, 72, 99, 108, 110, 135, 165, 178, 179, 187, 189, 219, 226, 235–237, 240–243, 264, 265, 273, 279, 290, 297, 303, 311, 317; *so* translated as part of the binome

"harmony" (合和), 15; *also* translated as part of the binome "moderation" (和成), 68; *also* translated as "soften," 131
harmony, harmonize (合), 49, 51, 60, 235, 240, 279, 288, 304, 313; *so* translated as part of the binome "harmony" (合和), 15; *also* translated as "unite," 51, 207, 241; *also* translated as "is matched with" and "match," 76, 276; *also* translated as "endorse" and "endorsement," 87; *also* translated as "directions," 95, 290; *also* part of the binome "circumference" (合抱), 204; *also* translated as "accord with," 220; *also* translated as "fitting," 227
Heaven, Heavenly (天), 4, 13–22, 24–26, 33, 34, 36–39, 41, 42, 44–46, 49, 51, 53, 54, 58, 61, 62, 71, 74, 76, 80, 89–92, 94, 95, 99, 101, 108, 112, 114, 117, 127, 130, 132–136, 139, 155, 160, 172, 176, 185, 188, 189, 193, 195, 200, 207, 209, 217, 229, 235, 236, 241, 248–250, 253, 255, 257, 259, 260, 263, 266, 268, 271, 275–280, 286–288, 293, 294, 297, 298, 303–306, 309, 310, 313, 315, 317, 319; *also* translated as "cosmos," 2, 245; *also* translated as "destiny," 271
Heaven's mandate, Heavenly mandate (天命), 25, 99, 120, 248, 260, 271, 272; *also* translated as "Heavenly destiny," 274
"Heavenly function" (天機), 269
Heguanzi 鶡冠子, 15, 43
hell, hells, 1, 13, 14, 35
Hengxian 恆先, 37, 41, 48, 50
Hesiod, 256
honesty (誠), 90, 112–114, 127, 130, 160, 176, 177, 216, 225, 227, 232,
261, 290, 291; *also* translated as "to make true," 214
honor, honorable (尊), 25, 167, 216
honor, honors, honorable (貴), 104, 113, 148, 158, 160, 163, 167, 257; *also* translated as "revere," 18; *also* translated as "precious," 26; *also* translated as "value" or "valuable," 50, 128, 130, 135, 168, 227; *also* translated as "venerate," 139; *also* translated as "exalt," 150
Hou Ji 后稷, 303
Huang Di 黃帝 (1st of the Five Thearchs; aka the "Yellow Emperor"), 300
humble, humility, modest (謙), 17, 149, 225; *as* part of the binome "humility" (謙遜), 124; *also*: two other graphs translated as "humble" (屈), 269, and "humility" (後), 314
hyperbole, hyperbolic, 14, 27, 43–45, 97, 99, 109, 119, 131, 162, 221, 270, 285, 289, 292, 313

imagine, imagination, imaginative, 5, 9, 12, 28, 29, 35, 42, 54, 62, 75, 102, 112, 118, 131, 132, 203, 220, 242, 286, 289, 290, 303, 308
impartial, impartiality (公), 127, 148, 149, 159, 177, 181, 196, 238, 264; *also* translated as "broadminded," 106, 149
impartially, impartiality, without partiality (無私), 16, 249; *also* translated as "not selfish," 151
incantor (祝), 65, 226; *also* translated as "prayers," 288
inclinations (情), 78–80, 85, 87, 91–93, 95, 104, 118, 121, 136–139, 155, 159, 176, 219, 221, 240, 255, 260, 272, 274, 276, 278, 299, 301, 303, 312, 319; *also* translated as "emotions," 53; *also* translated as

inclinations (情) *(contiunued)*
"circumstances," 148; *also* translated as "truth," 226
indications (表), 137, 138, 227, 262
intellectual history, 1, 3, 4, 8, 15, 28, 82, 101, 128, 147, 213
intention, intentions, intending (意), 23, 28, 74, 97, 102, 104, 125, 261; *also* translated as "attentiveness," 72; *also* translated as "conviction/s," 103; *also* translated as "awareness," 132, 133, 310; *also* as part of the binome "delusions" (惑意), 135; *also* translated as "meaning," 159, 225; *also* translated as "thoughts," 176, 214, 219; *also* translated as "conjecture," 222; *also* translated as "suspected," 223
introspective, introspection, 55, 131–135, 237, 262, 295, 310, 311
"investigation of things" (格物), 103, 135, 194, 214, 216

Jilu 季路, 64
joy (說, 悅, 兌), 209, 228, 265; *also* translated as "gladden," 72; *also* translated as "pleasures," 90, 92; *also* translated as "please," 157; *also* translated as "delighted in," 275; *also* another graph translated as "joy" (愉), 178, 273; *also* another graph translated as "joy" (樂), 319

kind, kindness (惠), 19, 164, 165, 176
king, kings (王), 18, 20, 108, 116, 148, 149, 156, 177, 180, 181, 236–238, 244, 267, 300, 304
Kongcongzi 孔叢子, 125
Kongzi 孔子, 4, 5, 25, 29, 56, 57, 60–62, 64, 70, 79, 81, 82, 96, 97, 120, 125, 145, 146, 150, 152, 156, 160–163, 166–169, 172, 175, 179–184, 186, 188, 191, 192, 195, 196, 198–200, 202, 208–210, 213, 216, 218–220, 222, 223, 226, 228–233, 239, 251, 252, 254, 257, 258, 264, 267, 284, 285, 298, 304, 305
Kongzi jiayu 孔子家語, 57, 61, 136, 200

Laozi, *Laozi* 老子, 7, 8, 19, 23, 26, 27, 29, 36, 38, 39, 49, 81, 111, 119, 121, 124–126, 128, 130, 131, 134, 135, 169, 170, 173, 174, 183–187, 191, 192, 194, 201, 202, 204, 213, 230, 262, 264, 268, 303, 305, 309, 314
learn, learning (學), 10, 91, 110, 113, 120, 127, 145, 166, 168, 169, 196, 213, 214, 216, 217, 228, 229, 281; *also* translated as "study," 45, 230, 265
Liezi 列子, 318
Liji 禮紀, 3, 25, 58, 60–62, 91, 94, 99, 103, 110, 112, 113, 134, 149, 150, 152–155, 157, 158, 165–168, 170, 171, 175, 176, 178, 182, 187, 193, 194, 214, 216, 229, 236–243, 248, 250, 263, 286, 287, 294, 298, 299, 301, 303–305, 313, 314, 316
Liude 六德, 129, 146, 147
Liuxia Hui 柳下惠, 198
loyalty (忠), 87, 146, 147, 150–152, 295; *also* translated as "dedication," 181
Lu Duke Xi (魯僖公; r. 659–627), 147, 148
Lü Zuqian 呂祖謙 (1137–1181), 9, 10
Lunyu 論語, 25, 29, 45, 60, 61, 64, 70, 77, 79, 96, 97, 120, 143–146, 150–153, 157, 160–162, 164–166, 168–170, 172, 175, 179, 181–183, 188, 195, 196, 199, 200, 202, 208, 210, 216, 218–220, 223, 224, 226,

228–231, 233, 239, 251, 257, 264, 284, 285
Lüshi chunqiu 呂氏春秋, 15, 16, 40, 41, 43, 46, 53, 54, 67, 69, 72, 90, 95, 104, 115, 116, 118, 128, 133, 135, 137, 138, 144, 148, 151, 153, 154, 160–162, 168, 179, 193, 207, 220, 223, 227, 231, 235–238, 241, 250, 252, 255, 259, 262, 267, 272, 275, 283, 287–293, 295, 303, 307–310

mainstay (經), 15, 80, 114, 155, 175, 259; *also* translated as "established," 42; *also* another graph translated as "mainstay" (主), 149
Mengzi, *Mengzi* 孟子, 44, 45, 53, 55, 72, 73, 82–91, 96, 97, 119, 130, 136, 145, 149, 150, 152, 154, 159, 161, 162, 164–168, 175, 177, 188, 191, 198–200, 209, 230, 231, 250, 253, 254, 258, 265, 266, 272, 289
merit: see *achieve, achievements*
metaphor, metaphorical, 16–19, 22, 26, 28, 30, 44, 45, 65, 66, 71, 74, 84, 88, 103, 106, 111, 122, 123, 126, 127, 133, 147, 149, 154, 173, 177, 185, 187, 194, 199, 200, 213, 215, 221, 232, 268–270, 283, 289, 299, 301, 305, 307–309, 315, 316
"mind-fasting" (心齋), 76, 105, 106, 109
Mizi 宓子, 180
moderate, moderated, moderation (適), 68, 69, 118, 133, 179, 220, 236, 274, 310; *also* translated as "accords with," 278
Mother Earth, 194
Mother Nature, 17
Mozi, *Mozi* 墨子, 19, 20, 26, 46, 47, 62, 136, 144, 152, 154, 159, 162, 164, 180, 181, 230, 243, 244, 256–258, 300, 303

music (樂), 98, 165, 187, 205, 218, 235–242, 244, 317
Mu tianzi zhuan 穆天子傳, 146

natural principle/s: see *principle, (natural) principles*
nature, (human) nature (性), 19, 25, 34, 45, 49, 76–78, 80–82, 85, 87–95, 98, 99, 115, 118, 124, 136, 165, 167, 178, 179, 207, 216, 231, 240, 247, 250, 253, 255, 259, 272–276, 279, 300, 303
nature spirit/s, 13, 47, 180, 226, 298
Nazis, 162
Neo-Confucianism, 15
noble people, noble person (君子), 5, 6, 9, 24, 27, 55, 67, 70, 72, 73, 79, 82, 91, 96–99, 102, 103, 110, 113, 114, 116, 117, 120, 127, 129, 144, 147, 150, 152, 153, 159, 160, 166, 170, 171, 174, 179, 181–183, 187–189, 198, 199, 203, 205, 216, 217, 223, 224, 228, 231, 240, 244, 251, 253, 263, 300, 317
non-contrivance, uncontrived (無為), 25, 104, 107, 108, 121, 126, 131, 184, 276, 279, 309
nourish (養), 44, 68, 70, 72, 75, 85, 89, 90, 95, 114, 118, 122–124, 131, 156, 178, 217, 243, 273, 275, 279, 295, 297, 298, 308, 309; *also* translated as "provide for," 29; *also* translated as "sustaining," 259; *also* translated as "raising," 272
numinous (靈), 303–305, 307
"numinous rostrum" (靈臺), 305, 306
"numinous storehouse" (靈府), 265
nurture (育), 91, 99, 144, 241, 294; *also*, two other graphs translated as "nurture" (畜), 27, and "nurture" (孕), 241
Nüwa 女媧, 42

338   INDEX

One (一), 6, 126, 128, 130, 132, 133, 309, 310
open, openness, open-mindedness (虛), 15, 37, 49, 102–106, 108, 117, 144, 178, 309, 313, 314; *also* translated as "empty" and "emptiness," 46, 119, 289; *also* translated as "depleted," 154; *also* translated as "hollows," 205

"peculiar magpie" (異鵲), 126, 201
Peng Meng 彭蒙, 148
Peng Zu 彭祖, 74, 75
percipience, percipients (明), 34, 43, 53, 59–61, 90, 104, 109, 121, 127, 145, 147, 160, 169, 177, 178, 189, 193, 216, 217, 264, 286, 289, 293, 296–305, 311, 312
perspective, 7, 125, 132, 150, 152, 181, 224, 281, 306
philosophy, philosophical, 1, 3–5, 8, 10, 28, 34, 35, 55, 64, 69, 169, 213, 218, 233, 243, 270, 284
Plato, 8, 169, 195, 200, 205, 232
politics, political, politicians, 1, 3, 4, 138, 143, 148, 151, 152, 169, 188, 196, 200, 201, 206, 218, 224, 249, 252, 255, 270, 272, 290, 304
precept (紀), 16, 304
principle, (natural) principles (理), 15, 21, 39, 73, 87, 89, 94, 114–118, 127, 134, 138, 153, 159, 160, 168, 177–180, 187, 189, 193, 205, 216, 226, 227, 231, 237, 241, 247, 252, 279, 311–315, 317; *also* translated as "patterns," 49; *also* translated as "conduits," 69; *also* translated as "externalities," 104; *also* translated as "organize," 188; *also* translated as "understanding," 260; *also* translated as "make reasonable," "reason," and "reasonableness," 274, 296; *also* translated as "rationalizes," 303
"principle of charity," 7, 26, 28, 29, 41, 96
profligate: see *excess, profligate*
proper, propriety (義), 17, 44, 64, 83–88, 90, 92, 145–147, 153, 155, 156, 158–160, 163, 165, 167, 179, 180, 184, 186, 187, 189, 220, 221, 224, 231, 235, 236, 241, 243, 251, 253, 258, 287, 317; *also* translated as "why," 153; *also* translated as "intentions," 221
Protagoras, 205, 307
protocol (禮), 65, 70, 83, 84, 86–88, 98, 146, 147, 150, 153–160, 166, 175, 187, 218, 235–239, 241–243, 251, 253, 258, 301, 317; *also* translated as "proper," 165
prudent, prudence (詳), 189, 287
prudence: see *careful, carefully, caution, cautious, prudence*

Qi Duke Huan (齊桓公; r. 685–643), 18
Qi King Xuan (齊宣王; r. 319–301), 149
qi-substance/s (氣), 15, 35, 37, 39, 40, 42–48, 50, 51, 54, 57, 58, 60, 61, 63, 67–70, 73–76, 80, 85, 92, 106, 108, 118, 126, 130, 132, 135, 154, 158, 236, 242, 273, 279, 280, 285, 286, 291, 296, 304, 305, 309; *also* translated as "passions," 104
Qu Yuan 屈原, 261, 266

real, reality, reality-based, realization (實), 104, 132, 158, 220, 225, 226; *also* translated as "to fill," 72; *also* translated as "truly," 80; *also* translated as "veracity," 108; *also* translated as "replete," 154; *also*

translated as "truthfulness," 177, 227; *also* translated as "fruitions," 193; *also* translated as "verify," 227
"rectification of names" (正名), 220, 222
regulate (節), 67, 68, 94, 98, 99, 118–120, 125, 133, 137, 159, 237, 238, 273; *also* as part of the binome "immoderate" (過節), 124; *also* translated as "orderly" and "orderliness," 155, 165, 189; *also* translated as "proper," 157; *also* translated as "timing," 205; *also* translated as "circumstances," 249; *also* translated as "moderate" and "moderation," 252, 310; *also* translated as "affiliations," 299
religion, 3, 4, 22, 28, 65, 115, 185, 213, 284
resentment: see *animosity, blame, enmity, resentful, resentment*
respect, respectful, respectfully (敬), 18, 51, 64, 98, 145–148, 154, 156, 161, 164, 165, 170, 171, 174, 189, 243, 284, 300, 306, 308
Ru, Ruist, Ruism (Confucianism), 4, 22, 129, 179, 196, 200, 213, 219, 230, 267

sadness (哀), 40, 72, 91, 92, 98, 99, 101, 205, 290
sagacity, sagely (聖), sages, sagely people (聖人), 24, 39, 43, 46, 71, 82, 101, 108, 112, 119, 121, 123, 130, 133–139, 146, 148, 159, 171, 172, 175–179, 181, 183, 187, 191, 193, 194, 196, 238, 241, 253, 273, 293, 295, 297, 300, 301, 304, 313, 314, 317, 318
Scholars' texts (子書), 3, 4, 6, 8, 11, 12, 14, 20, 28, 29, 192, 226, 260, 284

science, 12, 174, 180, 181, 185, 220, 252
self-cultivation (修身), 1, 157; *also* translated as "cultivate your person," 75; *also* translated as "cultivating oneself" and "cultivate ourselves," 89, 265; *also* translated as "cultivate our persons," 166
selfless, selflessness (無己), 16, 125, 281, 318
semblance (象, 像), 42, 132; *also* translated as "appearances," 95; *also* translated as "shape," 242; *also* translated as "compares," 294
Shang Yang 商鞅, *Shangjun shu* 商君書, 203
Shen Dao 慎到, 148
Shennong 神農 ("Spiritous Farmer"; 3rd of the Three Sovereigns), 287
Sherlock Holmes, 138
Shijing 詩經, 3, 13, 17–19, 55, 65, 144, 145, 147, 156, 161, 180, 182, 252, 272, 303–305
Shizi 世子, 175
Shizi, *Shizi* 尸子, 4, 69, 106, 146, 149, 151, 154, 164, 173, 175, 176, 196, 204, 213, 292, 293, 305, 319
Shujing 書經, 3, 17, 18, 101, 145, 148, 160, 170
Shun 舜 (5th of the Five Thearchs), 4, 5, 137, 250, 275
Shuowen jiezi 說文解字, 38, 41
"sitting and forgetting" (坐忘), 109
situation: see *circumstances, situation, position, the "dynamism" of a particular situation or location*
skillfulness (技), 315; *also* another graph translated as "skilled" (工), 65, 271; *also* another graph translated as "skill" and "skillful" (巧), 76, 125, 231
Socrates, 169, 195, 200, 285

INDEX

Song Rongzi 宋榮子, Song Xing 宋鈃, 318
soteriology, 1, 2, 12
soul, 1, 13, 14, 34, 35, 54–56, 59, 63, 65, 102, 131, 199, 213, 313
soul as *hun* 魂-soul, *po* 魄-soul, 36, 54, 58–63, 131, 313
spirit/ous/ness (神), 36, 41–43, 47, 49, 51, 53, 54, 60, 62–66, 70–72, 76, 121, 130, 131, 133, 137, 177, 193, 201, 241, 261, 279–281, 283–298, 300, 304, 305, 308–315, 319; *also* translated as "*kami*," 47
spiritous people (神人), 293, 317–319
spiritous percipients/percipience (神明), 34, 53, 59, 217, 297–303, 311, 312
substance, native substance (質), 34, 78–80, 93, 155, 157, 160, 167, 196; *also* translated as "substantiate," 103
Sunzi, *Sunzi bingfa* 孫子兵法, 194, 204, 205
syncretism, 11, 12

Taiyi shengshui 太一生水, 297
teachers (師), 70, 87, 88, 116, 150, 155, 181, 229–232, 281; *also* translated as "master," 261
thearch (帝), not including "Five Thearchs," above, 108, 145, 180, 287, 288, 294
Three Sovereigns (三皇), 287
Tian Pian 田駢, 148
timely, timeliness (時), 168, 191, 200, 207, 210, 265, 275; *also*, another graph translated as "timing" (節), 205
"torch of (slippery) doubt" (滑疑之耀), 175, 186, 281
tranquil, tranquility (靜), 15, 16, 28, 37, 39, 52, 53, 55, 94, 97, 98, 104, 105, 108, 121, 134, 170, 174, 178, 189, 214, 264, 273, 279, 289, 291, 295, 296, 301, 309, 313, 314, 316, 317; *also* translated as "to quiet," 76; *also* translated as "stillness," 240, 274
Tyson, Neil deGrasse, 194

uncontrived: see *non-contrivance*

verification (驗), 227; *also* translated as "checked against," 115
virtue, virtuosity (德), 6, 16, 27, 47, 49, 55, 63, 82, 108, 122, 134, 143–151, 153, 164–166, 170, 175, 176, 178–180, 183, 188, 201, 214, 216, 226, 228, 238, 240, 264, 268, 277, 279, 287, 291, 299, 302, 304, 308, 313, 317, 318

way, ways (道), 17, 19, 21, 24, 25, 44, 45, 73, 87, 90, 92, 99, 102, 105, 112, 113, 117, 129, 130, 133, 137, 143–145, 148, 149, 153, 157, 158, 161, 163, 166, 167, 181–183, 189, 196, 198–201, 206, 214, 216, 217, 219, 229, 230, 238, 240, 241, 249, 253, 257, 258, 263, 274, 275, 300, 302, 309; *also* translated as "carry out," 80; *also* translated as "the path of," 110; *also* translated as "guide/s," 120, 151, 238; *also* translated as "conveyed," 183
Way (道), 22, 26–28, 39, 40, 43, 106, 108, 110, 111, 114, 144, 172, 177–179, 183, 185, 186, 202, 206, 209, 269, 273, 288, 294, 296, 299, 304, 311, 314, 315, 317
will, willing, willpower (志), 23, 47, 67, 73, 86, 102, 105, 106, 118, 217, 255, 291, 295, 296; *also* translated as "intentions," 34, 92, 137, 196, 281, 286; *also* translated

as "aspire," 103; *also* translated as "set [my] mind on/upon," 120, 166; *also* translated as "set [your] heart on/upon," 143, 167; *also* translated as "purposefulness," 166; *also* translated as "attention," 201, 288; *also* translated as "aims," 221; *also* translated as "attitude," 266; *also* translated as "conscious," 273; *also* translated as "determination," 295; *also* as part of the binome "content" (滿志), 315

wise, wisdom (智, 知), 64, 80, 82–84, 86, 106, 108, 113, 114, 119, 127, 129, 133, 146, 167–170, 176, 203, 207, 208, 226, 228, 229, 238, 253, 284, 292, 300, 310

Woodworker Qing (梓慶), 75, 76, 105, 111, 112, 125, 277, 278

Woman Crookback (女偊), 196–198

world (天下), 1, 24, 37, 90, 99, 130, 135, 148, 149, 158, 159, 164, 166, 173, 180, 183, 184, 187, 196, 200, 207, 214, 224, 242, 244, 249, 251, 254, 263, 275, 279, 300; *also* translated as "the most," 153; *also* translated as "the realm," 153

worthy, worthies, worthiness, worthy people (賢, 賢人), 62, 148, 151, 154, 176, 191, 230, 237, 253, 265, 317

Wuxing 五行, 146, 238

Xiaojing 孝經, 64, 161

Xingzi mingchu 性自命出, 81, 90, 92, 155, 228

Xinyu 新語, 1, 45, 220

Xunzi, *Xunzi* 荀子, 18, 20, 24, 25, 30, 33, 34, 47, 50, 53, 70, 73, 75, 80, 82, 86–93, 97, 102, 105, 108, 114, 115, 119, 120, 123, 125, 127, 129, 136, 147, 148, 150, 153, 155, 156, 158–161, 163, 164, 169–172, 174, 176–178, 188, 189, 191, 193, 196, 198, 202, 206–208, 216–222, 227, 229–232, 238, 240, 242, 248, 249, 255, 258–262, 265, 274, 275, 277, 279, 280, 291, 292, 294, 300, 302, 311

Yan Hui 顏回, 229

Yan King Kuai 燕王噲 (r. 320–312), 149

Yanzi, *Yanzi chunqiu* 晏子春秋, 111, 112, 114, 230, 242, 288

Yao 堯 (4th of the Five Thearchs), 4, 5, 75, 122, 123, 137, 145, 275

Yellow Springs (黃泉), 280

Yi Yin 伊尹, 198

yield to others, yielding, the ability to yield (讓), 145, 147, 149, 150, 187; *also* in the binome "deference" (辭讓), 83, 87, 150, 154; *also* translated as "deferred," 266

Yijing 易經, 3, 17, 42, 48, 147–149, 166, 171, 179, 203, 228, 247, 260, 262, 263, 283, 286, 292, 299, 303, 313

Yin 陰, Yang 陽, Yin-Yang 陰陽, 6, 20, 35, 36, 38–43, 45, 47, 48, 50, 54, 58–61, 67, 69, 71, 80, 114, 134, 135, 144, 148, 155, 171–174, 191, 192, 207, 226, 235–237, 241, 248, 261, 283, 297–299, 307, 310, 312, 313, 319

Yu 禹 (1st ruler of Xia dynasty), 75, 229, 230, 258, 259, 284

Yucong 語叢, 45, 93, 125, 158, 225

Zai Wo 宰我, 60, 188

Zen, 111, 168, 296

Zengzi 曾子, 151

Zhao Jingzi 趙景子, 59

Zhongxin zhidao 忠信之道, 152

Zhou King Mu (周穆王; r. 956–918), 146
Zhou King Ling (周靈王; r. 571–545), 304
Zhou King Wen (周文王; r. 1099/56–1050), 13, 177, 180, 181, 230, 305
Zhou King Wu (周武王; r. 1049/45–1043), 181, 230
Zhuangzi, *Zhuangzi* 莊子, 22, 25–27, 29, 49, 50, 53, 55, 57, 58, 67, 70, 71, 73, 75, 76, 81, 82, 101, 103, 104, 106, 108–110, 119, 121–127, 129–132, 134, 139, 148, 154, 161, 163–165, 175, 176, 178, 184–187, 196, 197, 199, 201, 202, 205, 206, 208, 209, 217, 220, 224, 225, 229, 230, 232, 236, 244, 248–251, 254, 264–271, 275–281, 287, 288, 290, 293–296, 298, 301, 302, 305–310, 313–315, 317–319
Zi Zhi 子之, 149
Zichan 子產, 59, 60, 67
Zilu 子路, 97, 210
Zixia 子夏, 188
Zuozhuan 左傳, 19, 40, 41, 54, 59, 67, 80, 94, 146–152, 155, 160, 170, 175, 203, 214, 240, 260, 287, 300, 304

www.ingramcontent.com/pod-product-compliance
Lightning Source LLC
Chambersburg PA
CBHW031433230426
43668CB00007B/512